Fairfield Porter

Fairfield Porter
a life in art

Justin Spring

Yale University Press
New Haven and London

Frontispiece

Fairfield Porter, 1958.
Photo by John Jonas
Gruen. Courtesy John
Jonas Gruen.

Designed by Daphne Geismar.
Set in Minion by Amy L. Storm.
Printed in China through World Print.

A catalogue record for this book is available from
the British Library.

The paper in this book meets the guidelines for
permanence and durability of the Committee on
Production Guidelines for Book Longevity of
the Council on Library Resources.

10 9 8 7 6 5 4 3 2 1

Library of Congress Cataloging-in-Publication Data
Spring, Justin.
Fairfield Porter: a life in art / Justin Spring.
p. cm.
Includes bibliographical references and index.
ISBN 0-300-07637-1 (cl.)
1. Porter, Fairfield.
2. Artists – United States Biography.
3. Art critics – United States Biography.
I. Title.
N6537.P63S66 2000
700′.92 – dc21
[B]
99-30563
CIP

When I paint, I think that what would satisfy me is to express what Bonnard said Renoir told him: make everything more beautiful. This partly means that a painting should contain a mystery, but not for mystery's sake: a mystery that is essential to reality.

August 3, 1968

   – Fairfield Porter, letter to Arthur Giardelli
     Great Spruce Head Island, Maine

Contents

Preface

Fairfield Porter – "perhaps the major American artist of this century," according to the poet and critic John Ashbery (*Newsweek*, January 24, 1983) – is a painter whose significant achievement, in the most narrow art-historical terms, was to create a singular and distinctively American vision out of two disparate styles of painting. The first – intimate, sensual, and representational – had previously been explored by the French painters Vuillard and Bonnard. The second style – violent, colorful, and abstract – was the Abstract Expressionism of de Kooning. But Porter was more than an innovative painter: he was a philosopher-artist who spent his entire adult life participating in the American art and literary scenes not just as a painter but also as a critic, poet, observer, supporter, collector, and devoted friend. His life story demonstrates a rare continuity within the history of American art, for he wrote brilliantly and perceptively about the art world from the time of his arrival in New York in 1928 until his death in 1975. There were few, if any, movements within American art during this period with which he was unfamiliar, and he was personally acquainted with many of the most substantial artists. He also had a firsthand acquaintance with an extraordinary amount of Western art, from Ancient Greece through Picasso. His lifelong immersion in the conflicting theories of art which existed in America from the mid-1920s on gave him a rare breadth and depth of knowledge which informs not only his criticism but his personal correspondence as well. Though well versed in artistic, literary, and political theory, he was beholden to none of them; anti-academic and valuing plain talk above all else, he preferred art to ideologies and always identified himself first and foremost as a painter.

Because as an artist and a critic Porter was slow to develop and even slower to realize anything approximating success, he spent the early part of his life looking at, thinking about, and publishing his thoughts on other people's art. As a result, Porter's biography is more than just the story of a man who made paintings, or a chronological appreciation of those paintings (for he began creating his first memorable artworks only in his early forties). Instead, this is the story of a man of encyclopedic intelligence, born into an exceptional (and exceptionally privileged) family, who, after a period of youthful travel, was vitally engaged in the American art scene for over half a century.

This biography is less an art-historical account of the creation of individual paintings (a good account of which has already been published) than it is an intimate literary and intellectual biography of a painter who was also an exceptional critic, writer, poet, and thinker. It is a highly personal story of a brilliant and talented man, beset by personal demons, who considered himself a failure for the first forty years of his life and only in his last twenty-five began to realize his great talents. Finally it is, to a lesser extent, a portrait of a marriage and of a family that will, I hope, contribute to both a scholarly and a popular understanding of the artist and his work.

Writing a biography that speaks to both art-historical and literary audiences is a daunting challenge, perhaps because the two groups have never agreed upon the purpose or significance of biography, or the way it ought to be written, or what it ought to include. Art scholars have noted that biography is a useful, if not essential, component of their studies; although it is not always necessary to reconstruct all the intimate details of an artist's life to comprehend a work, doing so does have a role in verifying scholarly interpretation. Scholars of literature see a broader relationship between author and work and are bolder in their analyses of and speculations upon life incidents – as, indeed, are general readers. Porter himself chose an interpretive model for his monograph on Thomas Eakins and took a similarly humanistic approach to artists in his study of American artists for *Art News*, which is one reason I have chosen a literary rather than an art-historical model for my own project. But perhaps a more important reason for choosing to write a critical (or "literary") biography of Fairfield Porter is that, simply put, his life and work are clearly worthy of such an investigation, and his poetry, criticism, and voluminous correspondence give insight into the daily life and thoughts of a working painter who was closely attuned to the artistic, social, and literary discourse of his day. Porter was chiefly a painter, but the writing he has left behind affords a rare and valuable glimpse into the working life and thoughts of a twentieth-century American artist.

In writing this biography, I have tried to trace the development of Fairfield Porter's aesthetic. Throughout his life, Porter created art that was closely related to his intellectual preoccupations, whether literary, political, or philosophical. Had he not painted a single canvas, Porter's thoughts on art would be exciting and worthy of exploration, but these thoughts are particularly valuable to a biographer in the context of Porter's work and life, for in both Porter chose the sensual realm over the merely intellectual, favoring, in his own words, the "ultimate reality" of immediate physical experience over much that he had previously learned from his family and teachers. With Porter, the choice to practice art was nothing less than a metaphysical decision.

As fascinating as I find Porter's theories on art, I have not attempted a comprehensive examination of Porter's artistic theories in this biography, any more than I have attempted a comprehensive description of his paintings. Interested viewers and readers should consult Porter's critical writings and paintings directly, for, as Tolstoy observed (and Porter agreed), "a good work of art can in its entirety be represented only by itself." This biography should serve instead merely as an introduction to Porter's art and his ideas on art and to the way both were intimately connected to incidents in his life.

Porter's background, family life, and personal affairs claim a significant portion of this biography. Porter was a reserved and somewhat private man, but he was also a natural observer and an engaging correspondent who shared details of his life (in conversation, in letters, and in paintings) as easily and openly as he shared his home. His letters – clear, direct, affectionate – reveal a side of his personality which was invisible to most acquaintances. An awareness, through these documents, of events in his domestic life should be valuable to an appreciation of both his art and his criticism, for home life was, after all, the source of his inspiration and the subject of his greatest works.

The knowledge that Porter was of two minds about the home life he depicted so beautifully is important to an understanding of his paintings as well as to an understanding of the artist who created them. Then again, it is equally important to understand that Porter's ambivalence toward marriage, parenthood, and his bisexual awareness is only one aspect of the life he chose to lead, which was that of father and husband. Porter's understanding of and reconciliation with his social and sexual nature occurred late in life, simultaneously with his great achievements as an artist and a critic, partly as the result of psychoanalysis. My exploration of these aspects of Porter's private life is based on a wish to chronicle his professional achievements and hard-won self-knowledge. But I would hope as well to use that understanding to address the difficult situation which developed in the Porter home during the last two decades of Porter's life, concerning his and his family's virtual adoption of the Pulitzer Prize – winning poet James Schuyler.

It is only right and fitting that a painter who created intimate paintings should be the subject of an intimate biography, particularly since, in his work as an art critic, Porter himself often chose intimate details from the lives of artists he wrote about in order to express an understanding of and appreciation for their work. Moreover – and this is significant – no other major American artist of the twentieth century has painted his children, wife, intimate friends, or home as much as Porter did. These are not simple images, and the lives described are similarly complicated and in some cases, quite tragic. Yet they constitute a sort of "family album," as Anne Porter, the artist's wife, described her husband's first one-man exhibition to her mother in 1952. They require more comprehensive understanding of Porter's family and world, just as Porter's critical work requires an account of his long education as artist and critic. In this book I provide, as best I can, an accurate and responsible reconstruction of both.

I would like to add a note on transcription. In quoting from original letters and documents, only sometimes have I made corrections of spelling, grammar, and punctuation, and then only to avoid confusion to the reader. At the same time, I have avoided the use of *sic* except when absolutely necessary. Readers may therefore assume that misspellings and misuse of grammar in quoted materials are in the original and that they have been kept intact because of the spirited tone such inconsistencies often lend to the work.

Acknowledgments

Many people helped me in the difficult seven-year project of researching and writing this book. To begin with, I would like to thank the artist's family, particularly his widow, Anne Porter, without whom it could not have been written. Mrs. Porter allowed me unprecedented freedom in my research and never sought to control or influence my project. Her thoughts and comments on the manuscript were invaluable to my understanding of her husband, his work, and their life together.

I would also like to thank Fairfield Porter's four surviving children – Laurence, Richard, Katharine, and Elizabeth – each of whom helped me with my project to the best of his or her ability. Of the extended Porter family, I would like to thank Barbara Birch, Steve and Marcy Porter, and Margaret Straus. I especially thank Anina Porter Fuller and Gertrude Porter for hosting me during a stay on Great Spruce Head Island, an experience that aided immeasurably in my understanding of Fairfield Porter's life and world.

Many friends and acquaintances of Fairfield Porter and his circle were generous in sharing their recollections of Porter with me, among them John Ashbery, Ellen Auerbach, Bill Berkson, Rudy Burckhardt, Paul Cadmus, Robert Dash, Jane Doscher, Peter Doscher, Jane Freilicher, Henry Geldzahler, Arthur Giardelli, Mike Goldberg, John Gruen, Barbara Guest, Connie Herrick, Dr. Mary Johnson, Wolf Kahn, David Kermani, Kenneth Koch, Joe LeSueur, Emily Mason, Ilse Mattick, Paul Mattick Jr., James McCourt, the late James Merrill, Alvin Novak, Ron Padgett, Darragh Park, Larry Rivers, Peter Schjeldahl, Edith Schloss, David Shapiro, Rose Slivka, Sidney Talisman, Vincent Virga, Jane Wilson, Trevor Winkfield, and Penny Wright.

For help with Porter scholarship, I would like to thank the editor of Porter's forthcoming letters, Armistead Leigh; the editor of his critical writings, Rackstraw Downes; the author of *Fairfield Porter: An American Classic*, John T. Spike; and particularly the author of his forthcoming catalogue raisonné, Joan Ludman, whose patience and scholarship have been an inspiration to me. The late Tibor de Nagy, Andrew Arnot, and Eric Brown, of the Tibor de Nagy gallery, and Betty Cunningham, formerly of the Hirschl and Adler Gallery, have also been most helpful with questions related to Porter's paintings.

For help with James Schuyler scholarship, I would like to thank the editor of his journals, Nathan Kernan, and the editor of his forthcoming letters, William Corbett, who was kind enough to let me read through his collection of Schuyler letters at his home in Boston. Extracts of James Schuyler's unpublished correspondence in this biography are under copyright (© 1999) by the Estate of James Schuyler and are reprinted in this book by permission of the estate.

I would like to thank Maureen O'Hara Granville-Smith for granting special permission to publish several extracts of letters by her brother, Frank O'Hara. These extracts are under copyright (© 1999) by Maureen Granville-Smith and are reprinted by permission. I also thank the following for allowing me to quote from their unpublished correspondence: Jane Freilicher, Arthur Giardelli, Ilse Mattick, the Estate of Eliot Porter, the Estate of Ruth Porter, and the Estate of Richard Stankiewicz.

A number of libraries and institutions were particularly helpful to me as I researched this project. I would specifically like to thank Rodney Phillips and Phil Molito at the Berg Manuscripts Collection, New York Public Library; Mary-Jo Kine of Hay-Harris Library, Brown University; Susan Wilson and Fiorella Superbi of Villa I Tatti in Florence; Leslie A. Morris of Houghton Library, Harvard University; and Brad Westbrook and Linda Corey Claassen at Mandeville Department of Special Collections, University Library, University of California, San Diego, La Jolla. I would also like to thank the Archives of American Art in Washington and its branch office in New York for making the Fairfield Porter papers available to me. Alicia Longwell of the Parrish Art Museum, Southampton, New York, was also very helpful to me as I reviewed the Fairfield Porter materials in the museum's archive.

Amherst College supported this project with a one-semester Copeland residential fellowship. I would like to thank Professor William H. Pritchard, the staff of Frost Library, the staff of the English Department, and the staff of the Amherst College Computer Center for all their generous help and support.

Andrew Botsford, arts editor of *The Southampton Press*, and Sheridan Sansegundo, arts editor of *The East Hampton Star*, allowed me to write about Porter and related topics while I was working on this manuscript. Stephen Donadio, editor of *The New England Review*, also showed his support for this project by publishing an excerpt from the manuscript.

My literary agents, Susan Schorr and, later, George Nicholson, worked hard to find a proper home for this manuscript, which did not find a publisher until it was completed. At Yale University Press, I owe a great debt to my editor, Judy Metro, for seeing the value of my project, as well as to my manuscript editor, Mary Pasti, for her many insightful comments on the text. The editorial intern Sarah Rubinstein helped obtain photographic permissions for many of the works of art reproduced in this book.

I would like to thank the following friends for their helpfulness: Edith Aronson, David Beitzel, Robert Boynton, Jan Carter, E. Patrick Johnson, Rick Alan Kinsel, James Ledbetter, Holly Montague, Nicholas Nicholson, Ingrid Schaffner, Stuart Shils, Lee Smith, Pari Stave, Darren Walker, Ken Widener, and (especially) Karl Willers. My mother, Sharon Johe, and my sister, Margaret F. Spring, have also been tremendously helpful and supportive of this project. Most of all, however, I would like to thank Anthony Korner.

I would like to note, simply for the sake of scholarship, that apart from the small stipend attached to the Copeland residential fellowship at Amherst College, I received no financial support for the researching and writing of this biography, neither from public sources nor from private contributions. Specifically, I would like to note that I received no funding from either the extended Porter family or the Fairfield Porter Estate.

1

Family and Home

Fairfield Porter was not one to boast of his ancestry; he rarely mentioned his distinguished relatives and forebears, even later in life to those friends who would have been intrigued by them. Asked about his family background in 1968, Porter merely said, "I think I have ancestors who came over on the *Mayflower*. I'm not sure but I think I do." They dated back, he thought, at least to the seventeenth century.[1] Porter knew that he could also claim leading New England intellectuals, clergymen, and statesmen of the previous century as kin. But his ancestry was just coincidental to his project of creating visual art, and he was temperamentally disinclined to think more highly of himself because he was descended from several leading American families. Moreover, his politics were such that he disliked the idea of being associated with any particular class or of claiming precedence through background.

In fact, throughout his life he suffered because of his distinguished associations. As a man interested in the socialist movement, moving among leftist intellectuals, he was thought of as the dilettantish son of a rich man, too closely bound to society by money and family to be taken seriously as a revolutionary. As an artist, too, he was often viewed as an amateur, a gentleman painter moving among bohemians. So Porter's vagueness regarding his background may be the result of defensiveness as well as indifference.

Then again, vagueness regarding background seems to run in the extended Porter family; among the surviving Porters, only one family member keeps a copy of the family tree, and he has been notably unwilling to share this information freely, even with other family members. Fairfield's older brother, the photographer Eliot Porter, wrote only a small amount about his family background in his several memoirs. Fairfield Porter's children have few, if any, records about their ancestry, apart from one copy of an unpublished biography written by their father's maternal grandfather.

In the Porter family, similar modesty prevailed where money was concerned. Fairfield Porter grew up rich, but no one in the family cared to discuss where their wealth came from, what could be done with it, or even how much of it there was. Except for an occasional mention of a tuition check or spending money, Fairfield's early family correspondence rarely takes money as a subject. Perhaps this was because the money had come into the family almost by accident, and no one in Fairfield's immediate family had a keen interest in business or was overly concerned about furthering the family fortunes. James Porter, Fairfield's father, perhaps to compensate for the amount of time he was forced to spend managing the family business, spent money freely on his hobbies – boating, architecture, and travel – and on furnishing his homes. But within his lifetime the real estate empire that he managed dwindled significantly, in part because of the introduction of income tax and in part because of the Great Depression. Cultured, scholarly, and aloof from commerce, James Porter and his family exhibited behavior much more typical of the landed classes of the eighteenth or early nineteenth century than of the entrepreneurs of the late nineteenth or early twentieth, for their preoccupations, like those of a distant cousin, Henry Adams, were spiritual, social, and intellectual. Neighbors considered Ruth and James Porter "Victorians in the best sense of the word," "cultural aristocrats"[2] divorced from the mundane preoccupations of the money-making classes. From childhood, Fairfield Porter remained true to his parents' studied in-difference toward money and, even as his family's wealth vanished, main-tained a Chekovian aloofness toward improving his finances (to the end of his life, his painting, writing, and teaching earned him very little). Even so, in his attitude toward both his ancestry and his finances, he was as much a product of his rarefied background as he was a rebel against it. There, as in his criticism, painting, poetry, and correspondence, Porter evinced a deep respect for tradition which is best understood as a response to and product of his immediate and extended family histories.

Porter's background is exceptional in the world of twentieth-century American visual art, for he came from a family that had participated for more than a hundred years in the intellectual and political life of the country; many of his Abstract Expressionist contemporaries, by comparison, were first- or sec-ond-generation immigrants or European refugees. The intellectual and artistic inhibition that Porter felt during the first forty years of his life (and to some extent thereafter) was due at least in part to his awareness that he came from a brilliant and historically distinguished family and that his family's intellectual standards and expectations for him were high, even if he chose to practice fine art. Through the influence of his learned and socially engaged parents, he grew up in possession of an exceptional "gentleman's education,"[3] with a compre-hensive awareness of politics, literature, art history, and the pressing social problems of the day. His development into an artist was therefore slow, because he grappled for nearly twenty years with questions about the nature and relevance of contemporary art before creating any significant work, and even in the midst of his career, while creating his best paintings, he was constantly pondering the intellectual importance of what he was doing and why he was doing it. This rigorous questioning lasted to the end of his life.

Finally, Porter grew up in an intellectual rather than a sensual household, to be more a scholar and critic than a man who takes his chief inspiration and delight in the color, light, and textures of the physical world, so, in a sense, he needed to disregard his education in order to free himself to paint. His struggle was not so much the struggle of a rich young man trying to shake off the burdens of background and class as it was a struggle between systems of belief, in which painting itself (in conjunction with art criticism) stood for Porter as a kind of credo. Porter's painterly sensuality – an incredibly particular and American sensuality, one so relaxed and all-embracing that his work is sometimes misconstrued as a thoughtless recording of the commonplace – eventually triumphed in a body of paintings which are among the most significant of twentieth-century realism. But painting was not at all the sort of thing he was ever expected to do.

Born in 1907 in Hubbard Woods, Illinois (a village later called Winnetka), Fairfield Porter was descended on both sides from old New England families. His mother's side of the family was the more distinguished. Ruth Porter, née Ruth Wadsworth Furness, was the great-granddaughter of General Peleg Wadsworth, a general in the Army of the Revolution, and her grandfather Alexander's sister, Zilpah Wadsworth, was the mother of Henry Wadsworth Longfellow. As a girl, Ruth, who was born in 1875, had met the august Longfellow in his Cambridge home, where she was appalled when her little brother James spat out a piece of candy proffered by the renowned poet. But she could not have been too terribly embarrassed, since she was no more than seven years old at the time.[4]

Like many New England intellectual families, the Furnesses were involved in abolition and the women's suffrage movement. Though he never saw combat, Ruth's father, Major William Eliot Furness of Philadelphia, had commanded a Massachusetts brigade – Third Regiment, U.S. Colored Troops – in the Civil War.

To what degree Ruth Porter valued her New England background is hard to know; like her son, she was not one to trade on her family name or boast of her connections; and while the many letters she has left behind attest to an abiding awareness of her many relatives and ancestors, she seems to have had no vested interest in trumpeting their importance. Still, as a cousin of the author of "The Courtship of Miles Standish," she was surely aware that New England roots run deep and that New England memories are long-lived. Her active curiosity about other people and her ability to obtain information about them through conversation were in fact a constant source of humor within the family.[5]

The question of roots must have been of some importance to Ruth, for despite her many family connections to New England, she was a transplant. Her parents had moved to Chicago after the Civil War, where Major Furness, a Phi Beta Kappa graduate of Harvard who had studied to be a Unitarian minister, chose to practice law. Ruth Furness was transplanted yet again through marriage, when the wealth of her husband, James Porter, lifted her out of a world of reform-minded middle-class professionals and placed her into the isolated role of a wealthy suburban matron. Throughout her life, Ruth struggled to remain au courant with literary, artistic, and political developments in the world beyond Winnetka; she fought off boredom and isolation with the skill and grace of a heroine from Pushkin or Tolstoy – and the fact of her isolation may help account for her love of nineteenth-century Russian novels, a love she imparted to her children.

She was a woman of remarkable intelligence and industry. By the age of fourteen she had written and illustrated two little books for the amusement of her family: "Gleanings from Popular Authors: Illustrated Poems" and an "Illustrated Old Testament."[6] The former, stitched together with thread, is the work of a girl as intent upon lampooning popular styles as upon sharing great literature with her family. "My object in setting this work before the public," she wrote in her introduction, "is mainly to encourage love of poetry in the infant mind. Love of prose is inherent, but love of poetry is rather an accomplishment." Ruth's schoolgirl scrawl emphasizes the quiet hilarity of such precocious didacticism.

But she had a serious mind. According to her son Eliot, Ruth's strong social conscience developed at Bryn Mawr, where she "made several lifelong friends who became associated with Jane Addams' Hull House in Chicago ...

1
Ruth Wadsworth
Furness at her Bryn
Mawr graduation
in 1896. Photographer
unknown. Courtesy
Mrs. Fairfield Porter.

[who] encouraged her emotional bias towards a liberal point of view" (fig. 1). After graduation in 1896, she returned to Chicago, where she worked briefly as a grammar school teacher. After marriage to an old childhood friend five years her senior in 1898, she did not work outside the home. Rather, she ran a scrupulously ordered household on Chicago's North Shore, devoting herself to her husband and redirecting her educational zeal to the rearing of five children. When not tending to the needs of her family, supervising two household staffs, keeping up with the many details of the family's two homes (and, later, yacht), or working for a large number of charitable causes, Ruth read novels, poetry, newspapers, reviews, and magazines, including *The Nation*, *The New Republic*, and countless small leftist periodicals.[7]

As the daughter of Unitarian abolitionists and as a woman whose own political leanings had always been egalitarian, Ruth probably found her financial elevation through marriage problematic. The many obligations of being an affluent wife and mother denied her the opportunity to work as a teacher or reformer and in many ways kept her from doing what she might have done best. Nonetheless, and despite her husband's conservatism, she remained staunchly and actively liberal, continuing after marriage to believe in the necessity of changing the American class structure, which she perceived as unfair to workers in general and to working-class racial and ethnic minorities in particular. As a friend recalled, "Her intense sense of justice made her a brave leader in many quite advanced reforms. ... Her intense sympathy for the Jew when discriminated against, for the negro, as well as the proletarian under-dog of every race whom she saw unfairly treated, are too well known to require comment. Her zeal for education, for ... reform, for civil rights, for planned parenthood, brought her into prominence. ... She was an intellectual, valiant and unusual woman ... outspoken in the New England way."[8]

Recollections of Ruth Porter tend to describe her principles and activities more than they do her personality, which was active and outward-looking and could seem "awe-inspiring," "severe," and "impersonal."[9] She could be very funny in her correspondence but was rarely confessional. Even her children remember her most strongly as an instructor and role model rather than a confidante. "It was through my mother's influence that I learned racial and religious tolerance, or more correctly, was not exposed to social prejudices," Eliot Porter recalled. "Not until I [left home] did I learn about ethnic distinctions and how they subvert personal and social judgments. The term 'Christian' being uncommon in my family, I did not place myself in any particular religious category, nor did I know the distinction between Jews and non-Jews ... we thought of [Negroes merely] as the 'freed people'. ... Because we were exposed to a variety of political views we learned political tolerance. My father was Republican throughout his life, whereas mother, when women attained the franchise, voted Democratic or for third-party candidates, which encouraged in her children a tolerance for unorthodox political views."[10]

Ruth's strong beliefs were attributable to her Unitarian upbringing. Unitarianism is a liberal form of Protestantism that stresses the free use of reason. In the nineteenth century, Unitarians appealed for their views to both the Old and the New Testaments as interpreted by reason, but most contemporary Unitarians base their noncreedal religious beliefs simply on reason, conscience, and experience, feeling that ultimate religious authority lies in the self and that moral and ethical living is the supreme witness of that religion.[11] Ruth was intimately acquainted with Unitarian thought because her father had trained to be a Unitarian minister. In a memoir about her mother, she made special note of that upbringing, writing that she was "glad that the Unitarian exaltation of humanity ... made us free of unhappy prejudice against Jews and Negroes" (to which she added, with characteristic honesty, "though our beliefs were not much tested by experience").[12] Ruth formally abandoned Unitarianism for agnosticism after marriage to James Porter (who was, astoundingly for that time, an atheist), but she saw that her children were raised with a Unitarian conscience: all grew up with a strong sense of moral values and social responsibility.

When not educating her children or working for social reform, Ruth led a busy and engaged life: she hosted a neighborhood reading group (which continues to meet to this day), involved herself in community affairs, did volunteer work, and maintained an extraordinary level of daily correspondence. A neighbor later remembered her boundless physical energy: "I can see her now leaping along difficult and dangerous trails in the Canadian Rockies, rushing up a two-hundred-foot-high orange-hued sand dune in the Sahara after an exhausting day of travel, racing up hills in the Virgin Islands, plunging into the blue waters of Honolulu – always eager, never flagging, keeping pace with her ever active and unusually gifted husband."[13]

Ruth's liberal views on child rearing were in large part a continuation of the theories of her mother, Lucy Fairfield Wadsworth Furness, "a woman of great perfection of character,"[14] who in a pamphlet on bringing up children had advised that "the chief and best part of a child's education, even in book-knowledge, must come from the home ... [particularly] religious instruction. ... If possible, I would have a child's mind unbiased by any dogmas or creeds until old enough to read the New Testament for itself and reasoningly, as it might any other biography."[15] Ruth, in time, also wrote on the education of the young, advising parents to read both fiction and poetry aloud to their children from a very early age and cautioning them against many contemporary children's books: "Between the Scylla of inferior literary material and the Charybdis of candor and self-revelation on every theme imaginable," she observed in an article entitled "Children's Reading," "one must with sympathy and advice direct the small craft of a child's curiosity."[16]

As a child, Fairfield was directed by his mother in art as well as in fiction. Ruth preferred the classic children's illustrators Walter Crane, Randolph Caldecott, and Kate Greenaway, but she also admired the contemporary illustrators

Howard Pyle, Maxfield Parrish, and Jessie Wilcox Smith. Her judgments about illustration were sharp. "When I find children delighted with the harsh colors and unsympathetic drawing that distinguish the pictures of the tiresome *Oz* series," she wrote, "I [feel] more discouraged at the perversity in grown people who buy such books than at the lack of taste in the children." Fairfield, even as a small child, was thus long aware of the use of critical judgment in looking at pictures.

Literature, illustrated or not, was certainly much more important to the family than any of the visual arts were. When not tending to the endless details of domestic management, Ruth Porter read – either silently to herself or aloud to her children. According to her son Eliot, she "had so highly developed the art of reading aloud that, as she herself sometimes admitted, she could continue automatically and without evident break for moments at a time after she had actually fallen asleep."[17] She also wrote poetry. Her verses were simple and strongly felt, and the published ones usually concerned her children. A number were published in the "Line o' Type or Two" section of the *Chicago Tribune* – as, for example, this poem, "To a Little Boy," published when Fairfield was nine years old (but probably about his brother Edward):

> My little boy with tousled mien
> And shoes and hands not over clean,
> Whose jokes are nine times out of ten
> Incomprehensible to men,
> Your comic spirit renders birth
> To innocent and wholesome mirth;
> And through the grime of hands and ears
> The whiteness of your soul appears.

In a family that did not demonstrate or discuss affection easily, poetry was indispensable, for the reading and writing of poetry made allowances for feeling. Fairfield Porter, at a very early age, found poetry to be a crucial form of communication; it remained so all his life. His mother was a poet; so was his wife; so were his lover, his friends, and several of his children. He expressed his love for all of them through poetry. Significantly, at the time of Ruth Porter's death in 1942, her ashes went unclaimed, but her poems were published in a pamphlet which was distributed among her family and friends.

While Ruth Porter was socially quite active, her husband was a shy, private man who was, at his best moments, whimsical, extravagant, widely accomplished, and impishly good-humored. James Foster Porter was handsome and fastidious, a man of great intellect and application, but he also had a dark side. Frustrated in his vocational ambitions, he was often awkward and withdrawn and was subject to sudden fits of temper. The personal peculiarities for which Fairfield Porter was legendary in his adulthood – his long silences, indifference to social niceties, temper tantrums, and abrupt, unexplained appearances and departures – were behaviors he inherited from his father.

James Porter came from a distantly New England background but had grown up in the Midwest. The Porter family had been early settlers of the Connecticut River Valley in the small farming town of North Hadley, Massachusetts, and, according to family legend, the Porters had entered the educated classes when one son, too weak to work the fields, had taken up law instead.[19]

Edward Clark Porter, James's father, was an Episcopalian minister from Chicago who married Julia Foster, a woman so extremely pious that she was said to close her eyes when she brushed her hair "so as not to be tempted to vanity."[20] After marriage the couple moved from Chicago to Racine, Wisconsin. They soon had two children, Maurice and James, the first of whom died in infancy. A few years later and quite unexpectedly, Edward Clark Porter died as well, of a ruptured appendix. Julia, shaken by her double loss, moved back to Chicago with her remaining son, James, then five.

Julia Foster Porter was widowed but not without resources; in fact, she was rich. Her money came from a family property that had belonged to her father, a farm on the swampy shores of Lake Michigan which had been divided equally among his three daughters at the time of his death. Early on, Julia's two sisters, Clara and Adele, had sold her their shares in the farm and moved to the more civilized world of Peterborough, New Hampshire. Thus Julia gained sole possession of a large property in what would soon become the most valuable land in the Midwest: that area of downtown Chicago now known as the Loop.

So far as James was concerned, this wealth was problematic, for it gave his lonely and possessive mother too strong a hold over him. Her money required his constant attention and bound them together. Even after James had married and started his own family, Julia Porter expected to reside within his home. In family recollection she was bitterly disappointed when James insisted on building her a house, where she could live with a companion and her household staff, even though the new house was just a few hundred feet away from his own. She expressed her anger by leaving the dinner table abruptly and retiring in silent fury to the front hallway, where she sat for some time by herself.[21]

A pious widow, Julia Foster Porter devoted herself to philanthropy, endowing a children's charity hospital, Maurice Memorial Children's Hospital, in honor of her deceased firstborn son and, after her second son left home, adopting two girls from an orphanage. Eliot Porter remembered her as a woman who had "assumed lifelong mourning, dressing always in long, full black shirtwaists that buttoned closely around her neck. A costume of such formality, together with an inherent reserve, inhibited spontaneous expressions of affection by her grandchildren." Ruth Porter later suggested to her daughter that Julia Foster Porter's asocial tendencies had a direct relation to those of Ruth's husband.[22]

Though raised in a pious household, James Porter, who was always deeply interested in natural science, announced while still a teenager that he was agnostic. According to Eliot, "My father became a dedicated protagonist of the scientific interpretation of natural phenomena with an unshakable belief in causality and a fierce rejection of purpose as a driving force in the universe. Under the influence of Darwin's writings, [he] professed agnosticism; in later years he went beyond such qualified skepticism and pronounced his disbelief in a God or the need for a supernatural explanation of existence." The highly religious Julia Foster Porter doubtless felt her son's pronouncement as a great blow.

Despite their differences over religion, James was very much like his mother: grave, generous, and principled. Like her, too, he was retiring by nature, unreasonably shy, and (particularly later in life) prone to angry silences and periods of deep depression. "James was essentially non-communicative," his daughter-in-law Anne remembered. "If we went out on the boat, he would sit at the back of the boat, looking away at the water."[23]

After attending Harvard (class of 1895) and attaining a master's degree, James Porter began a career as a biologist. But by twenty-six he had given up, in part because poor eyesight made use of a microscope nearly impossible but also because, according to a letter from Ruth, he was "dissatisfied with it as a career." The scholarly Ruth supported James in his decision, writing a friend with determined optimism in the same letter, "For my part I like the idea of drawing houses much better than that of drawing bugs!"[24]

After a secret engagement – James had abruptly proposed, then departed alone on a four-month tour of Europe – James Porter married Ruth Furness in June 1898. They took a summer-long honeymoon in England and Italy, where they toured cathedrals and other monumental structures of interest to James. While overseas, they collected photographic reproductions of these and other masterpieces; the reproductions were hung first in New York, where James studied architecture at Columbia University, and later in Chicago, where the couple returned in 1899.

James's first intention in moving back to Chicago was to work in an architectural office, but he was soon forced to give up on this, his second career, in order to help manage his mother's real estate holdings. The disappointment he felt at having to give up his own ambitions for the sake of family money lingered with him always. "He never got to exercise his artistic nature," one family member later observed. "His was a surrender to duty."[25] Fairfield Porter grew up thinking of his father as a man of talent and vision who had been forced to raise and support a family rather than pursue his creative inclinations. Fairfield's own deep ambivalence to the duties of parenthood are probably best understood in light of his father's experience.

One consolation for James upon entering the family business of money and property management was that, with plenty of cash and a degree in architecture, he was free to design, build, and furnish his own home and a home for his mother. The site he chose for the two buildings was a bluff overlooking Lake

Michigan. Rather than facing directly out over the lake, his house faced south to catch the winter sun. A pergola designed to look like a temple descended south along the sloping lawn to Julia Foster Porter's house.

The James Porter home was, as Eliot described it, "a large brick Greek revival house with Ionic pilasters at its corners, an entrance portico and facade featuring Corinthian columns, and Doric columned porches on each side of the house ... [James's] admiration of classical architecture was based on its purity of function and design expressed by the mathematical precision of Greek temple construction, which he meticulously maintained in the features he incorporated in his house."[26] In later years Fairfield Porter proudly declared it "one of the most beautiful Greek Revival houses in the United States."[27]

The grounds and surrounding neighborhood were a paradise for children. Apart from the beach, the house had access to woods and marshland, ravines and gullys, large sloping lawns, a brick terrace overlooking the lake, a long, downhill driveway, a tennis court, a barn, and stables.

James built a home for his mother on the same bluff but in a very different style, one that he felt most suited her temperament: a half-timbered cottage screened by trees, facing away from James's house. Its mock-Tudor exterior was boxy and graceless. Its interiors, with dark woodwork, leaded windowpanes, and dark green and brown grasscloth wall coverings, were beautifully detailed but claustrophobic. Photographs of the bluff, with two such very different houses so close together and yet not facing one another, make an odd impression (fig. 2). Forced into close proximity with his mother, James Porter seems to have chosen to express through architecture an important psychological truth about their relationship.

The derivative nature of the building styles that James Porter selected seems to indicate he was not an innovative architect. In later years Fairfield

2
The two homes designed and built by James Porter
on the bluff overlooking Lake Michigan in Winnetka.
Julia Foster Porter's house stands on the left.
Photographer unknown. Courtesy Mrs. Fairfield Porter.

Porter, whose own work was thought derivative, imitative, and old-fashioned, suggested that the success or failure of the houses should not be judged by the styles in which they were built but rather by their functional and structural integrity and practicality:

[Modern architects] would have said [my father's house] was a monument, not a functional building. But as a matter of fact, it's very, very much more functional [than a modern building] because it's more practical ... the difference between a modern architectured house and what my father made was simply that they gave up the look of the classical monument and decided to make something that had the look of something else. ... It's just a change in fashion. ... A house is a machine for living – Corbusier likes this phrase – but you see a house by Corbusier and it always leaks, the rain comes through the roof, he doesn't keep out the weather ... [a Corbusier house] is just an amusing and tricky thing.[28]

By remaining impervious to fashion and sticking with a style he loved, James Porter was, in his son's estimation, being equally innovative, if in a way unacceptable to contemporary views on architecture. The same sort of thing could be said of Fairfield Porter's painting. Traditional but innovative, he refused to yield to a dominant style simply for the sake of being fashionable. Throughout his life, Fairfield Porter, who as a young man dreamt of being an architect like his father,[29] saw his life as a continuation of his father's life[30] and believed strongly in the validity of his father's creative work, limited in scope though it was and unfashionable though it may have been.

In truth, Fairfield Porter's relationship with his father was a complicated and exacting one. Every son craves the admiration and respect of his father, and among the talented and competitive Porter children, Fairfield sought to distinguish himself to his father through a shared love of art. Through his father, Fairfield would later claim, he had "acquired a wide ranging interest ... in architecture and the visual arts," once saying in an interview, "I think the chief influences on me as a child were my father's interest in art and architecture,"[31] and adding that "being a painter was somehow related to my father."[32] (From his mother, by comparison, Porter felt that he had merely inherited "an interest in people and an aptitude for writing.")[33] Fairfield's early tragedy was that not only did James reject him personally (James "disliked Fairfield"),[34] but he also disparaged his son's ability ("Father never completely understood Fairfield's aspirations or his first immature attempts to express them," and "James was doubtful that Fairfield had the necessary talent").[35] The eager son claimed a shared bond with the father; the father rejected not just the son but (perhaps more woundingly) the son's claim to the bond.

By the time construction on the Porter home was complete, James and Ruth already had a two-year-old daughter, Nancy. Shortly after moving in, Ruth gave birth to her first son, Eliot, in 1901. Eliot was followed by Edward in 1904, Fairfield in 1907, and John in 1910.

When John was born, an event occurred which had a resounding effect on Fairfield and which indicates that Ruth and James, though enormously supportive of their children's educational development, lacked an essential understanding of their emotional needs. As Fairfield's wife, Anne, later recounted, "Fairfield's real name is John Fairfield Porter. He had been known as Johnny until he was three, and he knew his name and recognized it. But when his little brother was born, his parents decided to name the baby Johnny, and so they started calling John Fairfield simply Fairfield. The same day, they took Fairfield to the barber shop. I suppose they thought they were encouraging him to think of himself as a grown-up boy, by giving him a grown-up boy's haircut. Well, they cut all his hair off and changed his name, all in the same day, and he never forgot that day."[36]

The Porters' detachment from their children's emotional vulnerability was perhaps typical of its day. Wealthy parents in the early years of the century spent little time with their children, leaving them instead to trained servants (Ruth's mother, Lucy, even wrote, "To me, there is no greater blessing to a mother than a faithful nursery-girl").[37] To some extent, too, this detachment was typical of the traditional New England manner, which rarely discusses feelings or indulges in sentiment. But in other ways the Porter family was exceptional in its detachment.

The Porters did not celebrate Christmas (James being, after all, an atheist), and birthdays, too, were "non-events."[38] Mealtimes, the traditional moment of a family's coming together, were notable in that the Porters made a regular practice of bringing books to the table and, upon finishing the meal, immediately falling into a silence broken only by the clearing of throats or the rustling of a page. Nearly everyone who visited the Porters, either in Winnetka or at their summer home in Maine, remarked on the stillness.

The changing of Fairfield's name and later incidents indicate that he lacked an essential emotional awareness and support from his parents, with the result that he grew up unable to locate his own emotions, much less communicate or acknowledge them. Fairfield's son Laurence suggested that his father "could seldom express his tender and vulnerable feelings verbally ... the emotional damage done to [him] by his father's coldness and remoteness was obvious." In like manner, "his involvement with me was sporadic and impulsive ... nearly always shaped by the adult point of view, with no sense of the effect on the child."[39] As a result, the young Fairfield sought emotional instruction and refuge in poetry, literature, and art, where emotion could be freely, if privately, acknowledged.

The size and decoration of the Porter home in Winnetka, at once classically imposing and academically austere, suggest the sort of people Ruth and her husband knew themselves to be: cultured people dedicated to creating an environment in which they could instruct and educate their children (fig. 3). The Winnetka house is nobly proportioned, unlike the darkly fanciful house created for Julia Foster Porter (which may explain why, unlike the Julia Foster Porter house, the James Porter house still stands on its bluff above Lake Michigan). The interior had grand space, Vitruvian dimensions, and beautiful furnishings, but not much in the way of original art. James Porter preferred photographic reproductions of masterworks. In Fairfield Porter's recollection, the art on the walls was "just photographs. And you know those casts made in Boston' ... of the Parthenon frieze. We had maybe ten of them around the house."[40] An interior photograph shows a room hung with reproductions of Renaissance portraiture and, over one brick fireplace, a photograph of Michelangelo's *Creation of Adam* (despite Fairfield Porter's memory that "my father ... didn't understand the Renaissance at all. He didn't like it").[41] The house also had its share of oddities: a player organ, a greenhouse, and a room set aside for James Porter's biological specimens. Out of James Porter's taste for the Gothic (he loved Gothic architecture) came one of Fairfield Porter's earliest memories, of "a giant photograph of the cathedral of Amiens, a mysterious cast of some architectural detail, which I used to dream of as though it had a kind of conscious life, at least an awareness of me, that was, though not overtly hostile, very cold and unsympathetic."[42] Here again, architecture gives form to an otherwise unarticulated emotional truth.

Given the emotional distance and intellectual preoccupations of the parents, the Porter children relied upon several members of the household staff for emotional support. There was the governess, Miss Probst, who taught the

3
Fairfield Porter and Ruth Wadsworth Porter in the driveway at 1085 Sheridan Road in Winnetka, circa 1910. Photographer unknown. Courtesy Mrs. Fairfield Porter.

younger boys German, because, as Fairfield recalled, "German was the prestigious foreign language for people to learn [until] the first World War."[43] (Later, Porter hired a young German woman to teach his own children and ended up falling in love with her.) The other staff member of greatest importance was Josephine Krup, the Swedish cook, who remained a close friend to Ruth Porter for over twenty years.

As Porter grew, he developed a reputation within the family for being bright but difficult; he was particularly known for throwing tantrums, "so much so that when Edward, as a child at a grammar school theatrical, observed Potiphar's wife onstage throwing a fit, he turned to his parents and remarked, 'Just like Fairfield.'"[44] Comparisons were frequently made between Fairfield and his little brother, Johnny, for "Fairfield screamed and cried all the time, and Johnny was sweet-tempered."[45]

In part, Fairfield's sensitivity was due to sensitive hearing; loud noises in contained spaces were upsetting to him throughout his life.[46] But Fairfield was frustrated by another problem as well, a reading disorder, perhaps a mild form of dyslexia, which made him read only half as fast as the other children.[47] Nonetheless, he was a voracious reader, with a fascination for the science fiction fantasies of H. G. Wells. One of his earliest preserved letters, written at age eleven to his maternal great-aunts Rebecca and Laura Furness (Rebecca had studied painting with Thomas Eakins in Philadelphia), describes a game he has been playing with his brothers Edward and John and his neighbors Barbara Mettler and Louise Fentress based on a Wells novel: "Edward John and I have just been playing with the Pulman train that we made out of the blocks. Louise and Barbara play with us most of the time. ... We pretend that the train goes around Edfaloba. ... We pretend everything in Edfaloba runs by sunlight and people store it to make a light in night time."[48] Edfaloba was an imaginary country located on Mars; the name is an acronym of Edward, Fairfield, Louise, and Barbara. "We drew maps of it," Porter recalled, "discussed it sociologically and that sort of stuff."[49]

So far as identities within the family were concerned, Eliot was the most accomplished, the handsomest, and the most independent. He shared his father's interest in science. Nancy was perhaps her mother's best friend, but she was "cold, self-righteous, and domineering,"[50] not the sort that would have enjoyed a mother's interference in her affairs. Fairfield, on the other hand, was both intelligent and malleable. He exhibited an interest in language, poetry, and literature from his earliest years, unlike his brothers Edward and John.

Significantly, Fairfield's first memory of looking at a painting includes his mother: "I remember being taken to the Art Institute [of Chicago] by my mother and ... the first paintings that I can remember in the Art Institute are [by] Giovanni di Paolo. I think it was because it had the *Beheading of St. John the Baptist* in it, which was sort of fascinatingly gory. ... When I was twelve [I remember seeing] an exhibition of Picasso, that Egyptian period, those great big heads. ... And I thought, if this is what painting is today, it's a significant activity."[51]

Ruth's encouragement of her son's artistic inclinations was a great help to him. Fairfield received early support from grammar school teachers as well, but as he recalled, "My art interest wasn't that decisive or active."[52]

By the time he reached high school – he attended New Trier, a public school which would eventually become one of the best in the nation but which at the time was merely a "good ordinary public school"[53] – he had developed into a quiet, introspective, and socially awkward adolescent, paralyzed by self-consciousness about his appearance, his lack of physical prowess, and a vague but persistent sense that he was somehow not acceptable, which came to him mainly from his parents: "Once all my brothers and my sister were photographed (I was about 12) and the pictures were all acceptable except mine (that is, to my parents) and I was sent back again and again to the photographer, until at last they decided to accept what the photographer had made, though they still didn't like it. I would have been quite content with the first photograph, but I hated each succeeding effort more and more. Ever since I have disliked pictures of myself: they are associated with a personality that exists in someone else's mind."[54]

Fairfield's dissatisfaction with himself extended to his name, for he disliked it and came to be known within his home as "Furl" and among his schoolmates as "Clam" or "Clammy." He had a hard time adjusting to high school, in part owing to his exceptional home education, which had qualified him to enter high school two years early, while physically immature. Porter's memories of his preparatory years were mixed: "I was rather isolated [there]. ... [it] frightened me. ... I wasn't very athletic. We [Porters] were all like that. But [my brothers] didn't have the disadvantage of being a couple of years younger than their group."[55]

On Sunday afternoons in Winnetka, James Porter took his children on nature walks along the lakefront, explaining the geology and natural history of the region, collecting rocks, plants, fungi, and fossil specimens as they went. James's interest in the natural world, combined with the impossibility of taking extended camping trips with his young children, led him to make a purchase in 1912 that would have a resounding effect on his family.

While visiting friends at a marine biological laboratory in Casco Bay, James Porter learned that a nearby island in Penobscot Bay was for sale. Several hundred acres large, Great Spruce Head lay halfway between the Maine coast and Deer Isle. The dimensions of the irregularly shaped island were roughly a mile long by half a mile wide, "small enough to be an island to children, yet large and varied enough to promise constant enjoyment."[56] There were no habitations on the island; two farming families had once lived there, and a small graveyard remained. The purchase price was ten thousand dollars.[57] Significantly, the island lay near Stonington, where the painter John Marin made his summer home and painted many of his famous watercolors of the Maine coast.

In the summer of 1912, James brought Eliot to the island to help lay out the site of the home he had designed. "Wild cattle [were] pastured on the hill's slopes by island farmers" and in recent years the island had been "overgrazed and repeatedly cut over for wood," making it "barren and open."[58] The grandly scaled house that James Porter designed and had built for his family, which was soon known as the Big House, was an extremely idiosyncratic structure. Sited on a northeastern headland at a significant distance from the cove which served as harbor and landing place, the building seemed more rustic pavilion than seaside mansion, its barnlike interior suggesting an elaborate campground shelter rather than a finished country home. With no insulation, paper-thin beaverboard walls, and large porches where only bug screens divided indoors from out, the house was warmed by a single large fireplace in the cavernous main hall (fig. 4). Each of the fourteen bedrooms featured little more than a bureau, a desk, and a sleeping cot. Electricity was only occasionally available, courtesy of a fuel-powered generator in a shed outside.

Despite its regal position overlooking the Barred Islands and Penobscot Bay, the building had an ungainly exterior, its structural lines compromised by the many screened porches which sprouted from all sides like fungus from a stump. The ugliness of the exterior may account for the lack of successful paintings of the house by Fairfield Porter.

The interior was much more successful. Years later, in a never-published collaborative effort with the poet James Schuyler, Fairfield Porter described the Big House with appreciation, particularly remembering its relation with maritime Maine's sensual, opalescent light: "The family cottage is commodious, very much in the style of its period, and the exterior and the interior spaces are handled, within the convention, in the most original ways: the living room – the scene and subject of many ... paintings – is two stories high with balconies at either end, off of which are bedroom corridors. To the eye, the room has the

4
Interior of the Big House on Great Spruce Head Island. Photographer unknown. Courtesy Mrs. Fairfield Porter.

5
Interior with a Dress Pattern, 1969.
From the Porter Collection
of Mr. and Mrs. Austin List.

serene proportions of a double cube. Beyond the windows there are open porches. This creates a soft and infinitely variable lighting."[59]

It was while exposed to this infinitely variable lighting that Fairfield Porter first felt compelled to create art, working first in pastels in emulation of his sister Nancy[60] and then in pencil, watercolor, and oils. One of Fairfield Porter's greatest paintings, *Interior with a Dress Pattern* (1969, fig. 5) would memorialize this interior, as would Eliot Porter, in his memoir of island life:

The large central living room, rising two stories to the roof, was flanked on either side by covered porches. On the southern-facing one, at the enormous table [seating twenty-two] we ate our meals in all weather. From the other end of the living room, the house continued into two stories of small rooms, the kitchen at one end with bedrooms above, the bedrooms on both floors at the other end. The upstairs rooms were reached by staircases that led to balconies. ... A huge brick fireplace capable of accommodating four-foot logs extended across most of the kitchen end of the living room. Above the mantle hung a plaster cast of one of the Elgin marbles from the Parthenon. The wood-work was stained dark brown and the beaverboard walls were painted chrome yellow. The floor ... was ... painted an oxblood red. The walls of the living room were decorated with an oriental rug, an embroidered Chinese dragon, India prints and Egyptian bedspreads ... Norwegian gargoyles, Japanese paper fish, and a ceramic plaque of sea horses, the emblem of father's first boat, completed the decor of the room. This heterogeneous and garish decoration had come about not as the result of any plan but through a process of slow accretion ... we accepted it uncritically and even took a certain degree of pride in it, a pride reduced only from time to time by the politely restrained, unenthusiastic comments of visitors. My mother, I believe, was more conscious of the room's atmosphere than the rest of us, for she once remarked that she felt as though she were living in a medium's parlor.

The final embellishment of the room was the result of father's passion for dragons. ... [My father] paint[ed] panels to fit the sloped ceiling of the island house's living room ... very boldly designed dragons in the most flamboyant colors obtainable. When the dragons were installed [they] dominated the living room, stretching for thirty feet along its whole length. A violet, green and yellow beast, the male of the species, with huge red bat-like wings, occupied one side. On the opposite wall, a wingless female, equally garish, hissed at two young dragons, one of each sex, sporting on her tail.[61]

Yet another playful note was added to the living room by the four large toy sailboats made by the island caretaker, which "soon serv[ed] the double purpose of decoration and toy, for when we weren't using them they were ensconced in cradles on the balcony railings at the ends of the living room."[62]

Its great style notwithstanding, the Big House had few creature comforts. The shared bathrooms had cold running water, but the only available hot water came from the reservoir in the woodburning stove in the kitchen, which was available only after the supper dishes had been washed and then in an extremely limited supply. According to Eliot, "Preparing hot water for bathing was not often undertaken for the benefit of children. ... An early morning dip [in fifty-five-degree water] was [thought] the most healthy and invigorating way to start the day." Even James and Ruth Porter took ocean baths every morning, Ruth at one point writing to Nancy, "I have kept as clean as Tommy [the dog] on my private Landing Beach."[63] In another letter, referring to some visiting boys, she remarked, "They are very good about not washing and most of them are delightedly growing mustaches."[64]

"Meals at the big table on the porch," Eliot recalled, "were often shivery affairs, especially breakfast or supper during stormy or foggy weather. ... Every morning Father would tap and reset the barometer and announce the temperature to the guests. When the weather was particularly bad, he always did this, it seemed, with a certain gleeful satisfaction in the extremes of the Maine climate."[65] The meals themselves, often serving upward of fifteen people, were planned by Ruth and prepared in the primitive kitchen on a single woodburning stove by the hard-working Josephine, usually with the assistance of a summer helper or two.

The job of planning and cooking meals was complicated by the fact that a limited amount of groceries could be brought in by boat each week from the mainland. Rations were supplemented by vegetables grown on the island, in a garden which lacked irrigation: water had to be hauled in. Other food sources included the tiny wild blueberries and strawberries that grew in the meadows, the shoals of mussels which lay exposed at high tide, lobsters bought from local seamen, and milk from the island's one cow. But mealtimes were never luxurious: the common recollection of Porter children and visitors alike was of cold temperatures and hunger.[66]

In addition to buying Great Spruce Head Island and constructing the Big House, James Porter ordered "a custom-made motorboat with sleeping accommodations for eight people. He named it *Hippocampus*, Greek for 'seahorse,' or, more literally, 'horse monster.'"[67] In addition, he retained a sea captain, Monte Green, to pilot and caretake. A year or two after purchasing the *Hippocampus*, James purchased a small speedboat, the *Squid*, for short jaunts around the island. He also ordered a cement tennis court constructed for family use and made sure to have a canoe and other small craft available for the children and guests. The island, despite its limited comforts, was a natural paradise for children.

It was also an escape for James Porter into the natural world that he loved and the hobbies he cherished: marine biology, architectural planning, boating, and having guests. According to a grandson, "Signs of James' frustrated, restless energy were present everywhere on his summer island, in his many improvements such as bridges and trails, and notably in a large collection of marine life he had collected and preserved in Mason jars."[68] For a man who had given up dreams of architectural design and research biology to attend to managing real estate, the island was his private Xanadu, a place where fantasies – which eventually included a Japanese bridge, a working farm, an orchard, a special swimming cove, a lookout tower, an extensive series of wilderness trails, and a special cabinet for marine specimens – came true. With his wife, children, servants, and guests participating in his utopian kingdom as grateful, willing subjects, James let his idiosyncratic nature run wild. Construction and maintenance of the island and boats took significant time and energy, but with few distractions other than reading, hiking, swimming, and working in the vegetable garden, the children, eager for their father's affection, gladly participated in his many projects. (Laborers were always hired to help with the heaviest work.)

Meanwhile, the burdens of housekeeping and guest management fell primarily on Ruth Porter, who planned comings and goings, ordered groceries, supervised the two local girls who worked as maids, and consulted with Josephine over the daily menus. When not entertaining visitors, she read, watched over the children, worked in the vegetable garden, or spent hours picking and hulling the tiny wild berries that grew all over the island. Ruth was equal to any task, even the strenuous opening and closing of the house. Never too grand to roll up her sleeves, she lightheartedly remarked to her daughter in one letter, "My usual associations with our arrival is dead flies."[69]

Without friends, the Porter children spent an inordinate time in isolated pursuits or in each other's company (fig. 6). While the former encouraged their intellectual development, it also encouraged asocial behavior. Summers on the island intensified the mixed feelings that the Porter children had for one another, feelings which deepened and became less easy to deny as, summer after summer, they grew older there together.

6
The Porter brothers on the dock at Great Spruce Head, 1925.
From left, Edward, John, Eliot, and Fairfield.
Photographer unknown. Courtesy Mrs. Fairfield Porter.

Fairfield felt a strong loyalty to his siblings, but his affection for them was limited, as was theirs for him. He disliked his bossy older sister, Nancy, whose behavior is exemplified in a story told by Fairfield's son Laurence: "Once Fairfield as a little boy planted bulbs in the wild field around the Big House to make it more beautiful. Nancy pulled them all up, claiming Fairfield had not been given permission."[70] Fairfield's early exposure to his sister's overbearing personality, as well as the strong and watchful presence of his mother, contributed to a lifelong antipathy toward dominating women.[71]

Fairfield and Eliot had a more complicated relationship. Considering how strongly cast in his father's image Eliot was – handsome, stalwart, self-motivated, a devoted naturalist – he must have seemed quite formidable to Fairfield. But Eliot disliked keeping company with any of his younger brothers, instead spending time alone in the woods, observing birds and taking photographs, which he developed in a self-constructed darkroom. When forced to remain indoors, Eliot recalled, he liked to create explosions and stink bombs with his chemistry set, play practical jokes on the much-despised tagalong brothers, and remain in his room with his door shut. But on Great Spruce Head he spent nearly every day outdoors, much of the time photographing birds. The Porters had a long-standing family joke that "Eliot lost fifteen pounds in the nesting season."[72] Eliot's wife, the artist Aline Kilham, remarked, "His mother said Eliot was the sort of person who should have been a lighthouse keeper. ... [He's] intense, with blinders on."[73] Another family member who knew him as an adult put it more plainly: "[He] was essentially asocial. ... It was impossible to engage him in a conversation unless he had initiated it on his own terms ... we seldom saw him."[74]

Edward was the next oldest son and the family wit. He disliked island living. Ruth described his characteristic behavior in a letter: While Edward and his friends play endless games of bridge, "Fairfield and I look on and listen and do chores in the background ... [James] tried to send [Edward and his friends] on a cruise to Isle au Haut but they went into executive session and decided to go for just the day ... and ... played bridge with the side curtains down all the time there and all the way back."[75] When given a choice, Edward avoided going to the island and was the first of the family members to abandon it entirely. An amateur photographer and mountaineer, he eventually helped his father manage the family real estate firm.

John, the baby brother, was constantly compared favorably to Fairfield, and the two had little in common. Yet of all the brothers, Fairfield and John spent the rest of their lives in the closest proximity, both on the island and off. John liked power boating, athletics, and island maintenance and construction projects. His pragmatic nature led him to become the de facto leader and manager of the so-called island family, and a high-school science teacher in Bronxville, New York. Relations between John and Fairfield became particularly strained in later years, for Fairfield depended heavily on John to manage the island's practical affairs.

Island life could be claustrophobic, especially because of the lack of outside diversions. There were no radios, and in the early years even mail delivery was limited (to this day the island does not have a telephone). Moreover, it could be so physically uncomfortable that despite the exhilaration of fresh air, sunshine, and natural beauty, even the hardiest visitors could find the place a challenge.

The Porter children were generally resilient in coping with the hunger and cold, the icy morning baths, the bugs and the fog. In his memoirs, Eliot even recalled a year when "we had an epidemic of German measles that went undiagnosed until all of us had recovered." Until then, the family thought they were suffering from "brown-tail moth itch."[76]

Accidents, too, were endured with stoicism. Ruth noted, for example, that the *Hippocampus* "went very badly and at the wharf at Buck's Harbor gave up and drifted for four hours before George Haskell and Eliot could get her going. As we drifted past the float Fairfield had jumped out and fastened the rope to the float. Edward on the afterdeck got entangled in the rope which wound around his ankle and pulled him overboard – fortunately or I think he would have lost his foot." After the emergency "Fairfield was forgotten for a time and stood in the rain."[77] In another letter, she calmly recorded that "John and Fairfield and I were starting for Beach Island in the [little motorboat when] there was a faulty carburetor [and] the gas around the engine caught fire ... the whole thing went up in flame. ... Fairfield jumped in and swam to [the tender]. I thought we might have to jump too but Fairfield kept saying very calmly, 'Don't jump, wait,' and we were able to get in and row to the float ... [where] we watched her burn to almost nothing."[78]

An additional challenge to the nerves, though certainly less thrilling to endure, came from Maine's unpredictable weather, for during extended rains and thick fog the family were confined to the damp and drafty house, sometimes for more than ten days. At one point Ruth observed, "Yesterday it poured all day. ... it was a day when we had to rack our brains in order to keep those young animals occupied."[79] On another afternoon, according to family lore, James Porter, fed up with listening to Fairfield's collection of cowboy records on the family gramophone, took the entire stack outside and wordlessly smashed them all on the rocks below the house.[80]

Long spells of rain and fog were particularly difficult for the children as they grew into adolescence. No teenager likes to spend too much time under the eye of a vigilant parent, and Ruth Porter was nothing if not vigilant. One gets a sense of her restless desire to observe and record everything about her in her prolific correspondence. Though generally careful not to discuss her children's personal affairs in letters, she made a significant, if oblique, observation about Fairfield's sexual indecisiveness, when her son was still in his teens, writing to Nancy from Great Spruce Head, "I am now deep in Proust ... I read a long and also funny part in the beginning to Fairfield and Eliot who listened with great interest. I should not enjoy reading it all to Fairfield. I do not yet feel perfectly at home with homosexuality."[81]

While Great Spruce Head Island held a special place in the affections of the Porters, the family did not limit their summer activities, at least at first, to island life. Ruth and James Porter loved to travel, and before the children went off to college, the family took several trips together. Fairfield Porter recalled taking a trip to the Canadian Rockies "right after the First World War. It was about 1918 or 1919. [Father] knew the Canadian Rockies very well. We took a boat from Seattle to Alaska, and then took a boat back again to Vancouver and then went to the Canadian Rockies to a camp that was near Lake Louise." [82] Then, in 1921, James and Ruth, John and Fairfield, and Ruth's sister Margaret went to London en route to a Mediterranean cruise. "I remember in the National Gallery going to see the Leonardo *Virgin of the Rocks*. But I discovered something I didn't know from the photographs at home, and that was Titian – *The Rape of Europa*. And Veronese's *The Family of Darius Before Alexander*." [83] The Mediterranean cruise itself afforded Fairfield Porter an introduction to southern Europe, especially Italy, as well as North Africa. A travel diary by Ruth Porter suggests frantic sightseeing combined with determined onboard socializing between ports of call.

One port of call was particularly important to Fairfield. As he recalled to the poet John Ashbery,

I was in Athens in about 1923. It thrilled me as few other events have. I was surrounded at home by life size plaster casts of the Parthenon frieze, and impressed by my father's explanations (he had been an architect) of the excellence of Greek architecture, which did in no way disappoint me. ... Greece means a lot of things to me related to my father and my mother – my father taught me to be thrilled by Greek architecture and sculpture, and he loved mountains, as I did too, and [the] blue [of the Greek flag] is associated for me with my mother, because she looked well in blue, and was blue-eyed, and had a candid expression, and a freshness and strength like Greek writing, like Homer, and she had a fresh gift for language. Also blue means to me the first boy I was ever in love with, when I was about seven, who had starry eyes and was somehow completely inaccessible, though we played together. [84]

1957

By the time Fairfield Porter graduated – two years early – from high school, finishing 28th in the New Trier class of 159, he was an exceptionally literate and well-traveled young man, thoroughly prepared for the cultural and intellectual challenges which awaited him at Harvard. [85] Yet after some thought, his parents decided he was probably still too physically and emotionally immature to enjoy Harvard as much as he might. So James Porter interceded on his son's behalf, writing his alma mater and requesting a year's deferral for his son "on account of his youth." [86] The deferral granted, Fairfield enrolled at Milton Academy, just outside Boston, for a final preparatory year. He was not the first in his family to do so; Ruth's cousin T. S. Eliot [87] had attended Milton for the same reason nearly two decades before.

2

Milton and Harvard

When Fairfield Porter entered Milton Academy in September 1923, he was, like T. S. Eliot in 1905, a young man from the Midwest in need of another year's physical and emotional maturation before entering the university by which he had already been accepted (fig. 7). Both were cerebral, withdrawn, physically unimposing young men who had spent most of their time in the company of a close and supportive family dominated by a brilliant mother. At Milton, Porter experienced for the first time the shock of an existence outside the enveloping warmth of family and home and began to realize the sort of uncertainties and insecurities less sheltered and more socially adept adolescents had already been negotiating for years. He also began to reconcile himself to the pretentiousness and self-regard for which Boston and Harvard are well known. Coming late to

7
Porter as an adolescent.
Photographer unknown.
Courtesy Mrs. Fairfield
Porter.

a preparatory school filled with wealthy and socially prominent easterners (a large number of whom would enter Harvard the next year), Porter was made aware of his oddness and lived outside the tight-knit society of his classmates. It was a lonely, frustrating, and difficult time.

Nevertheless, Porter's admission application to Harvard suggests that he really did need another year to mature, for it is an unprepossessing document. Asked why he wished to attend Harvard, Porter wrote, "I am going to Harvard ~~because~~ [the word is scratched out] principally because my father went there and I know more about it than any other university. But I think from what I have heard, it offers better scientific courses than many colleges; and you can be more independent there than in other universities that I know anything about; for instance, fraternities are relatively unimportant there." Asked his plan for college life and work, Porter responded, "I am going to take a general course, mainly sciences, but I have no plan as regards college life." These are the only questions asking a response from the applicant, and as a document of Porter's thoughts about Harvard in his senior year in high school, it is remarkably telling: he is quite honest that he has no plans or ideas at all about what he will do.

Little from Fairfield Porter's life at Milton survives, apart from a humorous essay on a Winnetka neighbor and a few letters from him to his mother, with whom he remained a loyal correspondent for many years to come. From his room at Wolcott House, he wrote her that September:

There is one boy here who is morbidly interesting in that he is crippled for life and deformed. He is also very nice and rather quiet ... the boys think he was crazy when he first came because of some queer things he did when he came here first. A good deal of folklore has grown up about him. ... If he says very little at one meal it is taken with reverence and much respect as though he were a little bright boy telling his name and age and address.

September 1923

I went to the Unitarian church a week ago Sunday with some other boys who were not Unitarians and who were going to the "heathen church" as they said, because of the shortness of the service. They were much surprised and interested to hear that I have never been [to church] before.

Reading between the lines of this grim, funny series of understatements, one can assume that Porter has taken his own feelings of outsiderliness and applied them to the handicapped boy. Inexperienced at articulating his emotions, Porter demonstrates the parallel vulnerability of another, couching that vulnerability in a Dickensian manner his mother will accept because she finds it amusing, though the real-life situation is not amusing at all. His reference to the Unitarian church as "heathen" suggests Porter's dawning awareness that not only was his family's atheism exceptional among his contemporaries, but even Unitarianism could be looked upon as lax, radical, and somehow socially unacceptable.

Porter resented his parents' decision to send him to Milton. According to his wife, "He had a terrible time. ... He always said that it was a terrible waste. He didn't need to go to Milton to become more social. He was already social. If there was something he wanted to talk about, he talked about it. He talked to his mother all the time. He had no problem talking to girls. He treated girls and boys equally. He just disliked chatter and small talk. ... He spoke very well when he had something to say. He just wouldn't make talk for its own sake."[1]

The year at Milton did not make "Clammy" any more loquacious. With no real interest in putting himself forward, Porter made no friends among the Milton teaching staff and only one or two among the other students. In a letter home he noted, "Mr. Osgood [a teacher] threatens terrible things to us very calmly at the beginning of the period, and he generally carries them out."[2] In another, he chafed at the conventions and hypocrisies of boarding-school life: "All the boys from 6th class up to 2nd class must show an insincere respect for the 1st classmen, no matter how much of an ass any 1st classman may be."[3]

The stay at Milton, however alienating, served its purpose: accustoming Porter to life outside the home. This shy young man with his family's taste for silence and introspection did need preparation for the forced sociability of university life.

Milton also served as a good introduction to Boston and gave Porter time to meet his many Boston relatives. Porter's brother Eliot was by this time a senior at Harvard; occasionally Eliot or his friends paid his little brother a visit. Porter wrote his mother in November, "I rode again on Murray [Fairbank]'s motorcycle last Saturday to the Little Aunts. Murray was very nice: he kept asking me if I was comfortable and if I could hold my bag all right and so forth."[4] (The description of Murray's kindness apparently had a stronger effect than the ride itself, which is nowhere described.) The way Porter communicates his pleasure is indicative of the transparency of feeling he maintained with his mother throughout his college years.

The destination named in the letter is also significant. The Little Aunts – Rebecca "Rebe" Furness and her sister, Laura Furness, called "little" because both stood just over five feet tall – were a vivacious duo of great-aunts on Porter's mother's side. The sisters lived together on Lyme Street in town as well as outside Boston in Petersham, New Hampshire. Both households provided young Porter, who had known the aunts from infancy, with the delights and indulgences of a home away from home. Much of the furniture which figured in Porter's mature paintings was inherited from them.

Aunt Rebe and Aunt Laura were not Porter's only relations in the Boston area. Later in the month, Porter wrote his Aunt Peggy – Ruth's sister Margaret Furness, a Chicago librarian – about visiting another aunt, Adelaide Wadsworth on Cedar Street: "Aunt Adelaide has a queer new maid, very fat and tolerant looking, who seems to be deliberately experimenting with Aunt Adelaide while she waits on table. Aunt Adelaide whispered to me several times about certain fresh things she had said to her and fresh things she had wanted to say back to her."[5]

By early spring, Milton had become so disagreeable to Porter that, after going to Chicago to attend his sister Nancy's wedding, he simply "didn't go back to school."[6] Instead, he stayed home and pursued his own inclinations – reading, sketching, and taking his first painting lessons from a private instructor. As Porter recalled, "When I was sixteen I went to Milton Academy for a year, where I was so shy and homesick, that when I came home I was unable to talk to any-one older than twenty."[7]

Nancy, then in her middle twenties, was engaged to a man named Michel Straus. She was the first of the children to marry. The Straus family were no strangers to the Porters; Mary H. Straus, Michel's mother, had been a childhood friend of Ruth Porter's.[8] Michel, like Nancy, was interested in politics; through another mutual acquaintance, Betty Ickes, the daughter-in-law of Harold Ickes (U.S. secretary of the interior from 1933 to 1946), Michel would begin his career as a press liaison. Ickes became one of the most powerful members of the New Deal administration and eventually raised Straus to a position of bureaucratic promi-nence as deputy commissioner of reclamation under Harry S. Truman. Michel, "a big jovial man with a loud voice," was "characterized in a news-weekly story as 'The Most Arrogant Bureaucrat in Washington,'"[9] and his views on the necessity of developing and exploiting the environment ("he liked building dams and flooding canyons")[10] provoked shouting matches with the more conservation-minded Porters during cocktail hour on Great Spruce Head Island. Michel was a good match for Nancy. Ruth and James were delighted with him – Ruth in par-ticular, because through her daughter's marriage she was finally able, to her mind, to demonstrate her complete lack of prejudice against Jewish people.[11]

After the wedding, Porter and his brother John, the last children remain-ing at home, were taken by their parents on a trip to Europe. They sailed first for Southampton, England, where they embarked upon a cruise to Norway and Iceland. Later, Porter told his friend James Schuyler about being especially impressed by the views of the Norwegian fjords. Upon their return to England, the Porters hired a car and made a cathedral tour of England, Scotland, and Wales, stopping in western Scotland for another boat trip, this time departing from Ayre to tour the isles of Staffa and Iona;[12] the inspirational skies and marine light of these islands gave Porter great pleasure. In letters Ruth also records his excitement at seeing the cathedrals at Salisbury and Winchester. Porter himself, enjoying the company of his parents after his time at Milton, later described his father, ever the curious naturalist, leading his family into the wilds of suburban England: "We had just debarked in Southampton, and I remember my father taking a folding pocket rule out of his pocket to measure the daisies growing in front of a house we were walking past. They were six inches across. It was like one's first sight of an elephant."[13]

In 1924, Porter entered Harvard, which in the academic year of 1924–25 had 944 freshmen and a total undergraduate enrollment of 3,009. His freshman address was James Smith C20, a suite for two in which Porter had his own bedroom but a shared furnished study. Porter's tuition was $250, inexpensive compared to the price of the room, which cost $450 for the year but included heat and maid service. Meals cost nine dollars a week extra. To his mother in early October, Porter wrote, "I have the largest room which is very nice because it is sunny in the morning. The poster of York is over the mantlepiece ... Lincoln is in my room. ... I like Harvard very much and I am happy."[14] The Lincoln is not Lincoln Kirstein, who befriended Porter at Harvard, but Lincoln Cathedral: Porter, like his father, had brought back photographic posters of York and Lincoln Cathedrals from England that summer.

Of his roommate, Thornton Coolidge, he wrote, "[We] get along very well considering we think each other half-witted most of the time."[15] Porter's only real complaint about his dorm room was a telling one: "I just today found all three *Nation*s in a dark closet in the basement. They don't tell you when your magazines come, you have to snoop around and forage for them yourself."[16] Through acquaintance with *The Nation* at home, Porter had decided to take out his own subscription; he remained a devoted reader of this small leftist periodical throughout his life and eventually become its arts editor.

One of the great delights of freshman year was having the freedom to explore Cambridge and Boston. Thanks to his many relatives and his brother Eliot (now attending medical school), he was hardly alone. Letters home suggest that he went to the theater frequently; in one letter he compared a Boston performance of Shaw's *Saint Joan* favorably with the London production he had seen with his mother the previous summer.

Porter's family connections were strong in Cambridge, and though none were close relatives, a number of professors at the university shared family names, starting with the president emeritus of the college, Charles William Eliot. There were also Eliot Wadsworth, overseer of the college; Samuel Eliot Morison, lecturer in history; Charles Allen Porter, professor of surgery; William Townsend Porter, professor of comparative physiology; and Arthur Kingsley Porter, professor of art history. So far as names were concerned, Fairfield Porter was no outsider at Harvard.

Perhaps because of the many excitements at the university, Porter's freshman grades were weak, and his grades remained low through his undergraduate years; the tradition of the "gentleman's C" is evident in his transcript (his older brother Eliot, by comparison, achieved many A's). In his first year, Porter made two B's (in English and French) and three C's (history of philosophy, physics, and introduction to fine arts). The art class, entitled "Principles of Drawing and Painting and Theory of Design," was taught by Arthur Upham Pope, a young professor who later developed a devoted following. Porter had not wanted to take Pope's course, which was a prerequisite for any other arts course, including a course in classical art history that particularly appealed to him. He complained to Ruth that Pope's course was "all theory about colors and so forth and we do silly little painting exercises like making circles of gray, red and blue, etc, varying in value and intensity. And I had to buy $16 worth of apparatus for even that."[17]

Apart from an occasional mention of making up late assignments or writing a paper on Marcus Aurelius ("it had to be at least 10 pages long, so I managed to expand [each of my three] sentence[s] into a paragraph and stretch it out all very thin and transparent over 9 pages,"[18] Porter seems to have been less interested in his studies than in the many diversions of Harvard life, including an ill-fated journey to New Haven to see the Harvard-Yale football game. "I got soaked [in] the rain. I missed the evening train and they asked us to spend the night. Next morning I missed the first train but got a later one at 10 which went to Springfield. But ... I would have to take the Boston and Albany to Boston from Springfield and I hadn't money enough to buy another ticket. So I changed at Hartford and waited there 4 hours to get a train at 3 for Boston and got back at 6 Sunday. Hartford is very picturesque and I rather liked the wait. I liked everything but the game Saturday."[19]

The letters from Ruth Porter during his first semester at school, which have not survived, apparently urged Porter to be as social as possible; she was certainly eager for him to purchase both a suit and a dinner jacket and cut a good figure among his classmates. Porter, however, was equally stubborn in not wanting a dinner jacket. "I have not bought a suit, and I don't want a tuxedo for Christmas," he wrote on November 21; two weeks later, when planning his return for Christmas break, he wrote, "I will let you meet me if you won't talk about the tuxedo." After receiving a reproach from his mother on this comment, he wrote with pained clarity, "I do want you to meet me, of course. I was surprised you should ask me if you might, especially the way you did, that was the only reason I said it like that. I thought it was silly of you to say 'May I meet you?' because I have always wanted you to meet me. I don't know any time I didn't. I did not mean it the way I said it. I wish you would meet me."[20]

This rather extraordinary exchange suggests that Ruth felt college life was drawing her favorite son out of her influence. The last son at home, John, though beloved, seems to have been less a focus of Ruth's interests and ambitions, perhaps because he showed less academic promise; as she wrote her son-in-law, Michel, sometime later, "It looks to me as if Johnny would need constant coaching to get him into college."[21] Although Ruth worried that Fairfield lacked the proper clothes and haircut and social introductions, James Porter showed little concern for his son's progress, merely requesting through his wife that Fairfield remember to take plenty of exercise.

Returning to school after the Christmas holidays, Porter found himself increasingly interested in the theories of art being taught at Harvard, and he explained them enthusiastically: "Professor Pope has been talking to us about modern schools of painting. He says it is wrong to think they are mysterious or un-understandable, because usually they are much easier to understand than older schools. Usually queer modern paintings are merely patterns. He said artists have recently had the idea of making 'pure' art as music is 'pure', that is, it doesn't imitate or resemble any sound in nature, but of course it is harmonious."[22]

Harvard's Fine Arts Department limited its teaching of studio art to courses that would aid in the development of connoisseurship; knowledge of technique, rather than immersion in the latest contemporary theory, was the goal. Like many liberal arts institutions today, Harvard in 1925 did not think the practice of contemporary painting a discipline it could possibly teach. The department's most celebrated former pupil was Bernard Berenson, who had established a reputation for his connoisseurship of Italian Renaissance art.

In later years, Porter's assessment of what he had learned at Harvard was mixed:

I don't think I could have gotten a better education anywhere else at that time just as far as history and so on is concerned. In aesthetics it was weak. But the weakness came from that fact that there wasn't any relation to practice ... it was theory and the theory didn't go very deep. It was superficial theory. ... [At Harvard] they would say, "Here's the surface of the painting. And this is well-composed." Composition is the most important thing. And composition means that they analyzed it – I think Professor Pope did, too – repetition and sequence and probably another thing, I don't know what: Harmony, maybe. And I found out many years later that composition isn't good because something is repeated but because it is not repeated. It was just the opposite. If there's something that never occurs again in a painting, that's what is its unique quality.

Pope ... explained Analytical Cubism ... was like jazz, which I think is true. I mean that's an intuitive remark, but I think it's true. Also we were presented with the aesthetic theories of Berenson. And that was a very strong influence on me. I think that I can't even today look at Florentine painting without doing it in Berenson's terms.[23]

During the spring semester, Porter joined the Art Department of the Dramatic Club, making posters to advertise its plays. The activity is noteworthy because it is Porter's first "official" work as an artist, but he seems not to have been inspired by the opportunity. "We are allowed to make the poster anyway we want," he observed, "so long as all the dope about the play is on it."[24]

Porter remained interested in poetry. Harvard had a living tradition of poetry which may well have consolidated Porter's sense of the importance of poetry in his own mind – not just as the domain of his mother or ancestors but as a part of contemporary life. (Later exposure to the ideas of Alfred North Whitehead would confirm the relation of poetry to philosophical thought.) The poet who became Porter's favorite in years to come, Wallace Stevens, had attended Harvard approximately twenty-five years before. Like Porter, Stevens was an artist with an essentially philosophical nature. Seeking an alternative to systematized thought, Stevens looked for poetry in shifting surfaces, in varieties of experience, and in the literary alternatives presented by other cultures, particularly the Chinese.[25] Porter, in time, followed a similar path, seeking an alternative to the modernism of his contemporaries in what one poet has called his "religion of light."[26] The mature work of each, one critic has observed, shows "the complex presence of a man who combines a searching intelligence with a joy in the life of the senses; who longs to see life clearly, stripped of all illusion, but is equally fascinated by the transforming power of the imagination; who is above all devoted to his art, who never loses his sense of humor."[27] Porter was significantly influenced by a number of other Harvard poets in later years, including T. S. Eliot, John Wheelwright, John Ashbery, Frank O'Hara, and Kenneth Koch, but Stevens always remained his favorite.

Still, poetry and art were not all that Porter cared about. His letters to his mother, even as early as his freshman year, demonstrate his wide-ranging curiosity. As the poet and art critic Barbara Guest has observed, "His mind was formed before he began to paint, and he had interests that had nothing to do with his art. You don't find that in his contemporaries."[28] Certainly he was fascinated with politics and current events:

The Italian Club had an interesting dinner recently. A Mr. Bruce, Ph.D., had returned from Italy almost converted to Fascismo. He said he had been prejudiced against the Fascisti before but the food in the hotels was so good that perhaps they are pretty decent fellows after all. Such things, he said, impress the foreigner. [The letter then goes into a long description of the many positions taken by club members on fascism, re-creating the heated debate.] ... Everyone [at the club] felt nervous about the slightest display of warmth; a gentlemanly affectation of boredom seemed perhaps more seemly, but they enjoyed the evening all the more for the argument, I am sure. The president said that we had not come here to discuss politics, which was obviously untrue.[29]

March 1, 1925

By the end of his second semester at Harvard, Porter felt interested enough in the Fine Arts Department to submit a proposal for his concentration of studies as a fine arts major. But he was hardly proposing to paint; most of the required courses were in art history.

Of the decision to be an artist, which Porter made while at Harvard, he recalled at the end of his life, "When I decided to study art, art was considered of peripheral importance; the artist or poet was thought to be outside of the mainstream of life. I remember a neighbor whom I respected very much, who was disturbed by my decision, and told me so. This man was a businessman, and at the same time an inventor and a poet. He told me that his first reaction to anyone's wanting to be an artist was the thought that this meant deciding in favor of triviality. Then he thought of the Vatican Torso, the piece of antique sculpture which Michelangelo said was his master. Triviality meant to him decorative objects."[30]

Porter spent the summer of 1925 working hard at his painting on Great Spruce Head. He had company in this activity, for over the summer Ruth Porter had engaged a Latin tutor for John, a man named Mr. Woodberry who had studied painting in Paris before becoming a teacher at Eliot Porter's former prep school in Morristown, New Jersey. As Ruth observed to her sister, "Mr. Woodberry is a nice person to have [here] for he likes the dullness and finds lots to do. He enjoys the shell heaps & berrying & is excited [about hunting] cantherella [mushrooms]. He & F. are growing positively hectic over sketching & F's room is plastered with his works of art."[31]

By the Fourth of July, Porter had done enough painting with Woodberry for Ruth to remark, "Fairfield is sticking to his sketching and sometimes doing rather nice things." The lack of excitement in Ruth's observation may well have been a genuine ambivalence about the quality of her son's paintings or else may have come from general concern over Fairfield's development; the same letter contains her observation about not being comfortable reading Proust to Fairfield on account of her discomfort with the topic of homosexuality. Perhaps the example of Woodberry, a failed artist reduced to teaching at a prep school and hiring himself out as a Latin tutor, made her worry about Fairfield's future.

Three days later, in another letter to her sister, Ruth discusses the subject of "family complexes" (questions of sexual and emotional development were very much in the air; by Christmas, Ruth would have bought Eliot a full set of Havelock Ellis): "Part of the reason that most of us don't get such exclusive devotion [from our children] is because we don't believe in exacting it." One can reasonably suppose, then, that after much thought and worry, Ruth was determined not to monopolize the affections of her children, and in stating her beliefs to her sister she was also reassuring herself. Perhaps she was having trouble letting go of her children: by the end of summer she had decided to delay her departure from the island on Fairfield's account, telling her daughter, "It seemed best not to turn Fairfield onto the cold world nor to take him home [to Chicago] for a few days only."[32]

For his second year at Harvard, Porter decided to take art courses – one in ancient art, another in medieval, renaissance, and modern art, and a third in freehand drawing. He also took courses in history and biology. Classical and medieval art were two favorite interests of James Porter, and so was biology. James Porter seems to have been very much on Fairfield Porter's mind. In a letter to Ruth, Fairfield observed, "I get quite a kick out of telling people about [Daddy's] atheism. The other day O'Neil said that college makes of almost everyone an agnostic or an atheist, but that his parents would be sorry to think he was. So I said proudly that Daddy would be as displeased if I got any religion."[33]

As a whole, however, the letters from Porter to Ruth concern the comedy of his progress as a fine arts major: "I have just finished writing an essay on El Greco for my tutor, as I decided that I liked best the portrait by El Greco in the Boston Museum. ... I had to read a book on him and look at photographs of his pictures, and so I have a feeling that what I wrote is largely hot air. I don't entirely believe what I said. [But] my tutor liked my essay, he said it was exactly the sort of thing he wanted me to do. In two weeks I am to write an essay on Monet."[34]

Porter seems never to have doubted his vocation, only the intelligence and perspicacity of his teachers: Why couldn't they see that he was barely trying? Two weeks later, he had more good news, writing, "My tutor liked my essay on Monet very much. He said that I needn't study and write essays on old masters after this unless I want to because he thinks I can get all the facts from my courses, to enable me to pass the divisional exams in senior year easily. So I am going to write about contemporary Americans, after I have read up and written on Degas and Manet, to give me a basis for the rest of the French Impressionistic School."[35] Given permission to pursue his own course of study, Porter began looking about for a suitable subject. With no outside help or advice, he decided to write on the painter and illustrator Rockwell Kent.

His dry observations on fusty academicians continued in a letter of December 10, 1925, after he attended an evening with the aged and reactionary Denman Ross, a professor, art collector, and legendary opponent of modern painting:

A few days ago Dr. Denman Ross who is [a] high muck-a-muck in the Painting World ... invited students concentrating in fine arts to his house. ... He is the man whose theory of color design rules the teaching of painting at Harvard; the theory which in brief advocates painting a picture with colors which make a pleasant combination. But it is more complicated than that ... he is about 80 by his appearance, and he says that he is just beginning to develop this theory, which has been going on for no mean while ... then a tutor asked him to give us his opinion on modern art, and he said, "I'm afraid they won't like my opinion," but he gave it of course. We were continually urged to ask questions and, of course, dead silence reigned when he ceased talking. Finally the same courageous tutor thanked him for us and we silently walked out. Going away one boy remarked on the broken antiques and general mess in his rooms. "How does that go with his theory of order to design?" he asked.

December 10, 1925

After the Christmas holidays, Porter returned to school to face the Rockwell Kent paper. His great enthusiasm for Kent is manifest in a series of stylized woodcuts he created in the 1930s. At the time, however, Porter responded most strongly to Kent's interest in coastal Maine; he may also have seen and shared Kent's passion for architecture – for, like James Porter, Kent had studied architecture at Columbia. Though remembered today mostly as a decorative illustrator, Kent was determined to cross the boundaries between "high" and "low" art, and later in his career he used his artistic abilities to support political and social change.

Porter may also have been drawn to Kent because Kent was enjoying a vogue among Harvard undergraduates. According to a classmate, John Walker (who later headed the National Gallery), Lincoln Kirstein, founder of the influential Harvard literary review, *Hound and Horn*, had commissioned Rockwell Kent to create a cover for the new magazine, calling him "the best graphic designer of our time."[36] Porter was a follower of the Harvard literary scene (particularly *Hound and Horn*)[37] as well as a friend of Kirstein's. The poet James Schuyler recalled that Kirstein had a collegiate infatuation with Porter; Kirstein's brother-in-law, the artist Paul Cadmus, remembered Porter and Kirstein remaining in friendly contact in New York throughout the 1930s.[38]

The fine arts faculty were nonplussed with the Rockwell Kent project from the first. In January, Porter wrote his mother, "Mr. Kates let me put off my Rockwell Kent paper till next week. I asked Mr. Mower, my drawing teacher, if he could tell me anything about Rockwell Kent I could use for a tutorial essay. 'Nope. Not a thing,' he said. And when I asked Professor Pope, he asked, 'Why Rockwell Kent?'"

Met with bemused indifference by the fine arts faculty, Porter relied upon the literary set to shape his tastes. The decision to let a writer or editor guide his artistic opinions followed naturally enough from the Porter belief that literature, being closer to intellect, was somehow more important, less trivial than visual pleasure. The paradigm of literature also explains why Porter's letters home to his mother are at once so detailed and entertaining: they are a parallel form of creation, a reassurance to his family that, despite his uncertainties about his artistic project, he remains worthy and intelligent. If he couldn't get anywhere as an artist or art historian, he could at least provide his mother with an entertaining account of his failure. Comic buffoonery was a lifelong strategy for Porter, a calculated way of deflecting skeptical assessments of his talent. It informs nearly all of his early correspondence and, according to his wife, was an important aspect of his adult character.

Later in the same letter, Porter indicated that through the help of Professor Pope he had been able to gain access to an actual Rockwell Kent painting – not a great help to his project but at least a step in the right direction. Pope brought Porter, along with another tutor in the Fine Arts Department, to visit John T. Spaulding, a major Boston collector whose French Impressionist paintings were eventually given to the Museum of Fine Arts: "Downstairs Mr. Spaulding and Prof. Pope and a friend of Mr. Spaulding's in spats talked about pictures and collections and things they would like to buy in much the way people talk about radio sets. He showed us a very excellent Degas he had just bought. The Rockwell Kent was upstairs. I liked it very much; it was a snow scene on Monhegan."[39] To Ruth Porter, with her Unitarian ideals and interest in social activism, the description of these men sitting around gossiping about recent purchases and things they would still like to buy would have seemed more than silly – in fact, immoral. Just what her son was doing among them was a question that probably puzzled them both.

A few days later, while attending a poetry reading at a Women's Club, Porter met Countee Cullen. The famed poet of the Harlem Renaissance was a mere four years older than Porter, yet had already published a volume of poetry (*Color*, in 1925) and in little more than a year would publish *Copper Sun*. As a black poet working in traditional verse forms, he would undoubtedly have interested Ruth Porter, and in a letter home, Porter described visiting him that Saturday evening at Cullen's boarding house.

What Porter seems not to have known and what Cullen seems not to have told him was that they shared a last name, for Cullen's birth name was Porter (he had taken the name of his adoptive father, the Reverend F. A. Cullen). Cullen may have been sexually attracted to Porter, for whatever Porter might have thought of his own looks, he was strikingly handsome, and Cullen, though he married Yolande Du Bois (the daughter of W. E. B. Du Bois) in 1928, was homosexual. Yet the evening passed uneventfully. When they ran out of conversation, the poet contented himself with being "most extremely polite, and when I spoke open[ing] his eyes very wide like the Neal girls."[40] The evening ended with Porter giving Cullen lessons in Dutch whist.

On Porter's side, the visit indicates an openness toward blacks which was not characteristic of young men in that place and time, as well as, perhaps, obliviousness to his own sexual appeal. A meeting between a black man from Harlem (however distinguished the family) and a white one from Harvard – meeting as equals, privately, in the bedroom of a Negro boardinghouse, to discuss poetry and play cards – was not unremarkable. Late in life, Porter mentioned the comfort he took in the company of the black bourgeoisie, a preference he ascribed to an essential shared feeling of having been found "second rate."[41] Cullen, a prodigy, certainly did not consider himself second-rate; but then, what Cullen thought and felt seem not to have been of any great importance to Porter during the encounter. Wrapped up in his own preoccupations and ambitions, Porter shared himself and his ideas that evening as best he could, but no lasting friendship came out of the meeting.

Another social event rounded out the month of January. "I went to an At Home at the Christopher Eliots' Wednesday afternoon," Porter wrote his mother. "Besides all the relations on that side I had ever seen or heard of there were three times as many more. I think that party the worst kind of strain."[42] The Eliots were indeed a large and formidable clan, and Porter, disinclined to social niceties, was doubtless uncomfortable among them. Nevertheless, the introduction had been made. A month and a half later Porter wrote his mother: "I called on Margaret Eliot the other day because the Little Aunts wanted me to because she had asked me to come to a party and I couldn't go. I waited a long time in a desolate bare antechamber while Cousins Lottie and Marian wondered in loud voices who had come at this hour ... then cousin Margaret appeared and talked very rapidly and giggled about the bare room ... I handed her the *Transcript* when I went and which reminded me of T.S. Eliot's poem that ends, 'Cousin Harriet, here is the *Boston Evening Transcript.*'"[43]

The Porters were avid readers of T. S. Eliot, Fairfield in particular. With his love of the new, Porter had been impressed by *The Waste Land*. But apart from a luncheon or two at the home of the Little Aunts, Porter did not get to know his brilliant older cousin, in part because within the year this literary celebrity permanently established himself abroad. T. S. Eliot's brother, Henry, however, was a frequent visitor to Great Spruce Head. Ruth was delighted to be the cousin of a poet of such renown and hoped her children would come to know T. S. Eliot through Henry. She wrote her daughter: "When you see Henry ask him to send Eliot [Porter] Tom's [T. S. Eliot's] address in London and Cambridge. I hope that Henry has seen all the criticism about T.S. lately in the *Nation* and the *New Republic*. ... Fairfield gets *Time* as well as high-brow periodicals like the *Dial*, and all the scientific and liberal weeklies pour in three times a day."[44]

In support of Fairfield's enthusiasm for poetry and art, Ruth carefully chose a book for her son that March, a biography of Blake. Porter immediately sent her an enthusiastic note of thanks, touched by his mother's thoughtfulness and interest, saying he would "count the book as a birthday present" and adding, for the benefit of his much less attentive father, "Tell Daddy I do take exercise, I walk into or out of Boston, or both, whenever I go there, which is something."[45]

Soon Porter wrote again, saying, "Last week at an exhibition I liked very much I talked to some girls about the pictures. Later I met one of the girls again at another exhibition. We passed judgment on everything at that gallery and went to another. Then she showed me a fourth exhibition of a different sort at the Library."[46] Porter seems to have felt that by actively exercising his critical judgment and by spending time with girls he was doing things that would gratify his mother. Two weeks later, reaching her in Naples, he added, "I have been reading *The Analysis of the Sexual Impulse*, which Eliot [Porter] lent me ... that is one of the Havelock Ellis [books] you gave Eliot for Christmas."[47]

None of Porter's intellectual development was reflected in his grades. His academic insouciance during his sophomore year resulted in two C's in art history and a B for freehand drawing. Still, the tone of his letters implies sophistication rather than cynicism, and engagement rather than indifference. Aware even as a sophomore that no one in his department had a deep interest in contemporary art (and beginning to sense that painting was what he intended to pursue),[48] he had clearly decided to enjoy whatever education was available to him but not take the judgments of his professors too seriously. To a young man settling into a painterly vocation, college grades were of little concern.

From Great Spruce Head on July 2, Ruth made an observation which describes in passing her feelings toward Boston society: "[Our guests] the Smiths are very cooperative & friendly with everyone & have the usual limitation of experience

& literal-mindedness with a superficial humor so characteristic of Boston. They play bridge and like the boat." The remark is startling because it is so uncharacteristic; her letters are rarely so overt in their judgments. Perhaps she was disappointed by the provinciality of Boston now that she was taking so many visits there, for apart from visiting her sons and the Little Aunts, she passed through Boston twice yearly on her way to and from Great Spruce Head. Perhaps also, having developed an active and socially committed life on the shores of Lake Michigan, she was disappointed at the quality of mind both she and her sons were encountering in that city. At any rate, she seems to have craved more substantially engaging company and, perhaps to her own surprise, began to find it in Fairfield. Three days later she wrote:

We had an excitement last night at the bridge table when Fairfield announced *July 5, 1926* that he was not a mechanist. Nor will he admit the horrid charge of being a vitalist which is all that is left for him according to James. He is a straight agnostic. When he has time he is going to read Whitehead's book, the new prophet at Harvard. All this was very startling to James though as far back as the spring vacation Fairfield was murmuring things to which James paid no heed about the mechanists not explaining the beginning of things any better than the vitalists. Johnny was very funny winking at me across the table and trying to bring back the discussion to the bid, in which John was not at all interested, just playing to oblige.[49]

Of Ruth's sons, Eliot had just been graduated from Harvard, Edward was on academic probation, and John, at sixteen, seemed not to be heading for college at all (he later attended Wesleyan). Ruth's husband was caught up in the fantasy of his many island projects, most recently the delivery, by barge, of a farmhouse designed by himself and constructed in the Greek-revival style (a barn designed in the same style followed shortly thereafter; see figs. 19 and 54). Faced with a lack of intellectual stimulation, Ruth's investment in Fairfield's company increased by the day.

Ruth's mention of Whitehead is significant, for Whitehead had a lasting effect on Porter's writing and thought. The excitement over Whitehead was family wide; the Porters eventually had all Whitehead's books with them on Great Spruce Head. As the grand old man of philosophy and mathematics at Harvard, he was causing a sensation among faculty and students throughout Cambridge. But the Porters' interest in Whitehead was more specific, for they shared his fascination with metaphysics, that speculative field of philosophy which concerns the principles, structures, and meanings that underlie all observable reality and which seeks to understand the nature of being. As an analyst of both religion and science, Whitehead would have been very much at home at the Porter bridge table – and, for that matter, elsewhere on Great Spruce Head Island – for he took great consolation in poetry and nature,[50] both of which were to be found there in abundance.

Fairfield's announcement that he was a straight agnostic, not a vitalist or mechanist, would have been appreciated by Whitehead, whose emphasis in teaching was always on clarity, specificity, and definition of terms. Whitehead insisted that the task of philosophy was to frame a coherent, logical, necessary system of general ideas in terms of which every element of our experience can be interpreted. He would certainly have been interested in the scientifically based thought which had led James Porter to declare himself an atheist, for the outright denial of the existence of God is an extreme and unusual position. Fairfield Porter, believing that God is unknown or unknowable (a straight agnostic) still needed, according to James, to address the question of whether life could be completely explained by the laws of physics and chemistry (the mechanist view) or whether life was in some part self-determining (the vitalist view). Porter's refusal to choose between mechanism and vitalism suggests that he had been dipping into Whitehead that spring; the book to which Ruth refers is probably *Religion in the Making* (published that year, 1926), but Porter's refusal to choose between mechanism and vitalism suggests that he was already aware of the critique of scientific materialism offered by Whitehead in *Science and the Modern World* (1925).

Returning to Harvard for his junior year, Porter immediately enrolled in Whitehead's course "Philosophical Presuppositions of Science," which met three times per week at noon. His other courses for the year included "Renaissance and Modern Architecture," "Art and Culture of Italy in the Middle Ages and Renaissance," a course in medieval sculpture, and two introductory courses in anthropology.

Whitehead's course was perhaps the most exciting one that Porter took at Harvard. More than forty years later he was quite clear in the lasting questions it had posed:

What I got from [Whitehead] ... was the importance of having very clear terms in your discussion and knowing what they mean ... [I realized that] you don't use synonyms. You don't write good English in the sense of never repeating yourself. If you are sure of your terms, you repeat yourself. Because that's what you mean. ... I also realized reading [Whitehead] that even if you used symbols, you can't get away from poetry.

[Whitehead also] taught us that Hume's criticism was practically unanswerable. ... Hume's idea is that all you know is one sensation after another: you do not know the connections between them. And that was what [Whitehead] was concerned with doing, finding an answer to Hume, who he thought had not been adequately answered by Kant. ... What I like in painting – I mean, partly what I like in painting – is to rationalize what I like in painting. Because it seems to me to relate to that [idea of Hume's that all you know is one sensation after another]. I mean I like in art when the artist doesn't know what he knows in general; he only knows what he knows specifically. And what he knows in general or what can be known in general becomes apparent later on by what he has had to put down. And that is to me the most interesting art form. ... in other words, you are not in control of nature quite, you are part of nature. ... the whole question of art is to be wide awake, to be as attentive as possible.[51]

Whitehead's interest in the questions surrounding the metaphysical conundrum posed by Hume – How does one know what one knows? – and Whitehead's sense that one could approach such knowledge through both poetry and direct experience of nature, persisted in Porter's mind for the rest of his life, and found ultimate expression in his mature painting and late criticism. And yet Porter seems not to have applied himself very much in the course with Whitehead. As he told the woman soon to be his wife several years later, while she was studying with the distinguished philosopher at Radcliffe, "Whitehead told us that it might be wise to write a thesis summarizing his lectures – which I took to mean that I could choose to be unwise if I felt like it, but on the day he handed the theses back, noticing that he had not handed me back mine, he said, 'Did I yet get a thesis from you?' and I said no, and he said very very gently, 'Well you know that was rather wicked of you. You will write one won't you?' I did therefore write one and I felt really rather more wicked than I had ever felt before."[52]

Apart from his studies with Whitehead during his junior year, Porter concentrated on art history, rounding out his coursework with two introductory anthropology courses. By the end of the year he had achieved only two B's (one from Whitehead, one in medieval sculpture); the rest of his grades were C's. Just what else Porter was thinking and doing during this period has not been preserved in any of the Porter family letters, nor is there any record of Porter's one surviving watercolor from that period, *Roofs of Cambridge* (1927, fig. 8).

But his junior year was not without incident. During one of Ruth's visits, Porter was brought along to Sunday lunch at the home of Henry and Katharine Minot Channing, where he had his first encounter with Anne Elizabeth Channing, then sixteen, whom he married five years later. In her words:

I attended the Winsor School in the suburbs of Boston. A family named Fisher was in Cambridge temporarily. They were from Winnetka, and Ruth Fisher was in my class. When the time came for the family to move back to Winnetka, Ruth [Fisher] still needed to finish up school, so she came to live with us. When Fairfield's mother came to visit Fairfield at Harvard, she came out to see Ruth [Fisher], and she brought Fairfield along. Eliot came, too. And John Porter showed up in the driveway on a motorcycle. It was really quite a scene.

I'd heard about Fairfield from the Fishers. They kept talking about this neighbor boy who'd decided to become an artist. And he had no talent. They thought it was a terrible thing. You can't become an artist if you aren't talented, they said. But from everything they said I knew I would like him. I was looking forward to meeting him.

I was sixteen. I never wore makeup in those days – women didn't – but when a gentleman came to call one powdered one's nose. Everyone did. My mother had some face powder, and my sister Barbara did, too. I didn't. I was too young. I found some talcum powder upstairs in the bathroom and I used that instead. I came downstairs with a big white nose. And that was how Fairfield remembered me. As the little girl with a big white nose. He drew a caricature of me like that ... at the time he called me "Prince Bulbo." That's a character from a Thackeray novel, *The Rose and the Ring*. I remember Fairfield and I went to look at a little calf we had at the time. It had no name. I said, "I wonder what we should name it?" and he suggested I call it "Nome" because that means "no name."[53]

There may have been another reason for the visit. Eliot Porter, back in America after a semester at Cambridge University and travel in Austria, had recently met and fallen in love with Marion Brown, a young woman from Hinsdale, near Chicago; the two had quickly married.[54] One of Marion's bridesmaids, a Bryn Mawr classmate named Barbara Channing, had been put up with the Porter family for two nights while participating in the wedding. A poised young woman of intellect, Barbara Channing had immediately hit it off with Ruth Porter, and Ruth had decided to ask Barbara to visit the Porters on Great Spruce Head. Thus Ruth's visit was as much to visit Barbara's parents and introduce herself as it was to see Ruth Fisher.[55] Ruth Porter may have been eager for company that summer, for she had already decided to give Fairfield and Edward a summer on their own in Europe – they were planning a walking tour through France – and Eliot would be in Paris on his honeymoon.

8
Roofs of Cambridge, 1927.
Parrish Art Museum, Southampton, N.Y.,
Gift of the Estate of Fairfield Porter (1980.10.120).
Photo by Gary Marnay.

3

Russia and New York

Few details of the walking tour in France that summer of 1927 have been preserved. Porter and his brother Edward arrived by way of Cherbourg[1] and proceeded down through western Normandy, stopping at Coutances, where Porter was so impressed by the small town's Romanesque cathedral that he recalled it with great admiration in an interview forty years later. But why he should have done so is unclear. The sculptural reliefs had been smashed during the French Revolution, the simple Clunaic design was derived from other, more magnificent buildings, and few of the original stained glass windows remained intact. Perhaps the building impressed Porter because he saw it early in the trip or else because its three-tiered arrangement of windows gave the austere building a sophisticated interior light. More likely, however, having experienced the airy, high Gothic and vertical Gothic architecture of England, he found the Romanesque style impressive in a new way. Certainly his enthusiasm for Romanesque grew when he returned to Harvard that fall and studied with a top scholar in the field, Arthur Kingsley Porter. And the fact that Coutances was bombed during World War II may well have made the memory of it more dear to Porter.

From Coutances, Porter traveled to Mont-St.-Michel before continuing south through the fortified medieval cities which divide Brittany from the rest of France. From there the brothers continued even farther south, into the Loire.

Despite the love of Gothic cathedrals which Porter had professed to share with his architect father during the 1924 tour of England, he seems to have spent the summer of 1927, apart from visits to Chartres and Rouen, developing an enthusiasm for the grand domestic architecture of the Renaissance. Along with images of train stations and landscapes, Porter's pencil and ink sketches (made with the sure, steady hand of a drafting student) include the renowned chateaux of Chenonceau and Azay-le-Rideau.

Porter's interest in beautiful houses (visiting them, building them, living in them, making paintings of them) would be lifelong.

Stripped of art and furnishings during the revolution, most of the Loire chateaux are primarily worth visiting for their architecture, though the more historically interesting fortified chateaux of Blois and Anjou (the Porter brothers visited both) have more to offer the student, including designs commissioned from Leonardo, who spent his last days in the Loire as the guest of Francis I. Still, Porter and his brother, free of their parents' overwhelming zeal for instruction, were probably having a more relaxed vacation than usual, with Edward, not overly interested in art history, seeing to it that they explored rural France at their leisure.

Porter's vacation was changed by a chance encounter with his brother Eliot in Paris, where he was honeymooning with Marion Brown. As Porter recalled, Eliot and Edward were out for a walk when they "met a neighbor from across the street in Winnetka, Illinois, who was going to Russia with a group of American journalists, economists and labor leaders. And they were in a bad way. They needed some money. And my brother said that *I* would like to go to Russia. And [the friend] said, well, I think that can be arranged if he'd give us some money."[2]

The friend was Arthur Fisher, the father of Ruth Fisher, the girl whom Ruth Porter had visited at the Channing home outside Boston. Fisher, a lawyer who had been a conscientious objector during the First World War,[3] was traveling with "a group of labor leaders and economists like Stuart Chase and Paul Douglas," as well as a few journalists and the superintendent of the Winnetka public schools. All wanted to see how the ideal society of the Soviets was shaping up, and, calling themselves the American Labor Delegation, they planned to visit and observe the Soviet Union as guests of the state, conducting a survey of business and labor conditions while there. Once they arrived in Russia, the expenses of the trip were to be picked up by the Russian Union of Trade Unions, but getting to Russia was proving more expensive than the group had thought. By providing them with cash, Porter had the sudden good luck to be included in a once-in-a-lifetime adventure.

The trip appealed to Porter because of his long-standing interest in Russian literature, specifically Dostoyevsky. But anyone following leftist politics and interested in the rights of the working class (as both Porter and his mother were) would have been reading and talking about developments within Russia. The fall of the Kerensky government to Lenin and the Bolsheviks in the October Revolution of 1917, the First World War, the Russian civil war, and the struggle for power between Stalin and Trotsky after Lenin's death in 1924 had provided an ongoing drama to readers of the American leftist press. For Americans interested in alternative forms of government, Russia was a grand, frightening, and distant experiment; though already marred by acts of violence and terrorism, it had not yet descended into the horrors of collectivization and genocide (Stalin's first Five-Year Plan went into effect in 1928). Russia was being covered inadequately by American newspapers. To see Russia firsthand was a rare opportunity.

The first leg of the journey, which began at the end of July, was to Berlin, where Porter and two Winnetka acquaintances were to depart by airplane for Moscow. Edward accompanied Porter as far as Berlin on the train, teasing his brother for striking up conversations with older women. As Fairfield told Ruth, the French lady he met on the train "is not one of the ladies more than fifteen years my senior whom, according to you, I intend to marry. Edward continually and gleefully quotes to me your dig about old ladies."[4] The comment is fascinating because of Ruth's prescience: by the time he married three years later, Porter had had a sexual encounter with an older, married woman.[5]

After eleven days in Berlin, Porter and two other members of the group boarded a small airplane owned by Deruluft, Deutsche-Russische Luftverkehrs-Gesellschaft. The fifteen-hundred-mile flight to Moscow was undertaken at the speed of one hundred miles per hour; the flight was broken by a brief refueling stop, where Porter quickly wrote his mother, "This is at Riga in Latvia where we are stopping for a few minutes on a 15-hour flight from Berlin to Moscow which started out at 3 this morning. I am with the Washburnes who are also in the party. We 3 are the only passengers, the other trade unionists & experts are coming later by train, and are stopping at Warsaw one day." This was the last time on his Russia trip that Porter would successfully post a letter to America; Ruth did not hear from her son again for over a month.

For a young man who had grown up listening to his mother read aloud from Tolstoy, the Moscow of 1927 was so appalling a revelation that it could be comprehended only through laughter. Porter told an interviewer forty years later,

Everybody in the streets [of Moscow] looked as though they had just come in from milking the cows. They didn't look like city people. And the city was like a sea with big swells which had frozen. Red Square looked like a great big wave of pavement. And it was shabby and junky. And there were a lot of wooden houses outside … we flew in by plane and you looked down and there didn't seem to be any roads anywhere. There just seemed to be worn places where grass didn't grow, which were roads, I guess, and little trees – all second growth. And as you came down and approached Moscow there didn't seem to be any reason for there being a city there. I mean it was as though you'd find a city in the middle of the Northwest Territory or the woods or something. Nothing led up to it … And there were glass houses on the way in from the airport to the city, completely glass with bulbous domes. And I said, What are those things? – they looked like greenhouses – and they said, Oh, those are the former summer houses of the nobility. It looked like Coney Island. And the church on Red Square, you know, the famous church [St. Basil's], was like something on Coney Island … very small and painted on the inside like the decoration in candy boxes of about 1912. And the walls were greasy from people's overcoats pressing against them.[6]

Reporting to his mother, Porter wrote:

September 15, 1927

Moscow ... seemed like the craziest sort of city you could imagine ... [it] at first looks shabby and dirty ... the streets are wide and the square enormous. ... There are really only two degrees of wealth, the ordinary populace and the beggars. ... After a while one gets used to the poorness of the people, which is made up for by the fact that everyone is much healthier looking than in any city in foreign countries. ... Every day you see in the filthy Moscow river many people swimming or sun bathing on the edge of the river. ... [Since the famine] all the peasants ... always boil water and milk before drinking it, but they keep to their former casual and rather dirty housekeeping and living conditions.[7]

He also includes, in an aside, his impression of the embalmed Lenin, a corpse now in its third year on Red Square but not yet housed in the impressive granite, marble, and black labradorite mausoleum which would be constructed by Shchusev three years later: "I went into [Lenin's] tomb and saw him. It is very impressive. He is so well preserved that it seems he is about to move. ... He is very small and rather handsome."[8]

After the rest of the American group arrived, Porter accompanied them on their rounds of interviews with government officials. When Arthur Fisher and many others in the delegation contracted dysentery, Porter went on interviewing rounds on Fisher's behalf. "He sent me around to [see] American businessmen. And it was very difficult. It took all day to find one address and get there in a droshky over these streets in Moscow paved with round stones as if from the beach. All the streets in Moscow and particularly Red Square [were] like a great big gravel beach."[9] Porter neither spoke Russian nor read Cyrillic, and (then as now) many Moscow street addresses were incomprehensible even to Moscow natives. Moreover, since Porter's droshky drivers were illiterate, they were as unable to read the addresses as Porter himself.

The first highlight of the Moscow visit was seeing two great collections of Impressionist and Modern art which had just been opened to the public after being warehoused since 1923. The Shchukin and Morosov collections had just been installed in the Morosov town house at Prechistenka Street.[10] The house served as a chilling suggestion of what life held in store for the artist and collector in the new Russian state. "I saw that Shchukin and Morosov collections of Modern art. These great houses of rich merchants were all sort of askew like this, they were settling. Everything [is] out of whack."[11]

The Shchukin and Morosov collections featured some of the most exciting art of the late nineteenth and early twentieth centuries (the contents of the two collections are today divided between the Hermitage and the Pushkin museums and constitute the bulk of Russian holdings of early twentieth-century European art). Shchukin had been a champion of Matisse and Picasso;

Morosov had a passion for Cézanne. Other major artists – Degas, Monet, Renoir, Pisarro, Bonnard, Vuillard, Vlaminck, Derain, and Marquet – were featured in their collections as well. Porter's first exposure to the work of Vuillard and Bonnard, artists who would later be of paramount importance to him, must therefore have been a strange one: these artists' celebrations of intimate French bourgeois life and interiors must have seemed bizarrely out of place in the neglected Russian Art-Nouveau mansion peopled with curious workers and suspicious bureaucrats.

Another early highlight of Porter's trip was his audience with Trotsky, which Fisher and the rest of the party attended despite their illness. The great revolutionary "was on his way out; he was something like Commissar for Foreign Concessions," Porter recalled to a political historian in 1974.[12] Nonetheless, Porter was thrilled to be included in the meeting and, when not taking notes, drew sketches, including one of the leader (fig. 9). Though Porter had no great enthusiasm for Trotsky's politics until the early 1930s, when Trotsky was creating opposition to Hitler,[13] and, later still, during the Moscow Trials, Porter was aware that Trotsky had been a major leader. Porter was particularly impressed by Trotsky's ability with English (he may not have known that Trotsky had once been a journalist in New York). He wrote Ruth Porter:

September 15, 1927 Trotsky was smooth and charming and clever. We spoke directly to [him] and he answered through an interpreter, but if the interpreter gave the wrong English word he interrupted with the exact one. The questions were written and the first six, which were about Trotsky's differences with the party, he refused to answer specifically and gracefully prevented Arthur from reading them. ... The most interesting question ran, "There being no civil liberties in Russia, how can it be said that 85% of the population support the present government?" To which he answered that there is a difference between economic and political democracy, and that even countries that boast our bourgeois civil liberties don't give full opportunities to the proletariat to express themselves ... we pretend to theoretical civil liberties which don't actually exist because all the press is owned by capitalists, and that Russia which makes no pretense towards such liberties has actually much more freedom of self-expression than is theoretically boasted. They accuse us of hypocrisy. There is one mistake that Russian communists almost always make which is to consider America divided neatly into two distinct classes – the bourgeois and the workers. They don't know that most "capitalists" in America work very hard, and that many "workers" own bonds and investments.[14]

The experience of meeting Trotsky had a lasting effect on Porter, particularly during the late 1930s, when, after being denounced in absentia at the Moscow Trials, the exiled politician sought to clear his name from Mexico. Porter not only went door-to-door in Winnetka collecting money for Trotsky's legal defense but also briefly entertained the notion of inviting Trotsky to come live with his family on Chicago's North Shore.

As a diversion, Porter and the rest of the group took a few days away from their work in Moscow to visit St. Petersburg, which had been renamed Leningrad just three years earlier. "Leningrad is shabbier than Moscow, because it's poorer ... the Leningrad buildings are all peeling," he wrote.[15] Later he commented that "the streets were all tar blocks, which I had never seen before, except that my father had a tennis court once made of tar blocks. ... [At the hotel] there were little bullet holes in the plumbing and in the pictures on the walls. And I thought that was [from] the revolution. I was told no, no, that wasn't [from] the revolution; it just hadn't been repaired. Before the revolution the aristocrats used to entertain themselves by shooting in their hotel rooms. Russia was so strange that it seemed to me probably true. ... It wasn't that Russia was strange because of the revolution. Russia was just strange anyway."[16]

When the group returned to Moscow, Arthur Fisher's dysentery had become so severe that he was advised by Russian authorities to take a vacation in the Crimea, and Porter accompanied him south to the resort town of Semeez on the Black Sea. He wrote, "Most of the healthy looking people in our sanitarium had incipient tuberculosis, it was an example of Russian preventive medicine ... which consists of simple health measures like sunlight and sleep and much good food. The Russian curative medicine, which Arthur experiences, is rather old fashioned ... many bottles and powders to be taken five times a day with long Alice-in-Wonderland labels ... including strong doses of opium, and

9
Porter's sketch of Trotsky, made during an audience with Trotsky in Moscow, summer 1927. Photo by Justin Spring. Porter's sketch courtesy Mrs. Fairfield Porter.

a very rigid fantastic diet."[17] Porter, left to his own devices, sketched and painted watercolors, one of which, *Black Sea* (1927), looks like a Marin watercolor of coastal Maine. While in Semeez, Porter was able to observe corruption among the communists up close, noting that "the sanitarium … was supposed to be a sanitarium for incipient tuberculosis. But there were a lot of people who were there just because it was a nice place to spend a vacation if you had some pull."[18] The skepticism with which Porter later regarded the Socialist and Communist Parties in the United States was probably rooted in his firsthand observations of Soviet communism at work.

As soon as Fisher could travel, the two embarked on a return plane ride to Berlin, departing from Smolensk. But the plane got only as far as Königsberg before being forced to land because of rain and headwinds. "As Arthur says, a plane trip is pretty severe punishment," Porter wrote his mother. "The 8 hours [in the air] was God awful. You can only sit still in your seat on the verge of air-sickness and hope that you won't really be sick."[19] From Germany, Porter departed immediately for America, where his senior year at Harvard was about to begin without him. Porter had been in Russia for only five weeks, but the experience remained vivid for the rest of his life, strongly influencing his thought and work until at least the mid-1940s.

After the thrill of Russia, Porter must have found it difficult to reconcile himself to a senior year in Cambridge. His grades for the year (two D's and four C's) suggest as much. His courses included "Races and Cultures of Europe," "Primitive Religions," and two courses in Continental European history, which covered the period 1815–1914. As part of his distribution requirements, Porter also took a course in mathematics. But the only course that seems to have been of any importance to him that year was Fine Arts 14C, "Romanesque Architecture," taught by Arthur Kingsley Porter. Erudite, charming, and suave, the professor "was discovering things as he gave them to us," and this sense of participating in the act of writing art history seems to have made a deep impression on Porter, so much so that even the forced jollity of an afternoon tea party at his faculty home was rendered tolerable. In a letter to his mother that November, he comments about "tea at the Kingsley Porters on Sunday afternoons" that "Mrs. Porter keeps separating you from the person you have just begun to be inane with, saying 'Now you've talked together long enough.' Thornton [Coolidge, Porter's room-mate] says he is afraid to go there because the only time he was ever there, he became involved in a long discussion on The Snake In Art. But I like even the difficulty at the Porters."[20]

Before Arthur Kingsley Porter died – just six years later, swept out to sea when he fell from a rock on the coast of Ireland during a storm [21] – Fairfield Porter, through his studies with the renowned professor, not only learned about the Romanesque but made a valuable social contact, for it was through Arthur

Kingsley Porter (as well as Porter's Harvard classmate John Walker) that he was welcomed, four years later, by Bernard Berenson at the Villa I Tatti.

Porter's indifferent college record reached a low point in 1928, when, as the result of skipping a final exam in anthropology, he fell short of the graduation requirement by one-half credit and was excluded from the list of graduating seniors. Porter maintained in a letter sent from Great Spruce Head that he had thought the exam was optional for seniors, but his professor replied from his own summer home that failing to take tests was "not done at Harvard."[22] After much wrangling and apologizing, Porter was finally granted a makeup exam during the summer, and received a course grade of C. He took a bachelor of science degree (essentially a humanities degree minus the Latin requirement) and was graduated during the next half-term while on probation and in absentia. In the Harvard class album he lists "painting" as his future profession.

Porter moved to New York in the fall of 1928 to study at the Art Students' League. He resided in a boarding house on Fifteenth Street in a first-floor suite that he shared with two friends, Wendell Reynolds and Hans van Weeren Griek. Reynolds was the Dickensian little boy Porter had described to his mother from Milton Academy as "morbidly interesting in that he is crippled for life and deformed ... also very nice and rather quiet." Despite his hunched back, Reynolds was making a start for himself as a journalist and remained friends with Porter until Reynolds's heavy drinking led to a falling-out six years later. Hans van Weeren Griek was a new acquaintance, a Dutchman recently arrived in New York who was studying, like Porter, at the Art Students' League.

Porter had chosen to live on Fifteenth Street rather than at a more convenient location (the Art Students' League was much farther uptown, on Fifty-seventh Street) because Greenwich Village was a center for artists, intellectuals, and bohemians. Porter's life in New York was much more social than it had been at Harvard. "I didn't really much meet people on a basis of easy give-and-take until I went to the Art Students' League, [where I] didn't feel I had any apologies to make for myself."[23]

For Porter, the question of how one went about being a contemporary painter was still unanswered, and the Art Students' League provided only a semblance of structure to his artistic explorations – it was less a school than a meeting place for artists of every sort pursuing independent goals. Still, New York was the capital of the American art scene, and the Art Students' League was its foremost school, thanks to the many successful working artists who taught or had taught there, particularly the members of the Eight. So far as Porter knew, it was the best possible place to study painting in the United States.

The Eight, a group of American painters who had united in opposition to academic standards in the early twentieth century, were no longer rebels but among the most respected painters of the day. The best known of the group was their leader, the legendary art teacher Robert Henri; others were Arthur Davies,

Maurice Prendergast, and John Sloan. Their realistic and analytical ideas about art were based on the feeling that art should be much more a part of everyday American life. Many in the group were former newspaper illustrators. Their disciples were already going off in different directions – some, like Thomas Hart Benton, affiliating themselves with regionalism and a definition, through art, of America, others, like Edward Hopper, following a more private and lyrical vision, and still others choosing to illustrate the political and sociological struggles of the Common Man. Most New York artists, according to one contemporary source, "immersed themselves in social and political currents, familiarizing themselves, more or less deeply, with the ideas of Bellamy, Henry George, Nietzsche, Tolstoy, socialism, individualism and the labor movement. ... [they] 'cared more for life than for paint.'"[24]

Porter's exposure to the Art Students' League immersed him in such thinking and guided him toward the politically and philosophically focused art that he practiced, unsuccessfully, for the next fifteen years of his life. His political enthusiasms (and those of his family) predisposed him to the idea of creating a socially relevant art. But he was aware of other ideas as well, thanks to the innovative gallery owner Alfred Stieglitz, who championed the cause of many nonrealist and nonpropagandistic artists. Porter was a great fan of Stieglitz, who had been introducing ideas about art to the New York art scene since 1908, when he opened his 291 Gallery. By exhibiting Europeans like Rodin, Matisse, Toulouse-Lautrec, Cézanne, Picabia, Rousseau, Picasso, and Braque and championing Americans like John Marin, Marsden Hartley, Arthur Dove, Edward Steichen, and Georgia O'Keeffe (whom he married in 1924), Stieglitz had become the most exciting and controversial promoter of new art and artists in America. Porter attended exhibits at Stieglitz's gallery regularly and within a year had met him socially, thus beginning a long acquaintance that would last until Stieglitz's death in 1946.[25]

Artists and activists shared close quarters in Greenwich Village, and artists' conversations of the late twenties and early thirties were as likely to be about politics (particularly the socialist and labor movements) as about painting technique. Porter, coming from a family background where politics was a part of everyday discussion and holding the memory of Russia still firmly in his mind, must have felt right at home. His living situation – sharing rooms with a journalist – mirrored the general tendency to mix politics with art. As he explained to an interviewer in 1968, "Journalism [in the 1920s] was somehow the way that painters got a connection with the world. ... Radical journalism. Or else the American painters were expatriate or they were isolated."[26] The most celebrated example of the marriage of politics with art was the mural cycle installed at the New School for Social Research, just three blocks south of Porter's boarding house, in 1930. *Mankind's Struggle*, by José Clemente Orozco, featured portraits of Lenin and Gandhi and scenes of revolution in India,

Mexico, and the Soviet Union. Orozco was very much an art celebrity; Porter attended a conference in the 1930s at which he was given a standing ovation for his work.

Greenwich Village in 1928 was as artistic a neighborhood as existed in America, but it was not the shady bohemian ghetto it had been during the first two decades of the century. Once an Italian neighborhood (many Italians still ran restaurants, cafes, markets, and boarding houses), the Village was now not just a home for artists and rebels but an increasingly fashionable gathering place for people of all backgrounds and politics. Fancy hotels like the Brevoort and the Lafayette, noted for their "distinguished intellectual and cosmopolitan clientele," were popular watering spots.[27] Thanks in part to the great surge in American prosperity during the 1920s and in part to the area's old-world buildings and raffish, anything-goes character, Greenwich Village had become a playground for the young and adventurous. A good example of the recent changes wrought by new wealth was the construction, in 1927, of One Fifth Avenue, a luxurious residential skyscraper on Washington Square, just a few doors down from the building where Edward Hopper lived in a one-room walk-up studio with shared toilet (Hopper, like many long-time residents, despised the new building).

Museums and galleries were also establishing themselves in the neighborhood. The year before Porter came to study at the league, the Museum of Living Art opened on the ground floor of 100 Washington Square East, just ten blocks south of his boarding house. The gallery eventually contained works by Man Ray, Gaston Lachaise, Cézanne, Brancusi, Matisse, and Juan Gris and included Picasso's *The Three Musicians*, Leger's *The City*, and Mondrian's *Composition in White and Red*. Exhibits at the museum later featured the works of such American artists as Marin, Demuth, Sheeler, and Hartley. On Eighth Street, beside the Clay Club, a sculpture center, Gertrude Vanderbilt Whitney was remodeling three houses and covering them with a pink stucco facade – they became the Whitney Museum of American Art, which opened in 1931. Intent on "help[ing] create rather than conserve a tradition," the Whitney also exhibited innovative American painters of previous generations, including James McNeill Whistler, Albert Pinkham Ryder, Winslow Homer, and Thomas Eakins.[28]

As a young man of means who came to New York to experience the new movements in both art and politics, Porter was lucky in that his father, much as he disparaged his son's talent, had no very strong desire to see him otherwise occupied. From the time of Porter's graduation in 1928 until James's death a decade later, James Porter made over a small trust income to his son, which left him free to pursue his art. Porter lived modestly (his one indulgence being the occasional purchase of the work of other artists), but even so, he was careful in his dealings, for among bohemians financial independence, though envied, instantly conferred a secondary artistic status. And in an art world concerned with the oppression of the worker and the tyranny of capitalist imperialism, it was difficult to admit to living off one's parents. Indeed, Porter's innate self-consciousness about his money worsened over the next decades, mainly because so many of his acquaintances had such a strong (if misguided) impression about the depth of his financial resources.

Porter's two years of study at the Art Students' League were largely spent working in a life-studies class. His time at Harvard had increased his knowledge of art history but done little for his art. He possessed drafting skills. *Roofs of Cambridge*, a 1927 watercolor, resembles a competent commercial illustration; it was probably completed as part of his Harvard classwork. But his ability to render the figure and to paint in oils was extremely limited, as the small amount of work that survives from this early period demonstrates.

Porter's two memorable teachers at the league were Boardman Robinson and Thomas Hart Benton. Retrospectively, Porter was much more enthusiastic about Robinson than Benton, but he looked to neither as an authority on painting: "I suppose what I was thinking of [when I started painting] was, what I've got to do is learn how to paint. And there isn't anybody who can teach me. I've just got to learn it. ... I just set about copying the way things looked and trying to get the concept of reality down."[29]

Robinson, a cartoonist and book illustrator as well as a muralist and painter, was a less formidable teacher and, according to Porter, a more sincere and engaging presence. But Benton had more influence on Porter over the next decade. Certainly Porter remained in touch with Benton after leaving the league and went so far as to visit the Bentons on Martha's Vineyard during his honeymoon. No letters survive between Porter and Robinson, and Porter did not write about Robinson's work, whereas he did write, quite critically, about Benton's.

Porter's relationship with Benton was complicated by the fact that Benton was an influential teacher and artist and, to Porter, an important person to know, even though, as their relationship progressed, Porter realized that he disagreed with much of what Benton thought, as well as how he taught, and even eventually took issue with the sort of person Benton was. In a letter to his mother written several years after studying with him, Porter wrote, "That pose or manner of being uneducated ... is getting more and more pronounced in all his official utterances. ... I don't like his attacking Stieglitz because Stieglitz is 'mystical' or 'talks too much' when it is, after all, a fact that Stieglitz is the only man perhaps in the world who shows pictures and doesn't do so out of a profit motive."[30] As an intellectual young man from an intellectual background, Porter found Benton's anti-intellectual posturing more than a nuisance. In 1968 he recalled that "Robinson was a more interesting man [than Benton] ... he would bring ideas from the outside to the class. And Benton's style as a man was that there is a body of knowledge and it is three feet long and three feet wide and one foot thick, and that's it. He had also what James Truslow Adams calls the "mucker" pose. ... He liked to pretend, he liked to act as though he were completely uneducated and, you know, just the grandson of a crooked politician. I found that sort of tiresome."[31]

Apart from Benton's anti-intellectualism, Porter disliked Benton's canny awareness that to establish one's painterly vision is, in effect, to market oneself as a personality and as a creator of a certain kind of product. (Another of Benton's students during the 1930s, Jackson Pollock, had fewer objections to Benton's way of thinking, though he, too, ended up renouncing his teacher.) In an effort to pass himself off as the embodiment of the regionalist spirit, Benton claimed kinship with his midwestern heritage and embraced a jingoistic reading of American history. What Porter most deplored in Benton's behavior was not just its simple-mindedness but what he perceived as its insincerity – an insincerity based upon commercial motivations – which cheapened the artistic endeavor. Benton not only celebrated commerce; he saw painting as a form of commerce and trumpeting one's identity as a way to move the product. For Porter, cultivation of sales, notoriety, and a celebrity persona (an idea which passed successfully and influentially from Benton to Pollock to Warhol) was unthinkable.

The irritation that Porter felt with Benton may also have been with his tendency to proselytize, a tendency more than matched in another great teacher of painting who was just then establishing himself in New York, Hans Hofmann. Porter was amused, years later, to recall an experience involving the two teachers: "I heard about [Hofmann] first when I was studying with Benton ... he was just out of Germany. And Benton had written something in *Arts* magazine called 'The Mechanics of Form Organization' ... Hofmann had said, 'Oh, that's very good – those articles by Benton. He used all my ideas.' And Benton was very annoyed by that. He had never even heard of Hofmann."[32]

Apart from his relationship with Benton, Porter soon felt frustrated at the Art Students' League. The classes "were life classes. They were drawing. Nobody taught painting there. I mean you could paint if you wanted to. But they didn't know how to paint. There wasn't anybody in the league who knew how to paint. None of the teachers did. I don't think anybody in America knew how to paint in oils at that time. Maybe Sloan did. But he put it aside ... there were certainly very good painters in America, but they weren't in the mainstream."[33]

Painting was indeed taught at the Art Students' League, but perhaps what Porter meant is that painting was not taught *well*. Painters arriving in New York soon introduced an entirely different awareness of the medium (Willem de Kooning is the most famous example, but there are many others). Porter later realized that he had come to New York to learn painting too early and that the only instruction available to him when he arrived was not very good.

Frustrated as he may have been with the Art Students' League, Porter soon found himself moving among a much more interesting set of people, artists among them, owing to a chance social encounter with an older couple who lived upstairs at his boarding house. "I left my room to go to the bathroom ... and when I came back a man came down from upstairs and introduced himself. He had seen a painting in my room by Harold Weston [through the door, left ajar]. He knew Harold Weston and he invited me up to his apartment. He and his wife had a collection of Marin, O'Keeffe, [Bluhmner, Kunyoshi][34] and Dove and so on ... they were friends of Stieglitz."[35]

Arthur Schwab, who managed a paper factory, and his wife, Edna "Teddy" Bryner-Schwab, had set up in Greenwich Village as art collectors. They made a point of meeting and knowing all the exceptional people in the art and literary worlds and were of course friends with Stieglitz, who had sold them a number of paintings. The Schwabs were good friends to Porter in the decade to come. "I met Marin at their house ... I also met [the critic] Paul Rosenfeld, who influenced me very much."[36]

Rosenfeld, much less well-known today than in the 1930s, was a music critic as well as a writer on Modernism in both painting and literature. He was an important person to know, not just for his insights but for his connections. Porter's friendship with him lasted many years. He was one of the first New Yorkers to whom Porter introduced his bride, Anne Channing Porter, two years later; Anne Porter described him to her mother as "a bachelor art critic ... who is kind and friendly and the exact opposite of hard-boiled. He lives in a big apartment with a mauve carpet and beautiful pictures, alone with his piano and his feeling for the arts."[37]

Rosenfeld's conversational style was similar to that of another writer and art critic with a strong musical background whom Porter met twenty years later, the poet Frank O'Hara. As Porter recalled, "I remember telling [Rosenfeld] I didn't like Odilon Redon. And he said, 'What's the matter? – Is he too ultra-violet?' And I thought, 'That's exactly it!' ... He had this impressionistic way of talking which was extremely accurate, you know. Beautiful."[38]

10
A studio portrait of Anne Elizabeth Channing, circa 1927. Photographer unknown. Courtesy Mrs. Fairfield Porter.

Through the Schwabs, Porter developed a strong-enough acquaintance with Stieglitz that by 1930 Porter had introduced his brother Eliot to him, thus making a vital connection that led to Eliot Porter's first exhibition of photographs at Stieglitz's An American Place gallery almost a decade later. As Eliot Porter recalled,

Fairfield's probable motive behind introducing me to Alfred Stieglitz was his hope that Stieglitz would be willing to look at and constructively criticize my photographs. In his gallery An American Place Stieglitz also exhibited his own photographs and those of a select group of others. Soon after Fairfield's introduction Stieglitz did agree to look at a group of my photographs. He treated me kindly, contrary to what I had been led to expect, but his comments were far from encouraging. He said they were all "woolly." ... Photography, he added, requires a lot of hard work. I had the audacity to return a year later with more photographs, when his remarks were again noncommittal and his advice again was to work harder."[39]

In the spring of 1931, Porter, who had by then finished studying at the Art Students' League,[40] took a weekend trip to Bryn Mawr, outside Philadelphia, to visit a Winnetka neighbor, Dorsy Gerhart. Porter may have done so as a favor to his mother, since Ruth had a passionate interest both in Bryn Mawr College (she was an alumna) and the lives of her neighbors (including the Gerharts) and was probably also eager to see her son romantically attached. Gerhart, in turn, invited Anne Channing, a classmate, to join them (fig. 10). Anne remembered Porter from his visit to her home outside Boston several years earlier; she had heard a great deal about him since then, both from her classmate at the Winsor School, Ruth Fisher, and from her own sister Barbara. Anne's curiosity had been piqued by observations within the Fisher family that Porter wanted to be an artist and by her sister Barbara's enthusiasm for the Porters. Anne had long known that she was a poet, and in Fairfield she felt that she had found a kindred spirit: an intelligent young man from a similar background who was following an artistic vocation rather than a more conventional way of life.

Anne lost no time in writing her sister of the meeting: "F. came down for the glee club, and he and his friend here, Dorsy Gerhart, took me to supper, breakfast, a long Sunday morning in the sun and lunch (from three to four!) I enjoyed so much seeing him and hearing about you all from him. He certainly is one of the nicest people imaginable."[41] What she did not mention was that she and Porter suffered from a certain shyness and had got off to an awkward start. She said later that

[Dorsy, Fairfield, and I] all had breakfast together. It was spring, I remember, because we ate out of doors. I was wearing a pair of white sneakers I'd brought back from Ireland. I felt very self-conscious. They were very white. Fairfield was looking at them. And I said, "I got them in Dublin." He looked at them a long time, then said, "They're very large."

I liked him ... He was very simple and direct. Very unaffected. Most Harvard boys talked about how many beers they could hold; Fairfield and I talked about Dostoyevsky. I remember he had a penknife and he was using it on the table, working at it, trying to make the table fall apart. I remember I got on the other end to see if I could do the same. Not to be destructive, just to see if it was possible to make the picnic table fall apart. It didn't. But we had fun.[42]

By summer, Anne had been invited along with her sister Barbara to visit the Porters on Great Spruce Head Island. Here Porter and Anne came to know each other better, but Porter's attraction to her was not decisive; for a while he held both sisters in equal esteem, writing to both of them when he departed in the fall for what he thought would be a year of art study abroad. Porter's diffidence during his early courtship with Anne – and the postponing of that courtship to travel abroad – is very much like the courtship of James and Ruth Porter more than thirty years before.

Anne Elizabeth Channing came from a Boston family of distinction, and her background, like Ruth Porter's, featured a large number of progressives and intellectuals. Unlike Ruth Porter, however, she came from great wealth – a situation she found troubling from earliest childhood. Born on November 6, 1911, in Sherborn, Massachusetts, she was the fourth and last child of Henry Morse Channing, a lawyer, and Katharine Minot Channing. Henry's father, Walter Channing, had been a psychiatrist who founded and ran a private sanatarium, first in Brookline, then in Wellesley, specializing in the care of individuals suffering from nervous disorders, including alcoholism. Katharine Minot had been orphaned in adolescence, losing her mother at fourteen and her father at sixteen; she and her brothers had been reared by their bachelor uncle Laurence Minot.

From the time of Anne's birth the family resided in a large house, Little Pond, built by Henry Channing before 1910 on a vast tract of farmland which had long been owned by the Channing family. There, Anne, her two older sisters (Barbara and Katharine), and her brother (Laurence) grew up in a brick Georgian-style manor house whose front drive was an eighth of a mile long – a house so large that, as one friend of Porter's recalled, "it was the only house I ever actually got lost in."[43] Anne herself felt the house too grand, "more like a public library than a home."[44]

Henry and Katharine Channing were dedicated athletes, and Katharine, having lost both parents at an early age, was so concerned with her children's health that she encouraged them to spend extraordinary amounts of time outdoors, just as the Porter children had been so encouraged on Great Spruce Head. Like Ruth Porter, Katharine Channing had a great love of literature, though her tastes were not so intellectual; in the evenings she too read aloud to the family, introducing the children to poetry (Browning, Coleridge, Tennyson, and Poe, among many others) as well as fiction. Katharine Channing did not write poetry, however; for a woman of her interests and background, "it would have been unthinkable."[45]

56

During the harshest winter months, the entire family lived in Boston at the Marlborough Street home of Anne's great uncle Laurence Minot. It was to this great uncle that Anne Porter in 1994 dedicated her first and only volume of poems: the kindly older man who "wrote down and illustrated my poems for me before I learned to write."

Anne received her earliest education in Washington (where her father worked for the wartime government as a Dollar-a-Year Man). She attended the Holton Arms School. Upon returning to Boston she attended a dame school called Mrs. Newcomb's until the age of ten, when she transferred to the Winsor School, in the Fenway. There her early writings were published in the school literary journal, and she won the literary prizes for several years running (she was included in a published anthology called *Singing Youth* at fourteen). But she did not enjoy school or the typical social life of a girl of her background. According to her sister Barbara, "Anne [was] in rebellion all through her adolescence. She didn't relate well to people [and] was very different from other girls. She lived very much in her own private world."[46]

Anne loved poetry, and in recognition of that love, a family friend who was descended from Thomas Wentworth Higginson gave Anne a letter that Emily Dickinson had written to Higginson congratulating him on the birth of a daughter. Anne kept the treasured letter for many years (Fairfield Porter featured it in several of his paintings of her) before donating it to the Emily Dickinson Papers at Harvard University.

Anne Porter's strongest memories of girlhood were of a life lived mostly alone and mostly outdoors, and it was there that she became aware of her spirituality, a spirituality which, aside from bedtime prayers, her family had not encouraged. Through a children's magazine called *Our Dumb Animals* she had learned of St. Francis and felt a natural closeness to him; she increased her awareness of St. Francis through a Protestant text by Paul Sabatier, which she found in the attic of her home. Knowing of Anne's interest, her mother presented Anne with two more books about St. Francis. At the age of fifteen or sixteen, she began to pray for an hour or so every day and, as she describes it, "became sure of the presence of God."[47]

Anne's family background was not very religious despite the later claims of the gallery director John Bernard Myers in his (often inaccurate) memoirs that she was "descended from a long line of Unitarian ministers."[48] The one exception was her great-great uncle William Ellery Channing (1780–1842), the great preacher, author, and apostle of Unitarianism who advocated tolerance in religion and championed a number of progressive ideas concerning slavery, war, labor problems, and education. Another Channing, Walter Channing, Anne's paternal great-grandfather, is memorialized in a statue on Boston Common for his achievements in medicine; but a joke among the Channings, who came to America from England in 1730, held that the family was more famous for its connection to May Channing, the woman who, after poisoning her husband, became the last woman in England to be burned at the stake (Thomas Hardy commemorated her in a poem).

The Channings were known for their involvement in government, law, and medicine. One ancestor of Anne's was the attorney general of Rhode Island during the American Revolution; another – Walter Channing – was among the first to use anesthesia in delivering babies. At least one antecedent was a poet: her paternal great-great-grandfather, William Henry Channing, a friend of Emerson's who, like Emerson and Alcott, was a radical utopian.

On the Minot side, Anne came from an immediate background noteworthy for principled female rebellion. Both her grandmothers had been suffragists; her maternal grandmother, Elizabeth Van Pelt (from Elizabeth, New Jersey), had refused to marry until she had finished attending Cornell University and become one of the first women in America to obtain a university degree. She married William Minot, a Boston trustee who became one of the city's richest men. Unfortunately, he and his wife died young, leaving Katharine Minot, Anne's mother, to forgo her own education in order to raise her little brothers in the home of her bachelor uncle. But Katharine educated herself (studying Greek, among other things); her awareness of the importance of learning was only increased by her lack of a formal education. Perhaps as a result, two of her three daughters attended Bryn Mawr College, and the third pursued a career as a schoolteacher.

Anne Channing had been unconventional from childhood. According to her sister Barbara, "being a debutante was the last thing on her mind. She had hated school and disliked all but two or three girls. She never got over her bad experience at school. She didn't relate well to people ... I remember at eighteen she was very pretty, and Anne and I were on a ship. The boys on the ship would try to chat her up and come away baffled by her."[49]

By the time Porter reintroduced himself to her in 1931, Anne had grown unhappy with life at Bryn Mawr. Though she excelled in her studies, she found the small, all-women environment claustrophobic and artificial, so much so that she had already applied for a transfer to Radcliffe, where she hoped to continue her studies while living at home. Though Radcliffe rarely accepted transfer students, the authorities gave Anne preferential treatment because of her exceptionally good grades and because she was descended from distinguished Harvard and Radcliffe alumni on both sides of her family (many of whom had left before taking degrees).[50] Anne, for her part, was keen on attending Radcliffe because Alfred North Whitehead had visited Bryn Mawr from Harvard during the academic year of 1930–31, and impressed her with his brilliance and charisma. Anne received an A from Whitehead while studying with him at Radcliffe and later recalled "how vast and wonderful his discussions were" and how much she had enjoyed them. "They were on the edge of [my] ability to comprehend, and in that way like poetry."[51]

4

Travel and Study
in Italy

During the summer of 1931 on Great Spruce Head, the same summer in which Anne and Barbara Channing came to visit, Porter and his mother were, to judge from their letters, reading and sharing thoughts on *The Possessed* (today better known as *The Devils*), Dostoyevsky's novel about atheist revolutionaries. Porter's interest in all things Russian had increased during his years in New York, and when he and his mother departed on their trip to Italy that fall, Porter brought with him both a copy of *The Possessed* and a critical work on Dostoyevsky.

Among New York artists and bohemians of the late twenties and early thirties, Dostoyevsky's appeal was enormous, for to be interested in him was to be interested in the fate of contemporary society. The fate of Russia was a topic of great concern among leftist intellectuals: Russia was a working model of socialism in action, and the success or failure of world socialism seemed to depend on the success of that model, which was now being usurped by Stalin's authoritarian regime. Dostoyevsky's interests – in radical politics, in the fate of Russia, and in the character of the Russian people – thus spoke to contemporary concerns. Moreover, the politically conscious artists and writers of the time hoped, like Dostoyevsky, to make significant statements on society, religion, psychology, and morality through their works. Dostoyevsky himself was a cult hero to many leftists, since he had been imprisoned as a radical activist when he was a young man.

Dostoyevsky's late novel *The Possessed*, which concerns the attempted overthrow of a provincial town by nihilist radicals, was considered by many Americans of the thirties to be a prophecy of present-day political developments in Russia and elsewhere. The novel appealed to Porter for its prescient description of the political demagoguery and group psychosis which had featured so largely in Russian (and world) politics in the years since the Russian Revolution. Published in 1867 in response to the growth of nihilism, the novel describes the collapse of Russian society in a microcosmic provincial town. The instigators of the collapse are a small circle of bloodthirsty, God-denying radicals. No one who had followed the rise of Stalin in the late twenties and early thirties (as Porter had) could have helped noticing similarities between Stalin and the fictional radical leader Pyotr Stepanovitch Verhovensky.

For Porter, the novel probably had a personal resonance as well, for aside from being a story centered on the actions of two men at the beginning of their adult lives (Stavrogin and Pyotr Stepanovitch), the novel features two comic characters who bear a certain resemblance to Porter's mother and father. Varvara Stavrogin, the widowed mother of the novel's erratic central character, Nicholay Stavrogin, is a wealthy provincial lady who has channeled her many social and intellectual frustrations into the education of a son who suffers from periodic bouts of wildly asocial behavior. A strong-willed woman of independent means who keeps a sharp eye on all comings and goings within the village, she craves a husband, but rather than lose her autonomy by remarrying, she maintains an intensely emotional but otherwise unsatisfying relationship with Stepan Verhovensky, a poor, feckless former university lecturer, self-styled intellectual, and failed father of a sociopathic son. Ruth Porter resembles the intrusive, well-meaning, but frustrated Varvara; James Porter resembles Stepan Verhovensky in that both are introverted and emotionally withdrawn. Though James Porter's finances were exactly the opposite of Verhovensky's, Varvara's command of domestic arrangements is quite similar to Ruth's management of the Porter households, as least so far as Fairfield Porter observed them.[1] The squabbling which takes place between Varvara Stavrogin and Stepan Verhovensky over Varvara's son is a comic version of the very real tension that existed between Ruth and James Porter over Fairfield's prospects.

Ruth's decision to finance Fairfield's trip – according to Eliot Porter, his year of art study overseas was financed entirely by their mother[2] – had an enormous effect on Fairfield's outlook and ability as an artist and critic. Not satisfied with what she had seen and heard of his art studies in New York and intent on helping him, she decided to give him the best possible exposure to European art – in her opinion, the late medieval and early Renaissance painting of Italy. In Eliot's words, "Father never completely understood Fairfield's aspirations or his first immature attempts to express them[, but] Mother ... was more sympathetic, albeit not informed about the prevailing vogue in painting."[3]

From Fairfield Porter's own point of view, the decision to travel to Italy may have seemed partially misguided; he knew from Stieglitz that the most exciting contemporary art was being created in Paris. But Ruth Porter was working from the older assumption that every young man of artistic inclinations should take the Grand Tour – and she was paying for the trip. Porter might have been able to convince his mother that the greatest artistic developments were not happening in Italy, but he seems not to have tried. His growing interest in contemprary mural painting in New York probably played a part in his decision to travel to Italy, for many of his journeys within Italy would be to view frescoes.

The S.S. *Conte Grande* left New York on September 11, 1931. Porter and his mother made two sightseeing stops (at Palermo and Naples) before disembarking at Genoa on September 22. No letters survive from the first part of their journey through Italy, but Ruth kept a record of it in a tiny notebook which was preserved by Porter after his mother's death. The wire-bound memo pad holds their itinerary, as well as Ruth's notes on the hotels in which they stayed, the meals they ate, and the prices they paid. The mother and son proceeded to Milan (for the museums, the Duomo, and Leonardo's *Last Supper* at the Basilica de Sant'Ambrogio), Mantua (for the extraordinary frescoes by Mantegna at the Ducal Palace and perhaps the Mannerist frescoes of Palazzo Te), then Verona (for the *pinacoteca*, the Roman ruins, and the Pisanello frescoes at the Chiesa di Sant' Anastasia). Curiously enough, they did not stop in nearby Vicenza, home of Palladio and site of many of his great villas; perhaps the time was too limited for Porter to indulge his interest in architecture. Instead, from Verona, Porter and his mother took the train to Padua, where Porter had what was perhaps the most profound and influential aesthetic experience of his early years: he saw the Scrovegni (or Arena) Chapel, the small and architecturally quite simple building whose entire interior is covered with frescoes by Giotto.

Porter spent three days in Padua gazing in wonder at these marvelous, jewel-toned frescoes, with cycles describing the Last Judgment, the life of the Virgin, the Annunciation, and the story of the Virgin's parents, as well as the infancy and miracles of Christ, his Passion, Crucifixion, Resurrection, and Ascension. Giotto's simplicity, his use of strong architectural presences, and his talent for rendering an intuitive psychological awareness of his subjects through innovative composition, basic human gestures, and broad areas of emotionally charged color are very much what Porter would achieve in his best paintings many years later. Porter's lifelong passion for Giotto, whose images he kept tacked to the walls of his studio, suggests that these similarities are more than coincidental.

At the time, however, Porter found the frescoes interesting for another reason. In the New York art world where he had been studying, both American muralists (including Benton, Edward Laning, and Jim Guy) and Mexican muralists (José Clemente Orozco, Diego Rivera, and David Alfaro Siqueiros) were championing the "public" art of the mural for its didactic and democratizing possibilities. Giotto and others whose work Porter saw in Italy (including Piero della Francesca, Ghirlandaio, Masaccio, and Pontormo) were masters of fresco, an art form which, like mural painting, had been designed for the instruction and enlightenment of the masses, though with a religious rather than political end in mind. As he toured Italy, Porter became increasingly excited about the possibility of taking on a public commission to create a work which would reflect his politics and beliefs and would be available to all viewers, not just a privileged few.

In addition to the Arena Chapel, Porter spent time in Padua admiring the magnificent Mantegna frescoes in the Church of the Eremitani, just next door, and visiting the Pinacoteca Civica and the Basilica del Santo, home to the sacred remains of St. Anthony. From Padua, Porter and his mother took the short train ride east to Venice, where they spent a week looking at art and admiring the light, which was surely at its most exceptional under the cold, clear October skies. Porter had a brief opportunity to acquaint himself with the superb coloring of the Venetian masters (Tiepolo, Titian, Tintoretto, and Veronese), an experience which would be of particular importance to him in later life, when he reached a breakthrough in his own painting by copying a small Tiepolo study at the Metropolitan Museum of Art in New York.

In Venice, Porter also saw Andrea del Verrocchio's equestrian monument to Bartolomeo Colleoni mounted on its tall pedestal in the Campo SS. Giovanni e Paolo (also known as San Zanipolo). Porter thus knew the statue well when he read of it twenty years later in Wallace Stevens's influential essay on reality and the imagination, "The Noble Rider and the Sound of Words." Stevens's description of the statue impressed Porter as the best possible sort of art criticism: a description which develops poetically rather than scientifically, out of "analogies" and "imaginative identification," and whose end, like that of poetry, was (to paraphrase Stevens), "without imposing, without reasoning at all, to find the eccentric at the base of design."[4]

Porter was both amused and impressed with Venice as a spectacle, writing to Anne Channing (then studying with Whitehead at Radcliffe) that the city was "like a combination amusement park and highbrow museum."[5] From there, he and his mother traveled south into the Marches, passing through Rimini, Pesaro, and Urbino and over the Apennines to Arezzo (where they lingered over Piero della Francesca's famed fresco cycle, *The Legend of the Holy Cross*) before at last reaching Florence.

Their hotel, the Hotel Roma on the Piazza Novella, was catty-corner from the Grand Hotel Minerva, where Ruth's cousin Henry Wadsworth Longfellow had lived while translating the *Divine Comedy*, and at the far end of the piazza from the Church of Santa Maria Novella, which contains the dazzling sanctuary frescoes by Ghirlandaio (as well as others by Filippo Lippi and a crucifixion by Giotto). Though day-trips to Prato, Pistoia, Pisa, and Lucca took up their first days, and tours of the many Florentine museums those that followed, Porter and his mother both eventually visited Santa Maria Novella and came away impressed by the Ghirlandaio frescoes. Ruth Porter observed how Ghirlandaio painted "such nice portraits of his contemporaries"[6] – an observation suggesting that her taste was guided not so much by politics or religion as by a humanist appreciation of character. Portraiture was a field in which her son would eventually distinguish himself, but at the time he was much less interested in it than his mother, preoccupying himself instead with questions of color, composition, and technique.

As Ruth Porter's time in Italy drew to a close, she saw that her son was suitably housed for the duration of his stay by moving from the Hotel Roma to a new, less expensive boarding house, the Pensione San Giorgio on the Arno, where he would stay after she left. Ruth knew that she had given her son an invaluable experience by traveling with him through Italy, and she continued to help him even after she had departed through the gift of her continuing financial support. Porter, perhaps sensing the strain the trip had had upon his aging mother and perhaps sensing her loneliness in Winnetka,[7] wrote home frequently after her departure. His letters, always addressed specifically to her, are characteristically bright, comic, and tender, full of diverting anecdotes and entertaining observations.

In 1931 wealthy Americans were only just beginning to realize the enormity of the Depression, and cultured sons and daughters of the American upper- and upper-middle classes were still traveling overseas to study art and culture. By chance, Porter soon encountered an acquaintance from Harvard, John Walker, who was just then embarking on a brilliant curatorial career by working for Bernard Berenson as a research assistant at Villa I Tatti. Walker, a wealthy young man of good family, had achieved brilliant marks at Harvard and arrived bearing a letter of recommendation from Paul Sachs, director of Harvard's Fogg Art Museum. Despite their many philosophical and political differences, which distanced them later in life, Porter and Walker struck up an easy friendship.

Walker immediately convinced Porter to change pensioni, moving from his quiet and comfortable lodgings on the Arno to the eccentric Casa Bertolini, just behind the train station on the Piazza della Indipendenza, a somewhat untidy residence favored by artists, writers, and art historians. (This pensione should not be confused with the fictional pensione of the same name in E. M. Forster's 1908 novel, *A Room With a View*; Forster based that pensione on the Pensione Simi, on the banks of the Arno, and renamed it after a hotel proprietor he had met in Milan.)[8]

Apart from Walker, Porter soon met Elizabeth "Tissie" Nottingham, a liberated young woman painter then in the midst of a torrid affair with a local Italian. Nottingham was, like Porter, copying masterworks in the Pitti Palace and, later, in the Uffizi. In a letter to his mother in early November, Porter wrote,

I moved, a few days after you left, to the above address, which is where John Walker who works for Berenson (Harvard '30, just my age) lives & where Italian is spoken at meals. I know no more Italian however. The teacher I have been having is really next to useless. I have started copying at the Pitti: "La Donna Gravida" of Raphael & Elizabeth Nottingham is copying also Raphael in another room. I am doing it in tempera. ...

At the pensione are a Prof. Knight of Political Economy of the University of Chicago who lends me *The Nation*, which is as you doubtless know an old Porter custom, and a very old and really rather nice English *Signorina* who speaks Italian fluently but with a terrible English accent, & who sits at a separate table during meals because she will not bother to speak italian, for I think she is firmly convinced that the Italians don't speak English only out of spite. ...

... *Signora* Bertolini speaks absolutely perfect and unlimited English which she learned as a child at an English school in Florence (she is Italian) & she has been to England & America – visiting friends at Blue Hill, Maine [a short distance from Great Spruce Head Island]. ... she has been to a Harvard-Yale baseball game. ... Her husband, *Commandatore* Mariani is a buffoon, almost in the manner of Dostoyevsky's buffoons. He puffs at meals & acts the child, & shouts *È!* And thinks it witty to call me *Signore Pianta* ... and when his wife says "Porter!" he says "*È! Pianta, Porter, tutto cose insieme.*"

... Through John [Walker] I have extended my social life – I have had dinner twice in casa Baron & Baroness [Egbert and Ada von] Anrep [refugee Baltic landowners and the sister and brother-in-law of Berenson's personal assistant, Elizabetta "Nicky" Mariano]. ... They speak English when we go there. ... Both times I tripped over Baroness Anrep's train & almost tore her dress & [was] a little ill at ease at the thought. Dress suits are never worn by Italians according to John ... because Italy is a country where men do not dress to suit their womenfolk, but to suit their own comfort (heh, heh). [The joke here regards Porter's ongoing battle with his mother over the purchase of a dinner jacket.] I have also met through the Anreps an American painter & his wife, named Blow [Dick Blow and the writer Nancy Hale], who live here.

... Last Sunday [Bob Pratt, a Ph.D. student] & John Walker & Rachel Albertson (the secretary of Mrs. Berenson) & Elizabeth Nottingham & I were driven by John in his Ford to Poggio a Caiano – the summer Medici villa – which was lived in by Medici even in the 19th century in fact until not long ago. An English painter friend of John ... invited John and me [to see a Castagno fresco in the Chiesa della Santissima Annunziata that is covered and rarely shown]. I also saw the Andrea del Castagno *Last Supper* – which I hadn't realized from photographs to be so wonderful as in actuality it turned out to be.

This is about as full an account as I can give without getting palsy or a haemorrhage & so I will abruptly stop.⁹

To be welcomed among the Berensons was to associate with some of the most brilliant and cultivated company of the day. In the fall of 1931, Edith Wharton was staying with the Berensons. Other regulars at I Tatti included the Byronic Italian literary figure Count Umberto Morra di Lavriano (whom the poet James Merrill met in Italy twenty years later and wrote about lengthily in his memoirs),¹⁰ the young novelist Alberto Moravia, Count Gugliemo degli Alberti, and Berenson's protégé, Kenneth Clark (who soon after departed to direct the Ashmolean Museum at Oxford). Through his marriage, Berenson was brother-in-law to Logan Pearsall Smith, who was present at I Tatti during Porter's visits, as was the poet R. C. Trevelyan, just then engaged in the translation of one of Porter's favorite poets, Giacomo Leopardi.

But Porter's enthusiasm for Berenson and his set should not be confused with a general enthusiasm for the world of the wealthy and the well connected. His letters suggest that he was more excited by the quality of conversation in the Berenson household than by its social magnificence or material opulence. Though Berenson could be a terrible snob as well as a difficult and exacting host, he was also a wit, a conversationalist, and an intellectual and was always eager for company. Intelligent young men of good family who had attended his alma mater were almost always welcome to lunch at his home.

Berenson, sixty-six in 1931 and by then the author of forty books, may have seemed happy and secure to the young Porter, but in fact he had recently suffered a number of major crises. His wife, Mary, had become an invalid following a suicide attempt. Berenson himself was just emerging from a scandal arising from his dealings with Sir Joseph Duveen, and Berenson's finances and reputation had suffered enormously as a result. He had recently lost nearly 70 percent of his personal income, and by the fall of 1931 his finances were so precarious that he was considering the sale of I Tatti.[11]

In addition to these enormous personal and professional setbacks, Berenson was disturbed by the Italian political situation and the recent, horrific developments in Stalinist Russia and Nazi Germany. Everyone at I Tatti (from Baltic refugees to intellectual opponents of Italian fascism) was convinced that the world political situation was nearing a crisis. "As early as December 1931 [Edith Wharton] had been speaking to Berenson about 'this angry sombre world,'" her biographer writes. "More than ever … Wharton saw her small circle of friends, devoted to the arts, to beauty, to good conversation and the graces of life, as a last stronghold in a collapsing civilization. Reflecting on 'all the shattering, crashing, smashing that has gone on in the world,' she suggested to Berenson that they should all 'go up on the Consuma Hill' – the Berenson's summer home – 'like Boccaccio's set, and try to forget all about it.'"[12]

From all outside appearances, however, I Tatti in 1931 was an oasis of civilized calm and a delightful rural getaway from the noise and bustle of Florence. Porter, at Walker's invitation, probably bicycled there for lunch, just a few miles over even ground, for the villa is not atop the breezy hills of Fiesole but at their base, just above the tiny town of Settignano, where Michelangelo had been wet-nursed. The thin stream that straggled down the hill beside the Berenson property was none other than the Torrente Mensola mentioned in Boccaccio's *Decameron*.

The two young men would have reached the villa not by the road along the border of the property but from the gate at the foot of the garden,[13] strolling directly up the ilex walk or else wandering up an ascending series of boxwood-and-gravel parterres into the *limonaia*, a winter storage house for the frost-sensitive lemon trees. From there it was just a few steps across the terrace to the villa, which, though grand, was no larger than Porter's own home in Winnetka. Berenson had renovated his house as a showplace for the art he loved, collected, wrote about, and sold, and it may have seemed more like an art showroom to Porter than a home.

Berenson craved company at lunchtime and made a point of having new people visit him then. According to his assistant, Nicky Mariano,

The coming and going of guests was a standing feature of daily life. We used to compare I Tatti to a big rumbling bus. Some passengers got on to descend at the next stop, others occupied it for longer trips. A number of unknown Americans armed with letters of introduction would be invited for a meal, would go through a bit of "third degree" by B.B. [Berenson] about their work, their interests and beliefs, would be taken over the house and only in exceptional cases would be seen again. Others were brought to I Tatti for some definite reason that aroused B.B.'s interest and curiosity. Shyness or awkwardness did not put [Berenson] off if he felt real gifts lay hidden behind them. Sometimes his inquisitiveness led him to ask tactless questions and even to say offensive things ... he did not want to be taken too seriously and could easily be laughed out of his over-pedagogical, not to say priggish, moods.[14]

Lunch itself was an event. Again, according to Mariano:

Guests staying in the house or guests from Florence or from the neighborhood would gather in the small eighteenth-century *salotto*. ... Meals at I Tatti were always a very informal affair. B.B. has been accused, I know, of being a snob ... but he kept completely free socially and saw people from every walk in life. ... What B.B. cared for was to get in touch with intellectually stimulating people or to have a gay time with agreeable and cultivated members of good society. ... Particularly pleasant and carefree was the after-lunch gathering for coffee and liqueurs. ... Between luncheon and tea was generally a drive combined with a walk. ... In the open air B.B. was as happy as a lark, waved his stick at the view, walked briskly except when the conversation took up his whole attention or when light and color were particularly beautiful.[15]

Berenson was probably amused to meet an intelligent young Harvard graduate pursuing a vocation as a contemporary artist, for Florence was no bastion of modernism, and Berenson must have found Porter's New York tastes and opinions an invigorating change from Kenneth Clark's. "I remember telling him that I liked Tintoretto and Rubens because I'd learned to like them from Thomas Benton," Porter recalled. "And he said, 'Yes, I know what you mean about them but the best painter of all is really Veronese, or Velázquez.'"[16] Whatever his feelings about young Porter's opinions, Berenson saw that Porter was invited back.

Though he could be dismissive of ambitious young scholars, Berenson seems not to have been at all unkind to Porter. As Umberto Morra recalled, "Berenson was generous with his time and with his attention ... [he] enjoyed conversation; for him it was equally a 'game of the spirit' and a total concern, something both beguiling and altogether serious."[17] Porter, used to the free play of ideas in a home environment, was unabashed at the idea of entering into a serious and wide-ranging conversation with an eminent scholar. And since there was nothing at stake in Berenson's estimation of him, Porter probably felt much more at ease with Berenson than did the many young art historians who were intent on securing his good opinion and recommendation.

Porter's interest in Russian history, literature, and politics gave him an advantage with Berenson. According to Mariano, "Everything regarding Russia had a special place in B.B.'s heart, from its earliest historians to writers on recent events, from accounts of the first colonizers of Siberia to the diaries of the Dekabrists [Decembrists], from the great classics of the nineteenth century to novels reflecting life in Soviet Russia."[18]

The shared enthusiasm for Russia may well have encouraged Porter not only to begin a series of illustrations of *The Possessed* but also to sign up for Russian lessons in Florence. "I have started taking Russian lessons at the Berlitz school," he wrote his mother soon after her departure. "I have had about 7 lessons & I now say sentences. The first day I wanted to arrange hours with him & he said, "*io parlo solamente Russo*" which made him like a God – he understood me, & what I didn't understand, & I felt like a poodle being trained to do square roots." Soon afterward, Porter began planning what he hoped would be another extended visit to Russia.

Nonetheless, he continued his quiet daily life in Florence, copying every day in the cold museum, sharing his lunch with the lovelorn Elizabeth Nottingham, and returning home to the pensione in late afternoon to listen to American records and read American magazines. As he wrote his mother in late November, "I have finished my Raphael [copy] and am starting soon on Pisselino [*sic*]. ... I have had lunch again with Berenson and made a hit with him, John says." But Porter does not dwell on Berenson in the letter, preferring instead to discuss Professor Frank Knight, the political economist from the University of Chicago who had lent Porter copies of *The Nation*:

Prof. Knight has left [for] Chicago. I liked him more & more all the time he was here, & miss him now. He would like to meet father because he likes father's being a thoroughgoing atheist. He himself is an atheist emotionally, but not a materialist. He is very quizzical and full of doubt about all things, & it comes from much knowledge about all subjects, which includes political economy, history, philosophy, languages, physics, biology, mathematics & art. ... His wife is on the Governor's unemployment commission & admires Herman Adler [the psychiatrist husband of Porter's paternal grandmother's adopted daughter, Frances].[19]

November 28, 1931

Clearly politics, family, current events, and metaphysics were still on Porter's mind, even while he was copying Raphael in the Pitti Palace, visiting the great churches and museums of Tuscany, or having lunch with Bernard Berenson.

Porter's next choice for his copying exercises was significantly related by subject to his liberal and progressive views, for he chose to copy a predella of the martyrdom of Cosmas and Damian, the twin saints whose great miracle was the grafting of the leg of a black man onto the body of a white man. Because they were the patron saints of the Medici (*medici* means "physicians" in Italian), images of Cosmas and Damian abounded in Florence, the most famous of them being Fra Angelico's altarpiece and predella for San Marco, which shows the miraculous graft. Ruth, with her long-standing membership in the NAACP and her history of activism on behalf of the American black, would surely have approved of an image of the miraculous joining, but the predella that Porter chose to copy (probably because it was convenient to him in the Uffizi) was an image of their martyrdom by the little-known artist Pessellino (also known as Pessello or, more commonly, Giulliano Giuochi).[20]

Porter's description of Professor Knight's departure shows his loneliness. Late fall is always a melancholy time, and Porter, though surrounded by art, was far from home. John Walker was not often at the pensione these days, and when Porter did spend time with him – usually traveling to the Tuscan and Umbrian hill towns to look at art – he was beginning to realize that their minds worked quite differently. As an artist, Porter questioned the relevance and validity of the art that he saw, while Walker, as an art historian, admired each work as a curator would. Upon returning from Siena, Porter wrote, "I don't admire Sienese painting very much more than before. John does because his taste is a critic's taste and ... comes from his Harvard and Bernard Berenson training."[21]

Porter continued the difficult and lonely task of teaching himself how to paint during what would have been, in America, the Thanksgiving holiday. By early December, perhaps feeling discouraged, he started planning a post-Christmas trip to museums in Austria and Germany. "I am now copying Pessellino in the Uffizzi and doing it badly but learning a good deal," he wrote his mother. "Alex [Haberstroh, a painter friend in New York] wrote to me that Daniel[s, a New York gallery owner] said of my pictures 'I don't want this year to chance a new painter, but I would like to keep these paintings to show to friends and critics.' So I shall leave my paintings there. ... We are now full up here [at Pensione Casa Bertolini]. ... John is leaving here for Czecho Slovakia & then Vienna where I hope to meet him about Christmas, & then we will visit an American family in Switzerland ... then I am going to Berlin ... and then back here to Rome."[22]

Shortly after Porter wrote this letter, a new lodger arrived at the Casa Bertolini who would have great importance in Porter's life. Porter mentions him first to his mother in a letter of December 12, after describing the exceptional snow and cold in Florence and the progress of his Russian lessons: "I talk Italian to the Oxford student Arthur Giardelli, because he wants always to talk Italian. He is here for his Christmas vacation to learn Italian, which he really already knows."[23]

Arthur Giardelli had just arrived from Oxford, where he was studying at Hertford College. He and his family had very little money; he was being educated at Oxford on scholarships and was in Florence at his parents' great expense to cram for an important scholarship examination in Italian. His father, a schoolteacher in the unfashionable London suburb of Bermondsey, had found the pensione through the Italian Institute; Giardelli had no idea that the place was popular with the Berenson set. Handsome as well as artistically, musically, and athletically accomplished, Giardelli, four years younger than Porter, was glad to have a companion in Florence, and the two became friends.

Porter and Giardelli had a great deal in common, beginning with family politics. Giardelli's father and mother were teachers, and both held liberal and progressive opinions. The Giardellis felt strongly enough about racial equality that they took in dark-skinned foreigners and Jews as boarders, in defiance of the racist conventions of their neighbors. Through contact with the Indian immigrants who had lived in his home, Giardelli had already become interested in the teachings of Gandhi, an interest that led him to a lifelong involvement in pacifism.

Giardelli's father, Vincenzo, had, like James Porter, decided to raise his children without religion; as a young man, Arthur Giardelli (whose background was partly Jewish)[24] spent Sundays in the different London museums with his father looking at art, an activity which "took the place of religion."[25] He began realizing his artistic talents early on; after an indifferent preparatory education, he overcame his dyslexia to excel in his final two years at Alleyn's School, Dulwich, where he was ultimately presented the school's art prize by the head of the Royal Academy at a ceremony held in Dulwich Picture Gallery. By the time he reached Oxford, Giardelli was caught up in Italian romantic and medieval poetry. Leopardi was strongly in his mind at the time of his journey to Florence, but his great idol, and the poet he eventually wrote about at Oxford, was Dante.

Though short, Giardelli was ruggedly athletic. A photograph of him as captain of the house football team at Alleyn's School, the year before he went up to Oxford, shows a strongly built young man with warm, forthright blue eyes and a large head of thick, dark, wavy hair. He was equally energetic in conversation, frequently punctuating his observations with an enthusiastic giggle.

Giardelli's beguilingly childlike manner had a deep effect on Porter, whose experiences among the rarefied Berensons and in Florence generally had been isolating. "Wednesday which was a hot day," Porter wrote just before Christmas, "the English Oxford student, Giardelli and I went out in the country taking our lunches. We talk Italian all the time."

For the duration of Giardelli's stay, the two took walks through the wintry countryside and visited museums and churches, discussing poetry as well as English and Italian painting wherever they went. Porter brought Giardelli to see the Fra Angelico altarpiece and predella of SS. Cosmas and Damian in San Marco, which featured that painter's rendering of the miraculous leg transplant. On another cold, bright afternoon they went into the country to paint watercolors; Porter presented his painting to Giardelli as a token of friendship, telling him to "destroy it when you grow tired of it."[26] Shortly afterward, Porter wrote a poem dedicated to Giardelli and presented it to him as a gift. The unnamed painting, a blue and brown watercolor in the style of John Marin, is still in Giardelli's collection; the poem, which Giardelli kept through the 1930s, has disappeared.[27]

In the evenings, in his room at the pensione, Porter began sketching Giardelli for his first illustration of *The Possessed*, an image which, though of little art-historical interest, reveals Porter's preoccupations and state of mind (fig. 11).

The illustration which Porter created out of this drawing of Giardelli (and incidentally, it is the only illustration for the novel which Porter ever completed) describes a moment late in *The Possessed* in which the fanatical Kirillov (Giardelli) is preparing to commit suicide, which he believes is the ultimate assertion of self-will. Pyotr Stepanovitch Verhovensky, the psychopathic revolutionary ringleader, who has come to convince Kirillov to sign a false confession (for a murder Pyotr Stepanovitch has committed) enters the darkened chamber: "When [Pyotr Stepanovitch] reached Kirillov he stopped short again, still more overcome, horror-stricken. What struck him most was that ... the figure did not stir, did not move in a single limb – as though it were of stone or wax. The pallor of the face was unnatural, the black eyes were quite unmoving and were staring away at a point in the distance."[28]

The scene describes the psychological torment arising from fear of acting on one's will. The key to the scene lies in Kirillov's monologue on the rationality of suicide. As the evil Pyotr Stepanovitch urges him on, Kirillov mutters,

If there is no God, then I am God. ... If God exists, all is His will and from His will I cannot escape. If not, it's all my will and I am bound to show self-will. ... I want to manifest my self-will ... I am bound to shoot myself because the highest point of my self-will is to kill myself with my own hands ... to do it without any cause at all, simply for self-will. ... Man has done nothing but invent God so as to go on living, and not kill himself; that's the whole of universal history up till now. I am the first one in the whole history of Mankind who would not invent God. Let them know it once and for all. ... I can't understand how an atheist could know that there is no God and not kill himself on the spot. ... I am killing myself to prove my independence and my new terrible freedom![29]

While dramatic, this moment is not the climax of a novel that features madness, idiocy, abandonment, arson, child rape, and several gruesome murders. One wonders, then, why it captured Porter's imagination. Perhaps because Kirillov's state – of standing on the brink of the unknown, of believing in the supremacy of one's own will and yet simultaneously doubting one's own sanity and being paralyzed by fear – is something Porter knew well. Kirillov's statements are, after all, the same metaphysical conjectures Porter and his family had wrangled with for years: the question of whether or not God exists, whether a man actually shapes his own destiny or has it shaped for him; ultimately, how one can know what one knows.

Metaphysics aside, Kirillov's anguish has a parallel in Porter's own moment of sexual indecision. For a young man becoming aware of his own sexuality – according to Porter, his first awareness of a definite and undeniable physical and emotional attraction to men came during his Florentine acquaintance with Giardelli[30] – the crisis of sexuality is a crisis of self-determination. Porter, alone in Florence and out of reach of all family and friends for nearly the first time in his life, was, as he later admitted, facing that crisis.

In Dostoyevsky's novel and Porter's illustration of it, the scene takes place in a bedroom, with the stronger man holding a gun to the weaker and urging him on. To perceive Kirillov's suicide as somehow related to a sexual act takes no great stretch of the imagination. (Similar moments of political and metaphysical revelation achieved through socially deviant sexual acts have been described by Gide and Genet.)[31] To the crisis of Kirillov's existential questioning, then, Dostoyevsky adds a shadowy awareness of psychological coercion by the manipulative other: Is Kirillov enacting his own will or that of Pyotr Stepanovitch?

The model for Kirillov was the younger man for whom Porter felt an extraordinary confusion of feelings. Porter's image of Kirillov describes the nameless terror which precedes the moment of self-definition – not the act of pulling the trigger but the unendurable moment which precedes it; not the act of sleeping with one's beloved but the anguish of wondering whether such a thing is actually possible. The choice of scene to illustrate seems to suggest that

11
Porter's lithograph for *The Possessed*, made at a lithography studio in Rome in 1932. Arthur Giardelli posed for Kirillov (*right*). Courtesy Mrs. Fairfield Porter.

Porter realized the crisis of his own sexuality both in his mind and in his art even if he did not demonstrate his attraction in any physical way.

The image of Kirillov and Pyotr Stepanovitch remains, of all the surviving works in the Porter oeuvre, the only image of a confrontation between two men. For the rest of his life, apart from his mural work, a few commissions, and several figured landscape paintings, Porter painted landscapes, still lifes, and images of his wife and/or the poet James Schuyler with one or more of the Porter children. On rare occasions, he painted double or triple portraits. But even in paintings of two or more people, the subjects do not interact. They exist in what seems to be self-imposed isolation, each secure in his or her private realm.

Giardelli recalled Porter as "seem[ing] to have all the time in the world. And there seemed to be a sort of inner serenity about him; nothing seemed to upset him or put him off. ... We used to walk everywhere during that time. I remember we went up to Monte Morello in the hills, and once to Fiesole. Fairfield and I both liked taking very long walks. Coming from England, I wasn't put off by the cold, and a walk of ten miles would have been nothing to me then." Intrigued by Porter's tales of life at I Tatti, Giardelli asked him if it would be possible to go to lunch with the Berensons, which Porter arranged.

The lunch was not a success. Berenson seems to have taken a dislike to Giardelli, perhaps because of the latter's youth, lack of polish, or vaguely Semitic looks. Giardelli recalled, "When he asked how I liked Florence and I went into ecstasies, he said, 'Actually, it's a sink of iniquity.' He was very cool and dismissive about Dante as well, and I remember that I was crushed by his remarks ... there was something about him I just didn't like ... he put down everything I valued."[32]

But Giardelli was given a sympathetic lunch companion in the person of R. C. Trevelyan (whose translation of Leopardi was published ten years later, in the midst of World War II), and from a safe distance across the lunch table, Giardelli was able to listen to Porter and Berenson discuss fresco painting. As Giardelli wrote Porter in 1933, "I remember an argument you had with Berenson on the subject of moderns painting fresco and I remember how keen you were then to do some fresco painting."[33] Apart from recommending Ghirlandaio, Masaccio, and Pontormo to Porter, Berenson had strong opinions about modern fresco painting, since his wife, Mary, had commissioned the French painter Réné Piot to do a fresco cycle for his library in 1913, with such disastrously gaudy results that Berenson immediately had the paintings covered, and he kept them covered to the end of his life.[34]

The conversation was an important one for Porter, who dedicated the next seven years of his life to designing, discussing, and creating murals in which he sought to combine the color and design that he had absorbed in Italy with the socialist ideals that he found so exciting in New York. (Porter's first published critical article, "Murals for Workers," was a guide to public murals in

New York City.) But Porter's enthusiasm for murals in general and the fresco technique in particular came as much out of a reverence for the Italian Primitives and Renaissance fresco painters as it did from contemporary styles and politics.

Giardelli left Florence for England just before Porter went off to meet John Walker in Vienna.[35] Porter saw his new friend off at the station, the two parting with vague promises of a get-together, either in London or at Oxford, if and when Porter came to England in the spring. But no specific plans were made, for Porter was thinking of going back to Russia and could not commit to any timetable.

Porter told his future wife months later that he was bisexual, an assumption that he based on the time he had spent with Giardelli, even though, according to Giardelli (and judging from later correspondence), there was no physical relationship, only a deep emotional attraction.[36]

Twenty-six years later, in 1957, after a period of marital estrangement, psychoanalysis, and contemplating a sexual relationship with a man (who, perhaps not coincidentally, resembled Giardelli in age, looks, and temperament), Porter wrote his old acquaintance, in response to a chance Christmas card:

I think of you very often. You meant a great deal to me, and it means much to *1957* me that you remember and write. I don't think I will write more now. I would like to, but I have lost the sense of who and what you are, and any letter in such a case is like a message in a bottle. You get it – but who are you – now – and did I ever know who you were? Does one ever know another person?

And the doubt must be greater when there is such an inarticulate intimacy as we had; we were shy with each other. I think our importance to each other came from something each of us had to give in the way of support that the other needed and had not really found before. For instance I, as an American, had no interest whatever in the social concerns you could not avoid as a poor boy, a scholarship student at Oxford, where as you told me your grandparents' humble origin would have made a curiosity of you if your friends knew it. And what you gave me was something equal and opposite; if you had been an American I would have been afraid of you and considered you beyond me because of your good looks and ordinary athletic abilities. I hadn't such a friend as you at home; but suddenly I had one in Florence, the unattainable became simple. For this I am always grateful. These things count, I hope you know, and I hope what I say will not seem strange to you. I loved you, and I think you loved me.[37]

To this, Giardelli, an artist and teacher who had long since married and fathered two children, responded: "Indeed, I have often thought of you, but I never analysed our relationship and was quite surprised to read your analysis of it, which was no doubt correct. I suppose that was how things were – although I don't know: words seem to pin down an experience & yet the truth of the matter flutters off."[38]

5

Home to America
and Marriage

Porter's travels in Austria and Switzerland in late 1931 and early 1932 are not well documented. In one letter to John Walker years after they had journeyed there together, Porter remarks how much fun they had in Vienna. In another to John Ashbery, written in 1957, Porter recalls a moment of sexual self-consciousness: "I like the descriptions of the Baron de Charlus [Porter had been reading Proust], reminding me of [older, homosexual] men whom I met sometimes when I was in college. The coldness of d'Argencourt meeting young Proust with Charlus leaving Mme. de Villeparisis was like an official in a Viennese hotel that was almost empty when I was twenty-five and brought home a friend once to show him a copy I had made of Pesalino (the one in the ... little guest room) and I was much embarrassed, and I guess so was my friend, who stayed only long enough to look at the copy."[1]

Porter's travels in Germany gave him not only an opportunity to see the great art collections of Berlin, Dresden, and Munich but also a chance to experience the German political situation firsthand. The political unrest in Germany resulted, little more than a year later, in the Nazi seizure of power. Thanks to the German that Porter had learned from his governess, he was able to read the newspapers ("I understand a quarter," he wrote. "It is a little like James Joyce's *Work in Progress*"),[2] meet communist friends of friends, and attend political meetings. In later years, Porter recalled being "disturbed by the Communist attacks on the Socialists which I heard first in the Berlin Workers' School [of the Communist Party] in January 1932," an incident which caused him to reconsider his feelings for Trotsky (who was now advocating an alliance of communists and socialists to stop Hitler, which Porter thought sensible). Porter was distressed by the lack of awareness and, in many cases, intelligence of the communist students at the Berlin Workers' School: "The people ... seemed to consist of mostly rather stupid, inattentive middle-aged women, at a loss for what to do with themselves." He was also distressed by the general lack of awareness among German communists of the imminent threat of Nazi totalitarianism. "We were assured that there was nothing to fear from Hitler, for Bruening was himself a Fascist: we already had Fascism."[3]

Porter had plenty of money for travel – enough "to go to China and back on"[4] – but his time in Berlin seems to have been solitary and joyless. His one contact there was a young communist woman whom he had met through the Schwabs in New York. When not visiting museums, reading newspapers, or attending political meetings with her, he wrote letters home, his attention turning increasingly toward Anne Channing, who was beginning her second semester at Radcliffe. In a tender and humorous letter to her, he wrote, "I took a course with Whitehead out of which I remember chiefly Whitehead, and R which meant 'the relationship of extensive connection' and aleph ... which I think stood for a kind of infinity and was used only because he had run out of English and Greek letters." He also recalled, with equal mischief, that Whitehead "has a daughter who has an impediment in her speech which interrupts her at interesting points of the conversation so that she half-stutters and half-sneezes and covers her mouth with her hand. ... I never learned the proper technique with her – I didn't know whether to finish her sentences for her – sometimes when I tried that, I finished it wrong, which only increased the violence of the malady ... or whether I should just freeze like the people in 'Strange Interlude' when another character was thinking."[5]

Porter already thought of Anne Channing as a source of friendship, consolation, and amusement. Now, through letters, the two began to think of love.

From Berlin, Porter went to Dresden, both to look at art and to visit an old friend and next-door neighbor from Winnetka, Barbara Mettler, who was pursuing a life in modern dance as a student of the internationally renowned Mary Wigman. He described the visit to his mother: "I gave Barb Mettler and ... her friend ... a couple of lectures on the paintings in the Dresden Museum and I learned a lot from it. I am sure that I know more about painting and am a better judge than any critic; or than any professor or graduate of Harvard who is interested in it." Porter seems to have meant this statement in all seriousness; apparently nothing he had learned previous to his journey to Europe was comparable to the education he had given himself since arriving. The grandiosity of the statement may simply reflect the much-needed ego boost that had been given to him by his childhood friend. Then again, Porter liked holding forth on art; it made him feel worthy and secure. He came from a family that valued knowledge and education above all else. For a young man uncertain of his talents as an artist, the role of teacher and lecturer must have been reassuring.

Disappointed with the holdings of German art museums, Porter went on to observe dryly to his mother that few of them were "as beautiful and as graphic and as alive as the Hygiene Museum in Dresden." The one great recorded artistic highlight of Porter's visit to this fabled city, which would be almost completely destroyed in the coming war, indicates his preoccupation with Dostoyevsky: "I saw the Claude Lorrain landscape in Dresden that Stavrogin dreamt about [in *The Possessed*]," he wrote. "I will try to remember to send you a postcard of it."

On the last stop of his trip through Germany, Porter went to Munich, where he developed his connoisseurship by examining the many paintings by Rubens at the Alte Pinakothek. These paintings were especially interesting to him since they had been heartily recommended by Thomas Hart Benton. "I am getting to be quite an expert on Rubens; I think I can tell what he did himself and what his school partly executed from his designs. One thing that very much interests me is that his paintings done on wood are much brighter and livelier than those on canvas. ... I understand what Benton meant when he said once that when people say to him that they don't like Reubens it is as if they should say 'I don't like the sky,' or 'I don't like the ground.' "[6] He also wrote, however, that "my opinion of Munich kunst [art] went way down [as a result of my visit]; the pictures by Germans in the German galleries are mostly terrible, some are good, which means equal to Eakins or Homer in America. Munich kunst is on the decline: many galleries have closed and the Riber of modern French paintings has moved away ... [the art students there] are all very excited over the two rooms of modern French and German painting in the Neue Staatliche Gallerie which is not so good as the Birch Bartlett Collection [at the Art Institute of Chicago]."[7]

Much of Porter's information on the art community and art students of Munich came to him through a chance encounter with a young painter he had known in New York, Frank Rogers. "I met an acquaintance of the Art Students League ... who is studying [in Munich] who says the [Munich] students ... haven't elementary ideas even of the fundamentals of painting."[8]

Rogers, meanwhile, wrote home to a girlfriend about the same encounter:

1932   As I was coming home from class I bumped into a fellow I had known at the League in New York ... his name is Porter. ... I once went to dinner with him and thought him a bit too intellectual. His drawings were good but his paintings a little too intellectual tending towards mannerism. ... He is quite an unusual fellow. ... He met me at 5:15 and had to catch a train for Florence, Italy at 6:45. For several weeks he had not talked much with anyone – much art, that is. Neither had I and we were both bubbling over, so that into that hour and a half we tried to cram every new idea we had, both of us talking a mile a minute and interrupting one another. ... He's rushing all over Europe. ... He's nuts about Rubens and Giotto and Piero della Francesca ... this crazy nut is going from Italy to Russia (he's trying to learn Russian now). He wants to see what Communism is like. Ha!. ... During our conversation he turned to me and said, "Don't you sometimes feel that you're just *wonderful*? I do," he said. "Sometimes I'm so wonderful I want to tell everyone; they ought to know it. It isn't right that they don't." ... but the way he asked me in all seriousness. ... I wonder what this fellow,

Porter, will ever do. He's got lots of talent and appreciation of the old masters. If he doesn't let his intellectual side carry him away, he'll be good.[9]

From Munich, Porter departed by train once again for Italy, traveling overnight to Florence and then to Arezzo, where he found "a museum with some bum Signorellis & some excellent anonymous 18th century paintings. That is what makes Italian Art so superior; the pictures by *ignoti* are better than the pictues by famous native artists in Germany." His trip through Tuscany was hampered by the cold, for Italy was experiencing the worst winter on record. From Arezzo, where he once again visited the frescoes by Piero della Francesca, Porter took a two-day side trip to Sansepolcro, Piero's birthplace, to see work by the artist at the civic museum and the *Madonna del Parto* in the cemetery chapel at Monterchi. Writing to his mother, Porter observed, "I am beginning to understand Piero della Francesca. Albert [Friend, a classmate at Harvard] once said of some negro music he & I heard at a vaudeville in Harlem that it was 'the bare bones of music' & Piero della Francesca is like that. He is probably close to negro sculpture and that is why both are popular with modern painters. Both space and solidity are stated in as few and simple terms as possible."[10]

The space and solidity that Porter admired so much in Piero were one day hallmarks of Porter's own best work. The simplicity of Piero's figures and the way nearly all of them seem to exist psychologically in their own quiet and self-contained worlds are reflected in, for example, Porter's *Anne, Lizzie and Katie* (1958, see fig. 37), where Anne Porter's solid stance recalls that of a Piero Madonna. Porter's figures, however, are not so rigid or frontal as Piero's.

After a couple of cold and snowy days in the ancient university town of Perugia, Porter returned to Florence to collect his luggage and art supplies and make the train connection for Rome. Advice on where to go and where to stay in Rome may have been given to Porter by Berenson's assistant, Nicky Mariano, who had just accompanied Edith Wharton there a few months earlier. At any rate, Porter maintained his connections with John Walker and with others at I Tatti.

From Rome, Porter wrote, "I have found a pension in the Via Vittorio Veneto 146, called Francini, which is jammed full of Italians, whose station in life I have not been able to figure out. It is rather a cold place and if it doesn't get warmer I'll leave. The room is about as warm as say my room at home in the morning during a severe blizzard. ... Next week-end I am going to Cortona to meet John Walker & stay at Count Morra's house who is a friend of Berenson ... whom I met at the Anreps in Florence. I liked him very much. ... He's about 35 or more, a bachelor, who is lame from tuberculosis of the spine."[11]

Count Umberto Morra di Lavriano, the descendant of an old Piedmontese family of military traditions, was seven years older than Porter. He had come to the Berensons in 1925 to secure a favor for a friend who had been arrested by fascists. A man of great intelligence and sensitivity, Morra soon became a de facto member of the household, frequently accompanying the Berensons on trips and acting as both guide and translator. A friend to poets and a writer of belles let-tres, Morra managed his physical infirmity with the suavity of a latter-day Byron.

Porter's visit to Morra's house was postponed for several weeks because Morra shut down all but a few rooms of his grand home during the winter and could have guests only when weather permitted.[12] In the meantime, Porter haunted the public rooms of the pensione trying to keep warm and soon found the forced company tiresome. A letter from a friend in New York, Alex Haberstroh, informed him that the gallery which had kept his paintings to show clients had returned them again. The news, the bad weather, and the lack of friends in Rome all seem to have put Porter in a low mood. He worked fitfully on the first illustration for *The Possessed* at a nearby lithography studio (see fig. 11), painted an occasional watercolor, wandered the cold streets looking at architecture, or went to the unheated museums to look at pictures. He also read and wrote letters home. "I am getting quite homesick," he wrote Anne Chan-ning. "In Rome I spen[d] most of my time … playing bridge (modo americano = contract) in Italian & German." In another he mentions that he "went to a Marxist Worker's School class in current events the other night" but declines to describe it; it seems not to have interested him. On a slow Sunday afternoon at the end of February he wrote to his mother:

February 28, 1932   Barbara [Mettler's] friends Signore & Signora Moro introduced me to an Ital-ian futurist painter – who is a bum painter but a nice man who promised to introduce me to the leader of the Futurist movement. Maybe he doesn't really mean it, and if so I don't really care. My opinion of American painting goes up all the time, seeing modern Italian or German painting. He had an automobile race which was "much praised in Paris" & by Mussolini and is a wonderful pic-ture, and so very original, & to my mind it doesn't compare with what Alex [Haberstroh] does when he has a headache.

… Gertrude Stein is supposed to say to all the Americans who live in Paris who come to see her, "Don't you know it means death to live abroad?" If it means death in Paris it means so even more so in Italy. Those American boys [at the party I went to last night] were practically dead.[13]

Porter's loneliness came to an end three weeks later when John Walker came down to Rome in his Ford and took Porter to visit Umberto Morra outside Cor-tona. With time and distance, Porter had come to appreciate Walker's urbane company. Moreover, he was eager to travel again, particularly with those who were well acquainted with the many hidden treasures of the Tuscan hill towns. He was delighted with the dashingly literary and poetically impecunious Morra, who "entertained John and me by going sightseeing with us in John's car." Together they visited Montepulciano, Cortona, Pienza, "and many others whose names I have forgotten … all have museums and good pictures." The poet James Merrill remembered Morra as a great literary gentleman, "at once goatish and austere," whose "virginity, if that was what it was, gave him a good deal of license, especially (it seemed to me) in his friendships with young men."[14] Porter wrote to his mother about the encounter.

March 25, 1932

I have just got back from visiting Morra with John [Walker] who has gone back to Florence. There came to visit the day before we left a Sig. Alberti [Count Gugliemo degli Alberti, a Tuscan aristocrat and poet] who is a descendant of the Alberti who designed Sant Andrea at Mantua which you did not like. Entirely English was spoken, except by Alberti who speaks even better English than Morra but is I think annoyed by foreigners who will not learn Italian. ... Both Morra and Alberti have read much English and American literature. ... Morra had a volume of Emily Dickinson with the poems in it marked that he liked, & one was "The Soul Selects Her Own Society" & the last verse was marked twice and underlined:

> I've known her from an Ample Nation
> Choose one
> Then close the doors of her attention
> Like stone.[15]

He is writing a complete criticism of James Joyce & waiting for the progress of "Work In Progress" to go on with it.

Wariness of the Berenson world appears later in the letter, however. Whatever the fun of the travel to Cortona, Porter seems to have realized, after some time on his own, that he would never enjoy life among the Berenson set, in part because of its preference for wealth and breeding and in part because of its unquestioning adherence to Berenson's authority:

March 25, 1932

I have the impression that the summit of Italian society is Bernard Berenson. He is certainly the top of a certain intellectual-aristocratic society that includes Americans and Italians. When friends of Berenson's talk about each other, they criticize each other's remarks and conduct, they say so and so doesn't know how to grow old or so and so has been rather stupid of late in her or his remarks at the Berenson's, or Berenson says that such and such a callow youth they all know has more brains than Kenneth Clark, an Englishman who writes on artistic subjects. But they never criticize Berenson's (or Mrs. Berenson's) remarks. They mention them and then agree or tacitly disagree. ... Alberti calls Miss Mariano, Berenson's secretary, "custode del luogo sacro."[16]

To a young man of socialist, if not anarchist, sympathies (and Porter described himself as tending toward anarchism over communism during this period in a later letter to a political historian)[17] such pious adherence to the thoughts and opinions of one man must have seemed uncomfortably snobbish and totalitarian. All in all, Porter was slowly reaching the conclusion that Italy held nothing more for him and that the time had come to move on.

Meanwhile, he continued to correspond with Anne Channing, writing her from Genoa,

1932 I am here waiting for good weather so I can take the airplane to Barcelona. ... I wrote Barbara [Anne's sister] I was going to Russia, but after, on the advice of the Russian consulate in Rome, waiting for six weeks for a reply to a very polite note I wrote to the Russian government in which I said I was incapable of doing anything except simple, not too muscular unskilled labor, and that I had read much Dostoyevsky and had fairly good manners and perhaps they had a job waiting for just such a well brought up capitalist; after waiting for an answer that has not come, I decided to go to Spain. ... I am getting quite homesick [and] have decided or found out that I wouldn't want to live outside of America. It would take so damn long to get adjusted.[18]

Porter's decision to visit Spain may have come out of his conversations with Berenson on the subject of Velázquez, or his conversations with Morra about Spain, since Morra had acted as tour guide for the Berensons and Nicky Mariano when they all traveled through Spain together two years earlier.[19] The decision may also have come out of a desire to witness the struggle between communists and fascists, since Spain was on the verge of civil war, and Porter had recently been disappointed in his hope of returning to Russia. No letters exist of Porter's time in Spain, and only a sketchbook, filled with street scenes and notes on great paintings, exists among the Porter papers. From notes taken many years afterward by his friend James Schuyler, Porter is known to have visited the Prado and the Escorial; the notebooks suggest that he visited Toledo as well. Departing from Madrid, Porter stopped briefly in Paris before taking the boat train to London. There, after a brief visit with Arthur Giardelli's parents and his brother Wilfrid (with whom he played a great deal of chess), Porter went up to Oxford to be reunited with his friend.

The visit was awkward. Giardelli was delighted to see Porter but busy with his many school activities, for he was president of the Oxford University Musical Club and Union, played the viola in quartets and orchestra, sang in the Bach Choir, and played cricket and football for the Hertford College team.[20] Porter, with his strong and unexpressed feelings for Giardelli, must have felt out of place. His experiences there, sleeping on a sofa in the outer room,[21] must have reinforced Porter's feeling of disconnection and outsiderliness. Despite the timeless beauty of the place, he was eager to go home.

After his return to New York in May, Porter corresponded more frequently with Anne Channing, and he soon visited her and her family at Little Pond. By June they were planning a canoe trip together in Maine, accompanied by Anne's sister Barbara and Porter's friend John Dickey.

Porter's letters to Anne Channing that spring are moody; though beguiled, he seems troubled by his relationship with her. A note of May 21 is typical:

May 21, 1932

I feel this is all wrong and that we aren't clicking at all and I wish we could. I don't understand. Let's not imagine that we are in love, let's wait until we see each other again. I feel farther away from you than I ever have since that Sunday I named the cow.[22] But I am glad you aren't afraid of me, very glad and grateful. I wish we had been really alone more. With Love.

> I want you to be happy,
> Fairfield [23]

Anne, Barbara, Porter, and John Dickey went canoeing on the Penobscot River that June, in the middle of black fly season. The group outfitted itself in Millinocket, where, to the indignation of the Channing sisters (who were to share a pup tent), a clerk misread the situation and assumed them to be "women of easy virtue."[24] From memories of that trip downriver, Anne Porter wrote a poem in 1989 entitled "Lovers," which summons up the spirit of that youthful time:

> I can still see
> The new weather
> Diamond clear
> That flowed down from Canada
> That day
> When the rain was over
>
> I can still see
> The main street two blocks long
> The weedy edges of the wilderness
> Around that sawmill town
>
> And the towering shadows
> Of a virgin forest
> Along the log-filled river
>
> We walked around
> In a small travelling carnival
> I can still hear
> Its tinny music
> And smell its dusty elephants
> I can still feel your hand
> Holding my hand
> That day

When human, quarrelsome
But stronger
Than death or anger
A love began.[25]

Upon returning to Great Spruce Head, Porter proposed to Anne in his characteristically direct and unsentimental manner. "I was due to leave in a week," Anne Porter recalled. "I remember Fairfield saying to me, 'Do you think if we got engaged they'd let you stay all summer?' That was how we got engaged. He wanted me to stay." For the rest of the summer, Porter worked hard at his painting. He "painted nearly every day. I remember he was working in tempera at the time. I remember the smell of gesso and rabbit-skin glue."[26]

The love affair was not without its difficulties. After spending some time on Great Spruce Head, Porter and Anne "went back to Sherborn on the Boston-Rockland boat and F. told me about his (continuing) love for Giardelli." "He just told me that that was how it was, and we both lived with it."[27]

Porter had other reservations about marriage. As a young artist, he was of two minds about having a family or even leading a settled domestic life, even though Anne recalled that he "once said he wanted 6 children (maybe like Boardman Robinson)."[28]

Despite Porter's reservations, Anne remained loyal to her feelings for him and later that summer recorded her thoughts in a carefully worded letter to her mother: "About our plans, Fairfield's doubts are serious and sensible ones, which he shares with me, and which I respect, so that I hesitate for him. This has always been so, but I haven't wanted to explain it to you, until I felt truly sure about it myself, and could reassure you. I think that nothing *really* hurts except losing faith in a person one loves or in oneself, and that kind of hurt I feel sure wouldn't happen either to Fairfield or to me, so I'm not afraid of any decision we might have to make."[29]

News of Anne's acceptance of Porter's proposal traveled so quickly that by mid-July she could report to her mother that "the Henry Eliots gave us a beautiful soup ladle. I told Mrs. Porter I would eat soup with it, then maybe I could keep up with Fairfield who as you know eats soup at lightning speed, and who every day becomes a more necessary person to me."[30]

When Anne departed in late summer, Porter corresponded with her in a series of letters which record his observations on what seems to have been a bittersweet period for Ruth Porter as her grown-up children, so long the center of her life, began to go their separate ways. Porter's friend from New York, the artist Alex Haberstroh, came up for a visit and eased some of the pervading sadness with his comic presence:

September 9, 1932   Yesterday [everyone] left for the whole day, so Alex and I took off all our clothes. I wandered around sketching and Alex, sitting naked on the kitchen porch steps was surprised by a man in a straw hat, coat and vest who asked for Rupert [Howard, the caretaker]. Alex said he felt startled – it was like being caught stealing. He asked the man in to have piece of pie – and he refused and left his telephone number.

… Mother has been wanting to talk to me for some time and today she cornered me: "Do give me an opportunity to talk to you some day – out in the sun, about money arrangements." So she saw all right that I had been avoiding her.

I will leave here on the 15th to have time enough to get a blue coat, etc. and the marriage license.[31]

Ruth's anxiety about her son's future may have been intensified by the family money problems and by James Porter's depression, which left her increasingly in charge of family matters. As Porter wrote in his next letter,

Father almost likes Alex now because he plays bridge so well and very zestfully. Alex is quite fresh to him and says, "Gosh, you look depressed" to him. I think Father thinks he has an unfortunate accent.

… I miss you very much my darling mysterious girl. I wish you were here and we went swimming in the cove and I could duck you again and regret it again and sit on the bridge with you.

Mother is very sad these days; I think she regrets her lost youth. I feel depressed and then I think about a possible story about someone like Mother … growing old by getting sad at her children leaving her … and Father (not Father but imagined from Father) would be in it: a man who is innocent of the world and who is therefore not a successful father to his sons and Mother trying to be her sons' father without success because she is not a man.[32]

September 1932

The wedding, a "small, simple" one, with only family invited, was held on September 22, 1932, in the garden at Little Pond. The event was timed to accommodate the Porters as they passed through Boston to Winnetka from Great Spruce Head. As a concession to Anne's parents, the couple were married by a Unitarian minister, the Reverend Charles E. Park of Boston (and coincidentally, the father of the future abstract painter David Park), who allowed the couple to amend and rewrite their wedding vows. In the handful of informal wedding snapshots that survive, Anne carries a large bouquet of wildflowers (fig. 12). Porter wears a blue coat and white trousers, as does Henry Channing, the father of the bride. Ruth leans forward, exchanging remarks with Anne's mother, Katharine; James Porter stands slightly apart from the group in a dark three-piece suit and bow tie, his hands clasped uncomfortably before him.

The couple departed in a brand-new car, a deluxe Ford two-seater with rumble seat, trimmed in chrome, that, along with six hundred dollars for the honeymoon, was a wedding present from the Porters. As the young couple pulled away, the car stalled, to the amusement of both families.

Over the summer Porter and his wife had debated where to travel after the wedding. They had been offered a house in the Adirondacks belonging to a friend of Ruth's but decided instead to travel in the new car, basing their trip loosely on Porter's desire to see the great mansions of the American South, including Monticello and Westover. Their first stop, however, was Martha's Vineyard, where Porter wanted to call on his old instructor from the Art Students' League, Thomas Hart Benton. Taking rooms at a local inn, they visited Benton and his Italian wife, who looked, according to a letter from Anne Porter to her mother, "like the Sistine ceiling."[33] Porter, when not talking with Benton about his adventures in Europe, sketched and painted watercolors. Anne wrote poetry and played with the Benton's son, Tiepolo (also known as T.P.). Just before Porter proposed, Anne had been accepted into a nursing program at Boston Children's Hospital; now she was eager to start raising a family of her own.

From Martha's Vineyard, the Porters drove to the Adirondacks, where Porter's New York friends the Arthur Schwabs had them to stay. As Anne wrote her mother, "With our host and hostess we have terrific discussions of art, literature, politics and life. Fairfield says I talk literary criticism in my sleep."

The next leg of the Porter honeymoon was to Virginia, where the Porters toured Jefferson's home. On their way back to New York, an incident occurred in Carlyle, Pennsylvania, which brought their adventures to an abrupt halt. While crossing a bridge, their car was rammed by a drunk driver.

Anne wrote her mother, "I hasten to write you, in case you should see anything in the papers to worry you. We did have an accident, but as you can see we're hurt hardly at all. Fairfield has two stitches in his lip and I in my scalp and we're still in bed because of slight shocks, but feel perfectly all right. So don't worry about us! The man who hit us was drunk and has been arrested, so

12
Anne and Fairfield Porter's autumn wedding in the garden at Little Pond, 1932. *From left*, Henry Morse Channing, Katharine Minot Channing, Fairfield Porter, Anne Porter, Ruth Wadsworth Porter, James Foster Porter. Photographer unknown. Courtesy Mrs. Francis Birch.

it wasn't our driving that was dangerous." The car was seriously damaged in the head-on collision, and between repairs, doctor bills, and their stay in an "awful boarding house," the Porters soon used up all their honeymoon money.[34]

As soon as they were able, the couple returned to New York and looked for an apartment, taking rooms in Greenwich Village at the Hotel Brevoort. Anne wrote her mother, "We're both pleased and a little excited to be here at last, when it means beginning our real, grown-up everyday life. We discuss how to make coffee and what we'll do for exercise."[35] The Brevoort, despite the Depression and the many bohemian socialists lingering in its cafe, still had a certain grandeur. Anne Porter recalled that at breakfast the management required her young husband to wear a tie at the table and that the waiter presented an egg for her inspection before sending it to the kitchen for soft-boiling.

Because of the Depression, cheap apartments were relatively easy to come by. Within a week Porter had signed a lease for 122 Washington Place at $65 per month (the year before, the rent had been $120 per month). There, on the small street between Sheridan Square and the Sixth Avenue El, Porter and his bride set up their first home, which they kept for exactly one year. Porter immediately set about his work as a painter – and he preferred the word "painter" to "artist" since it expressed solidarity with the working class.[36]

In those early days of their marriage, Porter had no luck placing his work. He and his wife would "walk around to galleries, showing his canvases. That's how you did it in those days. You simply brought in the work."[37] No galleries were interested. Porter's work was not very distinguished, and in the midst of the Depression few people were buying art.

Porter and his wife were not in agreement about whether or when to raise a family. When Anne became pregnant shortly after the honeymoon, Porter expressed his ambivalence toward fatherhood. "He simply wasn't ready to have children and he wasn't at all excited when I told him I was pregnant," she recalled. "He showed me a John Marin watercolor he'd just bought. I didn't understand his behavior, and I felt it very deeply. I understand now that he was young – only twenty-five – and an artist, and his mind wasn't on having a family. He had always been ambivalent about having a family, but I hadn't quite believed him when he said so. And I wanted to start having babies right away, and to have lots of them ... so that was a cause for unhappiness between us, right from the start."[38]

The couple went to Winnetka for Christmas that year, enjoying themselves with the Porter family and going out for long walks together on the shore of Lake Michigan. Porter sometimes sketched in the bitter cold with Anne keeping him company.

As winter progressed, Anne grew increasingly ill with morning sickness. In April she gave birth prematurely and lost the baby, a girl, an experience that affected her deeply. Porter "wasn't very sympathetic. ... He told me he had seen it and that it was very beautiful, and then later he told me that he had felt sorry for me as he was washing out my bloody underwear ... he wasn't good at expressing emotions and he wasn't very comforting. ... It wasn't that he didn't care. [But the Porters were] very far away from feelings and emotions."[39]

In some ways, Porter's perceived lack of concern for his wife's well-being may simply have been an attempt to minimize the enormity of her trauma by calmly reassuring her that nothing too awful had happened – standard-enough behavior for a man standing awkwardly in his wife's sickroom. Reflecting on the situation many years later, Anne Porter wrote, "I don't think & don't mean to say his reaction was abnormally 'cold' & 'awful.' Here was a *very* young man, only 25 ... with nothing yet achieved of his own in art, with his bisexuality, and with an immature wife who obviously wasn't very competent or realistic, & had no housekeeping skills, and around him in the world outside was the Depression, the sometimes chaotic art world and the approach of a world war. Of course I wanted him to be happy & excited about our child. But it wasn't realistic to expect this. He was unusually honest, so he told me that the miscarriage was a relief to him."[40]

As Anne lay in the hospital trying to make sense of her loss and of her husband's chilly response to that loss, her mother came down to New York and wrote Ruth Porter a note describing the situation:

April 13, 1933 I came to NY yesterday on the darkest wettest day I can remember – I was cheered and touched to find Fairfield waiting for me at the station & to have him so kindly and cordially urge me to stay in the apartment. He took me to the hospital where I found Anne looking pale, but seeming bright and well. She is not letting her disappointment prey upon her & is helping herself by planning the pleasant summer that she and Fairfield can have ... I should like to take her home with me, or follow me, for a few days rest & change. I should like Fairfield to come too, but I know that he wants to stick to his work.

I am enjoying being with him. I appreciate his sweetness & the way he has met this disappointment & the attendant difficulties. ... I hope everything will progress smoothly now.[41]

So began what would be, by the end of the decade, a regular pattern of separation: Porter remaining in New York to pursue his painting, Anne (and later the children) seeking the comfort and reassurance of Little Pond or the Channing summer home at Wareham, on Buzzards Bay.

That spring, on a visit to America, Porter's cousin T. S. Eliot came to visit Ruth and James Porter in Winnetka. Porter himself, alone in New York while Anne recuperated at Little Pond, attended a lecture by his distinguished cousin when he came east again to New York, writing Anne, "I went to the T.S. Eliot lecture with Albert [Friend] and sat at a table with Ogden Nash and a sweet dumb old lady director of the New School. ... T.S. didn't say what Albert expected, he said there is little difference between nonsense and great poetry ... Albert afterwards wanted to ask him something but hung about on the platform while people edged ahead of him. Albert and I then had some beer and then he spent the night here in your bed, but most of the night he read in the living room *Mont St. Michel and Chartres* and *The Brothers Karamazov.*"[42]

Whether Porter had obtained tickets to the table featuring Ogden Nash and the sweet dumb old lady through his cousin is not clear; Porter does not mention conversing with T. S. Eliot in the letter or even reintroducing himself. It may well be that Porter did not have much in common with his cousin, whom he had met again through the Little Aunts in Boston,[43] or else that he was awed, if not by Eliot himself, then by his international reputation. Nonetheless, within a month, when Porter was offered a chance to exhibit his paintings in a jewelry store, Theodore A. Kohn and Son, at 608 Fifth Avenue, the name of T. S. Eliot was summoned to explain Porter's intentions in the exhibition press release. As Anne, back in New York, told her mother, the publicity agent "wrote that F.'s method in painting abstractions is like T. S. Eliot's in writing poetry: i.e., a classical pattern and a contemporary subject. This applies to the abstraction where the composition is after Tintoretto and the subject is a trolley and buildings in Dresden."[44]

T. S. Eliot's name is mentioned again several weeks later when Anne describes to her mother the splendid literary and artistic life she has resumed in New York. "[At] the writer's party I went to at Paul Rosenfeld's ... I met an English poet named Ronald Bottrall, whom T.S. Eliot thinks is one of the best living poets. There was also Alfred Kreymbourg, Marianne Moore (a tall Bryn Mawr woman who looks like an abbess and is very cool, collected and intelligent), a novelist who has written a novel called 'Union Square,' a couple of unshaven young communists, etc. It was a very strange party, but fun."[45]

It would be easy to think that the recurring name of T. S. Eliot merely indicated the proximity of an artistic celebrity. But there is more to the mention of his name: an indication that Porter, even in the midst of his socialist-painter phase, was aware of literary paradigms and was measuring his contribution to visual art in literary terms. One could dismiss the press release which accompanied Porter's insignificant exhibition at the jewelry shop as an attempt to dress up some mediocre paintings with a lot of fancy talk about Modernism (Howard Devree, art critic for *The New York Times*, merely noted that Porter was a "solid but earnest talent").[46] Still, in light of Porter's later achievements, the comparison between his painting and T. S. Eliot's poetry is not far off the mark: Porter eventually used classical compositions (still lifes, landscapes, figured interiors, portraiture) to experiment with the nature of paint itself, which is surely, so far as New York painting is concerned, the "contemporary subject." Like T. S. Eliot, Porter drew on a thorough awareness of and respect for cultural precedents to make his individual contribution to the art of his time. In the desire to wed the modern with the traditional, to reconcile traditional continuity with modernist disjunction, these distant cousins were not so far apart.

As spring gave way to summer, the Porters made plans for Great Spruce Head, meeting up first with Porter's friend from Florence, John Walker, who was back in the United States on vacation. Walker had invited them to go cruising on his schooner. By late June the couple had arrived on the island with Porter's friend and former roommate Wendell Reynolds, where they enjoyed "a life of outdoor pleasures and rather unkempt domesticity in the big house ... swim[ming] and sunbath[ing] a great deal and read[ing] aloud."[47]

From Maine, the couple traveled back to Little Pond, where Anne's parents, perhaps wanting to stay close to their daughter after her miscarriage, had commissioned Porter to paint a fresco in their sunroom. Porter, who had been hoping to experiment in fresco since returning from Florence, was instructed in the process by a graduate student at Harvard, Barnet R. Rubenstein, later a professor at Vassar College. According to a letter written by Porter in 1972, "I painted [the] fresco ... from his account of how to do it, and then he came out to see it, and seemed impressed that I'd brought it off."[48]

Unlike the socialist murals on which Porter concentrated over the next five years, the Channing mural had a decidedly bourgeois theme. Though no photograph of the mural exists, a watercolor sketch does, portraying Henry Channing on horseback, his dog beside him, facing away from the viewer and looking over the grounds of his home toward the enormous pond in the distance. On the left, at the far edge of the lawn, Anne Porter stands beside a tree and looks toward the pond as well. The fresco was painted on the wall over the fireplace; a series of tile-sized frescoes depicting woodland creatures, painted by Porter's brother-in-law Pendleton Herring and by Anne Porter, later completed the project. Porter felt good enough about it to write Alfred Stieglitz at the end of July, "I have just finished a fresco for the Channings' house in Sherborn, Mass. My first successful mural commission."[49]

Upon returning to New York in the fall, the Porters prepared to move again, from their small apartment on Washington Place to a new one at 70 Bank Street. The new apartment, according to a letter from Anne to her mother, was "just what Fairfield always wanted and we feel as if we had a house." The place was larger than their previous apartment, with lower rent and (during their second year there, when they moved upstairs) access to the roof, which was good for Porter, who could go up there to draw. The roof would also be useful, they hoped, for airing the baby that Anne was expecting in February. In the months since the miscarriage, Porter had learned the depth of his wife's desire for children; her poems (five were soon to be published in *Poetry* magazine) were preoccupied with motherhood.[50]

That fall Porter enrolled in an anatomy course at the Cornell School of Medicine. Every morning, along with an amphitheater full of medical students, he observed the dissection of human cadavers. In the evenings he attended meetings of the Fresco Painters' League, a group of "about 10 members, 4 or 5 of whom have ever painted a fresco."[51] In both activities, Porter seems, consciously or not, to have been following a Renaissance paradigm in twentieth-century Manhattan: in essence, reinventing the way a contemporary painter should educate himself, looking not only to immediate precedents but also to the distant past for inspiration and guidance.

Porter was not alone in his taste for traditional methods, for during the 1930s a large number of European artists came to New York as refugees, and Porter learned about painting from them. He shared a studio with a Russian refugee painter, Simeon Braguin, during this period; Braguin, a portraitist, painted Anne Porter. When not in the studio with Braguin, Porter attempted to teach himself painting by copying pictures in the Marquand Galleries of the Metropolitan Museum, a practice he continued for over a decade. In the evenings he helped his wife with dinner, for she had been warned not to overexert herself for fear of losing the baby. Occasionally, as Anne noted to her mother, the young couple took a night out with other artists and their wives: "[Last night] we sat with [our fresco-painting neighbors] Mr. & Mrs. [Rico] LeBrun and Lewis Rubinstein at the Waverly Inn [and] had a violent discussion of the function of fresco in modern life. I think Mrs. LeBrun and Miss Cohen (who was with them) were positively frightened. After supper we separated, still muttering."[52]

As Anne's pregnancy progressed, she spent less time out of the house, but she hastened to reassure her mother that her husband was being attentive: "F … brings back stories of his experiences at night, and so I don't feel my life is limited. He knows the embalmers at the medical school, and the man who makes the skeletons, he describes to me the sea-lions and camels he has seen on the way through Central Park and also what jails are like because he was in one for a very short time for overtime parking when he had no cash to pay a fine."[53]

But Porter's concerns were not entirely lighthearted. With the Nazis sweeping into power in Germany, New York's leftist community was attempting to mobilize American public opinion, and many of Porter's Socialist Party friends were urging him to get involved in politics. As Anne wrote her mother that winter, "New York has been stirred in sympathy with Europe; Alex, our socialist friend, came to invite Fairfield to a very big demonstration about Austria. Alex told me it would be quite safe, there would be 200 policemen with no nightsticks. The next day I read in the paper *100 Hurt in Socialist Demonstration*."[54]

Meanwhile, Porter's career moved slowly forward. In January, shortly before the birth of his first child, Porter received news that a work of his had been "accepted by the Pennsylvania Academy, to be exhibited through February."[55] The painting, of a beloved stretch of beach on Great Spruce Head Island, had been a present from Porter to his wife.

6

Murals and Babies

At the time that Porter and his wife were preparing for the birth of their first child, Porter's friend Alex Haberstroh, a Socialist Party member, introduced Porter to Rebel Arts, a "national cultural organization," according to its promotional literature, "which recognizes the need of building a working class culture and ... the importance of using art as a weapon for the working class."[1] The club supported the Socialist Party, offering members the opportunity to participate not just in visual arts projects but also in a chorus, drama group, puppet theater, writers' group, dance ensemble, and camera club. The notion of an arts club as a weapon for the working class may seem outlandish today, but during the 1930s many such organizations existed, with varying political affiliations and degrees of radicality. The most popular was the John Reed Club, affiliated with the Communist Party, for which Porter had already done a small amount of artistic work for hire. According to two historians of the labor movement, these clubs "sought to change the entire structure of the art world, not solely the work produced; they wanted to revamp its goals, ideology and patrons, with the medieval or Renaissance systems as the models. ... it was the worker organizations, rather than the Church, that were to be patrons. Their art was intended to inform, educate and radicalize the worker. ... Art was to be by and for the working class. Not only was its content to be proletarian; it was to be readily understood by its patron, the ordinary working man ... instead of serving as a luxury product for the pleasure of the upper classes and the affluent bourgeoisie."[2]

Though Porter did serve as a member of Rebel Arts national advisory board, he was only incidentally interested in the organization. As a young man recently returned from Florence and aware of the enormous achievements of the artists' and artisans' guilds of the Renaissance, he was intrigued by the possibilities of a contemporary artists' guild. He was also seeking a connection between art and politics. But he was soon disillusioned by the mediocrity of the students and the rude and bureaucratic ways of Rebel Arts leaders.

In truth, Porter's interest in leftist politics came not from an affiliation with the Socialist Party but from a theoretical interest, best articulated by Trotsky, in art as a kind of "advance guard" of the revolutionary movement, preparing human consciousness for the political changes to come. Porter instinctively believed in Trotsky's notion that art should remain independent of any authority other than its own rules and principles, that "art, like science, not only does not see orders, but by its very essence, cannot tolerate them. Artistic creation has its own laws. ... Art [must] remain faithful to itself."[3]

Such theories on art and revolution attracted Porter; they suggested a leftist alternative to the nightmare of Stalinist communism while at the same time attaching enormous importance and significance to the work and thought of the independent creative artist. But this latter idea was not at all foreign (either literally or figuratively) to Porter. Trotsky's devotion to the idea of the responsibility of the individual, and the individual artist in particular, was very much in the tradition of New England radicalism; so far as art and the individual conscience were concerned, Trotsky was not far from Thoreau or, by extension, from the basic Unitarian beliefs which Porter had been taught by his mother.

But Porter's immediate decision to involve himself with Rebel Arts sprang not so much from interest in Trotsky or even Thoreau but from the persuasive abilities of Alex Haberstroh. Simply put, Haberstroh's interest in Rebel Arts made Porter curious about it. Porter was not a Socialist Party member – throughout the thirties, his nonaffiliation to any specific political party was a cause of friction between himself and his contemporaries – but Haberstroh took Porter's lack of ideological commitment in stride. He was eager to help Porter find both work and social stimulation in the projects and meetings which took place daily at Rebel Arts. Porter had already done a little freelance decorative painting for the John Reed Club; why not Rebel Arts?

Haberstroh had already made a mural for the headquarters of Rebel Arts, and he invited Porter to design one for the headquarters of the Queens branch of the Socialist Party. The design was accepted, and Porter got the commission. The subject, as he recalled, "was 'Turn Imperialist War into Civil War' ... it was in imitation of Orozco more or less."[4] Work on this mural took over a year.[5] As Porter began work on this ambitious project, Haberstroh encouraged him to join in other painting-related endeavors of Rebel Arts, some of which promised work for pay. By the end of the year, Porter was teaching a night class in figure drawing at Rebel Arts, as well as working with Haberstroh on sign painting and convention-hall decorating.

After the Porters' first child, John Porter, was born on February 20, 1934, Porter took up parenting with enthusiasm. The pride he took in his firstborn son is evident in the name he chose, for it was the name he himself had been given before his parents took it away from him and gave it to his little brother instead. Anne, writing her mother shortly after the birth, remarked on Porter's involvement and proficiency: "I wish you could see what a specially clever father Fairfield makes. He is better at diaper changing, and bubbling, than I am."[6]

Ruth Porter, perhaps feeling lonely in a house now empty of all children and interested in knowing about Anne's health and progress as a mother, kept in close contact with Porter that winter and spring, planning a trip east in late April. Porter, as ever glad for her support and interest, described his ambitious mural in a letter to her shortly before the trip:

April 1934   I have finished composing the war picture, and I have drawn from many models, mostly Socialists. Three comrades from Alex [Haberstroh]'s local, whom he got to pose for me, one an accountant, one (whom they were very proud of because he is a worker) a housepainter, and Alex. That took all one day ... they were all very busy, I guess over the taxi strike and getting ready to go to Washington. ... A member of the YPSL [Young People's Socialist League] got a dancer to pose a couple of days later at the Rebel Arts Dance Group, and while waiting for him to come I asked a woman who was behind a desk and wasn't doing much to pose as a person selling liberty bonds, and she said I might find a negro model that Friday night. Friday I went there and there was a meeting of people from different locals and some negroes, and after the meeting, which was about the Washington demonstration (arranging practical details) I asked a negro to give me fifteen minutes, and explained the purpose, & he was very obliging, I think he was delighted, he was a little confused about it all, and told a little Jew-

13
Turn Imperialist War into Civil War (mural lost; 1935).
Anne Porter can be seen at the center, breaking down the door.
Photographer unknown. Courtesy Mrs. Fairfield Porter.

92

ish girl and her mother who were waiting for him to help carry signs to the Penn Station to be ready for the next morning, "this is for the papers you know, this is for one of the other locals; it's the same work you know." The other negroes were not so dumb as he, but the inter-racial spirit is not as easy and pleasant as in the Communist party: here they all seemed a little deferential, the negro men wouldn't voluntarily sit next to white women. Anne [Porter] has been a model for a worker, for a starving mother, and for the woman member of the triumphant socialist state. It was for the triumphant socialist state that I wanted a negro. The idealogy of the painting is not pacifist, but "Turn Imperialist War into Civil War" [fig. 13]. In the beginning capitalists or munitions makers are starting soldiers off to war; the soldiers are prevented from seeing what comes next by flags that hide their view, on which, instead of crowns, are dollar signs, then comes destruction and so on and civil war, with soldiers and other people breaking in on the war profiteers who are dividing spoils, and above the socialist state, with a red flag and guns piled up to indicate Peace. I will try to have the finished picture photographed for you.[7]

The letter typically focuses on Porter's most recent art project and says nothing about Anne or the baby.

Ruth came east to see her new grandchild (and presumably the mural) shortly before May Day. She arrived to find her son hard at work painting placards to be carried in the May Day Parade, most of them reading, "Workers, Unite against Fascism." As Anne reported to her mother a few days later, "Today is the day of the big Socialist and Communist parades, when some of [Fairfield's] posters will be carried, but we aren't going, [Fairfield] is going to work on the mural and I don't want to go alone ... in case of a riot especially!"[8]

In the midst of her son's involvement with the May Day celebrations, Ruth suggested that he introduce her to Stieglitz and Paul Rosenfeld. Porter duly invited the two distinguished men to a home-cooked dinner in honor of his mother. Stieglitz's wife, Georgia O'Keeffe, rounded out the party. Anne wrote her own mother of the dinner's success, noting that Steiglitz "was quite gentle, talked all the time, and admired Johnny very much," later mentioning that Stieglitz had sat with his handkerchief in his mouth for much of the evening to entertain the baby. The meeting was an important one for Ruth, for she remained committed to involving herself in the progress of her son's career and wanted to meet and observe all those people her son most esteemed. As James Porter withdrew into depression and illness, Ruth transferred her energy to her adult children, encouraging them to invite their friends and associates to Winnetka and Great Spruce Head.

Accordingly, when the Porters and their new baby departed for their island summer, they found they had invited not only the erudite and politically conservative John Walker (now preparing to take up a position as assistant to the director of the American Academy in Rome) but also the coarse and engaging Alex Haberstroh of Rebel Arts and Edward Laning, a communist painter who had recently completed a significant political mural in Manhattan for the Hudson Guild.[9] The house was full, and passionate differences of opinion were the order of the day. Anne wrote, "We expect the Lanings (communist) and Alex (socialist) to visit us simultaneously, and I rather tremble at the thought of it. Fairfield and I considered making a rule that politics only be discussed in the open air. That would give a chance for the liberals to escape and also shouting is better out of doors."[10]

The summer of 1934 was not, however, as easy as the letter suggests. Porter and his wife were struggling with the new baby. Despite the joy of having a newborn in the house, there were tensions from living under the same roof with in-laws. The problem was compounded by a digestive illness of baby Johnny's, which "caused him to cry a lot."[11] Eliot Porter and Nancy Porter Straus had already set up small, independent homes nearby (Eliot's house was completed in 1929, Nancy's in 1933) to maintain a measure of peace and privacy for themselves and presumably their parents.

By late summer, everyone seems to have been suffering from frayed nerves and concern for Johnny's health. Anne wrote: "Fairfield and I feel very sorry because he hurt Jeanie's [the maid's] feelings in an argument about whether Johnny should be picked up when he cries. ... It is really my fault for telling Fairfield we should have a house here, so that our children can be naughty without our feeling apologetic. He champions my causes very fiercely sometimes."[12]

There were other tensions. Eliot Porter, now a father of two boys, was in the process of divorcing his wife; James was suffering from depression; Nancy Porter Straus and her husband, Michel, meanwhile, were entertaining New Deal administrators, some of whose philosophies about the exploitation of the American wilderness were very much opposed to the Porter concern for stewardship of land and resources. Anne Porter noted in a letter to her mother that "Fairfield [has just seen Harold Ickes, secretary of the interior] throwing perfectly good pencils into the water (irretrievably) to please his little boy."[13] Another letter describes Fairfield's friends "rowing around the island booming the *Internationale*."[14]

When the Porters returned to New York that fall, Porter began teaching an evening life-drawing class at Rebel Arts, spending evenings away from Anne and the baby, whose crying had now become a constant irritant. Along with motherhood, Anne Porter had achieved a small professional triumph: five of her poems were included in the October 1934 issue of *Poetry* magazine, and Paul Rosenfeld had decided to include two others in a hardcover poetry anthology entitled *The American Caravan*.[15]

Along with adjusting to life with a new baby, the Porters found their existence increasingly complicated by the late hours and irregular habits of Porter's artist and activist friends, most of whom, having decided that marriage was a bourgeois concept, lived in relationships of free love. To the dismay of the Porters, who had grown up in households run by former suffragists, they discovered that bohemian males of the 1930s, even those most passionately dedicated to the rights of the worker, routinely patronized or ignored their women, many of whom were not even introduced at social gatherings. Anne Porter found this combination of chauvinism, promiscuity, and hypocrisy-laden ideology difficult to reconcile with her own beliefs and distanced herself from her husband's acquaintances.

When life as an artist's wife in New York became overwhelming, Anne Porter retreated to her parents' home in Sherborn, where the class struggle was engaged once again, but this time on a different level. In a letter to her husband, she wrote, "Cousin Hope complained to Mother of Norman Thomas [the Socialist candidate for president] who married one of her cousins and borrows money from her family to educate his children. Cousin Hope thinks he ought to live in the woods with no property, because he is a Socialist."[16] But Anne was not without political allies in her parents' home; her mother eventually voted for Norman Thomas for president.

Back in New York, Porter, like his wife, was disturbed by the rough ways and undisciplined habits of his socialist companions, writing to his mother, "what I most object to in the Radical Movement is the irregular lives people lead, working until 2 AM and never getting up before 11 or noon. It would get me down if I worked more for them."[17] But irregular lifestyles were not reserved for political radicals. One painful incident involved Porter's old friend and former roommate Wendell Reynolds, then working as a journalist for *The Daily News*. Reynolds had been struggling for some time with a drinking problem. He appeared late one night at the Porters' doorstep accompanied by two prostitutes and upon entering became "loud and argumentative and he started swinging his crutches and breaking up the place. ... Fairfield scuffled with him and ... punched Wendell very hard, knocking him down, and threw him out of the house."[18] Porter broke with Reynolds permanently after that, and he and his wife began taking long weekend drives through the countryside looking for a new home away from the wild living and late nights of bohemian New York. "We hired a babysitter and went house-hunting together," Anne Porter remembered. "It was great fun, almost a vice!"[19]

That winter, as *Turn Imperialist War into Civil War* (which was painted on canvas) neared completion, Porter made plans to exhibit it in the show "Mural Painting in America – Contemporary and Retrospective." The exhibition, arranged by the Mural Painters Society, was to run for two weeks at the Grand Central Art Galleries in Manhattan – "a funny place," Anne Porter said, "where they play organ music all the time like a department store."[20] Porter was no stranger to the mural-painting scene; two of the three people running the exhibition (Edward Laning, Thomas Hart Benton, and Hildreth Miere) were his friends. The meeting at Grand Central Art Galleries of political radicals, art world celebrities, and society figures excited and amused Porter, who wrote Anne, then visiting her sister,

undated   I took the mural up to Grand Central Art Galleries to the Mural Painters show. ... Jacob Burk has a mural there and he came up to assemble it onto stretchers and was introduced to Hildreth Miere (a society woman type – a successful politician and businesswoman painter) and he grinned the Communist grin of a child asking forgiveness and she was curt and to the point like a school teacher. The Communist grin seems to say: "Yes I know you know I am a Communist, a bad boy, but I really feel friendly towards you." Her curtness seems to say, "Yes, I know you know I know you're a Communist, but come now, no persiflage, I have heard of Communism, I am sophisticated; what do you want me to do, anyway, wag my tail? Go on, get your picture ready and no nonsense."[21]

Not content with merely entering his mural in the show, Porter used the occasion to write an essay about the many murals which had been created in New York City since 1928 specifically for the benefit of workers, seeking to define their relative purpose and success. "Murals for Workers," Porter's first published critical writing, appeared in *Arise*, a publication of the Rebel Arts Club, in 1935.

Porter's writing is clear and straightforward, often delightfully so, as when, early in the piece, he observes, "The ideas [in a good mural] should be expressed well enough in painting terms so no description can be equivalent to the painting. In other words it should be good enough to require that you go and look at it." The essay abounds in equally succinct observations, including, "the painting of propaganda and the painting of ideas do not always go together."

Of all the murals for workers in the New York area, Porter finds the Orozco murals at the New School for Social Research to be the most effective, in part because "the austerity of the international style [of the building] is matched by the angular, bare-bones style of [Orozco's] painting" and in part because Orozco seems to Porter to have developed a style and vision particularly appropriate to the exploration of the Marxist vision of the coming world revolution. Diego Rivera's work, by comparison (at the New Workers' School) seems "confused and negative," "full of complaints but proposing few solutions."

Porter's notes on the different murals around New York City are sharply observant but unassumingly so. The piece is first and foremost a guide to New York City workers' murals rather than a criticism of them. Still, the most interesting part of the article, from an art-historical standpoint, is Porter's quietly devastating assessment of the work of his old friend and teacher Thomas Hart Benton: Porter, noting the lack of a political or philosophical viewpoint in Benton's murals for the Whitney Museum, writes, "Benton [has] a Missourian's suspicion of ideas ... he seems not to evaluate what he observes. ... His impression is like the impression you get of America from the New York *Daily News*." Porter's negative view of both Benton and his paintings was in fact considerably stronger than this. As he remarked shortly afterward to his mother:

> I think I made an enemy of Thomas Benton by my article on mural paintings because I showed it to him before it came out and I toned it down somewhat as a result of suggestions he made. That ... manner of being uneducated that you noticed [in Benton] is getting more and more pronounced in all of his official utterances. I think he feels both more and more successful and more and more persecuted. Sam Friedman [executive director of Rebel Arts] said I made an enemy of the I.W.W. [Industrial Workers of the World]. I don't care about the I.W.W. but I do about Benton because I learned a lot of what I know from him – but I also don't like his attacking Stieglitz.[22]

1935

Porter's decision to show his essay to Benton even though it was critical not only of his work but of his intelligence betrayed either an absolute faith in the truth or a shocking lack of discretion. Porter's love of truth, no matter what the cost to individual vanity, was his great strength as a critic (his words on Benton are apt), but cost him the good will of a great many people and proved hurtful in his personal relationships. Not surprisingly, Thomas Hart Benton disappears from Porter's correspondence and from his life after the publication of this short essay for a small and critically insignificant magazine.

After completing *Turn Imperialist War into Civil War*, Porter worked on other mural projects, including a collaborative effort with Haberstroh for the Children's Dressmakers local of the International Ladies' Garment Workers' Union, illustrating (among other things) the career of the labor leader Meyer London.[23] He competed for a government commission for a Long Island post office and submitted designs for murals for the Interior Department and the Justice Department.[24] But for the most part, Porter was excluded from government work parceled out by the WPA and other organizations because he was not on relief and was therefore not eligible to apply for the work,[25] so his mural-painting career is best represented by this first effort, now lost.

While working on his mural projects, Porter took two courses at the International Workers' School, one on American labor history taught by A. J. Muste (eventually the leader of the American Workers' Party) and the other on the history of the three Internationals, taught by Max Schactman. Despite the enthusiasm of these two inspiring figures, Porter found the day-to-day experience of socialist revolutionary life less than thrilling. His fellow students were a disappointment. As he observed to Ruth, "The art class I teach folded up for lack of members. ... Last Thursday was Passach or Passover so all last week radical activities in New York came to a temporary halt. Max Schactman was disappointed by the pupils of his class on the 3 Internationals voting a holiday last

Thursday. A. J. Muste was sick so probably he hasn't discovered yet the meaning of Passover. The May number of *Arise* may not come out, which is O.K. by me, and my only other obligation ... is a cover design for a leaflet of the Y.P.S.L. [Young People's Socialist League] ... (which I hate)."

Another disappointment to Porter was the lack of consideration shown by Socialist Party members for thoughts and ideas at variance with the party line. The ideas of Trotsky interested Porter most, but no one at Rebel Arts would consent to discuss Trotsky with him. As Porter wrote his wife about an *Arise* meeting, "They started to say to me, 'Well, why don't you join the Party?' and Alex [Haberstroh] said, 'Let him tell you about Trotsky' and Friedman sniffed disgusted, 'Trotsky!' Trotskyism to Friedman is synonymous with delayed adolescence."[26]

Porter's growing disenchantment with the Rebel Arts socialists, and with his own work for a movement which he had not joined and in which he did not quite believe, resulted in a decision, by mid-March of 1935, to move to the country and withdraw into a more contemplative way of life. "Next year," Porter wrote his mother, "I think I will (if I can) paint just for myself, & read a lot of stuff for a Marxian education."[27]

After a summer on Great Spruce Head during which Porter painted a portrait of T. S. Eliot's brother Henry Eliot, then a research fellow in anthropology at Harvard University, the Porters left New York City for a house, leased for one year, in Croton, Westchester. Country living appealed to Porter despite the severity of the winter and the constant need to chop wood for fuel, an exercise which soon turned an occasionally achy back into a severe case of sciatica which lasted on and off for the rest of his life. The Porters celebrated their first country Christmas with "a 'minimum Christmas tree' ([Fairfield] called it) because it [had] almost nothing on it, about 6 perfunctory looking glass balls and one roll of tinsel."[28] Porter occupied himself in early 1936 with a design for the mural competition for the new Justice Department building in Washington, D.C. Painting public murals was still his primary goal as an artist.

No sooner had the Porters established themselves in the country, however, than Porter began a habit of leaving his wife and children for New York. He did so out of a desire for stimulating company, political and artistic, and a disinclination to spend too much time in the vicinity of the ever-bawling Johnny. Anne Porter, pregnant with her second child, was lucky enough to have Agnes Cassidy, a capable housekeeper and nurse (about whom she later wrote the poem "A Deposition"),[29] to keep her company. When Porter returned, he often arrived with fellow artists and intellectuals in need of country air – so many, in fact, that Anne wrote her mother, just a week before the birth of her second child, "Sometimes it's as if we ran a hotel."[30]

By maintaining a certain independence of her own, Anne found she could make the marriage work. When particularly lonely or overwhelmed by the duties of motherhood, she visited her parents and sisters at Little Pond or their summer house in Wareham, on Buzzards Bay. When her time away stretched into weeks, Porter corresponded with her. One such cheerful, gossipy letter from Porter describes the carpentry work of his old friend Hans van Weeren Griek for the Theodore Roosevelts: "Hans is refinishing some furniture for the Theodore Roosevelts at Oyster Bay. They have a dog to whom you say, 'What would you rather do than work for a democrat' whereupon he rolls over and plays dead. Hans asked the servants whom they voted for, and they all looked sheepish and did not answer. Theodore [Roosevelt] can't talk without making a speech, and Mrs. [Roosevelt] says, 'Teddy, don't you think Mr. van Weeren could hear you better if you got up on a chair?' He pays no attention, and the children signal to Hans to pay no attention to pa."[31]

When visiting New York, Porter continued to attend lectures and political meetings, including editorial board meetings for *Arise*, which was, in Porter's words, "a Socialist imitation of *The New Masses*."[32] It was at an *Arise* editorial meeting that Porter met John Wheelwright, a poet, dandy, and eccentric who had been a generation ahead of Porter at Harvard and whose poetry Porter had read and admired in Lincoln Kirstein's *Hound and Horn* (fig. 14). Wheelwright, a Bostonian, had founded the Harvard branch of the John Reed Club in 1932 before changing his affiliation from the Communist to the Socialist Party.[33] Porter immediately warmed to this new poetry editor of *Arise*; Wheelwright's boundless enthusiasm for poetry and for the socialist movement, matched with his warmth, wit, and flamboyant charm, came as a welcome relief from the more self-important members of the Rebel Arts administrative staff.

14
The Boston poet and radical John Brooks Wheelwright in his coonskin coat. Photographer unknown. Courtesy John Hay Library, Brown University, Providence, R.I.

Few recognize the name of John Brooks Wheelwright today. The poet John Ashbery, a friend of Porter's in later years, is one of very few to write about Wheelwright, describing him as a "Yankee crackpot genius" who figures among the "cranks" of "mainstream American poetry" – a group which, for Ashbery, also includes Emerson, Whitman, Pound, and Stevens. Wheelwright's best poems are nonetheless remarkable: "the clear mystery, the cold passion, and the warm intelligence are there in equal proportion."[34]

Porter and Wheelwright had a great deal in common, starting with their backgrounds. Porter, though not a Bostonian, was sufficiently a product of that city to recognize Wheelwright as a renegade from the highest ranks of its oldest and most distinguished families. At Harvard, Wheelwright had been an editor of *The Harvard Lampoon* and *The Harvard Advocate*, acting librarian of the Hasty Pudding, and a member of the Poetry Society, the Stylus, and the St. Paul's Society. His expulsion from the university under bizarre circumstances was the stuff of Harvard legend.[35] His family history included suicide and manic depression. Like Porter, Wheelwright was bisexual and sexually confused.[36] Perhaps more important, both Porter and Wheelwright were cultured intellectuals following artistic rather than academic vocations with little support or understanding from family, friends, or political comrades.[37]

Porter was impressed with "Jack" Wheelwright's tireless work on behalf of the movement he termed "Rebel Poetry." Apart from his writing (he had published a volume of poems, *Rock and Shell*, in 1933), Wheelwright periodically edited and printed several small magazines of verse and held regular meetings of his Rebel Poets' Club in his mother's stately Beacon Street home. In addition, he taught a correspondence course entitled "The Form and Content of Rebel Poetry." At the time of his first meeting with Porter he was trying to organize a poetry talk show for radio.[38]

As Porter told Wheelwright's biographer,

I was thrilled to meet him at an *Arise* editorial meeting, and invited him to come out for the week end to my house in Croton that I had just rented and was awaiting my wife and baby son John in. I remember that week end we walked over the fields, while we exchanged views about social problems – my views differing from his in being more sympathetic to Trotsky, or perhaps we were equally attracted to Trotsky, and maybe I was slightly anarchistic. ... Wheelwright was quite familiar with the theoretical/polemical issues. I think he may have thought that socialism was a consistent development from American 17th century radicalism. He used to defend the Communists to me by saying they were the modern Puritans.

Porter introduced Wheelwright to the work of Orozco by showing him the murals at the New School for Social Research. Wheelwright commemorated the occasion in an affectionate handwritten poem entitled "Eye Opener," which he sent Porter in a letter by way of thanks:

His voice ascends and gentler tread. The stair
Well echoes till my eyes and ear drums fill
With his footfalls and tenderer gut[t]eral.
Each tongue had its say, but "you must reach"
Persistent he continues through his search
"For Oro[z]co's triumph pushing through
    found gloom"
With kindly voice and step he left the room, –
With sudden stern head behind me, he
    breathes, "Here!"

As at his brow's command argument stops,
his gait and tongue turn gentler again
and I let my lips rest while my eyes open
and see kind sounds of earth, noise-hunted, jade
like sundown tingle through darkling retrospect
and a sudden tread spring the day break erect
and stern trap hunter hunted and afraid
in their manhunt against persistent hopes.

This draft, which is not entirely coherent in its last stanza (it was later amended and published in *Mirrors of Venus* [1938]), is biographically valuable for the information it gives us about Porter's continued enthusiasm for the revolutionary murals of Orozco and his interest as well in exposing a poet friend to the power of visual art. (Wheelwright synopsizes the poem in *Mirrors of Venus* as "recovery of hope through Orozco's revolutionary conversion of Aztec mythology.") Porter again reported on Orozco to Wheelwright in February 1936, when Porter heard him speak at an artists' congress in New York City.

Upon receiving Wheelwright's verses, Porter wrote back, "Thank you very much for the poem. It is like seeing yourself in a snapshot or a movie that you did not know was being taken: in other words very interesting and strange and flattering."[39] So began a friendship which lasted until Wheelwright's early death, a friendship enriched by Wheelwright's enthusiasm for Anne Porter's poetry ("he was interested in my wife's poetry and my ideas").[40] In the coming years, Wheelwright accepted several of Anne's poems for publication by his small press and begged her to read her work aloud on his radio show, "Poetry Noon," broadcast live from the Miles Standish Hotel in Boston.[41]

Over the following three years, Porter collaborated with Wheelwright on several occasions, contributing six linoleum-cut illustrations to Wheelwright's *Vanguard Verse*, poems of which were originally published in the tiny, pamphlet-sized series Poems for a Dime and (in the case of longer works) Poems for Two Bits (fig. 15). The illustrations are competent but unre-markable, except perhaps in the elaborate credit that Porter sometimes gave for an image's inspiration. One, later entitled *Ruins*, was (according to Porter) inspired by both T. S. Eliot's line "sunlight on a broken column" and Wallace Stevens's poem "The Men That Are Falling," which Porter had recently read in *The Nation*. These statements again suggest how deeply Porter was involved in literary ideas as he practiced his art.[42] Of the other linoleum cuts, two illustrate Wheelwright's political satire "Masque with Clowns," two illustrate a narrative poem of social protest by Kenneth Whelan entitled "Murder at Pottsville," and the last illustrates the poem "Teacher's Oath Hearing," by Arthur Saxe, a satiric political poem about a leading Irish Catholic Boston politician, James Michael Curley, who served as both mayor of Boston and governor of Massachusetts despite pro-fascist sympathies.[43]

The friendship which grew during this collaboration resulted in a correspondence in which Wheelwright alternately urged Porter to join a political party, advised him on child rearing, and argued with him about the relative merits of socialism, communism, and anarchy.

Wheelwright's eccentricity, which Porter and his wife both cherished, served as a sort of safety valve for the tension he felt as an erudite and, some would say, effete member of the upper classes working on behalf of the proletariat. A typical story describes Wheelwright leaving "a dinner party attended by well-dressed Boston Brahmins. Jack came to the car in fancy dinner clothes with a raccoon coat, carrying a soapbox. They drove to a corner in Roxbury, and Jack got out of the car, put down his box, and started to orate. Crowds of curious people soon gathered, attracted mainly by his marvelous Brahmin accent and involved vocabulary."[44] Porter and his wife

15
Porter's black-and-white linoleum-cut cover for Wheelwright's *Poems for a Dime*, November 25, 1936.

responded to these stories with amusement and recognition, for they too were in conflict over their class origins and frequently wondered about the legitimacy of their engagement in cultural and artistic endeavors in a time of social and political crisis.

Writing in response to Wheelwright's repeated urgings that Porter join the Socialist Party ("Particularly should persons of our class get in contact with the masses through their political organs"),[45] Porter said, "I suppose I should answer your hope that I have joined the [Socialist Party]. I don't yet see joining any radical party, because I don't feel that I could then continue being a painter, or at least not an honest one. How can one both believe in revolution strongly enough to want to work for it and at the same time paint pictures? Pictures aren't useful enough. Alex [Haberstroh] may imagine he is serving both art and Socialism by making murals for local 22, but isn't he more likely using his Socialist connection to further his art?"[46]

To these troubling questions – questions which had made Porter feel like "a hypocrite"[47] – Wheelwright responded with reassurance: "So far as your career goes, consider it your chief contribution to the cause and no moral conflict will arise. A conflict must have arisen to have painting and socialism present a choice in your mind. Be a socialist painter, as another is a socialist cook, mechanic, lemon picker, or as with Engels, a manufacturer."[48]

The two men worked well together, and Porter did what he could to introduce Wheelwright's name among his acquaintances in the New York art world. After completing illustrations to Wheelwright's "Footsteps," Porter wrote his friend:

I saw Marsden Hartley and gave him "Footsteps" which I had just shown to some dancers. ... Hartley won't like it, because I think he is a reactionary. It was at his exhibition [at Stieglitz's gallery that] I saw him. I admire his pictures. He is hard to talk to because of his deafness, and because he is bitter and contemptuous, so that he turns your remarks into something absurd and silly. I gave him your address, and he sneered at its being Beacon Street, but cheered at its being at "the better end of Beacon Street." He probably prefers the poor and the Proletariat to "Society" but he is a reactionary just the same, I think. However, he is a real artist, who deserves better treatment from the world.[49]

undated

Porter's interests veered from the political to the personal in January 1936 with the birth of his second son, Laurence. Despite the suggestion by Wheelwright that they should name the baby Uriel after Emerson's rebellious archangel, the Porters decided to name him after Anne's brother and nickname him Leo. "Not Leo after Trotsky," Porter was quick to inform Wheelwright, "Leo after a lion because we imagine he looks leonine."[50]

Though Laurence's birth was an easy one, Anne Porter developed a case of Malta or undulent fever shortly afterward. In the days before sulfa drugs, undulent fever was a dangerous and recurrent malady in which the individual suffered prolonged bouts of low fever. For the next five years this illness drained Anne Porter's energy and prevented her from having another child.

Anne's illness was just one family worry. Starting around age two, Johnny Porter seemed to have succumbed to a mysterious psychological condition in addition to his digestive disorder. He was increasingly withdrawn, he disliked being touched and would not look anyone in the eye, and he had taken to injuring himself. Despite numerous consultations with doctors, the Porters were unable to discover the source of his disturbance and were unable even to determine whether the problem was emotional, developmental, or physiological in origin. In hopes of helping his son, Porter set his work aside and devoted long periods of time to Johnny in an effort to get his son to interact with him. The Porters also consulted frequently with doctors, hoping their son's strange and incomprehensible illness could somehow be cured.

Wheelwright tried to cheer the Porters,[51] but their psychological burden was enormous and continued to grow, for both family and doctors told them that Johnny's problems were their fault. "Back then," according to Anne Porter, "even the health professionals simply blamed the parents. Fairfield took it very hard. ... I suppose he must have admitted at some early point that he was ambivalent about being a father, and when Johnny had problems, everyone blamed Fairfield [even though] Fairfield spent years trying to bring Johnny out of it."[52] In later years Anne credited Fairfield for rescuing Johnny from the vegetative state that at least one famous doctor (Dr. Margaret Mahler) had predicted for him. Anne said that "largely it was because of all these hours [of attention] F. had given him in early childhood" that Johnny remained warm and outgoing. "No one gave him, F. credit – nor did he himself realize the amount of healing he had done."[53]

Meanwhile, Porter experienced a number of professional disappointments. He had not won either of the Washington mural competitions. A plan, suggested by Wheelwright, to create another *Turn Imperialist War into Civil War* mural for a socialist bookshop came to nothing. So Porter began yet another mural, this one featuring dancers from the school now being run in New York by his old friend Barbara Mettler, long since returned from her studies in Dresden with Mary Wigman. But the project never got any further than the ink studies Porter did of her students.

Finally, Porter's health began to suffer. The strain caused by this prolonged lack of financial or critical recognition, combined with the stress and sorrow of being unable to help his firstborn child, manifested itself in physical symptoms, mainly with attacks of sciatica and frequent colds.[54]

In October 1936, Porter's one-year lease on the Westchester house expired. In the midst of searching for a permanent home, Porter received word that Julia Foster Porter, Porter's paternal grandmother, had died at the age of ninety. A renowned pediatrician in Chicago had been recommended to Porter by friends of his parents, and so, after consideration, the couple decided to relocate temporarily to Winnetka, taking up residence in Julia Foster Porter's house, just across the driveway from Porter's parents. Though his artistic production had come to a virtual standstill and he was returning to his childhood home with nothing to show for his five years' work in New York, Porter left for Winnetka more concerned about curing his son's condition than establishing his career as a painter.

7
Winnetka

"It was fun driving west," Porter wrote Wheelwright shortly after arriving in Winnetka in October 1936. "On still bright days the Lake is a light blue-green the way the Mediterranean is supposed to be."[1] With hopes of finding capable treatment for Johnny and possibly even a cure for his illness, the Porters had motored west. But the life the Porters faced on Lake Michigan was hardly one of Mediterranean warmth. Their time in Illinois was complicated by illness and death within the family, continuing trouble with Johnny, growing feelings of guilt and incompetence in their parenting of him, and unrelenting (if unintentional) family scrutiny. The decline of the Porter family finances was a concern; the deteriorating political situation in Europe was another source of worry. And as Porter's political beliefs were challenged by the disinformation campaign being waged against Trotsky through Stalin's Popular Front and the Moscow Trials, so were his beliefs about his own political mission as an artist.

The large home at 1077 Sheridan Road was comfortable enough but hardly suited to their personalities, for it bore the heavy stamp of Porter's recently deceased grandmother. Months earlier, Ruth Porter had handled the sad work of clearing away Julia Foster Porter's possessions, writing her daughter, "I have been dipping in the dust of ages at 1077 [and] I hope never to see a family photograph again. ... Father is pretty good about my sending things to rummage sales & libraries, but I don't tell him about the loot I dig out of bottom drawers."[2]

The house had been built specifically to suit Julia Foster Porter's Victorian-ecclesiastical tastes. As Anne Porter described it, "Our house I call (secretly) the Parsonage because that is what it's like – two decorous dark parlours, with leaded lattice windows, big trees outside, – inside brown photographs of every conceivable Madonna ... furniture mostly the color of Pullman chairs and woodwork William Morris-like – sturdy pre-Raphaelite architecture."[3] The dim downstairs rooms, their walls papered with dark brownish green grass-cloth and trimmed in oak woodwork stained black, made most of the house unsuitable as a painting studio, but Porter set up his easel in a spare upstairs bedroom overlooking Lake Michigan and went to work.

In many ways, life at the Parsonage was much easier than the life the Porters had led in Westchester. Because the house shared its grounds with those of James and Ruth Porter, the maintenance of both was under the care of family gardeners and handymen. And the house, despite its Victorian look, had every modern convenience. Other resources of the elder Porters were also at the disposal of the Fairfield Porters – a situation not without its occasional ironies: "If I were going to a Socialist meeting in Chicago," Anne Porter recalled, "Ruth would arrange for the chauffeur to take me there."[4]

Porter did not lack for intellectual stimulation: *The Nation*, *Partisan Review*, and many smaller publications of the extreme left were all readily available on his mother's coffee table, and she hosted a steady stream of politically aware guests. But Ruth, however much in sympathy with her son politically, was an exacting and quietly critical presence; neither Porter nor his wife could ever be entirely at ease living under her close observation. James Porter, who had been much less involved in his son's taking up an artistic career, was politically disinclined to Fairfield's views and, despite his financial generosity, a constant source of quiet disapproval. Still, everyone in the family was aware that the move to Winnetka had been made out of need, not preference, and that Johnny Porter's requirements came first.

Age and illness were taking their toll on Porter's parents, and new strains had come to their household with the deepening of the Depression. James, having survived the recent death of his mother, was himself beginning a slow death from cancer. Ruth was experiencing constant back pain as the result of two "squashed" vertebrae.[5] The Porter real estate business, now being run by Fairfield's brother Edward, was in a slump, forcing the sale of a number of long-held properties.[6] Federal income taxes were eating away at the family's income; earlier that year Ruth had not even known if she would be able to afford to attend her Bryn Mawr reunion.[7] The nearness of Porter's parents – and his awareness of their mortality, their financial difficulties, and their unremitting scrutiny – distracted and disturbed Porter. No doubt the return to his childhood home had a melancholy effect on him as well. It did on his wife, who wrote her mother shortly after arriving, "Fairfield ... took me all over his house describing the Porter family as little children which was somehow very touching and I had to weep in the attic."[8]

Apart from the stress of living at home, Porter faced a much larger and more difficult problem: the lack of an art community in either Winnetka or Chicago. In writing an apologetic letter to John Wheelwright, for whom the Porters had been unable to secure a Chicago poetry reading, Porter mentioned the dismal state of the Chicago cultural scene despite its federal funding, mentioning that "'It Can't Happen Here' opened this week at the W.P.A. theater, and seems hardly attended, though the highest priced seat is 50 cents."[9]

Porter gave a dry assessment of the Chicago art community to Anne's mother, suggesting, in as cheerful a manner as possible, just how inadequate he found his new home: "I have met the Winnetka painters, who are a little lonely and therefore very friendly, and a few Chicago ones. There are some good painters here and as they all know each other they seem kinder about each other's work than the New York ones. There is room for hardly more than two cliques. ... There are about two art galleries here, and if you stay in a gallery for more than half an hour, the dealer suspects your sanity."[10]

Worse still, Porter's new acquaintances were incapable of comprehending the sort of art he had, up to this moment, practiced (or at least hoped to practice): a public, narrative art enjoining social commitment and world revolution. There was no support for such work in affluent Winnetka, except for a small number of socially aware wives of Chicago businessmen, among whom communism was fashionable.[11] Though Porter continued to work on his mural proposals while living in his parents' backyard and though his interest in politics remained as keen as ever, his new projects were far in spirit from *Turn Imperialist War into Civil War*. His first mural project in Winnetka depicted two boys standing at a birdbath.

He found little artistic inspiration in Chicago. European influences eventually appeared there – by 1938, Porter and his wife had met and dined with the director of the Chicago Bauhaus and experienced the ideas of Gropius and Moholy-Nagy.[12] But he felt little enthusiasm either for them or for their ideas. Still, he was fond of the city, writing in later years that "the people have the nicest manners in the world, friendly without being intrusive. There is a dignified modesty and lack of push and hurry. Chicago is ever so much better looking than New York, cleaner and better run. ... The difference between Chicago and New York is like the difference, in Russian novels, between Moscow and St. Petersburg."[13]

Upon arrival in Winnetka, Porter's first priority was not professional but personal: to find appropriate medical and educational attention for his son. Within two months, the Porters were consulting two doctors about Johnny and were in close consultation as well with Johnny's new nursery school teachers.

What had first been thought a behavioral disorder was now starting to affect Johnny physically. When Johnny refused to feed himself, he began to suffer from what seemed to be malnourishment. Rejecting solid food, he grew thin and his stomach began to swell. No one, neither doctors nor teachers nor family members, knew what to do. These new physical symptoms frightened the entire family and made all discussions of Johnny tense. That winter, despite constant colds and Anne's bouts of Malta fever, Porter and Anne struggled to ignore the many criticisms that were made of their parenting and to work with Johnny on a daily basis, encouraging him to feed himself and forcing him to eat.

"We are increasingly worried about Johnny," Porter wrote Wheelwright in the middle of a winter which was largely devoted to working with his son. "The new school psychiatrist whom we like, says he is misleading because his emotional development is normal, and it is hard to separate this from his intellectual development, which is retarded, why, and whether permanantly or not, no one yet knows."[14]

By early spring, three-year-old Johnny had become, in Porter's words, the nursery school's "no. 1 problem child." "The nursery school teacher came here every evening for a week to try to show us how to teach him to feed himself. After nearly two weeks of a strike on our part and a lockout on his, he refusing to allow us to guide him and we refusing to feed him, except milk, he now allows Anne to guide him, and will eat by himself even if she is in the room. ... he is now more cheerful than he has been for two years, and much more responsive and active ... at school they say he is behind his age in everything except music in which he is ahead about two years."[15]

By the beginning of April, the family was no closer to understanding Johnny's malady, but the physicial danger of starvation seemed to have passed. As Ruth reported to Nancy (the two were in constant communication), "Though Anne still has to sit by him, [Johnny now] feeds himself entirely with a great waste of food. He has difficulty chewing still because of the long period of purees for his sore little gums [but] yesterday he drank 3 glasses of milk at school, so the rejecting all the coarser food there doesn't matter so much. And he is talking more & more. I hope that Dr. Aldrich was too pessimistic about him. Anne & F. try not to do anything for him unless he asks or responds to their requests or orders. It has been a temptation to think & act for him."[16]

Porter attempted to compensate for his inability to help his son by keeping him company and indulging his son's peculiar whims. When Johnny became fascinated with spirals, Porter traveled to Skokie to construct a special staircase at a woodworking shop. "It is about 6 feet high," Anne wrote. "It's so impressive I feel we should build a house around it."[17] Porter eventually did so, incorporating the staircase into a tree house in the front yard, overlooking the lake.

In addition to his spiral staircase, Johnny loved playing with the building blocks that James Porter had bought years ago for Fairfield and his siblings. His play bordered on obsession, as Porter reported to Wheelwright:

Between his breakfast and ours, Johnny, like a patient spider, builds a structure of all the blocks in the front hall. If this web is broken he calmly repairs it, and if it is put away at night, it is there again by the time we come down in the morning, making passage difficult. I would like to know what he has in mind. He makes one kind of thing with the painted blocks, and an aqueduct, or, today, a wall made of blocks on the end of the big blocks, and of the little blocks he makes a round tower or a building with blocks laid flat like bricks, or a long train of all three and of the odd shaped blocks other structures, or he just arranges them very precisely just so on the floor. I have taken pictures of two different webs so far and I am going to take more pictures of further developments.[18]

undated

Porter's observation of the forms and his speculations on possible meanings of his son's constructions were thorough – justifiably so, for, from the photographs that survive, the building-block constructions were remarkable (fig. 16). The memory of these constructions inspired Porter to write the poem "Pick Up Your Blocks and Put Them Away":

> The angled words around a square
> Compose a fort of wooden walls:
> A blockhouse space of different air
> Whose life publicity appalls.
>
> And if regardless feet intrude
> The public air pours mixing in,
> Conforming, ruinous and rude
> Where shortly something clear had been.
>
> A play of words and play of blocks
> Make presences of empty space;
> Configurations mark the clocks
> A way that nature will efface;

16
One of Johnny Porter's mysterious building-block constructions, photographed at the Julia Foster Porter home in Winnetka by Fairfield Porter, circa 1937. Courtesy Mrs. Fairfield Porter.

Imaginary buildings put
Within the emptiness, to mask it,
Distinctions, till the conquering foot
Requires the neat, the random basket.[19]

This poem, as spare and elegant as a mathematical proof, suggests that Porter's interest in his son was more than dutiful, that it was a heartbreakingly complete artistic and intellectual identification. As Porter wrote, he way always "confusing [Johnny] with myself, and my disappointment with him with my father's disappointment with me ... all my father's and my own disappointment with myself is incarnate in Johnny."[20]

Still undecided about whether Johnny's difficulties were behavioral or physiological, the doctors warned his parents that their behavior toward their son had probably contributed to, if not created, his mysterious problems. One doctor suggested that Johnny's problems were the result of emotional coldness within the family. The guilt and anxiety created by such pronouncements were exhausting. As Anne wrote, "F. and I are doing what we can to help in discovering what [Johnny's] emotional difficulties are. We find it quite tiring to answer so many questions and be so very truthful."[21] Perhaps inevitably, the feelings of fear, anxiety, and guilt surrounding Johnny's condition, combined

17
Porter with his first-born son, Johnny, circa 1937. Photo by Ellen Auerbach. Courtesy Mrs. Fairfield Porter.

with the isolation of their living situation and Porter's vocational and familial troubles, took their toll on the marriage. When not painting or working with Johnny (fig. 17), Porter began taking long walks along Lake Michigan and even swimming long distances in its chilly waters; he spent long periods of time out of the house, traveling to Chicago and even New York. In the spring of 1937, not wanting to risk Johnny's health and perhaps needing a break from the rest of the family, the young Porters summered in Winnetka as the rest of the family took its annual trip to Great Spruce Head Island.

Despite their great concern over Johnny, the Porters did make a life of their own in Winnetka, frequently traveling into Chicago for political meetings and get-togethers. Anne Porter composed an anthem, now lost, which was sung at one May Day socialist rally; John Wheelwright deemed her composition "a tour-de-force."[22] For another May Day rally, the Porters topped their secondhand station wagon with a papier-mâché float for the Artists' Union depicting a worker crushing a swastika. "We can't help feeling," Anne wrote her mother, "that the combination of sculpture and station-wagon will be *extremely* quaint!"[23] Whenever possible, Porter escaped to New York to see art exhibits, plays, and friends; on at least two occasions, Anne Porter was able to leave the children behind and accompany him.

On an average day in Winnetka, Anne Porter, who had joined Ruth's "Monday Ladies" reading group and played the recorder in a small orchestra organized by a neighbor, endeavored to write both poetry and prose. Much of her time, of course, was taken up with household chores and childcare; she also spent a large amount of time on committee work for civil and workers' rights. Upstairs, Porter painted or read Marx, stopping to work with Johnny when his son returned from nursery school.

Their small home soon developed a reputation for chaos and disorder, for Anne's housekeeping was determinedly lackadaisical. Her style of household management was due in part to her disinclination to delegate work to household help, a disinclination based on her socialist views.[24] Her lack of delegation took Ruth Porter, who had always been meticulous in her own housekeeping and management practices, by surprise: "Anne & Fairfield's housekeeping is a constant wonder & amusement," Ruth wrote two months after their arrival, noting in another letter, to Nancy, "Anne ... has engaged a fat motherly cleaning woman ... I can't say cook or second girl because I am sure Anne has not defined Mrs. Dressler's work but is leaving it to work out like a natural phenomenon."[25]

Porter and his wife, in dealings with the senior Porters, both adopted a role which Porter had known as a child, that of the wayward but charming eccentric. When asked by Ruth to attend a formal dinner, Porter was at last compelled to wear the by-now-legendary dinner jacket which his mother had pestered him to acquire during his days at Harvard. Porter retaliated in an inventive way. As Ruth wrote Nancy, "Anne had never seen F. in a dinner coat before. He was 30 minutes late [for dinner] as he couldn't find any [shoe] black-ing. Anne telephoned that there was a light in the studio and she thought he was making progress: ... he was painting his shoes! But I served sherry and dewdads so 30 minutes wait wasn't hard." About her elusive, untidy daughter-in-law, Ruth added, "Anne looks like a little nymph caught in a drawing room. I love her better all the time."[26]

Part of the household disarray at 1077 was due to Porter's love of com-pany. In the spring of 1937, Anne wrote to her mother, "Fairfield is drawing all day from different models who are at lunch and supper and all but spend the night." Two days later she wrote again: "Fairfield has been painting and paint-ing ... we have been entertaining actors and professional acrobats at lunch and dinner."[27] Such bohemian comings and goings were new to Sheridan Road, even though the tradition of hospitality had long run in the family. Apart from artists' models, there were hungry socialist and anarchist guests as well, arriving wide-eyed and sometimes full of suspicion from the slums of Chicago: "Today six German Council – Communists ... came to spend the day," Anne reported. "Fairfield and I made a homeric stew the night before and wisely armed ourselves with paper plates and cups."[28] One senses that the indifferent housekeeping, apart from being habitual, may have served as a sort of apology on the part of the Porters to those houseguests who were less for-tunate in circumstance. By welcoming guests into chaos and serving them stew not on Julia Porter's prized Nankin china but on paper plates, the Porters were trying to meet the working class on some approximation of its own terms. Porter's communist friends, sensitive to nuance and ridicule and hard-ened by lives of real poverty, were not always able to appreciate the shy charm of such gestures.[29]

Politics was a frequent topic of conversation in the Porter family and occasion-ally a cause of heated discussion between Porter and his father, who, unlike his wife, believed firmly in the virtues of capitalism ("the evening was pleasant except for your Father's unwisely starting a discussion which was really a laying down of the law by him to the effect that ants bees and termites prove beyond the peradventure of a doubt the fallacies of socialism").[30] Fairfield Porter's enthusiasm, meanwhile, was for Trotsky, a man who was no more in favor among the Porters than he had been among the socialists of Rebel Arts.

Porter was not alone in his enthusiasm for Trotsky. To many American leftist intellectuals he was a compelling figure in need of a hearing. During his exile at the home of the muralist Diego Rivera and his wife, Frida Kahlo, in Coyoacan, Mexico, Trotsky had been condemned in Russia without being able to offer a defense of his past actions. American leftists were therefore mobiliz-ing to form a committee of inquiry, known as the Dewey Commission, to clear his name. But forming the commission and organizing the journey to Mexico required money. So Porter decided to pitch in, going door-to-door to collect money for the American Committee for the Defense of Leon Trotsky. As he wrote Anne's mother, Katharine Channing, in early January of 1937, "The editor of the *Socialist Appeal* in Chicago asked me if I would try to collect some money for Leon Trotsky, and I agreed to, (on the North Shore) and to my great surprise I have so far collected nearly $50. Everone is surprised ... one Communist argued with me, agree[ing only] that [going door-to-door] was a preposterous thing to do in this community, that it is a cause that is pretty remote from the interests of our neighbors."[31] Porter was more direct with his friend Wheelwright about the responses he received while making the rounds of his affluent neighborhood. "I got a list of about 20 people," he wrote. Most "gave something only because they were sorry for me."[32]

At home, Porter's efforts on behalf of Trotsky were not viewed charitably even by his mother, who wrote scathingly to her son-in-law, Michel, "We had a wonderful evening on Marx [recently] with Eliot [Porter] holding forth most winningly. He is the only son to whom James will listen with respect. We also have to listen a great deal to the Stalin-Trotsky controversy from Fairfield who is getting contributions from us all to pay Trotsky's way."[33] Ruth's scorn seems to be directed mainly against a man who could not even pay his own way. Trotsky's legal defense may well have seemed to her a vanity: useless squabbling over the reputation of a former leader. Still, her impatience was not just with Trotsky but also with her son – now a grown man who, like Trotsky, did not pay his own way.

What she may not have perceived was that to Porter, Trotsky was important as a contemporary political theorist and revolutionary intellectual with a fervent belief in leftist artistic and literary endeavor. Like many other artists and writers of the period, Porter saw in Trotsky a Promethean figure who believed in the crucial importance of art. (Indeed, Trotsky's thoughts on art eventually served as a basis for Clement Greenberg's critical justification of the American avant-garde.)[34] Trotsky's thoughts on art were all the more inspirational to Porter because, by 1937, confidence in the socially transformational power of art was in steep decline. Writing to *Partisan Review* in 1937, Trotsky had insisted that artists "must begin again with the struggle for artistic truth, not in terms of any single school, but in terms of the immutable faith of the artist in his own inner self."[35] This and other statements apparently struck a chord in Porter, whose lack of affiliation to any political party had derived not from political indifference but from his commitment to his art, an art that would, he hoped, make a difference to society – all of which may explain why Porter felt a responsibility to Trotsky. Porter felt passionately that Trotsky should be given the opportunity to clear his name – as, in time, he did, making a case for a Marxism unsullied by Stalin.

During his free time in Winnetka, Porter continued his ongoing project of completing his Marxist education by reading all of Marx. In addition, he began to read the news closely – and to doubt the veracity of much of what he was reading, in part because the Chicago papers were distinctly conservative.

"The newspapers [here] are even worse than the Boston papers," he wrote Wheelwright shortly after arriving. "There is a very dull tabloid, that isn't even especially sensational, and that is the only New-Deal paper."[36] Disturbed by the lack of adequate coverage in the newspapers, Porter turned to liberal periodicals but found them equally frustrating. "I used to read [about politics] – because my family got *The New Republic* and *The Nation*," Porter recalled in later years. "I felt – well, this liberal point of view ... is not true. It's an edited one. It's a censored one."[37] One result of Porter's reading was his decision to subscribe to an even greater number of small leftist periodicals which presented alternative news and views, including the Chicago-based *Living Marxism*, published by a group of anti-Leninist Marxists, the Council Communists. Another result, which had immediate repercussions on the entire family, was the decision of Fairfield, Anne, and Ruth Porter to participate in a boycott of the Hearst chain of newspapers.

The boycott was based on the Hearst newspaper coverage of the Spanish Civil War. To the dismay and outrage of the Porters, the Hearst papers had taken a strongly pro-fascist position on the war, delivering news supportive of Franco. At the request of a socialist acquaintance, Porter decided to hold a meeting in his home to discuss the possibility of a boycott. Shortly thereafter, a letter (containing thirty-seven names, including those of Porter, Anne Porter, and Ruth Porter) was sent out by a person who had been at the meeting, calling for a boycott and asking individuals to protest to anyone who advertised with Hearst. Hearst responded quickly, threatening to bankrupt the Porters with a lawsuit for promoting an illegal (secondary) boycott.[38]

The Hearst letter caused an uproar within the family. James Porter was furious with his son for unnecessarily exposing the family to financial ruin. He sent letters to his children denouncing the action and warning them that their interest in the family business was at stake. Porter rebutted his father's letter by mail, justifying his actions to his brothers (Eliot and John) and sister in a long letter:

I am writing this to give you another point of view from the one presented in *undated* father's letter. He wrote his letter without having seen the complaint of the Hearst newspapers, and without any knowledge of my and Anne's activities. ...

[We have] asked the opinion of Mr. Havinghirst of Northwestern University Law School about the case. ... He says that in 10 years of experience of such cases he has not seen a case with less merit. If it comes to a trial, it is not a difficult one to defend. ... There is a strong probability that it will not come to trial: for this is the kind of suit which is instituted during strikes by both sides all the time, and to his knowledge no such case has ever been brought to trial.

I have tried in this letter to give as reassuring a picture as possible of the situation as I can without being inaccurate. You can balance what I and Mother say against what Father says. Anne and I do not intend to allow you to suffer financially from this.

A letter from Eliot to Fairfield arrived at 1077 Sheridan Road shortly afterward.

February 24, (1939?) Thank you very much for your concise account of your relations with Mr. Hearst. Don't you, however, feel a little foolish ... to be sued for a paltry $50,000? I have always hoped there was enough spirit in you to make you able to libel Hearst to the extent of a couple of million. I am afraid you have sold out. ...

Seriously, now, you must not feel that the financial burden of their suit if it should be lost should be borne by Mother and Anne and you. It is a matter of obligation bound by our collective convictions that we should share it equally. It is mere fortuitous circumstance, for instance, that I was not involved, for if I had been living in Chicago I also undoubtedly would have been one of the defendants.

All of you have only acted in a way consistent with your convictions which are also my convictions. You have acted honestly and decently in the defense of social relations which we consider of permanent importance to a tolerable structuring of civilization. That these actions have come in conflict with certain legalistic principles indicated to me only that the legalistic principles are wrong. A fight which may in small measure lead to the acceptance of better principles is worth engaging in.

I shall be grateful if you will let me know from time to time the sequence of events in this case.[39]

Eliot's gallant response must have cheered Porter considerably, as did the dropping of the threatened action. But so far as his relations with the rest of the Porter family were concerned, the damage was significant and lasting. And in a sense, James Porter's concern about his son's political activities was not unreasonable, for during the period that Porter lived in Winnetka, his involvement in the American Artists' Congress, a group which eventually allied itself with the Communist Party, was recorded in government files kept by the FBI.[40]

As Porter continued his Marxian self-education in Winnetka, he found himself attracted to the small group of intellectuals known as the Council Communists. "In 1938, out of curiosity, I subscribed to all sorts of leftist publications, and from mistrust of the total CP-liberal line, I came across *International Council Correspondence*, later *Living Marxism*. ... Paul Mattick [the editor of *Living Marxism*] disillusioned me about Trotsky. I learned that Trotsky really believed in all the Leninist lying and authoritarianism and terror and, in contrast to his [Trotsky's] defender over the Moscow Trials, John Dewey, in the doctrine that the ends justify the means."[41]

After reading several issues of *Living Marxism*, Porter saw an announcement for a meeting. He attended the meeting and introduced himself.[42] Despite Mattick's suspicion of wealthy capitalists, the two men became friends, in part because the Chicago community of theoretical Marxists was a small one, in part because Mattick was a great lover of art, and in part because, being constantly hard up for cash to publish his magazine (or even to support himself), Mattick found in Porter a ready, if limited, source of financial support.

Porter's infatuation with Paul Mattick is easy to understand, for Mattick, three years older, was everything Porter was not: a working-class, self-taught, and – by the time of their meeting – seasoned revolutionary intellectual who had been writing, organizing, and publishing for nearly twenty years. As his widow recalled, "Paul was not a leader type, not a raging revolutionary. He was erudite, scholarly, and very level-headed … He was educated only until twelve, when he was sent to work, and he saw a lot of kids around him die of tuberculosis. He [himself] lived in constant pain [from chronic bronchitis]."[43] Mattick didn't just think or talk about politics; he lived and breathed it.[44]

At the time of their first meeting, Mattick was, despite his ceaseless work, experiencing deep financial and personal troubles; in fact, he was "desperate and on the edge of a complete breakdown."[45] An unemployed machinist with serious health problems, he had a great dream of writing a book, but his English was limited. His magazine, meanwhile, lacked funding and could only appear periodically. By 1939, Porter was not only helping to support the magazine but giving money to Mattick. Mattick accepted the money but begged Porter by letter to consider it a loan. When Mattick's financial troubles persisted, Porter helped create a Friends of Paul Mattick fund to enable Mattick to proceed with the writing of his book.

Porter was impressed by the level of dialogue he experienced in the company of Mattick and his fellow Council Communists. He preferred them because

their ideas seemed better than anybody else's. … They were among the few people in the world who had really read Marx all the way through, not just a little bit of it. And at the same time they weren't interested in measuring every opinion against Marx. … I liked these people … because they were bright, clever, and they seemed to me to be – well, they just knew more than American liberals and American Communists. … I suppose it's a kind of dilettantism on my part, but still, if you're going to be interested in things, you know, out of curiosity, there's no point in taking second best. … What impressed me most deeply about this group of Germans was not just that they were more intelligent or that they knew more than anybody else, but that their manner of discussion was something that I had never met with before. If anybody said anything at one of their meetings, they were never interrupted even if they talked for three hours. People just sat and listened until the person had said everything that he had to say before somebody else got up to say something. There was no interruption. There was no bullying. I admired that very much. … In short, it was democratic in the Quaker manner.[46]

The Council Communists appreciated Porter's intelligence but suspected his privileged background. They also seem to have felt sorry for him. "The way [Porter] walked, the way he talked, the way he was always so awkward, losing things – it was all psychological," Mattick's widow remembered. "Both he and Anne had grown up in worlds so privileged that they were really like children.

Fairfield never understood that you can't change the world by handing out money like Lady Bountiful. He threw money at every problem. Fairfield ... once said to me that he thought the only reason anyone listened to him was because they knew he had money. He was like that, very depressed."[47]

Mattick and the other Council Communists welcomed Porter into their midst, however, and he attended meetings regularly. Mattick had known George Grosz and other German artists in Cologne in the early twenties and enjoyed speaking with Porter about art as well as politics. Porter, in a letter to Stieglitz, noted that "so far the only friends who have noticed the Marin with pleasure are a German radical & his wife. But then they asked me if I didn't like Nolde whom they thought Marin resembled. They prefer of all artists today, Klee, Dix, and Ernst. They haunt the Art Institutes International water color & print shows to see German pictures. They have been here 13 years & are still, perhaps now especially, homesick."[48]

Through Mattick, who knew a great deal about Soviet politics and history, Porter began to see that his enthusiasm for Trotsky – however sympathetic that man may have been in his writing on art for *Partisan Review* – was misguided. Mattick reminded Porter of Trotsky's demonstrated tendencies toward Stalin-like authoritarianism, particularly during the Kronstadt Rebellion. Porter recalled, "I thought I was a Trotskyite. And then I met these radical German Marxists and they showed me, they demonstrated – they didn't say – that Trotsky was just another Bolshevik and that the trouble was with Bolshevism ... because of its method of organization [as] a centralized thing [where] one man dictates."[49]

Mattick's widow has observed that it was the idea of a society without central leaders that most appealed to Porter. "There was no party line in the Council Communists, no hierarchy of power. This was mind-boggling to Fairfield, who had been brought up to respect authority and work within the system. Fairfield caught a sense of the possibilities of an anarchic lifestyle through Council Communism."[50] Indeed, it was in the possibilities of anarchism that Porter eventually saw the potential not only for the sort of life he wanted to lead but also for the sort of art he wanted to create: an art which, while aware of its historical context, responded primarily to that which most interested the artist.

Porter attempted to share his growing infatuation with the Council Communists with Wheelwright: "Mattick is the leading intelligence in the group that get out *Council Correspondence*. ... [He] speaks terrible English, his syntax is German, though his vocabulary is perfectly fluent. I only went once because all the people there are supposed to be proletarians, and I was ashamed to let them know that I was not."[51]

He sent Wheelwright a copy of *Living Marxism* and asked for his response.

undated I like their intention that the magazine be the collective effort of the readers and editors and contributors. They ... run a forum now in an effort to influence the masses, the first had sixty people ... Since some of [the Council Communists] have the belief that communism is the probable inevitable development of society and all of them that Marxism is not a philosophy but a description of reality, they are freer from the minister-or-missionary-talking-down-to-his-audience than any other radicals I know – for anyone's real experience of society will be, in so far as it is real, Marxist. Also there is no interpreting of the word and no Marxian snobbery. And at the discussions where they are frankly out to enlighten there is not yet the spirit of having the last word and winning arguments by tricks. They are very serious. They want anyone, they do not insist on workers only, to come. And they do not hide their views to avoid antagonizing people. The whole thing was on a mature level.[52]

Wheelwright, however, was nonplussed by Mattick and by the Council Communist stance. "I was not at all impressed by the article you sent me. (1) I have not enough factual knowledge (2) I smell a death of hope and an amateur return to Wobblyism in it."[53]

After this exchange, Porter and Wheelwright began to part ways politically, Wheelwright becoming increasingly drawn to Trotsky, Porter to Council Communism. During 1938 the two maintained sporadic contact, in part through Anne Porter, who, having won the Mid-Atlantic Poetry prize from *Poetry* magazine for a dazzling series of poems, was being courted by Wheelwright to appear on his radio show, *Poetry Noon*. In one letter to Anne, Wheelwright wrote, "I feel guilty in that I have not written to Fairfield, but I just haven't. I hope to see him this summer and that I hear soon [from you] about the broadcast." Anne remembered her husband to Wheelwright: "Fairfield is painting & reading [Marx's] *Capital* & has arthritis in his back." But by November of 1938, when Wheelwright wrote Porter asking him to "help raise the money to buy Trotsky's archives for Harvard," enjoining him "to pledge and to approach graduates *entirely* free from all taint of Stalinism who will not blab to anyone also to make pledges,"[54] Porter simply declined, saying that he kept up with very few Harvard acquaintances and that those with whom he had maintained contact would not be interested in raising money on Trotsky's behalf.

Reasons for Porter's new political direction can be gleaned from his later assessment of Mattick: "Mattick's reaction to American intellectuals who were attracted to communism, Trotsky, etc., was a certain rather unspoken patronizing feeling, which I think was justified. He felt they were naive and dilettantish – not because they weren't proletarian but because they considered themselves 'leaders.' Mattick didn't think of himself as a leader." In other words, Porter's attraction to Council Communism seemed to be based partly on a rediscovery of humility, patience, and honesty, in both political and personal life, as exemplified by Mattick. These were Quaker values, just as the Council Communist meetings resembled Quaker meetings. He also recalled that what I got from them ... was that they were anti-theory. I mean what you do comes first and there isn't a theory which you then put into practice. You are what you are right now ... which also I like to think is a common American way of thinking: that action comes before theory. ... Matticks would [also] say that your means are your ends, that what you are doing are your ends – they are in no sense pie in the sky. ... He wanted people to be honest toward themselves. ... I think what I got out of my association with Mattick was a sense that if someone tells you what he thinks, you should look at what he does, [and ask,] "Does it express what he thinks he thinks?"[55]

In this sense, Porter's engagement with Council Communism seems less a dilettantish interest in theoretical Marxism than it does an ongoing interest in and faithfulness to principles which had long guided his family: the Unitarian values of honesty, service, and fellowship. The one great difference between the Unitarian and Council Communist values was in relation to authority. Porter and the Council Communists, watching the world descending once again into war, had no confidence in their leaders – fascist, communist, capitalist, or otherwise. Porter was going the radical way of Thoreau, finding ultimate authority not in government but in the free exercise of the individual conscience.

So far as his art was concerned, Porter was in a period of stasis preceding a moment of transition. Political murals were no longer of interest to him. His work in Winnetka, apart from some decorative commissions, consisted mostly of images of home life – houses, interiors, and family members – and Marin-inspired landscapes. Still, he began showing his work.

Porter's decision to exhibit was really a decision made by his mother, who by 1938 was growing impatient with the lack of real progress in the house next door: "F. is painting a lovely picture of Johnny on the chaise longue, with the room, open door and hallway beyond, very full of color," she wrote Nancy. "But he will probably get it just so far and then scratch it out as he does with most of his oils. I wish he'd send his watercolors somewhere ... some of them are charming. But he doesn't care about exhibiting unless he's satisfied himself."[56]

Ruth Porter's efforts on behalf of her son proved fruitful. Two of his paintings were included in an exhibit of local painters at the Art Institute of Chicago in the spring of 1938. Porter then held an exhibit at the New Trier High School, Ruth apparently strategizing for the exhibit to coincide with a statewide convention of the League of Women Voters in Winnetka.[57] Porter's first one-man exhibit took place a year later at the Winnetka Community House, again through the intervention of his mother, who felt that the time had come for one, whatever her son's opinions about the quality of his work. As Porter recalled, "[It] was sort of arranged by my mother. That was a family thing. She thought I wasn't enough known. She was pushing her son. She used the facilities at hand and got me an exhibition at the Winnetka Community House. ... it made me see what a lousy painter I was, I guess. ... I mean people were very polite and interested ... [but] I was interested in performance, not promise."[58]

The exhibition, which took place in April 1939, may have been all the more humiliating since Porter's brother Eliot had just been given his first show ever – with Alfred Stieglitz at An American Place. Apparently, Stieglitz had, upon seeing his latest work, informed Eliot, "You have arrived."[59] "His was the most sought-after art gallery in New York – indeed in the whole western hemisphere," Eliot noted in his memoirs. "To have work exhibited at An American Place was an honor that overwhelmed me."[60] To this honor was added the critical and (modest) financial success of the show.

Fairfield Porter must have been happy for his brother's success but torn apart by it as well. The Porters were a competitive family. Eliot had always been known within the family as the most talented brother and was favored by his parents for his industry and his intellect. Fairfield Porter had been known within the family as the artist; now Eliot had beaten Fairfield hands down in his own specialty. Fairfield Porter, already suffering from a lack of self-esteem on account of his inability to earn his own living or raise his own son, now had to face the realization that he was not even the family's best artist.

However difficult his time in Chicago, Porter continued to grow and develop as an artist. His interest in Council Communism exposed him to developments in German contemporary art. Like many artists of the period, Porter was becoming aware of contemporary European painting because of the influx of German and German-Jewish refugee artists and art lovers. He was on the lookout for inspiration, for both American Scene painting and the work of the Mexican muralists seemed, if not entirely dead, then at least far from current concerns.

Miraculously, Porter found that inspiration in December 1938 at the Art Institute of Chicago at an exhibition of the Intimist painters Pierre Bonnard and Edouard Vuillard. "I had never seen so many Vuillards before. ... And I looked at the Vuillards and thought, Maybe it was just a sort of revelation of the obvious, and Why does one think of doing anything else when its so natural to do this? When Bill [de Kooning] was first influenced, you know, by modern art, it was Picasso he was emulating. With me it was Vuillard."[61]

Still, his painting style did not immediately change. Porter's Vuillard-influenced paintings did not begin to appear until the early 1950s, roughly around the time that Vuillard received his first big retrospective exhibition in New York at the Museum of Modern Art in 1954, an exhibition which Porter, not coincidentally, reviewed with great enthusiasm for *Art News*. Still, Porter's exposure to the Intimist painters and to the idea of domestic intimacy as a suitable subject for artistic contemplation gave him a great deal to think about in Chicago in 1938. "It seems to be ordinary what [Vuillard]'s doing, but the extraordinary is everywhere."[62]

Just what Porter saw as extraordinary in Vuillard only becomes clear in his later writing on that artist. In the 1954 essay, he praised Vuillard for creating art that is "concrete in detail and abstract as a whole (which is opposite from Cubism) [in which] the existence of both the artist and what he looks at is doubtful: the narcissist's difficulties about his identity become the subject of art." Porter also praised Vuillard as "the artist who most profoundly expressed in visual terms the Third Republic," explaining that the privacy of Vuillard's Intimist interiors "is the essence of bourgeois life in France."[63] The idea that bourgeois life, particularly a psychological rendering of bourgeois life, should merit representation of any sort was surely quite new to Porter in 1938, steeped as he was in the socialist and revolutionary theories of art of that decade. Though he had been creating paintings of interior domestic scenes for some time, Porter had never before considered that there might be any compelling theoretical justification for doing so. Vuillard's moody images of domestic life, rendered in a personal and idiosyncratic painterly manner, bear an emotional complexity comparable to that of poetry. They seemed to Porter full of extraordinary possibility.

Porter's comments on the Bonnard paintings in the 1938 exhibition are equally revealing. "People look at Bonnard who don't like him or [who] maybe like him but have second thoughts about it," he observed. "They say it's too nice. What do they mean by that? They mean it's too pretty. They might mean it's saccharine. [But] they might also mean that they can't approve of the emotion that it gives them."[64] If, as he claimed, Porter was moved by the Bonnards, he may well have begun to think that art might serve a personal, rather than political, end – that is, that it could reflect a personal mood or feeling rather than a political agenda, that the sensation created by a painting could be, as with poetry or literature, sufficient unto itself. Ideas of this sort were surely reinforced by Porter's reading of the period. That Christmas, Anne's parents sent him a volume of the letters of Vincent van Gogh. In a note of thanks, Porter admitted, "I have wanted them for years."[65]

8

Three Homes in Westchester

Family correspondence from late 1938 describes an endless round of sickness in the Fairfield Porter family: colds and flu, Johnny's self-injuries and nutritional problems, Porter's sciatica, and Anne's continuing battle with Malta fever, which frequently left her exhausted and in low spirits. Porter traveled frequently, often going as far as New York to see art exhibitions and visit friends. Apart from wanting to escape the domestic claustrophobia of Winnetka and perhaps feeling overwhelmed by the frustration and sadness that came from working unsuccessfully with Johnny, Porter needed exposure to the art world to continue his work and reaffirm his identity. And he craved what his wife later described simply as "freedom." This freedom – Porter's abstract desire, at the age of thirty-one, for an unencumbered life in which he could continue to develop as a painter and, in time, make a reputation for himself – had been, he felt, compromised by the burdens and responsibilities of fatherhood. It was compromised further by his financial dependence upon his family, for their opinions were not ones he could easily disregard. More and more, Porter felt overwhelmed by the circumstances of his life and wanted to move back to New York to make a fresh start.

Porter's frequent absences did not go unnoticed by his mother. In a letter to Anne which has only partially survived, Ruth Porter took her daughter-in-law's side, writing, "If Fairfield were at home with me all the time I should be feeling too guilty to endure it, & should try to push him out of the house to take the train to you. ... James never left me for more than a few weeks."[1] Though Ruth Porter was careful not to interfere in her son's domestic affairs, her disapproval of his behavior toward his wife and childen must have been obvious to him.

By early 1939 both Fairfield and Anne were more than eager for a change of scene; they felt a move to New York necessary not only for Fairfield's career and Johnny's education (they were thinking of sending him to the New York Teachers' College School)[2] but also for the survival of their marriage. The move was long overdue; as early as 1937 Porter had written to Wheelwright saying that he wanted and intended to move back east. Anne Porter, without hinting at personal unhappiness, also looked forward to a change in household environments, hoping the new house would have "an outside studio for Fairfield, for the selfish reason that I don't want to be simultaneously responsible for the children's happiness and Fairfield's working conditions."[3]

Meanwhile, James Porter was nearing death from cancer. During the summer of 1939, the elder Porters did not make their usual trip to Great Spruce Head Island, for despite their hope that James would be able to take a final summer in Maine,[4] his health was failing rapidly (fig. 18). Ruth stayed with him in Winnetka, not knowing how much longer he would live. Porter and his wife enrolled Johnny and Laurence in summer school, planning to stay in Winnetka as well. But toward the end of June, with James Porter's condition unchanged, they made an impetuous decision. As Anne described it, "Fairfield said, 'Oh I wish I could see California' and I decided for once not to be negative about things so I said, 'Let's go right away while the little boys are in summer school.' Then Fairfield invited his Bavarian friend and to my joy and relief his fiancée can come too. ... We are going north to Oregon, then down the coast to San Francisco and home more or less through the Southwest, taking 3 weeks in all."[5]

The foursome traveled through the Pacific Northwest and down to San Francisco; Porter and Fritz Henssler, one of the Council Communists, continued as far as Mexico before heading home, so that, as Porter said, "I was in a foreign country just a little bit, just for lunch."[6] While traveling, Porter drew a great deal. Anne wrote her mother, "He was constantly thrilled by everything we saw and made some very good sketches."[7]

18
James and Ruth Porter in the late 1930s, shortly before James Porter's death. Photographer unknown. Courtesy Mrs. John Porter.

Porter reached Winnetka just days before his father's death on July 25. The passing of James Porter had been expected since the middle of that spring, and it happened without much drama during the night. Ruth Porter did not call upon her son to bid his father good-bye; she merely walked across the lawn early the next morning to tell her son and daughter-in-law the news. "The family was not at all expressive," Anne Porter recalled. "In fact, I would say they were given to extremes of restraint." All Ruth said to her that morning was, "Death is an indignity."[8]

No memorial service was scheduled on James Porter's behalf, and though his body was cremated, the ashes went unclaimed. With little to mark the occasion, the Porters simply proceeded with their lives, coping with their private grief in whatever way best suited them. Anne Porter wrote her mother, "Fairfield is well and his father's dying is a little easier for him because he foresaw it. ... I am still lost about whether to move or not ... but Fairfield really wants it sooner or later."[9]

By early fall, Porter knew that the time had come to return to New York. Though he was leaving his mother to live by herself on the rambling property at Sheridan Road, Porter could at least take comfort in the knowledge that she was a strong and capable woman with many friends. Moreover, Fairfield's brother Edward and his wife, Audrey, were living nearby in a Chicago apartment, and Eliot Porter, now embarked on his photographic career, was considering returning to Winnetka with his new wife, the artist Aline Kilham, for the birth of their first child in the spring.

During late summer the Porters had received good news: their sons had been accepted as day students at the Hessian Hills School in Westchester, one of the best-known progressive schools in the New York City vicinity. Coeducational, nonprofit, and nondiscriminatory with respect to race and color, Hessian Hills attempted to approximate in enrollment "a kind of cross-section of society, with high tuition fees for some students and for others a sliding scale of scholarships."[10] Though Porter believed strongly in public education, he had learned that his elder son needed more special care and encouragement than even the best public schools could provide. So, three years after leaving Westchester, the Porters found themselves returning there once again, and once again moving into a rented house. Their Winnetka housekeeper, Mrs. Davis, helped them settle at the Red Ridge House in Peekskill before returning to Chicago.

The little place was set alone in the fields, far from the nearest railroad station. Anne wrote, "F. is happy about the house, he really loves it and is only apprehensive about blizzards and like me always wondering if it were wrong to leave his mother."[11] Porter himself wrote, "[It is] so remote in the country that I almost wish we were nearer the station. It seems quite complicated to get into New York. Now I am not afraid of war any more but of winter."[12] Both the Porters professed to like the quiet, Porter suggesting to Paul Mattick that "the children are enough of an interruption."[13]

Visiting New York City, Porter attended many art exhibitions and took up again with his artistic, cultural, and intellectual friends. One of the first major exhibitions that Porter attended was the Picasso exhibit at the Museum of Modern Art, where *Guernica* was on display. There, by chance, in December 1939, Porter met his old friend John Walker and his wife, the former Lady Margaret Drummond, daughter of Sir Eric Drummond (later Earl of Perth). Porter and Walker had long ago lost touch. Walker, now a curatorial success, was the newly named director of the not-yet-constructed National Gallery of Art in Washington, D.C. Memories of I Tatti seven years earlier would certainly have been melancholy, particularly as the two men stood in the shadow of *Guernica*; the rise of fascism and the approaching war meant that Italy was now far out of reach. Porter's happiness for his friend's professional success was surely tempered by self-consciousness about his own lack of progress as an artist. Moreover, Walker's and Porter's political and social views were worlds apart. They continued to meet from time to time to see art exhibitions, particularly when Porter visited Washington, D.C., but they no longer sought one another out; their differences – political, professional, social – were simply too great.

A number of members of the Council Communist group were now making their way to New York, including Walter and Ellen Auerbach, German-Jewish refugee photographers who had been able to find work creating a photographic catalogue of the Lessing-Rosenwald print collection in the sub-

19
Porter with his brothers and sister on the dock at Great Spruce Head, circa 1940. James Porter's "Searsport" farmhouse is in the background. *From left*, Eliot, Fairfield, Nancy, Edward, and John. Photographer unknown. Courtesy Mrs. Fairfield Porter.

urbs of Philadelphia. The Porters' friendship with the Auerbachs, whom they had met in Chicago, was cemented in the summer of 1940 by a visit to Great Spruce Head which was meant to last just a week, but stretched out into a month, during which time the young refugee couple stayed not only with the recently widowed Ruth Porter but also with Eliot Porter.

Through the Auerbachs, Porter met a new group of artists and intellectuals residing in the Manhattan neighborhood of Chelsea: "They knew Edwin Denby and I met Denby through them," Porter recalled. "And through Edwin Denby I met the de Koonings and Rudy Burckhardt."[14] Denby was a poet and intellectual whose pioneering work in dance criticism raised him to cultlike status among aficionados of dance.

The Auerbachs made their first visit to Great Spruce Head Island at a difficult time. As Porter wrote Stieglitz in 1940, "I haven't been there for a long time & I have missed it [and] in this time of destruction I suppose I should feel as though it were the last good summer of my life, but I don't."[15] Porter's ambivalence certainly stemmed in part from his many unresolved feelings about his family: the memory of his deceased father, the presence of his widowed and grieving mother, the intensely worrying behavior of his two children (apart from Johnny's self-destructiveness, Laurence was becoming uncontrollably wild), and the presence of his now very successful brother Eliot, to whom Fairfield was inevitably compared (fig. 19). Then, too, there was Porter's estrangement from his wife, which had grown rather than lessened with their departure from Winnetka.

After his return from Great Spruce Head in the fall of 1940, Porter moved his family into yet another rented house, this one in a wooded area in Harmon-on-Hudson, and engaged a young German-Jewish refugee, Lilo Stern, to help Anne with Johnny. Porter kept on painting, but had little to show for it, and traveled frequently to New York City.

The family continued to grow. Anne's ability to have more children had been prevented, after Laurence's birth, by her Malta fever, but in 1939 her illness was cured by newly developed sulfa drugs, and in 1940 she received the news that she was to have a child. Unlike his wife, Porter was unhappy at the prospect of having another child.

Anne Porter later said, "F. told me once 'I *like* babies' and he did. He enjoyed his and played with them. He was proud of his children. But it would be hard to exaggerate how stressful a new child was for him. There must have been the fear of John's illness repeating itself in another child. There was the insecurity [and] anxiety caused by my inefficiency ... and maybe a reminder of all that happened to hurt and confuse him when his younger brother was born" and Porter's name was taken away.[16]

Porter's love for his children and interest in them informs many of his best paintings, from *Laurence at the Piano* (1953) to *Lizzie at the Table* (1958) to *The Mirror* (1966). But as a father he was often irritable and remote, and as an artist and writer, he found that his children came between him and his work (fig. 20). Perhaps he was simply exhausted. His early identification with Johnny and his close work with his troubled first son for nearly a decade seem to have left him with little energy or attention for his later children. For a man inclined to self-criticism and already aware of his lack of success as a father, husband, and artist, the news of yet another child may have seemed like yet another opportunity to be judged and found wanting.

Given his unhappiness at Anne's pregnancy, Porter may well have begun to question the permanence of his marriage, for among his Council Communists friends, marriage was an outdated and meaningless capitalist-bourgeois concept relating more to property than to human relationships, and not many of the Council Communists bothered with it or believed in it. The politically correct attitude toward human relationships was, they felt, one of free love.[17] The Porters had heard similar opinions from their socialist and communist friends in New York, but now, seven years into their marriage, Porter began to consider these old opinions in a new way.

One consolation for Porter in the midst of his domestic unhappiness was his return to his artist friends in New York. Porter quickly reestablished contact with the Lanings, Alex Haberstroh, and even Tissie Nottingham, with whom he had studied painting in Florence. He visited his old friends the Schwabs, saw Paul Rosenfeld and John Marin, and stopped in regularly to see Stieglitz at the gallery which now represented his brother Eliot. But if Porter had a specific social interest in late 1939 and 1940, it was in getting to know the writers and editorial members of *Partisan Review*.

The magazine, started as a literary review in 1934 by Phillip Rahv and William Phillips and allied to the American Communist Party through the John Reed Clubs, had revised its stance and resumed publication in 1937, this time critical of the communist movement. With backing from the artist George L. K. Morris (a member of the American Abstract Artists group who contributed an occasional column of art criticism), the magazine was run by Rahv and Phillips, Fred Dupee (a former editor of *The New Masses*), Mary McCarthy (the novelist and poet), and Dwight MacDonald.

As the historian T. J. Clarke has observed, *Partisan Review* was the center of "a considerable and various Marxist culture in New York at this time: it was not robust, not profound, but not frivolous or flimsy either ... and ... the pages of *Partisan Review* in 1939 and 1940 mirrored its distinction and variety and its sense of impending doom."[18]

Porter's interest, after supporting *Living Marxism* in Chicago, was to take part in the most important leftist intellectual publication of its time and specifically to persuade its directors (particularly Dwight MacDonald, whom he had met and dined with in Chicago in September of the previous year) to consider the ideas and writings of Paul Mattick. Doubtless he found such a mission critical at a time when the leftist movement in American politics was weakening with the approach of world war. Mattick himself hoped that with persuasion the New York intellectuals of *Partisan Review* would be won over to the Council Communist way of thinking. In a letter to Porter, Mattick even went so far as to suggest that "it would not be a bad idea to combine our work with theirs, and have one magazine instead of two ... but this is only a dream."[19]

Over the next few years, Porter's success in championing the ideas that he shared with Paul Mattick was limited. Indeed, *Partisan Review* itself soon suffered a sea change, becoming a magazine primarily of culture rather than politics. Trotsky, from his exile in Mexico, would refer to it disparagingly as "a small cultural monastery, guarding itself from the outside world by skepticism, agnosticism, and respectability."[20] But Porter did introduce the Council Communist ideas to the magazine and, a year later, introduced Mattick to Dwight MacDonald.

In the meantime, Porter derived satisfaction from merely influencing MacDonald's ideas. Writing to Mattick in 1940, Porter observed, "The editorial by MacDonald in *Partisan Review* ... had several ideas from me and you ... I recognize my phrases in letters and conversations with him, and my versions of your ideas. One minor point is the Merovingian-Carlovingian analogy to the fascist revolution, which he got from me ... [and] I remember defending to him the ideas which he now has adopted."[21]

Porter occasionally published rebuttals to magazine editorials. But he was not, unlike the young Clement Greenberg, interested in consolidating power for himself as either a critic or a theoretician, nor even in securing a position as a contributor to the magazine. Resolute in his determination to be an artist, he remained on the sidelines of the New York intellectual community, participating only tangentially in its discussions of politics and art in the coming decade.

Among the editors of *Partisan Review*, Clement Greenberg, then making a name for himself as a Marxist-inspired art critic, seemed the most interested in Porter's ideas. The two were in a constant state of disagreement and remained

20
Porter painting on Great Spruce Head surrounded by unidentified children, late 1930s. Photographer unknown. Courtesy Mrs. Fairfield Porter.

so for years, but each respected the other enough to relish their encounters: Greenberg in fact showed Porter hospitality on several occasions. One of the first pieces of art criticism that Porter presented to the magazine was an essay on the then unknown Willem de Kooning, a piece of writing which the magazine rejected and which has since unfortunately been lost. "[Greenberg] and MacDonald liked it," Porter recalled. "Greenberg said, 'It's very good; it's better than I could do.' He was polite."[22] Another time, Porter remembered, Greenberg "was annoyed with me for being 'opinionated' about art. He said I was conceited. But I felt he had come to an interest in painting later than I and that his firm classifications and judgments were somewhat sophomoric."[23] The artist Jane Freilicher, who saw Greenberg and Porter at loggerheads in later years, explained that "Greenberg was a bully, and he loved to make pronouncements. Fairfield's irritation with Greenberg came from the fact that they were both intellectuals, but Fairfield wasn't interested in making a name for himself as a critic, or in having critical influence, and he got fed up with that sort of behavior. Fairfield wrote criticism because he liked to think and write about painting. He didn't like the bullying or the pronouncements. None of us did."[24]

Porter's habit in criticism was to follow the Porter manner: to be straightforward, blunt, and combative, without much concern for hurt feelings. An early and telling example of such writing survives in the form of a letter of complaint which he sent not to *Partisan Review* but to *The Kenyon Review* after its publication of a criticism of Picasso by the former *Blast* editor and Vorticist painter, Wyndham Lewis:

I would like to make a criticism. Your article on Picasso by Wyndham Lewis was very bad. I think that like many literary people you have an indirect understanding of the visual arts, and that since Lewis is both a painter *and* a writer you thought he must be an art critic.

The criticism shows about Lewis, first that he looks at paintings through the spectacles of words, and without these spectacles he would be blind. He does not know the difference between the pictures and his talk about them, and his talk is about many things that are quite true and that relate to the pictures, but they are non-essential. ... The article [also] shows that Lewis paints from a written program, concocted in advance. He is a manifesto painter. In the end of his article he compares Picasso with his manifesto, and finds Picasso lacking. Picasso is not a manifesto painter, and the end of the article shows that what is at issue is the manifesto by Lewis, nothing else. It serves as an advertisement for the work Lewis is planning to do.

Lewis says that it is "no longer a question of defending Picasso against the abuse of the ignorant ... it is ... a question of saving art itself." But Lewis' whole criticism is ignorant, and Lewis' former defense of Picasso must have been motivated only by snobbishness. Who wants to *save* art, anyway? Certainly no one who is creative. Is art something that Lewis is fearful for? If so, it is Lewis, not Picasso, who is the antiquarian.

Also, [Lewis] is wrong to think that art is effective to change society. Art is symptomatic, not causal. It is a common vanity of the intellectuals to think that they lead and that they have the power to change society.

Lewis' boredom with abstraction is boredom with the limitations of his own impotence, and his anger with Picasso comes from a sense that Picasso is not bound by this idea, as Lewis was, but liberated by it, as Picasso is liberated by most of what he uses.

Lewis says: "A street in Timbuctoo is always so much more interesting ... than a street in one's home city." Again he reveals the cause of his own boredom as a failure of sensibility. He does not recognize the home street without the most superficial obvious trappings. What Picasso positively does, is to show hitherto unnoticed and essential aspects of the home street.[25]

The letter, which amounts to a tirade, is perfectly just (Lewis's criticism of Picasso was self-serving); it is also a good example of Porter at his most combative. In his later critical writings, Porter concerned himself with the direct appreciation of art rather than with squabbling over the ideas of other critics (with several notable exceptions, his head-butting with Clement Greenberg took place at parties, not on paper). Even in this early letter, Porter seems more interested (after his initial outburst of disapproval) in exploring the ideas of the artist rather than the critic.

Considering Porter's later achievements as a painter, his assertion that Lewis's boredom with the everyday street in one's home city amounts to a failure of sensibility is important, for the statement suggests that as early as 1941 Porter's aesthetic concern with the importance of the everyday was already well established in his own mind.

Unfortunately, Porter's direct response to art was off-putting to those interested in remarks to a general readership. John Crowe Ransom, editor of *The Kenyon Review*, was impressed enough by Porter's letter on Lewis to solicit another contribution for his magazine, but when Porter sent the de Kooning article, Ransom, like *Partisan Review*, declined to publish it, on the grounds that "it's about a strange painter and there are no accompanying reproductions to *show* what his effect is."[26] The rejection of the essay, saddened Porter for years afterward, for he felt that he had been the first to recognize de Kooning's genius.

In truth, Porter was ready to write art criticism at a time when the venues for publishing serious art criticism and the audience interested in reading it were extremely limited. Greenberg had secured a place for himself at *Partisan Review*, but he had done so through the publication of the landmark essays "Avant-Garde and Kitsch" and "Towards a Newer Laocoon," which addressed themselves as much to a political as to a cultural sensibility. Porter, who was not interested in establishing himself as a Marxist (or Trotskyite) critic – he had long since chosen the specific identity of artist – needed to wait another decade, despite his abilities and perceptions as a critic, before being able to publish his more personal and less programmatic opinions on art. But the letter to *The Kenyon Review* had one very specific effect on Porter's personal life: it astounded and delighted his wife and confirmed her in her resolve to stand by her husband as he struggled with his vocation. Upon reading it, Anne Porter told him, "I want to be around when this blooms."[27]

Porter continued to care passionately about all that was published in *Partisan Review*, sharing his characteristically strong opinions about the magazine with its staff in person and in print. But just what he was doing among the *Partisan Review* crowd is as much a personal question as an intellectual one, for Porter did not just enjoy these get-togethers; he needed them. After attending a *Partisan Review* party at the penthouse home of George L. K. Morris, whose art criticism Porter had recently blasted in a letter to that magazine as resembling "a fashion column in *Harpers Bazaar*,"[28] Porter wrote Mattick that Morris's place

July 4, 1941   is beautiful with inlaid wood furniture of what period I don't know, and modern, almost all abstract, paintings by Picasso, and Morris and others ... Morris impressed me as cautious and restrained ... he told me in a quiet voice that he did not only like abstract painting ...

... I like [Clement] Greenberg because when I see him he smiles most warmly and he does not look around the room for a way to escape. He is the only editor of PR who is not snooty at all. Greenberg and Reimann both expressed great admiration of you and they were both as drunk as I.[29]

The tone of these observations suggests that Porter was delighted simply to be among the *Partisan Review* staff, speaking with them as an equal. The pleasure was even greater since, among this group, money and people who had money were not subject to as much scorn, derision, and suspicion as they had been among the Council Communists. In New York, Marxist intellectuals were more sophisticated about, or at least less suspicious of, the rich; moneyed individuals with leftist outlooks were not altogether uncommon in their world and were routinely cultivated as sponsors. Besides, since 1937 *Partisan Review* had dedicated itself to cultural issues more than political ones. With the revolutionary movement teetering on the edge of extinction, many leftists were being forced to reaccommodate themselves to the status quo, and to admit to themselves that all culture, however revolutionary, was tied to the financial goodwill of the ruling class (Greenberg himself observed in 1939 that "it is to the [ruling class] that the avant-garde belongs ... attached by an umbilical cord of gold").[30] For Porter, intellectual exchanges among people who understood his background and did not condemn him for it must have been a refreshing experience.

The world was changing, and with change came loss. In September 1940, Porter and his wife learned that their good friend John Wheelwright, whose poetry and mind they so admired and whose struggle to reconcile his class background with his political beliefs so much mirrored their own, had been struck and killed by a speeding truck in Boston. Though Porter and Wheelwright had grown apart politically during Porter's time in Winnetka, news of his friend's death was a terrible blow; both Porter and his wife felt the loss for years to come.

When Porter was getting to know a new circle of intellectuals at *Partisan Review*, his love of politics and world events also led to an unusual introduction, one far outside his usual artistic-intellectual circles, which rapidly developed into a full-scale romantic infatuation. During Johnny and Laurence's first year at the Hessian Hills School, Porter made a chance acquaintance with a young woman named Ilse Hamm, known as Spatz ("Sparrow"), whose interest in politics was very much to Porter's taste. As he wrote to Paul Mattick in early December, "Johnny's teacher had [as an assistant] before the holidays [a Jewish refugee], a little girl whom we thought was a student at first, who is a pseudo Trotskyite. She worked in Germany in the Karl Marx School in Berlin which became something like Jewish School or something or other at Hitler's advent. She must look a little like Anne, because Laurence says she is 'Mummy at school' and Johnny calls her Mrs. Porter, to her slight embarrassment. Johnny says, 'Spatz *looks* like Mrs. Porter! She *is* Mrs. Porter!' again and again in a shrill voice."[31]

Hamm, a former student anarchist, had been involved in leftist protests against the Nazis in Berlin through 1938 and had been active as well in helping Jewish children flee the country for Sweden through the help of a Quaker organization. When, upon graduating from university at eighteen, she found that her teaching diploma had been taken away by the Nazis on a technicality, she realized her options in Germany were limited and escaped to New York, where she found work at the Hessian Hills School. She was not yet twenty years old.

Ilse Hamm was, by all accounts, a beauty,[32] and she was, by her own admission, fiery, flirtatious, and fickle. She explained that she "met Fairfield and Anne through Johnny. I didn't see much going on between Anne and Fairfield at the time; they didn't seem too involved with each other. They were just married with children. I was working at Hessian Hills ... and I liked Johnny, he was an extremely interesting child, and in his own way quite brilliant ... like [a] genius, only he had no idea who or where he was. It was genius that was not attached to anything. There was no person."[33]

Hamm was uncomfortable at Hessian Hills, for the former Luxemburgian anarchist had discovered that the school was "a hotbed of Stalinists, with a copy of the *Daily Worker* in every faculty mailbox." As she recalled,

I would sometimes think, what the hell am I doing here? I was no Stalinist. And I remember starting to talk to Fairfield, talking politics, and I realized we had a lot in common. So he'd invite me to come and visit them in Peekskill. I was new in the country and I knew absolutely nobody. Here he was, an artist, and his wife a poet, and they knew all about what was going on in intellectual New York. Fairfield was always extremely generous, and absolutely wonderful about introducing me around to artists and poets. He was very tolerant of my ignorance and clumsiness with language, and simply because I was with him, people accepted me. Being young and unencumbered, lively and flirtatious, easily flattered, I was great for him. He was so awkward, he needed someone like me to draw him out. And he liked being out and about, and Anne didn't. She was shy, and so vulnerable, and she had the children at home.[34]

With his wife preparing for the birth of their third child, Porter began introducing Ilse around town to his many well-placed friends and consequently spending a great deal of time with her in New York. Porter's letters to Hamm have not survived, but a letter from Hamm to Porter dated September 16 (probably 1940), indicates at least a brief romantic involvement, though she later claimed nothing physical had transpired:[35] "Those two days with you still live inside of me. Being outside – and in complete relaxation, clear and somewhat freed – strange, how often we get timid or even embarrassed – but I guess that's alright. Right now I won't say another word about it & don't think it would be necessary or even good."[36]

Anne Porter was not unaware of Hamm's existence. Both of her children talked about her, and Porter even confided that he was deeply in love with her. Anne recalled that he "was telling me almost more about his feelings for Ilse than I could bear to hear. He did this because he was a remarkably frank person, an exceptionally guileless person. He had no idea how much this could hurt, because he needed so much to talk about it ... what he told me was the truth about his feelings. ... I'm sure there was no cruelty *intended* towards me in [his] attraction to Ilse."[37]

Anne also sensed that her husband's infatuation had something to do with her pregnancy: "Whenever I had a child, it seems my relationship with Fairfield went through a particularly difficult period. He had such a strong ambivalence to being a father, I think he felt like he simply had to get away from it by doing something else, by having some other experience. Whether with Ilse, or with Jimmy [Schuyler], it seemed to me he was searching for something outside of his relationship with me."

At the time of their son Jeremy's birth in December 1940, Porter came to his wife with an extraordinary announcement.

Fairfield was having a very hard time. ... He was working on his painting but it wasn't going very well and he felt very cut off. He wasn't doing any [regular] criticism then, either. ... I remember I had just given birth to [Jeremy], and Fairfield came to see me in the hospital and told me that he had invited Ilse to come up with us to the island that summer to help with the children. And I remember saying to him, "Do you really think that's wise, considering your feelings for her?" ... And he said, "Yes."

I can't explain it, but in many ways, he was very innocent about things. He simply didn't realize what he was doing. Or else perhaps he knew that he needed a support I couldn't give him and that he had to have her there. Maybe he was right about that. I really don't know. [38]

At any rate, the invitation had been extended, and Hamm accepted. She spent the summer of 1941 with the Porters on Great Spruce Head Island.

During the preceding spring, Porter struggled to balance his infatuation for Ilse with his sense of duty toward his wife and children. He was particularly concerned about his eldest son, but in many ways Porter's concern for Johnny only contributed to his feelings for Hamm, who, apart from being attractive and intelligent (and looking very much like his wife), was able to help Porter in his conflicts with the staff and administration at the Hessian Hills School. Despite her youth, Hamm sensed how humiliated Porter was to have to defend his child from people who in many cases blamed Porter himself for Johnny's sickness. Porter's feelings for Hamm intensified as he watched her give so much of her attention to Johnny, with whom Porter felt a close personal identification.

Johnny, meanwhile, continued to baffle both doctors and teachers. His extremes of anxiety (as they were called) were such that, when provoked by touch or human presence, he screamed incessantly and hit himself in the face until he bled. Hessian Hills had hesitated to take him back for the 1940–41 school year and in the end would do so only on the condition that the Porters pay triple tuition to offset the burden of hiring an independent teacher to give him special care. Porter managed to free up enough money to pay for Johnny's immediate needs, but even so, everyone could see that the boy was getting no better.

Throughout 1940 and 1941, Porter maintained a correspondence with Paul Mattick which became increasingly intimate, often describing family matters as well as politics. Porter's affection for Mattick had grown as a result of the move to New York, and Mattick's for Porter – in part, surely, because the Porters took an active interest in Mattick's financial and physical well-being and helped underwrite the costs of his beloved magazine. But there was genuine friendship. Porter lent Mattick his copy of van Gogh's letters in 1940 and sent him copies of Anne Porter's poems. Porter also worked for a long time on a portrait of Mattick, which he intended to give Mattick as a gift but with which he was perpetually dissatisfied.

By 1940, Porter was confiding in Mattick on what were for him the most relaxed and intimate terms:

So far in my life I have very little felt myself part of a group. I get on better with one person at a time than with several. This quality was what made Fritz Henssler [another Council Communist] tell me I was spoiled – he felt I was undisciplined and selfish. And my reason for telling him he was spoiled was a feeling that his discipline meant mastery for Henssler.

    This problem of authority makes me think of my children. Laurence very much resents authority, and sometimes I get annoyed with him and cross at him for his negativism, but I am never sure that it is good for him for me to spank him (which I do out of anger) or that a kind of cold firmness is good either. I think the best thing would be to be always extremely affectionate and patient. But if there is really not much time as is sometimes the case, I don't quite know what to do. I think it is equally bad to give in to him as to be arbitrarily authoritarian. ... I like Kafka because for me he expresses in the most detail possible, with humor and with horror and always with great and beautiful tenseness all the combinations of the relationships between authority and the object of authority – and all the mystery or perhaps the unsolvable problems connected with it.[39]

Mattick, living alone in Chicago, enjoyed hearing of Porter's family and friends and, being unattached and lonely, inquired about the young German-Jewish refugee the Porters had included in their household, Lilo Stern. He was also interested to know about Ilse Hamm of the Hessian Hills School, whose Berlin background and anarchist political views drew him to her, sight unseen.

At the beginning of the summer of 1941, the Porters prepared to travel to Great Spruce Head for their second summer since the death of James Porter. Porter had made the arrangements with his mother by mail, informing her that Ilse, or "Spatz," would be coming along. Ruth Porter's concern for her son's unhappiness is evident in her response:

March 26, 1941 I think a great deal about your having more freedom to paint and I know that Anne does too. I said to someone ... that it didn't matter whether you had more time to paint if you could help with the problem of Johnny, and she said it did matter a great deal, to Johnny and Laurence as well as to you because children were very much affected by having their parents achieve success later in the childrens' development. That holds for Anne's poetry, too. ...

I am glad that your dear friend Spetz is coming to be with us. ... Of course I expect you to stay with me. ... I will give you your side of the house and one room upstairs for Spetz.[40]

The misspelling of "Spatz" was probably not intentional, but it points to a fundamental problem with Porter's bringing Ilse Hamm to Great Spruce Head – namely, that Ruth Porter had hardly heard of Spatz, much less thought to invite her into her home for the entire summer.

The summer began with an unfortunate incident. As Porter described it to Paul Mattick, "On the way up here Anne and Jeremy went ahead by train, and the children and Spatz and I by car. In Portland we were run into by another car, and had to go to the hospital. Johnny had to have six stitches taken in his forehead, Laurence got a splinter over his eye, and cried so much and complained of pain so much that he was x-rayed, and was found to be perfectly sound. Spatz got a broken nose, and a filling knocked out of a tooth, and I escaped unharmed. But it was pretty awful all around."[41]

The sight of Porter standing beside Hamm as the mailboat arrived on Great Spruce Head must have been disturbing enough to Ruth and to Anne; to see the injured children must have been frightening. Hamm later remembered Porter's own anxiety about their arrival: "The summer we went to the island, Fairfield told me, 'You're going to hate my mother.' I said, 'She's your mother, not mine. It won't bother me.' But he was right. I didn't like her at all. She was impossible. She was cold and abrupt and in charge of everything and she didn't like me one bit. ... Mrs. Porter was very interested in keeping a tight hold on her son."[42]

Hamm found other aspects of island life equally uncomfortable. The perceived coldness of the Porter manner was not one which she could easily comprehend, and the fact that Ruth considered Hamm as much a servant as a guest led to near confrontations. Ruth Porter "was not one to make anyone feel welcome. She never once touched the babies, even when they started to cry." Ellen Auerbach, who was briefly a guest of the Porter family during that summer of 1941, had a similar recollection of Ruth Porter's chilly manner. "When we got to the island, Ruth Porter, the mother, was standing on the dock. I remember her as awe-inspiring. She literally made me tremble. She was rather severe, the way she stood, the way she had her hair pulled back. You couldn't say she was a warm person. In fact, she was very intimidating, and she didn't go out of her way to make others feel comfortable."[43]

The primitive nature of island living required an additional adjustment for these recent refugees, who equated cold and hunger with suffering rather than (as the Porters did) with health. Auerbach remembered that "there was an austerity to their life that was foreign to me. I prefer things to be cozy and *gemütlich*. Their life was very solemn, very austere. ... it was not a warm and cozy family."[44] Hamm agreed: "It was always cold in the house and there was never enough food. Never! Fairfield was always hungry and there was never enough for him to eat. It was almost a psychological hunger – whenever [Mrs. Porter] left the room, all of us would give whatever food was left on our plates to Fairfield."[45]

The summer was not, however, without pleasures and surprises. The greatest surprise came from Johnny Porter. As Anne Porter remembered it, "Johnny had suffered so many developmental problems that we never even attempted to teach him the alphabet. But one day that summer of 1941, he picked up Dostoyevsky's *House of the Dead* and simply started reading it aloud." For the rest of the summer, the Porters encouraged Johnny, then only seven years old, to read aloud from both *Moby Dick* and *The House of the Dead*. Meanwhile, Laurence Porter, aged five, demonstrated his own precocity, writing surreal and exceptionally musical poems.[46]

Still, Porter struggled with his feelings for Ilse Hamm for all of that summer. To have her so near and yet out of reach frustrated him terribly. Hamm, for her part, enjoyed flirting with Porter and spending time with him but was not interested in him sexually.

That summer I remember we read *Moby Dick*. Anne introduced me to poetry, Fairfield to literature. But Anne was so busy with [the baby] Jeremy. I would go swimming – everyone swam naked – and I suppose Fairfield would be watching me. But I always knew where the limits were, even if he didn't. ... I may have flirted with him, but I could never respond to Fairfield in a sexual way. I just did not have those feelings for him. I suppose I knew that he was in love with me, but I was young, and I suppose I was being selfish, though I didn't think of it as selfishness at the time. Young people never know they are being selfish . ...

Fairfield was so troubled psychologically he really could not express love. ... People tend to end up like their parents, in spite of themselves. It was a very troubled family. I came out of a troubled family. I had no desire to go back into one.[47]

Hamm had also begun to notice what she perceived to be a "mean streak" in Porter. "One person he could be very cold with was his mother. I saw it on the island. He simply didn't care what she felt. The entire family was like that ... there was no concern for feelings."[48] To some extent, the difference was cultural. The New England manner of the Porters was quite different from the manner of both Ilse Hamm and Ellen Auerbach, who came from warmer, more expressive German-Jewish backgrounds.

Another source of unhappiness among the Porters that summer came from the changing ways of island life since the death of James Porter. After James died, Ruth Porter had sold the *Hippocampus*. The shock of its loss was considerable. Anne Porter remembered a day when she, Ruth Porter, and Ilse Hamm were looking out over the water. "The *Hippocampus* appeared, sailing past the island with its new owners. Ilse saw it and she got excited and pointed it out to Ruth. There was nothing wrong in doing that, but I remember the moment. Ruth saw the boat and turned white. That was when I realized what [Ruth] was going through."[49]

Porter, meanwhile, was struggling with financial obligations. He had been under severe financial strain for over a year, and he now had another child. His limited income meant that he could no longer afford to send money to Paul Mattick. On July 4 he wrote his friend, "I cannot keep up my monthly pledge to *Living Marxism*. I will send you money when I can. My income is reduced about a third, and our expenses next year will not be correspondingly reduced. I have been trying first to wangle a scholarship out of [Hessian Hills], and second, a larger scholarship than they were willing to give. In a sense they have me in a spot, because I can not take my children out because Johnny's psychiatrist has to go on some more, and if we move anyway next June, it would make too many changes for Laurence."[50]

Mattick, who was already deep in debt to Porter, could hardly object to Porter's need to economize. Instead, he merely asked for more details about Hamm and about life on the island. Porter replied,

July 27, 1941   Ilse Hamm ... is small, very pretty, childlike in appearance, with thick black hair and little features.

... Mother [Ruth Porter] feels less lonely this year, but it may be really that she is growing used to being lonely. She feels a gap between herself and me and my family, but that may be because we live in the same house. She says she wishes she could understand the things Anne and I are interested in. I think it is hard on her that we are very friendly with Spatz, because though Spatz is considerate and kind, she is 10 years younger than Anne, and shares our interest rather than Mother's, which only can increase Mother's sense of isolation.[51]

Mattick, whose knowledge of (and interest in) Ruth Porter was limited, responded: "It was a good thing that Anne went ahead [on the railroad train] with the baby [and avoided the car accident]. I also hope that the broken nose of Ilse will not spoil her features. ... Thanks for the description of Ilse Hamm; I might now be able to dream about her in my loneliness. Please give her my best regards."[52]

Porter apparently did so, giving Hamm a copy of an article that Mattick had written and asking her opinion of it. Through this introduction, Ilse Hamm began corresponding with Paul Mattick.

Porter's feelings for Hamm remained strong when he returned to Westchester in the fall of 1941, settling with Anne and the children into yet another old house on a year lease, this time in the little town of Croton. But Hamm's preoccupations lay elsewhere: she had a German boyfriend who was in detention, and she was trying to help his parents escape from Germany; she was also trying to earn a living and had taken a post as a schoolteacher in suburban Queens. Then, starting in October 1941, she came down with a life-threatening case of encephalitis which briefly left her blind and hospitalized.

Porter's sense of rejection by Hamm, or of the impossibility of his situation with her, may have partially prompted his decision, in the fall of 1941, to travel alone to California. The ostensible reason for the trip was to locate better public education for his children than was available in New York and, once a good school was found, to find a home nearby suitable for purchase. Porter had always enjoyed house hunting, usually in the company of his wife, but now, after a summer with his family, he wanted some time away to sort through his feelings. Despite his personal misery, his letters home to Anne Porter from this trip are both tender and amusing; the couple seem to have been in agreement with each other about the need for Porter to travel and look at houses and schools.

Anne settled into yet another unfamiliar house with her infant and two boys and tried not to let her loneliness get the better of her. "It's fun, like dressing up, to live in an 1885 house with plaster fruit and flowers on the ceiling," she wrote her mother.[53] But her observation suggests an atmosphere of make-believe. To stay on alone in a rented home, awaiting the return of a husband who had fallen in love with another woman, must have been almost unbearably difficult. Hamm found the social isolation of a bourgeois life in Kew Gardens, Queens, difficult as well. So, while Porter was away, Anne invited Ilse to stay with her and the children. Ilse accepted her invitation, for she was lonely and enjoyed Anne's company. "The truth is," Hamm later observed, "I always liked Anne the better of the two."[54]

9

Househunting and a "Bivouac"

Porter did not have any friends in California when he traveled there in 1941 to look for schools and a home, but through Paul Mattick he had been given the name of Kenneth Rexroth, a poet, painter, critic, and fan of *Living Marxism*.[1] Rexroth offered not only to host Porter in San Francisco but also to help him locate good school districts. The resulting brief acquaintance proved a pleasant diversion for Porter during a difficult period of his life.

Like the Porters, Rexroth had strong political opinions and held Christian-derived beliefs in ethical activism. Porter recognized him as a kindred spirit, writing Anne, "Yesterday I met Kenneth Rexroth, who is thin, tall, with a moustache and longish hair and a raconteur something like Jack Wheelwright: that is he acts out his stories with gestures and wiggles and vocal imitations, and like Jack he knows much about many things, and he paints good abstract pictures (Jack might have) and he is prejudiced and firm in his opinions, together with complete tolerance for 'any disagreement.' "[2]

Porter's next letter to his wife gave a more guarded assessment:

undated   I have [rarely] heard such a flow of filthy language and dirty anecdotes as from Rexroth. He tells these stories in male or mixed company, to men or women without any embarrassment or change in his manner. No one else talks that way. ... He talks in parables I can't fathom ... if you ask for an explanation, he doesn't come up, he just swims off sideways under water. ...

I think Kenneth Rexroth is lonely. He says almost all intellectuals are Stalinist. ... He has read seemingly as much as Paul [Mattick] and [Fritz] Henssler and he has no one to talk to about it – or he reads a new idea by [Dwight] MacDonald in P[artisan] R[eview] & he feels dissatisfied because he knows where it comes from and knows where it leads – but MacDonald hasn't caught up yet. ... But he loves mountain climbing and swimming, and he couldn't get the combination anywhere else [but San Francisco].

The Rexroths – Kenneth and Marie – did their best to point out the schools and neighborhoods that were best for children. Porter liked San Francisco, disliked Oakland, and thought Marin County prettiest of all, but sensed that all the areas were culturally and intellectually as barren as Winnetka, and he was quickly discouraged. Rexroth seemed to Porter a living example of the dangers of social and intellectual isolation. As his visit drew to a close, Porter observed to Anne, "I like Marie Rexroth better than Kenneth, who is kind and so forth, but his caustic despair, or bitterness, or hatred, or misanthropy depresses me. He makes me feel like a Hollow Man."[3]

During Porter's trip west, he corresponded not only with his wife but also with Ilse Hamm (Anne Porter also shared parts of his letters to her with Hamm). Porter's letters to Hamm have not survived, but he saved her responses to them until the end of his life. Hamm posted a sympathetic letter to Porter from the Porter home in Croton, where she was visiting: "I was so glad to get your letter yesterday – I've been thinking of you and wondering how things were ... It all seems so discouraging and I just hope there'll be still a place you can find with a good school, where people aren't quite like Rexroth and the houses, smell and atmosphere are the kind of thing you'd be able to live in."[4] Hamm also voiced a political sentiment that Porter, too, must have been feeling that autumn: "I don't think the revolution is going on now at all! Furthermore – it doesn't matter at all. If there *had* been a revolution all [the] confusion and destruction [of the war in Europe] wouldn't have been necessary."[5]

Disappointed by San Francisco, Porter briefly considered living farther south. He wrote Anne, "Sunday though it rained [the Rexroths] drove me down the Peninsula, which has one of those incredible coasts of high slopes down to wild sand beaches. ... [Rexroth and I] had a violent argument ... about 'modern' or 'progressive' education ... we ended the argument rather good friends."[6] Sadly, nothing south of San Francisco seemed to hold much promise for Porter; even Monterey seemed spoilt: "The few historical houses are like Pennsylvania stone houses. I saw from the outside one that was for sale, in a nice yard, which had been tampered by some damned artist and I suspect ruined. Artists ruin everything they touch. They are utterly without taste."[7] Porter's indictment of artists in this statement is odd, for he seems not to be thinking of himself as an artist, or else including himself in this expression of disgust. But the trip to California had been a desperate attempt to envision a new life for himself, and as the trip drew to a close, Porter may well have been in despair, for the idea of a life in California had proved a mirage.

Porter returned home from a trip of nearly six weeks at the end of November to the enormous relief of his wife and children. He found a letter waiting there from Paul Mattick requesting more financial assistance. Porter's response was characteristically generous and, for a man who rarely spoke of his feelings about money, revealing:

You say, the relationships with people always suffer, as soon as money enters. Probably this is so. But in our relationship money was there at the beginning, and it was a constraint, and probably [always] will be. If I help you a little, it lessens at least my own feeling of constraint, though it may increase yours. Also I do not have a very possessive feeling about my money, because it is like the rain, I never did anything about it, neither to make it, nor to enhance it. About 12 years ago friends of mine told me I used my money as a sort of cotton padding against the world. But I sometimes have a bad conscience about it, maybe because of the contrast between my ideological and my actual upbringing. This however is disappearing as I have more people in some way dependent upon me.[8]

Though Porter had little money to spare, in part because of the great expense of keeping Johnny at Hessian Hills, he sent Mattick what he could.

Within two weeks of Porter's return, the Japanese bombed Pearl Harbor, and the United States declared war. Though Porter had long known that a war was coming – a war which he considered to be the inevitable result of capitalist imperialism and which he had hoped could be stopped through the organized rebellion of the working masses (the theme, after all, of his mural *Turn Imperialist War into Civil War*), he was unable to remain philosophical about world events. The strain of his feelings was such that he began for the first time to feel a distance from Paul Mattick, whose detachment regarding the war was a committed expression of his belief: namely, that the enemy was not fascism so much as a rival form (or forms) of capitalism. Porter wrote his friend and mentor, "The war makes me feel uneasy and unhappy. I can not get to feel as objectively impartial as *Living Marxism* seems to. I wish the Germans would be defeated."[9] He did everything he could to help his German refugee friends, including writing letters of recommendation on behalf of Hamm and the Auerbachs to enable them to travel, since as enemy aliens their movements were now being restricted by the U.S. government.

Porter, meanwhile, after asking his wife to consider living with Hamm in "a triangle way" (a request she said she did not think she could manage),[10] announced to his wife that December that he had proposed to Hamm and that she had accepted him and that he wanted a divorce.

Anne said, "I went to Ilse and told her I didn't want anything and that I wouldn't make problems about the children. I didn't know what I was going to do – sponge off my parents, I guess – but I wasn't going to stand in their way."[11] Hamm claimed, however, that Porter had never asked her to marry him and that she certainly had never agreed, because she was already engaged to Paul Mattick. As she recalled many years later, "I think that the reason why Anne thought Fairfield had proposed to me and that I'd accepted and that he was leaving her for me was that Fairfield had told her so. ... He was never mean to me, but I saw it in his treatment of other people, and so did Paul. He was very cold and very angry, particularly towards Anne."[12]

In early 1942, Paul Mattick had come to New York to give a series of talks at the Institute for Social Research. Porter proudly introduced his friend around New York. "Fairfield was happy in introducing Paul Mattick to Stieglitz and Alex Haberstroh and having them like each other very much."[13]

During the same trip, however, Mattick had contacted Hamm, with whom he had been corresponding for some time. The two made a date. Mattick, who had parted with his first wife, Frieda, was lonely, and as Hamm remembered, he "was looking for a woman, any woman ... I remember we had a terrific fight about George Grosz. Paul was talking about [the] beautiful new paintings [Grosz] had been making since coming to the States. I said Grosz was a sellout. The fight went on for hours. He was going up to stay a week with the Porters, and he came back one day later. After that, we never separated. I didn't think it was going to be a lasting relationship at all, and neither did he, but it was. ... He stayed in New York until I was ready to go with him back to Chicago."[14]

No surviving letters by Porter record his feelings of betrayal upon learning that Mattick, whose work he had long helped to support, and Hamm, whom he had helped in many ways, had become lovers (fig. 21). But for a man who had already voiced the opinion that the only reason people liked him was because he had money, the news must have been personally devastating. According to his wife, Porter wrote a long series of angry, accusatory letters to Mattick, which he showed her – "he was very open about the whole thing."[15] Hamm, too, remembered Porter's anger: "I was in love with Paul. And this made Fairfield very angry, yes. He said he hated Paul and had slashed the portrait he'd done of Paul. How do I know? I know because [Porter] told me. Really – a grown man, slashing a painting! This is not grown-up behavior. But that was how Fairfield was."[16]

Within a few months of receiving the news that Hamm and Mattick were lovers, Porter learned of another more significant tragedy. Ruth Porter, who had begun feeling ill, entered the hospital in May 1942 for what her doctor considered routine exploratory surgery. During the procedure, which was conducted by a relative, she died on the operating table. Whether Porter returned

21
Paul Mattick and Ilse Hamm Mattick on the beach at Lake Michigan, summer 1943. Photographer unknown. Courtesy Ilse Mattick.

to Chicago immediately to settle the estate and attend a brief memorial service held by Ruth's friends on June 7 is not certain (a pamphlet of the service remained in his papers).[17] At any rate, there was no interment; Ruth's ashes, like her husband's, went unclaimed.

Porter's psychological condition was fragile. With no plans for the future, uncertain whether his marriage could possibly survive, grieving for the mother with whom he had recently experienced a difficult summer, and feeling like a failure as a father, husband, lover, and artist, he began to fall apart. He sent his wife and the children off to Anne Porter's parents' summer home in Wareham, on Buzzards Bay, took a furnished room in Manhattan at 141 East Fifty-third Street, and stayed there alone to think. At the urging of the Auerbachs, he considered psychoanalysis[18] and meanwhile read Freud and Karen Horney.

Porter had made no formal agreement to separate from his wife, but the rest of his family were soon aware that the couple had parted ways. Anne wrote her husband that "Nancy [Porter's sister] wrote me a very warm comforting letter, much of it about you, & I want to answer and tell her everything, if you don't mind. But you tell me if you do mind." Porter responded, "Tell Nancy anything you like, as much or as little, whatever you will."[19] He continued to confide his unhappiness to his wife, writing, in another letter, "I saw Albert [Friend] in town & he made me feel that all my life since 1929 was just a fantasy. But I *don't like* this feeling, as you don't like my imagining, as you say, that you don't exist. ... Life [here] is very private & lonely & Robinson Crusoe-ish, but I get a funny kind of satisfaction out of it. With my love to you and the boys."[20]

As the summer progressed, Porter's moods varied. At one point he wrote his wife,

1942   Thanks for your nice letter. I am getting to enjoy my room, it feels like home, though all I do here is loll on the couch and daydream, or read Karen Horney, *New Ways in Psychoanalysis* (I finished *The Neurotic Personality*) or play chess, or try to think about painting. ...I think one trouble with me, that is, a basic and ancient trouble, is simply puritanism and adolescent sex frustration or something quite classical and according to the old man. But I like Horney, she does not impress me as [being as] full of non-sequiturs as Freud is, non-sequiturs which assume that if two things are coincidental, the biological one is original. He is really mechanistic and very much like my father. It is curious that Father would not have understood this. Freud is so like what he attacks. Horney is more in line with my prejudices or assumptions, that is, she says the character structure is what causes coincidence of events in sexual, and in the laymen's sense, non-sexual fields. It really relaxes me to read her, and even Denby's conservative pessimism relaxes me, and so does writing letters.

Bill de Kooning has painted some surpassingly beautiful abstractions – one in pink and yellow, with a blue window, which expresses my delight in June at the island – the blue for the sky and water, the yellow for the Indian paintbrushes and the pink for the way you feel at the seacoast. But de Kooning him-self, though I like him, makes me feel uneasy, perhaps envious, perhaps guilty that I don't paint. Also I feel I am interrupting him, and that he is poor and I am rich.

... Give all the little boys my love, kiss them for me. [21]

By early July, Anne had decided not to stay in Wareham. Her sister Katharine had agreed to take care of the three boys while she traveled down to New York to live with Porter in his furnished room. "He was quite willing for me to stay with him and no matter what, we were never physically estranged from one another. I did go job-hunting though, knowing he might someday leave us." [22]

At some point, Anne returned to Wareham, and Porter traveled out to Chicago, where he visited Hamm and Mattick while seeing to the details of his mother's estate. "After his mother died, Fairfield came to visit me and Paul. I remember I said how sorry I was that she had died and that I hoped he would be okay. He said, 'Not at all. I concluded my relationship with her long ago.' It was such a cold, shocking thing to say, Paul had to get up and leave the room. I remember not knowing how to respond. Fairfield gave me a silver pin that had belonged to her – a Mexican silver pin. I still have it." [23]

Porter was not altogether direct with his wife about his plans. Anne Porter, as the summer drew to a close, wrote her husband from Wareham to mention a recent discovery: "Edward [Fairfield's brother] wrote a note about business & said at the end 'I've seen your new home & like it better than the one at Croton ... ' & I didn't even know we had a new home or anything about it, and I still don't know." In his desire to rise out of his depression, Porter, who was due to receive a lump sum of money from his mother's estate, had begun looking once again for a new home, perhaps as a way of sheltering the inherited capital from taxation. He answered Anne tersely on August 25: "I bought [a] house at 312 E. 52 for $13,250. But work has to be done, and it won't be ready until October 10 or so." He did not say directly whether he expected Anne and the children to join him in the new house. "When I left [Chicago] because of house business, I felt very low because of the old trouble. I hadn't wanted to ... I had wanted to see Spatz [Ilse Hamm]. ... I have to hang around [Manhattan] until my insurance policy is cashed through the Chicago office. Then I would like to come out to Wareham on a weekend. I don't know what to do with my busted life. But New York is better than the ache that is Chicago." [24]

Anne Porter stayed in Wareham with just the children and the cook, Margaret Bumpus, for company after September first. Everyone else was leav-ing, "& it will be funny here with Margaret the cook at one end of this big class conscious house & me at the other." But the large former hunting lodge which had been built by Anne's maternal grandfather was too isolated and too exposed to the elements for autumn habitation. When the peninsula on which the house stood was hit by a tropical storm, Anne Porter wrote her husband,

"The trees and everything are ravaged and the lawn is all covered with sand & weeds and I guess I am like [Laurence], I feel more at home in it like this than when there were lawns with people mowing them etc. ... I still feel rotten [about our separation] but I can somehow kick it aside & enjoy myself – it's a little like an unpaid bill. ... I'm off the word 'love' for the moment in any context but I would kiss you if you were here or vice versa."[25]

Leaving Wareham, Anne and the children moved briefly to Boston, where they stayed on a floor of her parents' winter home at 3 Exeter Street, a tall, narrow single-family residence in the Back Bay. The awkwardness of explaining the separation to others is manifest in a letter she wrote Porter after arriving: "Barbara [Anne's sister] invited me to dinner with Eliot [Porter]. I think Eliot was embarrassed to see me but anyway I'll invite Eliot & Aline [his wife] & the Kennedys & Barbara this weekend for a party when you come."[26]

Anne did not stay in Boston for long. By the end of the fall of 1942, Porter and his wife and children were once again living together under one roof, though with the understanding that their marriage might be winding down. Porter's interest in Ilse Mattick had not disappeared; he continued to spend time with the Matticks when they moved back to New York, and attempted to make love to her through the late 1940s. Porter and his wife nonetheless continued to know each other intimately during this period, as they did throughout their marriage.[27]

The purchase of a house was something new for the Porters, who had changed rented residences at least ten times in the previous decade. They had never experienced the sense of permanence and security that owning a home can bring, but unfortunately their new town house had not been purchased by Porter in an attempt to put down roots. For over a decade, Porter had been searching the New York countryside for a nineteenth-century farmhouse in which to settle, and he still intended to live in the country. With the war, however, life in New York was more convenient, and in any case the money which came to him from his parents' estate needed to be safeguarded against the depredations of income tax. So the house at 312 East Fifty-second Street was merely a financial investment during a period of national instability and personal indecision. Anne Porter later described it as a "bivouac."[28]

The plain four-storied brownstone had a kitchen and dining room on the ground floor, a living room and master bedroom on the main floor, and on the second floor two bedrooms for the two youngest boys, facing a converted bedroom in which Porter intended to paint. The fourth floor held Johnny's bedroom and two others which were to be rented out. Spacious and comfortable, the house also had a small backyard, which, while hardly a garden, was suitable for the needs of children and pets. The house had previously belonged to the singer and comedian Eddie Cantor, and for the first years of the Porters' residency, people occasionally came to the door demanding to meet the famed vaudevillian and movie actor.

At least one close friend who visited the house in 1942 remembers the extraordinary "colors of the walls. They were painted either a cool milk blue or a raw bluey pink, colors that I had not seen on bedroom walls before."[29] Using the home as a place in which to experiment with paint, Porter was able to experience new sensations of color and light, which eventually found their way into his work. But apart from some major repair work which Porter completed before Anne and the children joined him in late 1942, the house was not decorated in any conventional sense. Furniture had come to Porter through his aunts and his parents. Books and paintings were present in abundance. But not until three years later, in 1945, did Porter set about hanging his art collection. Until then, the house in New York remained, like the marriage, in a state of suspension. "I remember thinking it was a crazy thing to do, considering the state of our marriage," Anne Porter recalled. "We were breaking up, and we were buying a house."[30]

By the end of fall, Porter was also looking for a full-time job for the first time in his life. His income was shrinking, the cost of maintaining his family was growing, and the purchase of the brownstone had limited his access to capital. Moreover, despite being a father, Porter felt that he might be drafted. On New Year's Eve, Anne wrote her mother, "Fairfield is taking an aptitude test at the YMCA in case he gets a job if he isn't painting. It seemed necessary for a while, then we got some sort of an inheritance from Chicago which has taken away some of my anxiety about how to afford what Johnny needs." The aptitude test had amusing results. According to Anne Porter, her husband "scored 100 percent on science and very low on art."[31]

Porter found employment with the company of the famed industrial designer Walter Dorwin Teague at 444 Madison Avenue. As Porter later told a friend, "During the war I worked for the navy, though as an industrial designer who had navy contracts: it was very boring and futile work, and as soon as VJ day came I quit. I was never drafted because I was already doing something that the government considered useful enough: if they had drafted me they would have had to pay me to do what my boss paid me to do – why not let well enough alone?"[32]

After starting off with a dull job in the cataloguing department, Porter became "a draftsman on the staff ... [designing] for the Bureau of Ordnance, Navy Department."[33] He was soon a valued employee; while working for Teague he helped design a "shell-case ejector for shipboard cannon."[34] When, toward the end of the war, he grew bored with drawing gun mechanisms, he was moved to the company's model shop.

Employment was good for Porter in several ways. It removed him from his domestic environment, thereby easing the many frictions of day-to-day family life and perhaps helping reverse the deterioration of his marriage. It also gave him a valuable insight into the nature of the average working life, thereby alleviating some of the paralyzing guilt and self-consciousness he had always felt as a non-wage-earning member of society. As he later explained,

I had always felt a little guilty about being an artist, so to speak, and having no connection with the real world. And I saw working for this person [Walter Darwin Teague], who was considered to have a connection to the real world and engaged in a really useful activity, that his activity was no more socially significant than if he'd owned, say, a one-thousand-foot yacht and employed one hundred people to run it around. It was just his own entertainment. It didn't really matter. He would redesign things that were perfectly well designed already ... so after that I never felt guilty again ... I realized that probably a great deal of business in practical life is just as whimsical and personal as this. And why not do what you like to do?[35]

Throughout his years of employment, Porter saw his political friends and involved himself in intellectual speculation on the course of world events. Porter's friend Edith Schloss, a German-Jewish refugee, remembered one such gathering at the Porter home in the mid-1940s. The subject of conversation that evening was whether the Germans had constructed a "doomsday device" and, if so, whether they intended to use it on the world. (Unbeknownst to Porter, one of his brothers-in-law, the Harvard physicist Francis Birch, was at that moment sequestered in Los Alamos, New Mexico, participating in the creation of the atomic bomb. Birch's wife, Anne's sister Barbara, later said that "it seemed the thing to do at the time.")[36]

Edith Schloss specifically recalls the presence of Paul and Ilse Mattick and the absence of Anne Porter, who, having prepared dinner and put the children to bed, was leading an independent social life:

[I first met the Porters with] Heinz Langerhans [and] Leo Friedman [at their] one family house in the Fifties off Third Avenue ... Fairfield had opened the basement door into the kitchen for us and led us into the dining room at the back. [After dinner] we all went upstairs to the living room and the men went on with the political conjectures they had begun at dinner. ... Langerhans, the friend I was living with ... had been locked up in several concentration camps.

Paul was an outspoken man of great vitality and imagination, chunky features and brutal honesty. He was downright ugly, squarebuilt but not tall, the picture of the working class man. He was self-educated. No one could resist his blunt wit and ultimate good nature. He was much older than his new girlfriend, the relentlessly flirtatious Ilse, who he could not keep from touching all the time, even when immersed in the deepest political exposition. Both had come from Chicago to Queens for a limitless stay in the parlour of a little semi-detached house of a member of their group, the music copyist Boelke.[37]

Porter's affiliation with the Council Communist movement had always been tenuous, but his break with Mattick over Ilse Hamm (now Ilse Mattick; by her own account, despite indifference to the institution of marriage, "a legal mess compelled us to marry")[38] was not so deep that he had ceased to respect Mattick as either an intellectual or a source of information on recent developments in Europe. Rather, with the progress of the war, interest in the possibilities of Council Communism dwindled, just as, throughout the Marxist culture of New York, intellectuals abandoned the revolutionary movement – some taking more moderate leftist positions, others veering toward the extreme right. According to Ilse Mattick, "There was nothing going on. The group hadn't broken up, exactly – we were all still friends, but there was nothing going on politically."[39]

Despite a societywide falling-away from leftist political enthusiasms, Porter and his wife continued to attend socialist meetings. They did, however, regard these get-togethers with growing skepticism. As Anne Porter wrote her mother at the end of the war, "I go to meetings, held by the magazine 'Politics' whose editor we know and listen to papers on 'Socialism Should Be Utopian And Not Scientific,' etc. ... So few people seem really to discuss, or question, they seem only, as Fairfield says, 'waiting for a chance to say something rude.'"[40]

A decade later, Thomas B. Hess, editor of *Art News*, commented that with the end of the American communist experience, "there was nothing to do but paint. The self-directed community became self-oriented. Art replaced revolution in its eschatology. It was a moment of complete dedication to the revolutionary vocation of painting, a time for inspiration, for changing a way of life and a style. Never before in painting had art itself so preoccupied the artist."[41]

At that point in the war, however, Porter's main preoccupation was not with painting but with the Allied destruction of Europe and the spreading news of Nazi and Stalinist atrocities. Edith Schloss recalled, "One day Fairfield opened *The New York Times* and exclaimed, 'They've gone and bombed the Eremitani chapel in Padua, Giotto's chapel will probably be next!' We painters became very upset. Anne [Porter] could not understand why we made such a fuss, [why] the loss of human lives reported daily in the papers did not move us nearly as much as the loss of an old piece of art."[42]

The Allies had destroyed the Church of the Eremitani in Padua, annihilating the Mantegna frescoes Porter had so admired there in 1931. Knowledge that Giotto's masterpiece, the interior of the Scrovegni (or Arena) Chapel just a few hundred feet away, had escaped bombardment did little to calm him. The cathedral at Coutances, which had made such an impression on him in 1927, also suffered great damage by the Allies in July 1944, and Dresden, which Porter had visited and loved during his travels in Europe in 1932, was bombed flat on February 14, 1945. Porter's awareness that his own country was destroying the irreplaceable artistic heritage of Europe was a shock; it increased his distrust of big government and bureaucrats.

During the war years and the years immediately following, Porter's feelings for Ilse Mattick were slow to cool. As she recalled, "Fairfield spent a lot of time just hanging around us. Paul didn't mind that so much as I did. ... After Paul and I moved in together, Fairfield kept coming over, even after we had the baby. And when little Paul was growing up, Fairfield would buy him expensive presents – a little tin knight on horseback, for instance. Well, this sort of thing drove me crazy. I felt like he was trying to buy his way into our affections. It made me very angry. ... Paul was quite indulgent of Fairfield ... I often wished Fairfield would leave, but Paul wouldn't tolerate it."[43]

Porter, having reached an agreement of sorts with his wife that they would pursue independent paths, was attempting to make a go of his Marxist-inspired ideas about free love. Anne, in response, thought she should leave. "I didn't want to leave but thought I should offer. F. said two things, that 'he didn't want to have *nobody*' and that he wanted his children, and I sort of belonged with them. ... I said, 'You mean I belong with them like an old nursemaid?' and he said something like, 'Well, yes.'"[44] Anne Porter, though saddened by this response, chose to remain (fig. 22).

Within a year, however, she found that she had become attracted to another former member of the Council Communist group. Realizing the implications of having feelings for this man,[45] who was already married, she asked him not to come back to her house any more, not understanding that her words would be taken as an invitation. The man, who was moved by her situa-

22
Anne Porter in the backyard of the house at 312 East Fifty-second Street, circa 1944. Photo by Ellen Auerbach. Courtesy Mrs. Fairfield Porter.

tion and attracted to her, told her that he wanted to become her lover. The two went to Porter to discuss the idea with him. Porter's response was, according to his wife, that "it would only be a little inconvenient, 'like the chauffeur going out with the housemaid,' but otherwise it would be all right."[46] She later came to understand that her husband had other feelings about the affair but was unable to express them.

Both Porter and his wife were looking for a creative solution to their marital difficulties; neither wanted a divorce. Reflecting upon her affair in later years, Anne Porter observed, "It wasn't a good thing. ... But even now I don't perceive it as an infidelity. We'd agreed upon it. We'd decided to live this way, and during this time F. himself had a brief affair with someone we both knew. I certainly didn't count this against him as an infidelity."[47]

10

Living and Painting
in New York

The Porters' brownstone, despite its convenient location in midtown Manhattan, had its drawbacks for Porter, particularly in the location of his painting studio, just across the hall from his boisterous children. Indeed, the problem of reconciling his vocation to his duties as a parent had hardly been solved by the purchase of a home or by the taking on of a full-time job. By early 1944, Porter was looking at both office and residential space in which to set up a studio away from the children. He finally settled into an unfurnished room, far across town in Chelsea, at 116 West Twenty-first Street.[1]

Johnny Porter's problems persisted, adding to tension within the home. Porter habitually attempted to take his son's erratic behavior in stride, as when, writing one of his last letters to his mother, he noted, "Johnny actually hits Laurence, says, 'I will never!' when asked to do anything, threw a knife at Anne today, and is generally showing many signs of progress."[2] When they moved to Manhattan, both Porter and his wife still hoped Johnny would be able to live a normal life: they enrolled him at Emerson, which Anne Porter later described as a "progressive, 'we can handle it' type of school." By the mid-1940s, however, Johnny's psychiatrist, Dr. Edward Liss, "who was worried about the strain Johnny had been causing on the family,"[3] suggested that he spend the year with a woman named Sophie Lilienthal, who had once trained preschool teachers in a settlement house. She now lived full-time in Greenwich, Connecticut. Johnny stayed with her for a year. "Sophie devoted herself to him entirely," Anne Porter recalled. "She was very, very healing." Johnny came back "very much improved."[4]

Though their finances had declined during the Depression and with the onset of war, the Porters did not yet face severe financial hardship; apart from the special care Johnny Porter required and the cost of the children's education, their needs were few; indeed, throughout Porter's life, his friends and acquaintances remarked on the simplicity of food and dress in the Porter household, and strangers often mistook Porter and his wife for servants or caretakers.[5] The couple no longer had household help; by the time of the move to Fifty-second Street, Anne Porter was doing the majority of the housework, including cooking, cleaning, and dishwashing. The Porters were also restricted in their movements due to wartime shortages so that, following the unhappy summer of 1941, they were not able to return to Great Spruce Head Island until the summer of 1946.

The question of where to go in the summer became problematic when, in winter of 1942, Anne's family's summer home in Wareham was struck by lightning, caught fire, and burnt to the ground, with only the servants' wing left standing (this remnant was eventually made over into a new, vastly diminished vacation home, Windmill House). Since Anne and the children no longer had access to Wareham, Porter sought them a summer rental.

After much looking, he was able to secure a "big 100% non-picturesque house"[6] in Sayville, Long Island, "an hour and fifteen minutes from New York by train and just fifteen minutes from Great South Bay."[7] Porter, alone in the brownstone during the week, joined his family on weekends, using one of the rooms in the house as a painting studio. During this period, which was still one of marital unhappiness, Anne Porter "kept telling him things would get better"[8] both for their relationship and for his painting.

After Anne Porter began her affair in 1944, the couple shared the responsibilities of housekeeping and childcare but went their own ways in the evening. Eventually, though, as Anne Porter recalled, "F. began to get angry and upset about the affair, [so] I chose to end it. Perhaps psychoanalysis was helping me to see who it was I really loved. And to go on, I would have had to lie to F. and I didn't want to. Most of all, I sensed that with [the other man] something like true love was missing and always would be. But with F. though so very much was missing, some tiny spark was there. Something like a bond or like friendship, but indescribably more than friendship, it made me not want to lie to him or to leave him and I believed it would grow. It did grow and was the strength of our marriage."[9]

By 1945 the house on Fifty-second Street was furnished. As part of a general housecleaning, which coincided with preparations to accommodate new tenants on the top floor, Porter washed the walls of his home ("cheaper than paint and not so smelly," Anne wrote)[10] and hung all the pictures, including, as a centerpiece, the portrait of Anne from the early thirties by Porter's Russian friend Simeon Braguin, entitled *Young Woman from Tcherborn, Massachusetts.*[11] Porter's early copy of El Greco's *St. Anne, the Virgin, and the Baby Christ* hung in the kitchen downstairs.[12]

A 1945 insurance assessment combined with a memoir by a close family friend, Edith Schloss, provide a rare glimpse of the small art collection that hung in Porter's home at this time. Along with Porter's student copy, made in Florence, of the pradella of SS. Cosmas and Damiano (referred to in the valuation as "a copy of Pessellino's 'Flagellation of Two Priests in the Presence of the Crowned Head'") there was de Kooning's *Composition of Three Classical*

Female Figures, One with Pitcher Vase, described by Schloss as "a mysterious long oil of a procession of starry-eyed ladies [actually Elaine de Kooning] carrying odd vases. It was painted in the same pinks and blues of the walls of this house but there were chinks of sour green and orange as well. The figures were unfinished, half wiped away, and everything looked vaguely ritualistic, a bit like a weathered Pompeiian mural. But the clash of colors and the ambiguity were completely modern."[13] Another painting was by Orozco, *Vigil, Abstract Composition*, which Schloss described as "a row of armed Mexican peasants with large hats and cartridge belts – full of sickle-shaped repeats."[14] A John Marin watercolor which Porter had bought in installments from Stieglitz, *Movement – Cape Split, Maine* (1936), pictured "a jagged shape – of a sailboat riding an agitated sea against chunky islands grown with trees like hair brushes and a translucent sunset."[15] Other articles listed in the valuation appeared over and over in Porter's interior paintings of the late forties, fifties, and sixties: an Audubon *Birds of America* folio print of a raven; two Japanese woodcut prints (a number of which had been bought by Ruth Porter from Isamu Noguchi's mother, whom she had known at Bryn Mawr); many odd lots of silver with assorted different family initials; several Oriental carpets; and a great deal of eighteenth-century American furniture.

Within two years of this assessment, more work had been introduced into the Porter home, as is evident in Porter's 1947 painting of his wife, entitled *Anne at the Fireplace*, which exists in another version, entitled *Anne at 312 E. 52nd Street* (1947). Anne's framed letter from Emily Dickinson to Thomas Wentworth Higginson appears in the image, along with a series of photographs by Ellen and Walter Auerbach, the little de Kooning, and the Audubon print of the raven. In the foreground of the painting stands a rosewood tea table made for the couple by Porter's brother Edward. The depiction of Anne Porter is uncharacteristically racy (Anne described herself to her mother as looking "very alert and mischievous"). This composition of a young woman reclining in a furnished interior is perhaps the earliest suggestion of the great Vuillard-inspired interior paintings Porter would create in the next decade. But even now, Porter was turning his attention, pictorially, toward family and home. During 1942–47, nine of the thirty-one surviving paintings by Porter are images of his wife and children, usually shown within the house.

The Porters continued throughout the forties to welcome guests into their home for stays both long and short, but until they moved to the country again in 1949, they also had tenants. The first lodgers were a friend, Ted Mabely, and his acquaintance, referred to simply as the Colonel. By the mid-1940s the Porters were defying neighborhood conventions by renting the upstairs rooms to two black women, Roni McLeod and Lydia Tate, then studying to be teachers at Teachers' College, Columbia University. Through these two, who became lifelong friends, the Porters received early "sensitivity training,"[16] Anne Porter learning, for example, that "blacks did not appreciate being called Negroes and

Negresses,"[17] for she had (like other poets, including Wallace Stevens) used the word *negress* in one of her poems.

At the same time, according to Anne Porter, the downstairs portion of the house existed for a while as a sort of commune, with people coming and going as they pleased, often, unfortunately, taking things of value when they departed. Among many other items, Anne Porter's second wedding ring disappeared during this period (the first had slipped off her hand while she was digging carrots in her garden in Westchester).

As the war ended and with it the job with Walter Dorwin Teague, Porter turned again to his painting. During 1945 and 1946, at the suggestion of his old muralist friend Edward Laning, Porter began studying at the Parsons School of Design with Jacques Maroger, who before the outbreak of war had been a restorer at the Louvre. Maroger had in the course of his work developed a painterly medium which was reputed to be that of the Old Masters. The medium could be used to prime canvas but was mostly used in conjunction with oil paints to create paint that stayed put but was slow to dry and so could be reworked with ease. When Porter began working with Maroger, the medium was not commercially available and had to be cooked up at home out of one part lead carbonate, one part beeswax, and ten parts linseed oil. But a later, simpler recipe from Maroger which Porter used with equal success called for ten parts raw linseed oil boiled together with one part white lead, which was then mixed with equal parts mastic varnish and strained.[18] Boiling and decanting the noisome substance took up significant amounts of time and energy in the Porter home. "Fairfield and his painter friends talk[ed] late into the night about technique," Anne Porter recalled. "There wasn't the preoccupation with career or money or celebrity you have today. Nobody had any money. Egg, oil, varnish … all anybody talked about was technique."[19] The house, according to Laurence Porter, stank "of molten lead, linseed oil and eggs."[20]

The significance of Porter's use of Maroger's medium is open to debate. Many artists who knew Porter in the 1950s and 1960s considered it to be a kind of artistic snake oil, and Porter's advocacy of it to be misguided, if not downright silly. In truth, Porter's interest in Maroger's medium corresponds to his larger interest during the late 1940s in painting techniques, particularly the European techniques that he had seen and admired in the works of Bonnard and Vuillard. Moreover, his letters make clear that his friendship with de Kooning had made him painfully aware of that artist's formal training – a training that Porter had never been able to undertake in America. "I had a feeling that I had never learned how to paint," Porter recalled. "It was very difficult. … Then when I [studied] with [Maroger] he showed me this medium. It seemed to be so easy, natural, that I stayed with it only for that reason."[21]

Porter's interest in Maroger's medium also demonstrates his broad-mindedness – use of Maroger's medium was hardly in the mainstream – and his enthusiasm for traditional materials and techniques. If Porter could not paint like Titian or Tintoretto or Veronese, he could at least paint with the same materials used by a Venetian Master.[22] The interest in time-tested artistic tradition which had led Porter to attempt fresco painting in the early 1930s also led Porter to Maroger.

Still, Porter had enough perspective on Maroger and his medium to see the folly of growing too deeply enamored of a technique. Maroger "measured everything by what he called 'the Medium.' And if you spoke of Goya he would say, 'Well, he didn't have the Medium.' And that was all he'd have to say about Goya. The last person he was interested in was Fragonard, because he did have the Medium."[23]

Perhaps the most significant aspect of Porter's use of the Maroger medium was the way it altered his technique. Porter

found, after the war, that his painting had become tight in a way he heartily disliked, a result, possibly, of the drafting board and very little time for his own work. Here the Maroger medium was a help: it was difficult to handle and, to quote Frank O'Hara [in O'Hara's 1955 *Art News* feature "Porter Paints a Picture"], "if it is fussed with or changed too much it gets rubbery and unpleasant." This is no longer true. He had to learn to go with the medium, to let it have its way and to use it as it could or would be used. An instance of what Pasternak somewhere wrote: that life, in order to accomplish its purposes, turns our attention from itself. Thus the challenge of the mulish medium to the conscious mind helped free the hand.[24]

After finishing his study with Maroger, Porter set up his easel in the Metropolitan Museum and began copying Tiepolo's *Adoration of the Magi*. A small work, approximately eighteen by twenty-four inches, the painting appears to be a quick sketch for a larger project. The energy in its brushstrokes suggests an affinity to de Kooning: both artists have a lush way with paint handling. The primary masses of color consist of a pinkish beige ground (the foreground and the column against which the Virgin and child are seated) offset by ivory white (a ruined arch) and a bright, pale blue (the sky). The brilliance of the sky comes in part from the way it stands off against the pinkish beige and in part from the white mixed into the bright blue, which adds extra brightness. It is a blue that can also be found in Sisley and Pisarro,[25] but Porter found it first in Tiepolo and sought to understand it through copying Tiepolo.

While at work in the Metropolitan, Porter had an encounter which took on the aspects of personal myth. He was accosted by an odd and unpleasant-looking man, "a little man with very, very bad breath,"[26] a "Belgian painter,"[27] later described as "a Frenchman with a Dutch name who said he had known Degas, Renoir, Bonnard, and Vuillard,"[28] who eventually introduced himself as Georges van Houten.[29] Van Houten, known in Europe simply as Georges Houten, had exhibited nudes and landscapes at the Salon des Independents in Paris beginning in 1910.[30] He told Porter, "You have light in your pictures. Most of those copyists don't have any light in them."[31] After some discussion, Porter decided to pay van Houten for a series of lessons.

Porter's main interest, both in the Tiepolo copy and in the cityscapes of the period, was with the specific task of capturing light in paint. Tiepolo painted skies which are perhaps the most light-filled in all of classical European painting, and Porter, recognizing the beauty of this light, which he described to James Schuyler as "modern light,"[32] sought something similar. The importance of light may have become clearer to Porter as he studied with the older painter, or he may simply have realized as he studied with van Houten that light and the portrayal of light were of importance to him in his painting. At any rate, Porter credited van Houten for his sudden and dramatic improvement as a painter.

After three lessons with van Houten (who then vanished), Porter began a series of paintings in which he sought to portray the light of the city. New York, with its brilliant sunshine and clear northern breezes, seemed to him to have some of the most beautiful light in the world, and he was painting, he believed, "New York disguised as Venice."[33] Part of his improvement came from the adoption of a new strategy. Earlier "I made the mistake of thinking that I could do everything later instead of at the beginning."[34] But by using a watercolorist's strategy of blocking out areas of color and light, Porter experienced a new "freshness and mystery." His paintings seemed "softer, less literal and more alive," according to his wife. "They express him better."[35]

Porter's interest in the sensual color was reinforced by the extraordinary exhibition, in 1948, of the work of Pierre Bonnard at the Museum of Modern Art. Another exhibition that year – of paintings from the Kaiser Friedrich Museum – left an equally deep impression, but for reasons that have less to do with the pure dazzle of color and light and painterly textures than with the psychology of pictorial composition. The paintings were by Velázquez, and they haunted Porter for years: quotations from Velázquez's imagery crop up in many of Porter's late paintings, most notably *The Mirror* (1966). As Porter later told an interviewer, "I admired [in the Velázquez paintings] what might be called understatement. Although I don't like that word, really. The impersonality – I don't know what word to use. He leaves things alone. ... He is open to it rather than wanting to twist it. ... I think there's more there than there is in willful manipulation. ... I used to like Dostoyevsky very, very, very much. Now I prefer Tolstoy, for the same reason ... he is like Velázquez for me ... he's open and also knows when it's unimportant to pay attention. Chekhov and Tolstoy have that quality."[36]

Porter once again used a literary analogy to express a psychological understanding of what makes a painting work. The Velázquez paintings referred to are a series of Infantas. From the way Porter describes them, he seems to suggest that Velázquez, like Chekhov or Tolstoy, has found a focus for his work in the illustration of an interior psychological moment of his subject. The subdued yet focused awareness common to all three artists – Tolstoy, Velázquez, Chekhov – began to appear in Porter's own work during the coming decade.

In the mid-1940s, Porter decided to enter psychoanalysis, a decision that had a remarkable effect both on his personal life and on his abilities as a painter. Porter's interest in psychoanalysis had evolved out of his many consultations over the years with doctors treating Johnny Porter; but the more persuasive influence was certainly that of his German and German-Jewish friends, particularly the Auerbachs, who felt that Porter's unhappiness (which manifested itself in depression, anger, selfish and asocial behavior) could be ameliorated, if not cured, by a course of psychoanalysis. In New York, interest in psychoanalysis was widespread among intellectuals, as Anatole Broyard recalled in his memoirs: "In New York City [in the mid-1940s] there was an inevitability about psychoanalysis. It was like having to take the subway to get anywhere. Psychoanalysis was in the air, like humidity, or smoke. You could almost smell it."[37]

After reading Freud and Karen Horney during his miserable summer of 1942, Porter began the difficult process of analysis. He soon left his first analyst, however, for his wife's, for Anne Porter, who was also being psychoanalyzed, was experiencing good results with Dr. Erich Kraft. Kraft, a student of Freud's in Vienna, had moved to New York at the beginning of the war. Financial records kept by the Porters during this period suggest that the amount of time spent in analysis by both Porters was significant, up to four sessions per week.[38]

In retrospect, Porter felt that his analysis had been helpful and worthwhile both to himself and to his work. He wrote:

May 16, 1974   My analysts were Freudians. For all the while I was being analyzed, I hardly ever heard of the terms associated with Freudian talk. If I should (I don't remember precisely doing so) have used any word like ego, superego, id, even words like repression, libido, unconscious, the analyst would ask what in particular I meant. I once did use the term that I had heard from an acquaintance who had had a Jungian analysis, namely, anima. The analyst asked, "Who is she? – Perhaps Moira?" (Because he seemed to find that patients take a rhyming word to take the place of another). ... I think that some of my ability as an art critic derives from my Freudian psychoanalysis. The doctors always particularized – one would never know that any two people were at all alike.

... My analyst went to my show and said, "Shall I tell you what I think, or are you not interested?" I told him I was very interested: this was because he was a sensitive and very intelligent man, and I knew that what he said would be both simple and aware, and free from any sort of fashionable jargon, but instead direct, and to the point – to his point, i.e., honest. (I once quoted in analysis Jimmy [Schuyler]'s translation of Dante's sestina: "I have reached, alas, the long shadow," and his reaction was, "Can you give me a copy?"). ...

My first analyst would say things like, "Some people like to fight." They both always turned everything into ordinary non-technical language.[39]

In an interview, Porter gave a more abstract evaluation of his psychoanalysis, stating that the lessons he had learned from psychoanalysis were related to discoveries he had made about himself through painting: "Once I was psychoanalyzed. And in psychoanalysis of course you follow your free associations without criticism. And what you get when you're all through (or you're never all through) is that you get yourself. This is your shape. And you get it by following – not by ordering the thing or using your head – but by being unconscious ... what *is* the form is what is real and that is something that you can't get outside of in psychoanalysis or in art."[40]

While it would be difficult to prove a causal relation between Porter's psychoanalysis and the improvement in his painting ability, the chronological coincidence is striking, particularly since the very thing that had most interested Porter about Tolstoy, Chekhov, and Velázquez – the artist's surrender to impersonality, to leaving things alone – was the very sort of unconsciousness that Porter began to embrace in everyday life as a result of his psychoanalysis. In learning to surrender, Porter was not just achieving psychological relief; he was also learning to cultivate a psychological state which would become invaluable to his painting. "You get it by following – not by ordering the thing or using your head – but by being unconscious."[41] Porter treasured this state of openness and sought it for the rest of his life. In later years, he tried to induce it through different forms of meditation, including transcendental meditation and the yoga-like practice of *latihan*, often before starting to paint.

A more immediate and tangible result of Porter's work with psychoanalysis was his growing awareness of the enormous emotional pain that he had been suffering over the past decade. He also became aware that the future of his family was based, in no small way, on coming to a decision about Johnny Porter.

By now, Porter had been forced to admit to himself that his son was not getting any better. "Johnny grows more dignified and sweet-tempered all the time," he wrote his mother-in-law in 1947, "but the essential trouble remains. This is an inability to identify, which is the reason that he is irritating. He appeases people in order not to be bothered by their anger, but really he remains an egotist. He needs other people for their warmth and usefulness, but he doesn't know that he is of the same species."[42] Porter's certain knowledge of his son's great intelligence, combined with the difficulty of reaching him as a person, was a double heartbreak. Now he (and his wife) had to decide how to move on.

Through Porter's continuing struggle to gain medical exemptions on his taxes, many of Johnny Porter's medical documents have been preserved, including letters from different doctors testifying to Johnny's condition. We know from these documents that Porter discussed the future of his son with his analyst, because the analyst wrote one such letter, describing Johnny as "suffering since early years, if not from birth, from an organic nervous illness, possibly a schizophrenia."[43] Another specialist, Dr. Margaret Mahler, concurred with Dr. Kraft: "He is suffering from a chronic schizophrenic condition (*dementia prae-*

cox) with slight paranoid traits. The condition is of such long standing that much improvement or recovery cannot be expected."[44] (With the Porters themselves, Dr. Mahler had been blunter, telling them that their son would probably be reduced to a "vegetable" state by the age of twenty.) Years later, diagnoses suggested that Johnny suffered not from schizophrenia but from autism. *Autism* is a vague, umbrella-like term for a set of cognitive disorders of neurobiological origin which interfere with an individual's ability to process perceptual information, and so affect physical, social, and language skills. Experts on autism now agree that Porter and his wife did well to work with their son intensely all through early childhood, which may help explain why Johnny, far from descending into Dr. Mahler's expected vegetable state, eventually lived a well-adjusted life under managed care.

Still, during their time in New York, Johnny had become a medical, financial, and personal liability to a family on the brink of falling apart, and Porter and his wife needed to make a decision about him. Sending Johnny away was difficult and traumatic, but it was also necessary to the survival of the family, and so it was done. After his year with Sophie Lilienthal in Greenwich, Johnny attended the Devereux School, an all-boy boarding school in Devon, Pennsylvania. The Porters consoled themselves with the knowledge that Johnny was in capable hands and that he would return frequently throughout the year for holidays and vacations, as indeed he did to the end of Porter's life.

Perhaps to console themselves over the departure of their son and perhaps also to enjoy the greater freedom that his absence now permitted them, the Porters began devoting more time to each other. By the late 1940s they had largely reconciled. They even went so far as to purchase, in 1946, a small house in Sand Brook, New Jersey, in the hope of moving there together with the children. (They sold it again when they were unable to find adequate public schooling in the neighborhood.)

Both Porter and his wife also seem to have recognized during this time that an active social life for Porter was good for their relationship and for his morale as he struggled, at forty, with a continuing lack of professional recognition. Anne was "glad" Fairfield would see friends on New Year's Eve. "He should have lots of parties, especially with other artists."[45] And with the end of the war, a more active social life was possible for everyone: through the G.I. Bill, large numbers of servicemen were taking advantage of tuition reimbursements to enroll in art schools and immerse themselves in bohemian culture, with its promise of good times, stimulating conversations, available women, and, of course, art. As a memoirist of the period said, "After a war, civilization feels like a luxury … Education was chic and sexy … [We] had a blind date with culture, and anything could happen."[46]

Along with their old photographer friends the Auerbachs, the Porters were now on intimate terms with (among many others) Rudy Burckhardt and

Edith Schloss, Edwin Denby, Willem and Elaine de Kooning, the Lanings, Isabel Bishop and her psychiatrist husband Harold Wolf, Milton Resnick, and Nell Blaine. In February 1947, Anne "gave one dinner party for five painters not counting Fairfield. He brought out his watercolors for them – he hasn't looked at the watercolors for a long time."[47] These get-togethers often served as group strategy sessions for artists struggling to make a living. After a long evening with the de Koonings featuring arguments over whether "architecture [should] be functional, and, do modern artists need a new metaphysics," Porter and Elaine de Kooning decided to make money by trying for portrait commissions and came up with the idea of having Anne pose for them "looking as society as I can manage."[48] Porter was buoyed up by Willem de Kooning, for while Porter "found it depressing not to be recognized," Anne Porter recalled, "he admired de Kooning's cavalier attitude about recognition, which was 'easy come, easy go.'"[49] Porter admired de Kooning for other, more important reasons as well. Chief among them was de Kooning's single-minded dedication to his own visionary style of abstract painting.

De Kooning had not always been an abstract painter. In 1916, at the age of twelve, he had been apprenticed to a Dutch firm of commercial artists while attending evening classes at an art academy. Emigrating to New York City in 1926, he worked as a freelance commercial artist; from 1935 to 1937 he had worked with the WPA; and in 1939 he had designed a mural for the Hall of Pharmacy at the New York World's Fair. By the late 1940s he was devoting himself to abstractions, both large and small, and during this crucial period, Porter bought not only the two small paintings mentioned in the household inventory of 1945 but another, major painting, the *Pink Lady* (circa 1944), which Porter referred to confusingly as the *Pink Woman* (1943).[50]

Edith Schloss recalled a moment in Chelsea during the 1940s:

One day when I was visiting Rudy Burckhardt at his studio, Fairfield came in from his studio next door. Bill [de Kooning] arrived too, unpacking a painting Fairfield wanted ... it was shiny paint smoothed on paper. It was small. It had green in it, but mostly there was a lot of bright deep red, something then quite outrageous. There were some square shapes on it and a pod shape dancing on tentacles, a sort of bell octopus.

Bill had put the painting down on the table. Fairfield put his checkbook down on the table. He made out a check for 75, maybe 100 dollars. This was then an enormous sum. I was amazed. I was witnessing the buying of a living painter's painting.[51]

Porter's purchase was indeed remarkable in those early, impoverished days of Abstract Expressionism. But Porter's belief in de Kooning was so great that, apart from buying several of de Kooning's works and attempting to publish articles on his painting, he also tried, unsuccessfully, to introduce de Kooning to his influential old friend the critic Paul Rosenfeld. According to Edith Schloss, Porter actually brought Rosenfeld to de Kooning's loft, but de Kooning was so caught up in his work that he ignored their poundings on the door. The meeting never took place, and Porter's old friend died in July 1946.

Porter wrote more on de Kooning and cared more about de Kooning than he did about any other artist of his time. His feeling for de Kooning's work, which was based on Porter's respect for craft and for art history as well as radical innovation, is suggested by the observations that he made about *Pink Lady* in *Art News* in 1955: "The 'Pink Woman' ... in pink and greenish-blue, has a quattrocento look." It was made at a time when "painting was for him a matter of color-value relationships. ... One often hears the complaint that his figures of women are monstrous in their distortions [but] it is when his distortions are most twisted that he makes the most vivid similes between women and the commonest beauties of nature, like those in the Song of Solomon. ... Here is that shock or surprise that is so often the sign of original creation."[52]

From Porter's essay and from the observations Porter made to his wife in 1942 about his "surpassingly beautiful abstractions," it seems likely that Porter was discussing color-value relationships with de Kooning, which may account for the change in light and color that Porter otherwise ascribed to studying with van Houten and to copying Tiepolo and to looking at Bonnard and Vuillard. (Later critics have noted the relation of Porter's color to de Kooning's.)[53]

But Porter never directly emulated de Kooning, even during their closest acquaintance. Throughout the 1940s, Porter continued to create realist imagery – landscapes, cityscapes, and images of Anne and the children – using the tight, careful brushwork of American Scene painting. His real growth was in his awareness of color and light. Abstract imagery may have been all around Porter, but it is not found in his work from that time. De Kooning's influence is evident, however, in the gradual loosening up of Porter's brushwork, as in the small study *Painting Materials* (1949).

By the end of the war, Porter had taken a small painting studio at 116 West Twenty-first Street, just a few doors down from de Kooning's old studio at 143 West Twenty-first and just around the corner from de Kooning's current loft, shared with his wife, Elaine, on Twenty-second Street, in Chelsea. Porter may have appreciated the architecture of the neighborhood, which consisted of grand old turn-of-the-century warehouse buildings with good light and expansive interiors. Both the neighborhood and the buildings of Chelsea were perfectly suited to the needs of artists working on a tight budget, so much so that *Chelsea* was sometimes used as an adjective to describe a bohemian.[54] Stewart's Cafeteria, on Twenty-third Street and Seventh Avenue, was the local hangout for Porter and his friends.[55] (Another Stewart's Cafeteria, also an artists' hangout, was located in Greenwich Village.)

By keeping a studio in Chelsea but living in the East Fifties, Porter successfully managed to divide his life in two – much as he had during the previous decade, when he commuted into New York from his home in suburban Westchester. What was extraordinary and new about Porter's Chelsea studio was its proximity to a large number of friends; Rudy Burckhardt, Edwin Denby, the Auerbachs, Nell Blaine, Edith Schloss, and the Matticks all lived within a few blocks. The adolescent exuberance of this group, as well as its German-Jewish coziness and affability, is suggested in photographs of Porter taken by his friend Ellen Auerbach, including one showing him at his easel (fig. 23).

Porter still encountered Ilse Mattick, who now worked at the Hudson Guild Settlement House, just a few blocks north, on Twenty-eighth Street, and supported Paul Mattick in his writing. Porter's interest in Ilse Mattick had not lessened. But, according to Ilse, she kept her distance: "The problem with my relationship to Fairfield was that after a point he felt like he owned me, and he didn't. He was so awkward and wrapped up in himself that he never really knew what to do and could never really understand that I wasn't interested."[56]

In escaping home for this bohemian enclave, Porter was not alone; in postwar New York City, many people returning from the war were reinventing themselves as painters, writers, and intellectuals, and many of them were eager as well for sexual experimentation. "The first impulse of adolescence is to want to be an orphan or an amnesiac," a memoirist has observed. "Nobody in [Greenwich] village [during the 1940s] had a family."[57] The artists and intellec-

23
A 1944 portrait of Fairfield Porter taken in his Chelsea studio. Photo by Ellen Auerbach. Courtesy Ellen Auerbach.

tuals of this particular group also had an esprit de corps which enabled them to survive their poverty and lack of recognition. Edwin Denby recalled a typical evening discussion: "At one party [at de Kooning's studio] the talk turned to the condition of the painter in America, the bitterness and unfairness of his poverty and disregard. People had a great deal to say on this subject, and they said it, but the talk ended in gloomy silence. In the pause, [Arshile] Gorky's deep voice came from under a table. 'Nineteen miserable years have I lived in America.' Everybody burst out laughing."[58]

Even though Porter's life in Chelsea excluded his wife and children, it was necessary to his development as an artist. Along with the challenge of returning to painting, Porter, for the first time in a long time, was working among and conversing with like-minded artist friends, and the relief their company afforded him was enormous. After so much sadness and anxiety in the late thirties and early forties, the late forties were a time (selfish, perhaps) of reinvigoration and gradual renewal.

Naturally enough, Porter wanted to invite some of his Chelsea friends to Great Spruce Head in 1946. His desire for company arose, at least in part, from a need for further support. Porter's last visit to the island had been during the difficult summer of 1941, when, at odds with his wife and mother, he had struggled with his feelings for Ilse Hamm. Since then, his mother had died, Ilse had married Paul Mattick, and Porter and his wife had endured the most miserable period of their marriage. Porter's brothers and sister, having witnessed the near disintegration of the marriage, held various opinions on the subject, as well as opinions on Johnny; they also held opinions on Porter's continued habitation of the Big House, which belonged to Porter in name only. (Like Nancy and Eliot, John Porter had built his own snug house in 1938; the one remaining brother, Edward, who had never enjoyed island living, notified the family in 1946 of his financial withdrawal from the island community.)

That Porter, who contributed nothing to island life, should by default retain occupancy of its grandest home (and thus be capable of inviting the greatest number of guests to the island) must have seemed unfair to his brothers and sister. The house had always been inhabited by the family patriarch, James Porter, and Fairfield Porter, the fourth of five children, was (so far as they were concerned) the least responsible and accomplished of the lot. While Porter had always maintained an aloof indifference to his siblings' pronouncements, he was not unaware of their feelings. Returning to the island on the mailboat in June 1946 must have been daunting.

In the Big House belongings stood where they had been five years ago, when Ruth Porter had closed up the house in her usual way. Five years' accumulation of dust and dead flies may have lain on the countertops and windowsills, but otherwise not much had changed. Ruth's and James's belongings – her books and summer clothes, his marine specimens preserved in formaldehyde, their pencils and typewriter and gramophone – were there, just as they had always been. To step inside that house was to step into the memory of lives that had ceased to be.

The island, too, had taken on a Gothic quality. No longer "barren and open,"[59] as it had been in 1912, the woods had grown up over the island, giving it from a distance the brooding melancholy of a landscape by Caspar David Friedrich. Trees had fallen across the trails, and the houses, barns, and outbuildings were battered and in need of maintenance, for winter storms had taken their toll. Though nearing retirement, the caretakers, Rupert and Lottie Howard, had remained on the island for the duration of the war and had attended to the worst of the damage.[60] But the island had entered a long period of decline during which, according to Eliot Porter, "the wharf was damaged in a storm, the boathouse doors blew off, the electric plant failed and was not repaired, the tractor broke down, the house went unpainted, insufficient wood was cut, and the garden was planted too late."[61]

Anne Porter spoke for her husband when she wrote her mother that summer of 1946: "Both Fairfield and I, but I guess Fairfield the most, feel somewhat sad and bereaved in this house where we are so used to having his parents. It's hard for Fairfield to talk about things, which makes them hurt more. Oth-

erwise we're having quite a lovely time."[62] In another letter she observed that "Fairfield paints and takes the little boys on walks and I think feels happy in spite of the sadness he must feel in this house sometimes" (fig. 24).[63]

The Porters' friend and houseguest Edith Schloss remembered the melancholy of the Big House during her first summer on Great Spruce Head, in 1946 or so, in a memoir:

In the hall, tables, chairs and settees were hung with afghans. Berrying baskets, books and chess boards were scattered about. A frayed sneaker or two peaked out from under a chair ... the cozy summer life untidiness, as if stilled by an unseen wand [stood] in contrast with the exotic furnishings [dragons and chinese lanterns] above, [which] gave a half ludicrous, half sinister air to the scene. ... That first summer a fog hung down. There was greyness and clamminess. "There was also a fog of small children," Edwin [Denby] said later. There were family disagreements and I was bored. ...

[Fairfield had] left his parents decor ... faded bathing suits and greying summer clothes stirred stiffly in the closets ... in the upstairs front guest rooms with their view of the sea and their golden yellow paint, the beds were unmade [and the] porches were littered with sleeping bags and open books. ... The rooms in the back towards the woods were empty. The shady gloom of the close trees was made deeper by the wrong green with which [the guest bedrooms] were painted and by unappetizing jars full of murky liquids left by [James Porter] in which swam the denizens of the deep ... which no one had ever dared to throw away.

... The kitchen downstairs was paneled in wood and its shelves were graced by an immense set of flowered English china which no amount of breakage seemed able to reduce ... at the large long oaken slab of a dining table on the front porch Fairfield presided at meals, distributing food and justice. ... Right after the shopping trip to Camden, food was ample, then ... it grew ever more sparse. When once Jenny, the whitish untrimmed poodle, had dragged the last roast of lamb from the dining table and devoured it, Anne told her mildly: "But dear, didn't you remember we are on an island?" It was a long time until the next trip to Camden and we were reduced to stale biscuits, a few cans, and gathering berries in the woods like Hansel and Gretel.[64]

Schloss remembered, too, the disapproval with which the improvident Porter and his Chelsea guests were viewed by other members of the island community:

Fairfield's raggedy guests ... his refusal to build himself an island house of his own – were considered loose-ended, eccentric, even selfish by his family. That he went ahead painting without hope of selling, that he devoured philosophical books and talked about them vividly to anyone who would listen, was odd enough. ... No one in an old respectable American family, however rich, could take anyone who did not earn his own money seriously. ...

... There were cocktail parties the other Porters gave on their clipped lawn for their guests in neat summer clothes with hearty voices, at which Fairfield and his friends appeared looking threadbare and supercilious – the hippy intellectuals of the island – sauntering along barefoot.

Fairfield and his friends were not the only bohemians in the neighborhood. Close by on Bear Island, Schloss recalled, "Rosie Fuller, Buckminster's sister ...

ran a 'hippy' summer colony, only then there was not even such a word as 'beat.' ... Fairfield remarked that [Rosie] was very 'Chelsea.'" Schloss often saw people on Bear Island "naked in the sun, some making love."

Schloss's memoir of life in the Big House points to a particular awareness which has escaped many observers of Porter's paintings of Great Spruce Head: that the images of what appear to be a magnificent and comfortable country home are also images which describe a world that was Porter's conditionally and by default. This environment was not of his making and not one that he owned. The Big House never belonged to him psychologically; it was the home of his parents in which he, his wife, and children were, by the grace of his brothers and sister, improvising a life. Even the purchase of food supplies in town depended on the generosity of Porter's brother John, for Porter did not keep his own boat, and the old family motorboat, the *Penguin*, was frequently broken; the mailboat docked in the little village of Sunset, on Deer Isle, which had no real grocery store. So, though privileged, Porter's life on Great Spruce Head was not one of luxury or ease, despite the many summertime pleasures.

Great Spruce Head may have been melancholy, but Porter made progress with his painting there. The light and landscapes were inspirational, and island life offered few diversions other than reading, conversing with guests, and taking care of routine household chores (about which Porter, to the irritation of siblings, was notably indifferent). "Fairfield has really tossed off a great many pictures, which have an increasing lightness and freshness," Anne Porter wrote her mother at the end of one summer. "I think soon he will begin to feel that in his painting he has gone through Leah to Rachel, which is how it seems to me."[65]

Porter found little professional encouragement on his return from Maine to New York, only increasing financial pressure. Care for Johnny had been an enormous drain on his finances through the years, and so had the purchase and maintenance of the home on East Fifty-second Street. The financial crisis facing the family now concerned Laurence's education.

Growing up in the shadow of his troubled older brother, Laurence Porter had by necessity received less attention. From 1942 to 1944 he had been enrolled with Johnny at the Emerson School, which, being geared to the needs of troubled children, had hardly encouraged Laurence's extraordinary intelligence. In late 1944, however, Johnny was gone, and the Porters enrolled Laurence in the Dalton School, one of Manhattan's finest private schools, and one of its most expensive.

The popularity that Laurence enjoyed at Dalton during his five years there and the attention he received from teachers were crucial to his development. Laurence had suffered socially from his parents' peripatetic existence over the past decade. As he recalled, "My changing schools nearly every year and sometimes more often until 1944 prevented building any network of friendships ... I can't remember inviting any friend from school over to play until 1947 ... there just weren't many friends or relatives around during the New York years."[66] After his first few years at Dalton, his parents were unable to afford the tuition, and Laurence's hard-won security was once again in jeopardy. Ultimately the school offered Laurence financial assistance on the basis of his exceptional intellect. But even as it did so, Porter was once again planning a move, this time to an area which would (he hoped) provide a quality public education for his children free of cost.

Fortunately for their marriage, Porter and his wife were in agreement about the need to leave New York. "I still think it would be good to get Fairfield and the little naturalists into the country," Anne wrote her mother from Great Spruce Head. "We will make a little money when we leave New York, because our house, which wasn't expensive, is now in the UN area. Fairfield doesn't mind [moving] because he loves looking for houses – or would, if I didn't always insist so stubbornly on good schools."[67]

By 1948 the Porters had moved into a "happier time"[68] in their marriage. But when in late 1948 Anne learned that she was going to have another baby, Porter again found the news terribly distressing. He may well have felt that, although his wife supported his vocation as an artist, she was making a decision for the both of them by becoming pregnant, a decision which once again compromised his own plans and dreams and introduced the liability of another child in need of special care. Anne Porter had not "made" the decision to become pregnant any more than her husband had. Yet his emotional response to the news, however irrational, could not be denied.

Porter left his family frequently during his wife's pregnancy, searching New England and Long Island for a new home. His travel was, like the California trip of 1941, timed to manage his own stress, anxiety, confusion and emotional pain. He was not present for Katharine Porter's birth on May 20, 1949.

His distress also manifested itself in visits to Ilse Mattick, visits he told his wife about and later apologized for, even though his relationship with Ilse Mattick was no more than friendship – for Ilse, now married and a mother, had few warm feelings for Porter and no interest in taking him on as a lover. In fact, he alarmed her: "Fairfield was persistent. He simply could not understand the idea that I was not attracted to him. ... I once said to him, 'I'm not a fortress. You can't conquer me by force.' But he would just show up and hang around, hoping I would finally fall in love with him. I remember once he nearly attacked me in the street, grabbing me so hard he cracked three ribs. That was when I realized, 'This cannot go on.'"[69] Ilse allowed Porter into her home in deference to her husband's wishes but resented Porter's presence and rejected his advances with an irritation that bordered on disgust.[70] Her opinion of his behavior was based on the awareness that the 'freedom' he sought through her was illusory and that the love he professed for her was no more than a confused expression of his mixed feelings toward the life he had already created for himself with his wife and children.

11

Moving to Southampton

In 1948, as part of the ongoing search for a home in the country, Porter entered into negotiations for a house outside Boston which had been found for him by Anne's family and which stood just a short distance from Little Pond in Sherborn. Arrangements for purchase were well under way when a disagreement between Porter and his father-in-law made Porter realize the folly of living too close to his wife's parents. He decided abruptly to seek a home elsewhere.

In the spring of 1949, following the suggestion of his friend Eliot Atkinson, Porter ventured toward the east end of Long Island, to Southampton. Settled on the basis of fishing, farming, and the whaling industry, the area had historically been more closely aligned with New England than with the Middle Atlantic States and, thanks to its remoteness, had retained its New England charm. The salt air, brilliant sunshine, sudden fogs, late springs, and lingering autumns suggested to Porter a place in which he might stay close to New York

25
The house at 49 South Main Street in early 1949, shortly before Porter purchased it. Porter took this photograph for his wife, who was expecting a child and unable to travel. Courtesy Mrs. Fairfield Porter.

life and yet experience New England weather, light, and access to the sea. The decision was clinched when he found a house that spoke directly to his love of early nineteenth-century New England architecture.

The house at 49 South Main Street, built in the late Federal period, was decrepit and quietly grand. It might have been thought a mansion in some other part of the country, but in Southampton – which had a surfeit of propertied and architecturally distinguished country estates, having been the home of an affluent summer colony since the late nineteenth-century – the structure was known simply as the Captain Rogers house, after the wealthy sea captain who had built it some time before 1840. The Rogers house had been in the same family for over a century when Mary Rogers decided to sell. At the time that Porter came across the house in 1949, the owners had made only the most superficial changes in its interior and exterior. Porter immediately felt an affinity for the place. He photographed it for his wife, who, being in danger of miscarrying, was unable to come and view the house herself (fig. 25).

Anne Porter, to whom the burden of all housework had fallen owing to the decline in family finances, viewed Porter's photograph of the large, ramshackle place and its primitive kitchen with apprehension. She had struggled single-handedly to look after a four-story brownstone for the past seven years. But she was eager to return to country living and viewed the challenge posed by the Rogers house philosophically. "In fact, I was worried we'd end up in some place even more grand. This one was at least close to the town and its schools."[1]

26
The Porter family, minus Johnny, in the dining room at 49 South Main Street, shortly after moving to Southampton. *From left*, Jerry, Anne, Fairfield, Katharine, and Laurence. Photo by Ellen Auerbach. Courtesy Mrs. Fairfield Porter.

Just why Porter chose the sort of home he did is an important question, since many of his paintings over the next twenty-five years depicted rooms in the house or the house exterior and garden. In a sense, the purchase of this home (the only home, apart from the brownstone, he ever owned and lived in)[2] was a defining moment for his aesthetic. One can assume that after years of study Porter had become passionately aware of light and space, and recognizing just the sort of light and space he wished to inhabit and paint in the house at 49 South Main, he decided to buy it.

Along with its noble proportions and spacious interior, the house featured a pair of ancient horse chestnut trees in the front yard, overgrown hedges, a large, weedy back garden, and a great deal of peeling paint ("Fairfield was waiting for every last fleck of paint to fall off before he repainted").[3] In a town whose streets were determinedly prim, the Porter home stood apart, like an edifice from Hawthorne or Poe (or, for that matter, Tolstoy, Turgenev, or Chekhov). The painter Jane Freilicher observed that "it really was like stepping into a nineteenth-century novel."[4] The "chilly, inefficient and charming house,"[5] like the equally improbable Big House on Great Spruce Head, contributed an "almost gothic-novel feeling" to nearly all of Porter's paintings,[6] works whose "Vuillard warmth is continually tempered by a kind of cold New England breath."[7]

Rogers was forced to sell the house because of bankruptcy, and the price she asked was low: $25,000 for the seven-bedroom house and 78,500 square feet of land. The property ran from South Main Street to Lake Agawam and took in a garage, a toolshed, a barn, an arbor, a small orchard, and a meadow which ran down to the shallow, brackish lake. When Porter agreed to her price, Rogers included in the purchase a number of original furnishings, including a set of ladderback chairs and a table which had been around Cape Horn with Captain Rogers.[8]

With the conclusion of the sale and the completion of the most important renovations, the Porter family settled into the house in late 1949, the children enrolling in the Southampton schools very late, a full six weeks after the beginning of classes. A series of photographs of the Porter family, minus Johnny, were taken by Ellen Auerbach shortly after their arrival in Southampton; they contain a great deal of information about the house's interior (fig. 26).

The house was furnished by the Porters with a sturdy collection of antique furniture, carpets, and clocks ("mostly inherited from parents and great aunts")[9] which Porter treasured. He "*loved* things that had workmanship [and] beauty, upholsteries and paintings and wallpapers and antiques. He bought Shaker chairs and antique tables. He hated them to be damaged or broken, I think because he was a painter and recognized the work & gifts that go into making a beautiful object ... they weren't 'just' things to him."[10]

The house also featured a number of junk-shop finds, including the hanging lamp which appears over the dining table of so many Porter paintings and which bears an uncanny resemblance to the hanging lamps in dining tables in many Bonnard paintings.[11] (Porter, who never commented on the lamp, purchased it at roughly the time of the 1948 Bonnard retrospective at the Museum of Modern Art.) There was also a 1918 Steinway upright piano weighing nine hundred pounds, for the Porters were a musical family. To this was added Porter's growing collection of contemporary artwork and the pictures which had been passed down to him from his parents.

Porter made few interior renovations. He refinished the floors and installed a costly Scandinavian coal-and-wood-burning Aga stove in the primitive kitchen without bothering to remove the nonworking black cast-iron stove or the gas range which had succeeded it.[12] But he did take pains to repaint and paper the walls.

Porter was creative in choosing colors for the walls of rooms he would feature in his works. The downstairs rooms were repainted in colors Porter mixed himself: the living room, a soft pinkish beige; the dadoing in the dining room, a light battleship gray. Porter's preoccupation with subtly nuanced interior wall colors and the atmosphere they created had started on Fifty-second Street and even toward the end of his life, visitors to his studio remarked on the exceptional environment created by its interior of palest pink. (These colors stand in stark contrast to the garish colors that James Porter had chosen for the main room of the Big House, whose walls were Ming yellow, and whose floor was Chinese red. But Porter took a different sort of pleasure in those "inherited" interiors.)

Porter selected a range of expensive wallpapers for the Southampton house from Schumacher in New York for the walls of the dining room, front parlor, and little study, in addition to the stairway, upstairs hallway, and back bedrooms. These patterned or figured wallpapers brought a Vuillardesque complexity and liveliness to an otherwise austere New England interior.

The pinkish beige of the living room, an extraordinary color for a domestic interior, is reminiscent of Tiepolo, who constructed many of his paintings, including the *Adoration of the Magi* which Porter had so recently copied at the Metropolitan Museum, out of a pinkish beige ground. The choice must have been more than coincidence, especially when one considers that the trim (wainscoting, windows, doors, and fireplace) were painted Tiepolo's favored complement to that pinkish beige, ivory white. The blue skies in the windows beyond would have completed Tiepolo's color trio, had Porter wittily reworked Tiepolo for an American domestic interior. If so, subtle, historically based games of artistic quotation would have figured in Porter's works simply because they had figured first in his domestic environment.

Ellen Auerbach's photographs of Porter and his family taken in early 1950 indicate that Porter quickly hung art by various painters around the house. But Porter was not a "collector," nor did he intend to "curate" his home, even in later years, when appreciative artists (Leon Hartl, Joseph Cornell) presented him with works or when the sale of his own work enabled him to buy as well as trade the work of up-and-coming artists like Jane Freilicher, Alex Katz, and Larry Rivers. Though he was appreciative of the curatorial instincts of others, from Bernard Berenson to John Graham (his sometime Southampton neighbor),[13] Porter had no time for such endeavors in his own life, nor would his household support such an enterprise. Of Graham, a substantial painter and intellectual (as well as guru to Jackson Pollock and Lee Krasner), Porter wrote, "Wherever he lives, his home is a museum: its furnishings, from antique and second-hand shops and the five-and-dime store, reassemble a consistent workable house of no particular period in which each chair, painting or cooking utensil is set aside from such things by his recognition (which a visitor immediately senses) of a unique artistic or craft excellence. His houses illustrate a frame for civilized life."[14]

Graham, according to Porter, came to art "the aristocratic way: through connoisseurship."[15] Porter, in contrast, collected art but did not think of the art he collected as a collection, nor was his home a quiet, orderly place that lent itself to curatorial endeavors. In fact, his constant irritation with the state of the housekeeping at 49 South Main indicates the opposite: he frequently compared himself with the beleaguered Dagwood Bumstead[16] and had many conflicts with his children over their unwitting destruction of treasured objects. Similarly, his art collection was an organic accumulation of objects for which he felt or had felt enthusiasm – like the children's toys which lay scattered and forgotten throughout the house. Porter discouraged James Schuyler from writing about his paintings as a collection, for he did not feel that they were representative of his taste and disliked, too, the idea of being perceived as a collector,[17] probably out of a lifelong disinclination to identify himself with wealth or the "aristocratic way."

The Southampton home was always in a state of lively disorder. To the idiosyncratic mix of furnishings and paintings and wall colors was added the ongoing mess of three energetic boys (Johnny was living briefly at home), a newborn baby, and, in the words of one son, "a long succession of totally undisciplined animals who were destructive and often stupid."[18]

But even this disarray is worthy of consideration, for Porter not only featured it in his paintings but let it seep into his aesthetic. As the painter Jane Freilicher observed, "An 'unfinished' quality ... was part of Fairfield's aesthetic. The same sort of casualness you find in the household you find in his paintings."[19] If Porter had not in some sense accepted the untidiness of his home, it would not have appeared in his paintings, but it did (at least sometimes). Some of that untidiness was Porter's own; the crusted-over remnants of a family breakfast, for example, would often remain in the dining room for up to a week while he painted them. That his paintings celebrate the messiness or randomness of everyday family life is, in fact, one of the most notable and delightful aspects of his oeuvre, one which has found an enthusiastic reception in viewers and critics alike.

Porter had an aesthetic justification for this randomness. He felt that form

is discovery ... it's the effect of something unconscious. The dishes are in a certain arrangement at the end of a meal because people, without thinking, have moved things and then have gone away. And I think it's impossible not to get some sort of form if you don't think about it. If you do think about it, you can get chaos. But if you don't think about it, you get form. ... When I was in high school, doing algebra or something, I would see the doodle [I'd made] and like the way it looked. It had a certain spontaneity and freshness; it had a certain shape. And I would think, I'll do it again, I'll copy that because I like it. I would copy it. But the copy wouldn't have that freshness. It was only chaotic.[20]

The exterior of the house remained, for the duration of Porter's life, in a similar state of benign neglect, which seems, in retrospect, to have been an aesthetic choice. Porter made the most necessary renovations before moving in and bought himself a very expensive European stove and fancy wallpapers, but he seems not to have desired to do all those things that an average suburban homeowner would consider routine – repainting the exterior, trimming hedges, presenting a neatly ordered front garden to the street. But Porter and his wife had found, from their many years of living in rented houses, that a less tidy environment was atmospherically and emotionally more theirs and therefore more comfortable and welcoming. They furthermore seem to have taken a certain rebellious delight in the effect their housekeeping had upon their house-proud neighbors. In short, the majesty of the property on South Main Street combined with its severe neglect emblematized Porter's paradoxical stance toward money, property, and class – a deliberately provocative stance which both suburban neighbors and bohemian contemporaries found alternately charming and infuriating.

Twenty years in the art world had taught Porter that his leftist orientation and artistic vocation constituted a rejection of bourgeois culture. Yet he had come to recognize his attraction to the work of Bonnard and Vuillard, artists who had never found their relation to bourgeois culture problematic. Porter had a passion for architecture, possessed an independent income, and was in need of a home. So he wanted and bought a grand old home. But he had not moved to Southampton to become a suburban bourgeois; he had moved there to raise children economically and to create art in relative solitude. At age forty-two he was sure enough of his identity to purchase a place that suited him and to live in it just as he pleased. By buying a large, beautiful home and ignoring its upkeep, Porter was demonstrating that one could invest emotionally and financially in property and deny the significance of that investment (that is, of the money that made it possible), most visibly by neglecting the maintenance of the exterior, or public face, of the house.

Porter established for himself and his neighbors that in his home, the cultural and intellectual concerns of its owner took precedence over both stewardship of worldly possessions and participation in the many shared rituals of communal orderliness that are the essence of small-town life. Just as Porter and his friends had appeared "threadbare and supercilious"[21] at cocktail parties on Great Spruce Head, to the irritation of other family members, so now he and his family appeared before Southampton Village. As the Porter children soon learned, the members of this village were much less accepting than their island relatives.

The Southampton of 1949 was quite different from the Southampton of today, a busy beach community overrun by day-trippers and filled with year-round vacation homes. But contemporary Southampton is, if less tranquil, at least somewhat more cosmopolitan and in possession of the broader tax base required for the creation and maintenance of good public schools. Southampton in 1949 was, by comparison, a sleepy old village with much less money than one might have supposed from looking at its architecture. While the grand summer cottages in the estate section of Southampton were occupied by the very rich, these people were in residence for only part of the summer and had no great role in the life of the village or township. Apart from its summer colony, Southampton Village was known as the seat of Southampton township, a quiet potato-farming community and home to the local hospital. It was graced with examples of early American architecture, for the area had been settled in the second half of the seventeenth century, and thanks to the mild climate and lack of an expanding economy, many of the old buildings remained just as they had always been. The permanent population consisted of farmers, shopkeepers, doctors at the regional hospital, and retired people of independent means. While picturesque, the town was also racist, xenophobic, and – perhaps because of the influence of the affluent summer colony and a small group of families whose ancestors dated back to the founding of the settlement in 1648 – exceptionally class-conscious.

As a friend and neighbor of the Porters, Penny Wright, explained, "When we were growing up, the summer people were here only for the season, and they came here on a sort of circuit. They were up from Palm Beach. The same group of people every year. There weren't any city people. Nobody came out for the weekend. There was only one hotel in town – the Irving Hotel on Hill Street – and when it burnt down, nobody replaced it. There was no need for one. Weekending was unheard of." The rich summer people "came for the Fourth of July and left the day after Labor Day."[22]

At first, the Porters had little contact with their neighbors. Anne Porter recalled that "an old childless couple" lived on one side of them, and on the other side was a "very, very old couple with a chauffeured limousine." Shortly after their arrival, the Porters were surprised by a woman who wandered into their house, introduced herself as Princess Obolensky,[23] and demanded to know if the house was still available for summer rental (she had apparently rented the place from Mary Rogers the summer before). During the winter the neighborhood was largely abandoned. Southampton never was a place where Porter felt at home, and he violently rejected any suggestion that he lived in there out of any real feeling either for the town or for Long Island, once informing a journalist that "Long Island Regionalism ... has nothing to do with me. We moved here because I wanted to be in connection with New York, as a painter. It seemed a place that, if we couldn't afford to keep on going to Maine, would be a place where in the summer one could swim in the ocean. If you try to make something of our living in Southampton rather than in another place, you won't find much real material."[24]

When not painting or working on the house, Porter spent his time in Southampton doing yardwork with Johnny (planting only the most old-fashioned blooming shrubs – lilac, forsythia, and weigela), teaching himself to touch-type, and "spending endless days in the winter working at a newspaper progressive puzzle series; if you completed many rounds, you'd win a cash prize," according to his son Laurence. "He couldn't yet win recognition as a painter, so he wanted to win something."[25] He also read to his children. "We spent two years going through *War and Peace*," Laurence recalled. Porter's reading was "embellished by his enthusiastic, knowledgeable comments about Russian culture."[26]

But Porter, now in his early forties, had not yet reached a moment of Tolstoyan self-assurance. He was not at all satisfied with himself, and his children knew it. "I felt sorry for my father because he wasn't at all successful while I was at home (till 1953)," said Laurence. Porter knew his paintings were changing for the better, but he still sensed that his work was not yet worthy of a show. Life in Southampton, despite the pleasure he took in the house, was not helping his career as a painter.

Moreover, small-town life, particularly life in a grand old house fronting on South Main Street, offered much less privacy than life in any place the Porters had previously resided. Small towns are known for gossip and for a limited toleration of difference, and Southampton was no exception. In buying the large, decrepit house but making no improvements upon it, the Porters had attracted the critical attention of the village. Johnny Porter's odd behavior also attracted notice. Porter's apparent unemployment also seemed suspicious. There was no one like Johnny in Southampton, no father like Fairfield Porter, and no home like the Porter home. As Laurence Porter put it, "In the eyes of the community, we children were alien for at least four reasons: we lived conspicuously in a larger house than did any of our classmates ... our father did not have a 'real, regular' job ... the High School faculty did not respect confidentiality regarding test scores, and our [high scores] ... made our classmates and teachers acutely uneasy ... worst of all, the homosexuality or bisexuality of many of Fairfield's guests ... made most parents think the Porters were depraved, and they warned their children not to have anything to do with us."

The schools themselves were a disappointment to the children. Porter had assumed that a prim and seemingly affluent town would provide a quality public education, but he was mistaken. Porter's investigation of the school there had been intuitive rather than systematic. According to Anne Porter, "He wanted them to have at least an opportunity to study Latin. And he partly went by the *smell*. 'If the school smells of urine,' he said, 'it means the children are scared and unhappy.' "[27]

Unlike Winnetka, Southampton had no sizeable base population of upper-middle-class professionals and so had neither the resources nor the inclination to provide the best-available educational services to its most gifted students. And it gave little special care to its most troubled. Johnny, accordingly, attended the Southampton public school only briefly;[28] by age sixteen, his education was essentially finished. Laurence, meanwhile, after being so happy at the Dalton School, found his freshman year at Southampton High School shockingly different: "Had he not been socially unaware, [my father] would never have moved his family into a small, bigoted Long Island town. He had no idea of the situation into which he was placing his children. I resent the move to Southampton. That was a terrible mistake on both academic and social grounds. We children were ostracized from the community – except for the welcoming Methodist Church – and deprived of the intellectual stimulation that our parents didn't have to lose themselves."[29]

But Porter, unaware of his children's adjustment problems or perhaps unwilling to admit to them, blandly observed to Anne Porter's parents (with whom he was still on cautious terms since breaking off negotiations for the Massachusetts house), "Laurence and Jerry like the school. Laurence has been elected to the student council. He finds the work much easier than at Dalton, and I hope it will be enough of a challenge to him. Mr. Pincus liked Jerry's saying that this school is the least unpleasant of any he has been to. He thinks children should somewhat dislike school."[30]

Johnny was unable to adjust to Southampton life. "His intellectual development was about that of a ten-year-old; he read regularly, and loved cowboy music," his brother Laurence recalled. "Occasionally, he'd become so overwhelmed by anxiety that he was unreachable, but as he grew older, he slowly matured, becoming more considerate of others."[31] Within a year Johnny left for Spring Lake Ranch in Vermont, a rest and rehabilitation center. In time, Spring Lake Ranch proved inappropriate, and Johnny was placed with two successive foster families in Vermont, returning to Southampton and Great Spruce Head for holidays and vacations. His departure was deeply felt by the entire family, particularly his mother. But Porter felt liberated by the departure as well, later writing that it was only "after deciding, on advice from a psychiatrist, to send him to a foster home, that I began to have a career or life of my own … that I could concentrate on painting, that means paint without thinking of my supposed failure as a father in this one case."[32]

The one consolation for the remaining Porter children during their first year in Southampton was the Methodist church on the unfashionable north side of town. The Porters, who had been married in a Unitarian service, had never attended church regularly. Anne and the children did so now in the hope of finding a connection to the community. The Methodists proved more welcoming than either the Presbyterians (the church stood just opposite the Porter home on South Main Street) or the Episcopalians (the church was also on South Main, just a few hundred yards away). Within their year of arrival, Laurence and Jerry had received confirmation from the Methodists. Anne, Laurence, and eventually Katharine would sing in the choir. But Anne did not remain with the Methodists.

During the late forties, Anne Porter had begun to feel a growing awareness of religion. She had been drawn to the revolutionary Catholicism of the socialist religious activist Dorothy Day, who had helped raise Roman Catholic social and economic consciousness by political agitation, nonviolent resistance, and voluntary poverty, as well as by cofounding, in 1933, a monthly newspaper, *The Catholic Worker*. Anne Porter had known of Day since the early 1930s through a friend from grammar school; by the late 1940s, Day was a well-known activist who had been profiled by Dwight MacDonald in *The New Yorker*. Anne, long a follower of socialist and progressive movements, found Day inspiring and corresponded with her.

But Anne's attraction to Catholicism predated her awareness of Day, and it would be a mistake to think that her correspondence with Day caused her to convert. In fact, Anne Porter had been interested from childhood in the life and work of St. Francis of Assisi. At the age of fifteen, she had begun to pray for an hour or so every day and so became "sure of the presence of God."[33] Her specific interest in Catholicism had emerged in early 1949, while carrying her daughter Katharine. Overwhelmed with feelings of meaninglessness, she had begun reading Catholic hagiographies as well as the writings of Catholic saints and mystics, including Juliana of Norwich, at the cathedral library on Lexington Avenue, a short walk from the Porter home on East Fifty-second Street. Of her conversion, Anne Porter has observed, "The [Catholic] church itself seemed impossible & alien. But when I learned about Dorothy Day and the Catholic Workers I could see that the faith I'd met through St. Francis was still alive in the church."[34]

After a brief correspondence, Day directed Anne Porter to Father Joseph McSorley, an author and educator then in his mid-eighties who was also the retired Superior General of the Paulist Fathers. After more reading and studying, she traveled into New York to meet with Father McSorley for religious instruction and was finally received into the Catholic church on June 9, 1954, at the Church of Paul the Apostle on West Fifty-ninth Street.

The conversion had strong repercussions in the Channing family. Anne Porter's mother, who had been raised to think of Catholicism as a superstitious religion of the uneducated lower classes (most of the servants in the Channing home were Irish Catholics), was shocked and disappointed, blaming the conversion, at least in part, on the irregular life to which Anne Porter had been exposed through her marriage. "The pain for my parents in my becoming

Catholic wasn't anything I wanted. It just couldn't be avoided. It was pain for me, I hurt them," Anne wrote. "As for F., for him I think it was nuisance and enrichment, both together. I think of *course* it doesn't matter [that] he was closed to 'pietistic' things. He was open to spiritual ones."[35]

Anne Porter's departure from the Methodist church was a "grave personal loss"[36] for Laurence, for it meant that one of the adult Porters' few ties with the Southampton community had been severed, leaving the children to fend for themselves. But the greater shock to the Porter family may have been in Anne's decision to allow her inner life to take precedence over the needs and expectations of her family. Eventually they saw that her faith helped her to meet their needs more fully, but at the time, she seemed to them only to be asserting her spiritual and intellectual independence and formally declaring a change in her relationship to her family.

The move to Southampton and the birth of Katharine Porter marked a turning point in the relationship of Porter and his wife. Anne's affair had long since ended; Porter, though he remained absent from home a great deal of the time and though he still saw Ilse Mattick socially, seems to have reconciled himself to being a father and husband. In his first few months in Southampton, Porter attended PTA meetings with his wife and worked hard at settling in; as householders and parents, he and his wife were working as a team. And even as Porter began leaving Southampton for New York, he made time for an occasional night out with his wife. As Anne wrote her mother: "Fairfield and I have made ourselves a new custom. We tuck Kitty [the baby] up, I get all dressed up and leaving Laurence in charge, we go to a little nearby restaurant where we are all alone in the dudes' dining room with white tablecloths (the bar in the next room is full of men in caps), fried oysters 90 cents, and a cat that sits like a penguin beside the table waiting to be fed. This gives us a nice non parental feeling."[37]

Porter had no quarrel with his wife about her Catholicism. The two discussed her religious beliefs openly. Porter essentially respected his wife's mind enough to accept her faith and himself became increasingly interested in matters of spirituality. (In the coming years, Porter watched his two daughters and Johnny also become members of the Catholic church.) He did decline, however, to be remarried in a Catholic ceremony, telling his wife, "One wedding is enough."[38] Anne accepted his refusal gracefully while acknowledging that her husband's lack of opinion either for or against her conversion was typical both of his nature and the nature of their relationship. "Jimmy Schuyler was the only person to congratulate me on my conversion to Catholicism, except for one ninety-year-old Episcopalian lady who lived down the street, and my son Johnny, who said, 'It's nice to have a mother for a Catholic.'"[39]

Porter's trips to New York after the move may have had something to do with escaping a homebound life, but mainly he returned to New York to participate in the many goings-on in the art world. Still, even his adolescent son

Laurence knew that "the move to Southampton [had] made it possible for Fairfield to be in New York City and away from his family at the same time." By 1950, just a year after the move, Porter was spending several days a week in New York City in a small apartment at 500 East Eleventh Street that he was subletting from Walter Auerbach.[40]

Porter's living situation at Auerbach's was primitive but no more physically challenging than everyday life in the Big House on Great Spruce Head. As he recalled, "It was something like $18 a month. It was on Avenue A at Eleventh Street. The rain came in through the roof. But it had a stove. It was a cold water flat." The apartment was "a walkup in this little tenement," the painter Jane Freilicher remembered, "a very clean, well-run little building with a Polish superintendent who used to scrub the stairs."[41] Porter's apartment was on the fifth floor; Ellen Auerbach lived right next door.[42]

Porter's life in the city, when he was not painting, consisted of visiting friends or meeting them at bars like the Cedar Tavern or restaurants like Beatrice, as well as visiting galleries and museums. "He would come and go," Ellen Auerbach recalled. "He hated small talk. He just got right down to talking, so immediately that you would feel almost as if he'd been there for hours and you were just waking up to the fact that he'd been having a conversation. For years he would come by my apartment whenever he was in town, have one of those conversations, look uncomfortable, and then leave." Other friends recalled similar experiences with Porter, Jane Freilicher likening them to the sudden appearances and disappearances of the Cheshire Cat in *Alice in Wonderland*.[43]

During this period, Porter began meeting a younger generation of artists, writers, and poets. Some introductions came through his old friends Denby, Burckhardt, Ellen Auerbach, and the de Koonings. "The younger members of the group were busy at self-discovery, while the older ones assumed the role of father-confessors and sounding boards. [It was] a milieu brimming with activity and complex personal relationships," said the writer and dance critic John Gruen long afterward.[44] Freilicher remembered Porter as looking "like something out of *Boy's Life*. Very sort of American. Tall and lean and nowadays what might even be called preppy."[45]

During a get-together at the home of Rudy Burckhardt, Porter met the poet James Schuyler, then twenty-eight years old. As Schuyler remembered it, "I first met [Fairfield] through Rudy Burckhardt's sister, Helen, a friend of mine. ... [We] went to Rudy and Edith Burckhardt's for a little evening, not really a party but just an after-dinner thing, and Fairfield was there, looking very stern, in a black suit and black shoes, and not saying a word. But then very quickly he became interested in the young poets, John [Ashbery] and Frank [O'Hara] and myself. Our friendship just grew."[46]

Emotionally, mentally, and financially unstable, Schuyler, who would one day win the Pulitzer Prize for poetry, had already had an eventful life.

After an indifferent education, he had joined the navy, gone absent without leave in New York, and received a dishonorable discharge. At the end of the war, he used a small inheritance to travel to Italy, where he met and worked as a typist for W. H. Auden and became close friends with Auden's lover, Chester Kallman. In the early fifties, Schuyler (who is said to have had shock treatments while in the navy)[47] suffered religious delusions and was hospitalized at the Bloomingdale Psychiatric Center in Westchester, a treatment for which Auden may have paid. Schuyler was handsome, well-read, and, when he cared to be, charming and romantic. He had a fondness for older men and was involved briefly with Porter's friend Edwin Denby. Porter was intrigued by Schuyler and invited him to visit the house in Southampton, an invitation that Schuyler finally accepted in the summer of 1953. Porter's interest in Schuyler at the time of their first meeting seems to have been mainly as a friend. But his interest may also have been romantic, for Porter's letters to Larry Rivers, Frank O'Hara, and Schuyler from this period are unlike anything Porter had written to men previously and indicate that Porter was beginning to reconcile himself to his bisexuality – as does Porter's poem "The Young Man," written in 1952, which describes "homosexual" attraction (Porter's own word, in a letter to Schuyler of 1956). That Porter seems to have used the written word to clarify and understand his feelings suggests that the feelings were being understood in a new and unfamiliar way.

Porter's life in New York included the Artists' Club on Eighth Street, and though he found many of the Abstract Expressionists who made up its core group overbearing, he did attend lectures and meetings and occasionally spoke on panels.[48] As he described it, the club

started as a group of people – de Kooning, Kaldis, Milton Resnick, and maybe a couple of others who would meet in Washington Square at night after work and then go to Stewart's cafeteria on Sixth Avenue near Eighth Street ... But they were all very patronizing to me – who the hell is he – because I wasn't an abstract expressionist. Except Bill [de Kooning], who knew me, who wasn't that way. And I felt just the same towards them. I thought, who the hell are you; I'm really brighter than you think. So I just sort of kept away from them. But one of the first things I heard there was a talk that Bill [de Kooning] wrote out and didn't want to give because of his Dutch accent, which he felt self-conscious about. So [Robert] Motherwell read it. Motherwell introduced him by talking in this very patronizing way about really how good it is, you know, sort of patting Bill on the back. And his attitude sort of disgusted me. Because Bill has a connection with reality, a real connection with painting, and Motherwell just came out of a book and courses in philosophy at Columbia or something ... that talk was later given at the Museum of Modern Art.[49]

While making the rounds of museums and galleries, Porter found a ready sparring partner in Elaine de Kooning, a painter who was also a brilliant critic and conversationalist and who was then writing features and reviews for *Art News* magazine. Porter had written art criticism but had never had the opportunity to publish on a regular basis. He was given his chance one day as the result of an argument with Elaine at the Whitney Museum of American Art.

[Elaine and I] went to a show at the Whitney Museum, a retrospective show of [Arshile] Gorky. And she talked to me about how good they were. And I talked to her about how bad they were. We had a complete, thorough disagreement about them. But apparently I expressed myself so well that when she was leaving *Art News* and [its editor] Tom Hess asked her who she could recommend for a reviewer, she recommended me. I had just moved out [to Southampton] and I sort of jumped at the chance, because I had always thought I would be good at this, better than anybody. ... They liked me right away at *Art News*. As a matter of fact Frankfurter, who was the editor in chief, said I was so intense he'd give me a year. But I stayed for about seven years. And I could have kept on forever.[50]

The argument at the Gorky exhibit was about "who did it better and first."[51] Since Gorky and de Kooning had once shared a studio address, the argument was a friendly and almost trivial one between two friends about who knew the most about de Kooning's life in relation to his painting. But Elaine de Kooning appreciated Porter's intelligence, knew he was looking for something to do besides paint, and was sure of his devotion to her husband's work. Recommending him for the humble job of art reviewer at *Art News* was not a problem.

Porter's delight in writing criticism was not so much in the writing itself (the density and abruptness of much of his criticism, compared to the easy grace of his personal letters, suggest struggle as well as brilliance) as in being able to spend large amounts of time looking at art, thinking about art, and discussing art with people who were equally impassioned. The fact that he was being published in what was perceived by his colleagues to be the most important art magazine of its time was also significant to him, as was actually being paid money to express an opinion. The amount of money was negligible, but the psychological benefits of receiving it were enormous, even to a man wary of equating money with virtue.

Porter's talent was in paying exceptionally close attention to the work of art itself. The notebooks that Porter kept while making his rounds as a reporter show an extraordinary depth of involvement in the construction and composition of artwork. Artists were uniformly impressed by his concentration during studio visits; many felt that such attention was the highest form of praise. Porter's strongly focused presence (which had its asocial aspects: he was renowned for showing up at studios, looking at work, and then departing without saying many words) was in part the result of his upbringing. He had, after all, grown up in a home where people read aloud to one another in preference to speaking and were in the habit of paying more attention to works and ideas than to people and their feelings. But his focus on work was empathetic, and that empathy may have developed out of his long struggle to understand his son Johnny through the forms and signs that his otherwise noncommunicative son often produced (Porter's long involvement with the possible meanings of his son's building-block constructions comes specifically to mind). Porter himself described his method of approaching new work: "I would try as much as possible when looking at something that I had to review to cease to exist myself and simply identify with this so that I could say something about it."[52]

By the time Porter began reviewing regularly, he was so thankful for praise of any sort that the many positive comments (from editors and writers, but particularly from the artists he reviewed) made an enormous difference to his state of mind. He had begun, through his work as a reviewer, to feel connected with the world around him, and to imagine a place for himself in the New York art scene. Anne Porter noticed the difference, writing her mother, "Fairfield likes his part time job as critic and there is real *joie de vivre* in his short reviews – which are full of wit and sympathy and much knowledge acquired in solitude. ... *Art News* seems to appreciate Fairfield (hurray!) and has given him a book to review."[53]

In another letter, she wrote, "We have seen many painters lately who really admire Fairfield's paintings very much, which makes me very happy!"[54] Among these painters were Jane Freilicher and Larry Rivers, both nearly twenty years Porter's junior. Both were former students of Hans Hofmann (as were the emerging artists Nell Blaine, Wolf Kahn, Robert DeNiro, Paul Georges, Jan Muller, and Robert Goodnough) and had chosen, contrary to the prevalent mode, to work with the figure and with landscape. The two artists, then lovers, were showing at Tibor de Nagy, a new gallery at 219 East Fifty-third Street.[55]

Porter's introduction to Freilicher came by way of a studio visit shortly before her paintings went on view at Tibor de Nagy in May 1952. Freilicher and Porter had friends in common; she knew many members of Porter's old crowd, particularly the dance critic and poet Edwin Denby. Upon meeting Freilicher, Porter found that he enjoyed Freilicher's mind as well as her painting. Literary and witty, Freilicher was also politically aware, if not politically active; she had grown up in Brooklyn with a Trotskyite brother and tended to look on political radicals with sisterly skepticism. Still, she was impressed by Porter:

By the time I met him, I think Fairfield had become largely apolitical. Or perhaps I should say that the real passion or focus of his concerns lay elsewhere. I believe that he felt that technology, as an extension of capitalism, was what really threatened our society. So there was a continuity to his thinking; it wasn't as if he simply walked away from his earlier socialist concerns. Though one did have a sense that he had become something of a neoconservative. At any rate we rarely talked politics; generally speaking, we were an apolitical group.

All the same, Fairfield's political interests were not entirely foreign to me. I did know a number of Fairfield's earlier, more politicized friends ... [besides,] it was very much the "done" thing to keep up with that world [of leftist intellectuals]. I was an avid reader of *Partisan Review*. And other magazines, like *Transition*.[56]

Porter gave Freilicher an appreciative one-paragraph review of her May 1952 exhibition, praising her painting as "traditional and radical ... consciously imitative of masters of the Renaissance, but in a first-hand way," an assessment which Porter, so interested in Giotto and Tiepolo, would have been glad to see applied to his own work. In truth, with few serious artists of 1952 daring to create nonabstract work, Porter may have felt that he had found a young ally in Freilicher, who – candid, articulate, sharp-tongued, and often hysterically funny – soon became a close and valued friend. Freilicher, for her part, immediately recognized Porter's singular intelligence. Fairfield was

a very distinguished man and very unusual. He had tremendous education and memory. He could recall things for his use, things that he read. He had a lot of material, intellectually, at his fingertips. He had a lot of ideas about painting, but his main idea, in a sense, was that you shouldn't have ideas about painting. That painting was in a sense inspired play. He thought one of the things wrong with American painting was that it was somehow an extension of the work ethic in American life. The painter he loved most was Vuillard, whom he felt had a certain naturalness that was the thing that he was looking for in painting. ... There was something very Yankee and no-nonsense about him [and] his painting had that same kind of lack of decorum ... it was very natural and spontaneous. He was able to use any subject that came to hand. He could paint anywhere and anything. ... In a sense, his love of the playful aspect of painting was sort of deceptive because he actually had at his command all these ideas.[57]

While the new generation of artists responded to Porter's ideas and criticism with enthusiasm, Porter's close identification with this younger group was sometimes problematic for both him and them. Like Rivers and Freilicher, Porter was just beginning to exhibit, but unlike them, he had been working at his craft for a full twenty years. He had originally taken up his brush with a much broader sense of social and political commitment and had struggled intellectually with the many different styles and philosophies of American art from 1931 on. And he was, quite simply, an older person, with an older person's awareness of life's many sadnesses and complexities, as well as an older person's desire to share his experience and knowledge with people who have experienced and known less. The younger artists were, on the other hand, a skeptical generation, ebullient, personally ambitious, and essentially apolitical. As the editor of *Art News*, Tom Hess, said:

The experience of radical politics was, for most of them, a rather incomprehensible aberration by their elders which produced nothing but silly paintings. ... Instead, a number of them had contact with what, for want of a better label, can be called "G.I.ism," a working philosophy, not restricted to veterans, whose slogan is the admonition, "never volunteer." It embraces a belief in short aims, day-to-day cures for changing symptoms; larger problems are ignored. Destiny is considered a delusion; high ambition, a pipe-dream. What had been revolutionary is adapted to expressions of personal charm. No attempt that seems bound to fail, like trying to reach a mass audience, is made. References are understood by friends, and in such an intimate dialogue it is rude to appear overreaching, explicit or anxious. Manners are deliberately cultivated, irony and parody are the permitted vents for explosions of exasperation.[58]

As a result of these differing backgrounds, Porter and his younger artist (and poet) friends often grew frustrated with one another. To the younger generation, Porter's philosophical inquiries, free-ranging intellect, and high moral seriousness made him seem lugubrious, pedantic, even a crank. To Porter, the younger artists sometimes seemed callow, cheeky, and appallingly egotistical and self-involved. At the same time, after emerging from a profoundly unhappy period of his life, Porter needed and appreciated their enthusiasm and joie de vivre. Even if narcissistic, they were at least less fustily self-congratulatory than the Abstract Expressionists holding forth at the Artists' Club on Eighth Street.

Any artist practicing realist or representational painting in New York in the 1950s needed allies, for the unpopularity of representational painting during this conformist and politically conservative period is hard to comprehend in the present day. According to one source, "By 1954 a visiting English art critic [Geoffrey Wagner] could write [in *The Antioch Review*] that 'at the start of last season I counted eighty-one New York galleries showing contemporary art, of which only seven were exhibiting painting that could be called realist in the loosest sense.' Even as late as 1959, according to John Canaday of *The New York Times*, 'For a critic to question the validity of Abstract Expressionism as the ultimate art form was to inspire obscene mail, threatening phone calls, and outraged letters to the editor signed by eminent artists, curators, collectors, and critics demanding his discharge as a Neanderthal throwback.'"[59] Later critics have suggested that the "hegemony" of Abstract Expressionism was due to the virulent anticommunist, pro-capitalist politics of the time, since the realism of a generation before (the realism of socialist murals) had been programmatically critical of capitalism.

The critics and their theories, the art publications as well as the general press, the museums led by the Museum of Modern Art, the avant-garde art galleries, the clandestine functions of the CIA supported by the taxpayer, the need of artists to show and sell their work, the levelling of dissent encouraged by McCarthyism and a conformist era, the convergence of all varieties of anti-Communists and anti-Stalinists on a neutral cultural point, the cold war and the cultural weapons employed in its behalf, American postwar economic vigor and its sense of moral leadership, plus the explosion of a totally new kind of American-born painting that seemed the objective correlative of Greenberg's early announcement that "the main premises of Western art have at last migrated to the United States" – all these combined to make Abstract Expressionism the only art acceptable on a wide scale during the conforming 1950's.[60]

Porter, whatever his reservations about the younger artists, was facing an art world that was generally opposed to representational painting, an atmosphere of "cultural Stalinism."[61] As different as he knew himself to be from Rivers, Freilicher, and other young artists, he took his talented fellow realist and objective painters as he found them and was surely both glad and grateful for their company and support.

12

Young Friends

When Porter learned that Jane Freilicher would be sharing a house in East Hampton for the summer of 1952, he invited her to come to Southampton for lunch. Freilicher did so on Memorial Day weekend, arriving with her two housemates, Larry Rivers and a handsome young poet named John Ashbery. During the visit, the three looked at the paintings in Porter's studio. Rivers was by then a well-launched young artist already praised by Clement Greenberg in *The Nation* as a better composer of pictures than was Bonnard himself in many instances. Rivers recalled,

Our youthful exuberance for art and ourselves included his work. ... We began to look at [Porter's] work, and talked about it as we talked about everything else. We liked a lot of what we saw. ... All this attention lit a spark under Fairfield. At forty-eight [Porter was forty-five], twenty years older than the rest of us and even a little older than de Kooning, he began taking his own painting seriously. ... He paint[ed] more [and] moved out of Bill [de Kooning's] orbit. We all worked on John Myers and Tibor de Nagy to give Fairfield a show at the gallery. Working for an exhibition finally pushed his work into recognized quality.[1]

Porter was heartened by the artists' response, remarking to artist and critic Lawrence Campbell, "Larry and Jane seemed to like my paintings (which is something that always surprises me) and maybe I will as a result get an exhibition at Tibor de Nagy. I want to paint some pictures worthy of it."[2]

Porter's work from 1951 shows a new interest in color and the strong influence of Bonnard. Porter had responded enthusiastically (as had Freilicher, Nell Blaine, Wolf Kahn, and for that matter an entire generation of young painters) to the 1948 Bonnard retrospective at the Museum of Modern Art; a sense of the inherent sensual and emotional possibilities of color, texture, and nonliteral representation had made that exhibition a revelation. Porter bought a Bonnard-like painting from Larry Rivers during this period which soon claimed pride of place in the Porter living room. But Porter was still championing the cause of Vuillard; he had recently purchased two copies of a French monograph about him, sending one to his in-laws and keeping one for himself.[3]

The increasing sensual awareness in Porter's painting has been credited in part to Jane Freilicher, who demonstrated to Porter through her work (just as Tiepolo had, several years earlier) that brighter, more highly keyed painting held exciting possibilities. Both Freilicher and Bonnard contributed to Porter's awareness of color, as did the growing general enthusiasm throughout the New York art world for Impressionist and Post-Impressionist painting.

During the course of the afternoon with Rivers, Freilicher, and Ashbery, Porter found himself attracted to Ashbery, whose poetry he already knew and liked. As he recalled, "Before I met John Ashbery I saw his poem, *Little J.A. in a Prospect of Flowers*, which appeared in *Partisan Review* in about 1949. I couldn't have given a paraphrase of it; I couldn't have extracted an essence to substitute for it, but when I read it I thought that here was a new and absolutely first-rate poet. After I met him, and had completely forgotten this poem and this new and first-rate poet, hearing that he had once had a poem published in *Partisan Review*, I asked him to show me it. Then my original feelings came back to me."[4]

Porter's love of the poetry had predisposed him to admire the young man, who reminded Porter physically of his distant cousin T. S. Eliot.[5] Porter's physical attraction to Ashbery did not go unobserved by the other guests.[6] Porter maintained a friendship with Ashbery to the end of his life; he memorialized his feelings of that afternoon shortly afterward in a poem entitled "The Young Man":

> Young man with the narrow waist and thin
> Arms, and heavy beautiful thighs of youth,
> Whose green eyes under a foxy brush of
> Fair hair regard me with insolent love,
> Since you cannot forgive the father who fears you,
> Is contempt what you need me to convince you of?[7]

Porter sent a copy of the poem to Larry Rivers several months later, remarking that "Anne likes it, and J.S. [James Schuyler] writes that he does."[8] Several years later, Porter remarked on a revised version of the poem (with which he was never really satisfied) to James Schuyler: "'The Young Man' ... is a memory of my first meeting with John [Ashbery]. Do you think it is too homosexual? And if so, why not? I think it is not bad."[9]

The change in Porter's sexual awareness corresponds closely with the dramatic improvement in his painting if only because it constitutes one aspect of Porter's new, more accepting, less judgmental way of existing, a way he had learned through psychoanalysis and described as "being unconscious."[10] The new openness and relaxation that he was achieving in his personal relationships paralleled – or affected – his relationship with his painting, which also underwent a change of mood.

Mixing with this bright, clever and attractive young crowd, mostly male and mostly bisexual or homosexual, Porter seems to have been experiencing a sort of long-delayed adolescence. He wrote a friend, "You guess that I am very much occupied with my children. Well, perhaps not so much as you think. ... I think I am more involved with friends right now, who are all much younger than me – as if to make up for lost time?"[11]

Another aspect of the creative surge which Porter experienced during the early 1950s was his return to poetry writing. Porter had written poems during the late 1920s and early 1930s, for his wife and, in one instance, for Arthur Giardelli; he returned to poetry now, in part because he had met a group of young poets, including another significant poet friend, Kenneth Koch, whom he met in the summer of 1953 while visiting Jane Freilicher in Nyack, New York. Ashbery, O'Hara, and Koch had, like Porter and Porter's earlier literary friends, Wheelwright and Kirstein, attended Harvard, which may have given an additional fraternal chumminess to Porter's encounters with them: "I started to [write poetry] because I met all those poets who were published by the Tibor de Nagy gallery and they used to meet at the Cedar Bar and pull something out of their coat pocket and show them to each other. And I envied that very much. I thought I'd like to do that too. So I tried to see if I could and for a little while I could."[12]

Porter's enjoyment of these new friends is reflected in a Christmas letter to his sister-in-law Aline Porter of 1952, in which he writes, "The Tibor de Nagy Gallery also publishes avant garde poetry, very good. If Anne would write they would publish her. I like the poets whom I meet, whom Anne calls the de Nagy children, because they are all under thirty. I think I am the oldest person whom they [the gallery] sponsor. From feeling way out of things for years and years, I suddenly feel on the inside. It is naturally a good feeling."[13]

While Porter may have begun to feel on the inside during the early fifties, other members of his family were not so lucky. Porter's continual absence from the Southampton house was hurting his children, who were having a hard time adjusting to life in their new town and naturally craved their father's reassuring presence. Porter had been living part-time at home since early in his marriage, but during the years on East Fifty-second Street, he had been present, and his children had grown used to having him near. Laurence in particular was now at an age and in a situation where he needed his father.

Porter's children were aware of their father's emotional unavailability and accepted it, as children must. To some extent Laurence was able to understand his father's inabilities as somehow related to Porter's relationship with his own father many years earlier. "His upbringing had crippled him emotionally so that he could seldom express his tender and vulnerable feelings verbally," Laurence noted. "[His] involvement with me ... was sporadic and impulsive ... nearly always shaped by the adult point of view, with no sense of the effect on the child." In addition to having trouble in school ("During my sophomore year I sank into what I would now diagnose as a clinical depression ... without calculation, I went to bed for two months with a mild cold; I simply saw no point in going on"), Laurence had a brief fling with pyromania; his younger brother, Jerry, showed an indifference to schoolwork and developed a passion for violent games.

Anne Porter remembered Laurence's many difficulties during this period. "Laurence had it very rough. Changing schools, and having to fight all the other children who thought – who *knew* – that we were different. And on top of that feeling [that] his father [was] so critical [of him]. Laurence fell apart. His teachers said he just stared at them. And he didn't do any work or else did it terribly. And [he] had been such a wonderful student at Dalton."[15]

Southampton High School offered him few challenges and little encouragement. He recalled: "The guidance counsellor – a likable man – looked at the results of my Kuder Preference Test ... showing the highest interest in art and math, and suggested a career as an accountant in an art store. Since he was working the night shift of the first summer job I had (bellhop and switchboard operator at the Southampton Meadow Club), I wasn't sure how his guidance might help me improve my prospects."[16]

Schoolwork and vocational guidance aside, Laurence faced another problem: his manners were not like those of other children, and many new acquaintances viewed him askance. "I think Fairfield's greatest deficiency as a father – one that he could not help, nor even imagine – was to be unaware of the future of his children as social beings," Laurence wrote years later. "Anne and Fairfield showed us the joys of offering and receiving hospitality, but as far as any conventions of interaction and appearance were concerned, we were unwittingly raised asocial. ... Holidays, birthdays, and anniversaries were essentially non-events. My wife ... still is astonished at my ignorance of or unconcern with basic etiquette regarding greeting, eating, dress, thanking, and so forth."[17]

Local parents, suspicious of the Porter family's strange house and strange ways, excluded Laurence. "I was invited to only one party during my four years [at Southampton High School], when a girl's parents were out of town. ... I had no friends."

At the same time, Laurence Porter had enough self-confidence to reject the many prejudices he encountered in Southampton. "Parents made racial slurs without restraint." When three local black children were unjustly punished by the school, "Fairfield wrote a letter of protest to the Southampton paper," with the result that when "I won a local D.A.R. Essay contest on 'What America Means to Me,' the D.A.R. wouldn't let us in. They handed me the prize ribbon through the door."[18]

But perhaps the most difficult adjustment problem of all concerned sex. "After I won my first varsity letter (in cross-country), another boy in the locker room said to me in a friendly way, 'I thought that you were homosexual.'" Laurence's awareness of sexuality was limited, and he sensed that his acquaintances assumed him to be sexually deviant because he was from a different sort of family and home. Porter might have been able to reassure his son – had he been more aware of Laurence's problems – but Porter never gave his son any sexual advice, just allowed him to watch a cat have kittens, and was simply not in the habit of conversing with his son about his son's life.

While Porter may have been open with his wife about his sexuality, he was not so with his children. Laurence remained unaware of his father's bisexual identity until after Porter's death. "Because bisexuality was a hidden issue in our household, from the children's point of view, I got no explicit [sexual] guidance. ... I suspect that I subconsciously registered [my father's sexual feelings towards men] as a threat to our family."

Laurence felt betrayed and abandoned as a young man in Southampton and vaguely distrusted the reasons his father gave to explain his long absences in New York. In the coming years, Laurence would grow angry at what he perceived as his father's irresponsibility and self-indulgence. But angry and confused as he may have been, Laurence very willingly sat for "an extensive, sensitive series of portraits," especially from 1946 through 1960. "I was always happy to sit for paintings because it was a way of helping my father and being with him." Laurence was also "keenly interested in my father's work as an artist and as a critic because I was interested in him." In later life, Laurence was able to understand his father's depth of unexpressed feeling through the art he created during the period and through his poetry (Laurence has composed poems to his father in response). One poem by Porter, "The Beloved Son," written when Laurence was about to leave for Harvard in 1953, suggests Porter's own awareness of the lost opportunity for closeness. An excerpt follows:

> My heart is suddenly wrenched out of me
> And I might as well let go and be done with it
> And stay heartless, for what use could regret be
> If my heart must no longer follow him?
> . . .
> I think how carelessly I have regarded him
> With what little penetration I have known him
> And have not listened to the pleasant wit
> That marks the shrewdness of his watching mind.[19]

The anguish of the poem stands in marked contrast to the elegiac calmness of the Porter paintings of Laurence, particularly *Laurence at the Piano* (1953, fig. 27), one of Porter's most formally elegant and well-composed images. Laurence, practicing piano, is framed by the successively receding spaces of the front hall, living room, dining room, and doorway. Laurence's studious face is turned away from his father in three-quarter profile. He wears a blue checked shirt, dunga-

27
Laurence at the Piano, 1953.
New Britain Museum of American Art,
New Britain, Conn.,
General Purchase Fund (1990.7).
Photo by Michael Agee.

rees, and sneakers as he sits, in a relaxed teenage slouch, upon a black, straight-backed dining room chair. Along with the Tiepolo-inspired color combination of beige, blue, and white, the painting features a warm ocher floor in the foreground and an orange carpet in the living room, colors Porter chose again in *Katie and Anne* (1955). Patterned wallpaper, echoing Vuillard, is visible in the upper right-hand corner. Over the mantle hangs the Audubon folio print of the raven that appeared earlier, in the painting *Anne at 312 East 52nd Street*. Laurence's absorption in his practice evokes the same melancholy awareness of growth and distance expressed by "The Beloved Son," though in an entirely different, more spontaneous and immediate way; rather than delving into strong feeling and specific regrets, the painter marks a quiet appreciation of Laurence's simple physical presence, a presence which ended that year with Laurence's departure for Harvard.

By the end of the summer of 1952, Porter had been invited by John Bernard Myers to have a show of his work at the Tibor de Nagy gallery. The show opened on October 7. Just who was responsible for recommending Porter to Myers and de Nagy is open to debate; perhaps the most complete accounting comes from Porter himself, who that Christmas wrote his sister-in-law Aline, "Walter [Auerbach] told [Tibor de Nagy] about me, and Bill and Elaine de Kooning also recommended me ... and then two artists who were there [Rivers and Freilicher] also liked my pictures, and put pressure on for me, and I told them that I preferred them to all other galleries, which did no harm, and so they took a chance with my pictures."[20]

The risk to the gallery, Porter explained, was "that my pictures would look academic."[21] As a financially unstable enterprise seeking to define itself as cutting-edge, the gallery probably saw Porter's work as a risk to its image; the deciding vote on Porter's show may have come from Larry Rivers, for John Bernard Myers, then infatuated with Rivers, was open to his opinions.[22]

As Porter's first exhibition approached, the entire family grew excited about his debut. Anne Porter wrote her mother, "Will you give me names (and if possible addresses) of friends of yours in New York who might like to see Fairfield's pictures? ... The director of the gallery, John Myers, a warm hearted Irishman, chose *all* pictures of the children and the house and one of the sycamore tree – it's a sort of family album. I hope to get to the opening for an hour. Fairfield will drive me back here. On top of all that he has been asked to be membership chairman of the PTA, which he will try to do."[23]

But Anne Porter's excitement about the exhibition was considerably less offhand than she indicates in this letter. "I wasn't yet a Catholic, but on the way to the opening of his first real one-man show in New York, I found the Church of the Holy Innocents, I went to Mary's altar and said *please* have this show succeed – it's a matter of life and death! (I don't think my prayers made it succeed, however.)"[24]

The show was in fact a success, but Porter's later assessment of it was mixed. "They gave me a show and it was some new pictures and some old pictures and it was kind of a scrappy show," he thought. "Some of them shouldn't have been in the show. But people were interested. I think they were interested because it was realistic and realistic in a different way from what they were used to. And then artists were interested in it."[25]

There was no checklist or catalogue for the show, and there is no record of any paintings having been sold. But Porter's old friends Rudy Burckhardt and Edith Schloss attended. Schloss said,

I think most of us, including Bill de Kooning, loyal friends, tried to believe in this show but it was not easy. It was not that it was figurative when most work in those years was abstract, but that much of it was still awkward … .There was something blunt and brooding about these paintings, but most of all, something too rare in those times, they were very honest. In a show years later, when Fairfield's work was in full bloom – when it was clear he could perceive a scene and put it down and paint it all in one fluent whole – Bill and I were remembering that first show. We agreed it had been much better than we had secretly thought at the time. True, then there had been something tentative and inhibited, a sort of stumble between perception and execution. But thinking of the old pictures in the light of the new ones, we realized they already carried everything. Fairfield's determined directness and clear sight were always there. It was we who had not seen this.[26]

The reviews for the show were generally good. Lawrence Campbell, a critic and friend, wrote perceptively in *Art News* that "everything holds together. … Sometimes [Porter's] acute appraisal seems to extend into the thoughts of his subjects. *Katy*, though a little girl having breakfast, is thinking about being a fish or a bird. The stove in *The Big Studio* is not displeased at being cast in the role of prima-donna."[27] *The New York Times* critic, Howard Devree, also reviewed the show favorably; he was the same critic who had taken note of Porter's first exhibition, in the jewelry store twenty years earlier. Only James Fitzsimmons in *The Arts Digest* attacked Porter's work, for reasons that became all too familiar to Porter in the coming years: "There is too much taste and charm here … and also a slickness, a suggestion of the magazine illustration."[28]

Despite the lack of sales, Porter was buoyant enough about the exhibition to write, "It has given me a big boost. I like reviewing too. I am much prouder of my reviews than of my paintings. In fact I think that I could be the best art critic now writing in English. *Art News* also likes me."[29]

Porter's life had not changed as a result of the exhibition; he had not created a sensation. Nor would he. Porter struggled for critical and financial recognition over the next decades. But at least, at the age of forty-five, he had finally made his New York debut and established himself as well as an art reviewer.

In the month following Porter's show at Tibor de Nagy, the small group of painters and poets with whom Porter had become closely involved during the past year were shaken by a suicide attempt in their midst. When Jane Freilicher, after breaking off her relationship with Larry Rivers, began seeing another man, Joe Hazan, whom she eventually married, Rivers, in despair, slit his wrists.[30]

Rivers, an artist of exceptional talent, was also an "egomaniac"[31] prone to Dostoyevskian histrionics, renowned among his circle for high spirits, brilliant comic timing, drug abuse, and wild sexual behavior (all of which he chronicled in his memoirs). Porter respected Rivers's abilities as an artist. After the suicide attempt, O'Hara, who was nursing Rivers, telephoned Porter, told him of the emergency, and asked for help; Porter came to town in his 1949 Willis jeepster and picked Rivers up. As Rivers recalls in his autobiography, "We traveled in silence. About an hour out on the road talk began, obliquely concerning my Act. Suddenly Fairfield, reserved, restrained, taciturn as a Hawthorne minister, poured out his own past sufferings to do with his wife, Anne, trying to soften my sorrow. He had been waiting a long time to air these feelings, it seemed to me. To anyone. It cheered me up. In all the years I knew him he never spoke personally in that way to me again. Nor did he mention my suicide attempt again, not even when he did his portrait of me with my wrists bandaged."[32]

Porter's discussion of Anne probably concerned their temperamental differences for her one affair had long since ended and had never been perceived by Porter as a romantic betrayal.[33] He was certainly trying his best to be sympathetic. But he had found Rivers difficult company since their first acquaintance, writing to the critic Lawrence Campbell after the lunch with Freilicher and Ashbery the previous Memorial Day that "Rivers was like a tactful anthropologist visiting natives of an alien culture whose mores must be formally respected. It is clear that they are not his mores. He thought that we would find him strange (that we are not used to people like him), which made it strenuous all around."[34] Still, Porter recognized Rivers's essential unhappiness. He later told Rivers, "If I truthfully say that I have been through what you are now suffering it is only to let you know that you are not alone, maybe at the moment, but I remember, and it lasted for years,"[35] a statement which suggests that Porter was making reference to the permanent loss of Ilse Hamm to Paul Mattick.

In another letter, Porter counseled Rivers: "In the meantime, use your ego as much as possible for creative efforts because though love is mostly ego, much more than it is sex, right now you are frustrated egotistically in the love direction, so you have to find some substitute. It will not make you any happier, for sublimation is not possible, but it will count in the future, if you will have not wasted your time in vain efforts. Also forgive me for being so pompous, and talking about what is none of my business, and for my inability to properly understand, and for telling you to do what you are doing anyway."[36]

Rivers quickly made himself at home at 49 South Main Street. His autobiographical reminiscences of that time, written forty years later, retain something of the tactful anthropologist:

I stayed with the Porters and four of their five kids for a couple of weeks, in their white-columned house on South Main Street, practically in the center of town ... remain[ing] in my cosy room for the entire recovery reading *Swann's Way*. From the outside the house looked to me like a slightly run-down mansion; inside, dirty dishes and food would be left on the table until Fairfield finished using them as a still-life – which didn't detract from the room's inherent class. ... The house had a sun-porch, a fireplace in almost every room, a very expensive wood-and-coal kitchen stove from which every morning Fairfield pulled out his Irish oatmeal cooked overnight, and a specially built garbage container alongside neatly piled cords of wood waiting outside the kitchen door. Hanging casually on the living room wall was a de Kooning he'd bought when de Kooning didn't even have a gallery. It all filled me with the comfort and awe that I called class.[37]

In this and other passages, Rivers adopts a note of mockery in his observation of the Porters. But his response is sincere in its anxiety about class, for like many of Porter's new young friends, he came from a very different sort of background. Born Yizroch Loira Grossberg, Larry Rivers had grown up in the Bronx, the child of Ukrainian immigrants. The Porters had different ways. He responded to the uneasiness they caused him with humor.

At the same time, Rivers recognized character. Of Anne Porter he writes: "Fairfield's wife was a kind woman, but I found it difficult to make contact with her. She had a quiet smile that she held in place longer than expected. Her few but nail-on-the-head remarks came across with guru brilliance. She gets my vote for canonization. ... her [poetry] was delicately tinged with concern for the future of the human race. Unlike most humanitarians, she liked humans enough to invite some to live in her house. She had put her own work aside for a couple of decades to have five children and to take care of Fairfield's needs so he could be free to write and paint."[38]

Porter's feeling for Rivers seems to have been one of paternal indulgence tempered at moments with extreme irritation, perhaps because his desire to sympathize with Rivers's predicament was thwarted at every turn by Rivers's irreverent, ebullient personality.

As Rivers recovered, Porter painted his *Portrait of Larry Rivers* (1952). In it, Rivers, in a T-shirt, slouching in a straight-backed chair, rests his bandaged wrists on spread thighs and looks directly out of the painting with a knowing gaze. The stillness of the image conflicts with Rivers's own agitated personality. What may have begun as Porter's contemplation of the suicidal condition seems to have been commandeered by its subject and transformed instead into a portrait. The work, with its large areas of yellow ocher, may well have been done in homage to (the similarly suicidal) van Gogh, whose ninety-five-painting exhibition at the Metropolitan Museum of Art had caused a sensation in New York in 1949, as had Meyer Schapiro's recent book about the artist. Porter had lent his copy of van Gogh's letters to Paul Mattick shortly before Mattick met Ilse Hamm; looking at Rivers, Porter may have been thinking of his own past distress. Rivers's comment on the finished portrait was, "As a painting it seems flat and rather empty, except for a lot of yellow ocher."[39]

Toward the end of his stay with the Porters, Rivers began to wonder what to do with his eldest son. Joe Rivers, neglected by his father, was having emotional difficulties in New York. The Porters had helped Larry; maybe, Rivers thought, they would help Joe. He was correct. As Rivers recollected, "With Fairfield's approval [Anne Porter] volunteered to take Joseph in, offering her home and whatever her family could provide. She'd get Joe into the Southampton Public School. ... He was ... shipped to the Porter house."[40]

Joe arrived, and Larry Rivers departed, subsequently inviting himself by letter to the Porter home for Christmas. After a few days Porter replied,

undated   Yes do come for one or two days if you feel so inclined. Christmas is like this for us: there are more people (the children home from school), there is less for them to do, so they hang around the house making a mess and smashing things, and feeling hurt and unjustly treated if I object ... therefore I don't want any additional children to increase the mess and the damage. Also because it is a holiday all the house work is done by parents; nobody wants to come and work because they have a similar problem at home, and it is Christmas, the season of jollity, during which it is bad manners to be anything but gay.[41]

Joe Rivers (whom Porter described as "superficially tame")[42] remained with the Porter family for the balance of the school year. Joe's large and destructive dog, Tristy, did not last quite so long; after an attack of diarrhea, it was banished to New York.

Rivers moved to Southampton that May, eventually purchasing a home just two blocks from Porter's own. But a friendship did not develop between the two men. Porter later remarked apropos of Rivers, "I am tired of being a person whose function for other people is that I appreciate them."[43] Incidents involving the Rivers household and the Porters' adolescent son Jerry drove the families further apart. Anne Porter, however, continued to look after the Rivers family; according to Rivers's autobiography, she taught Rivers's mother-in-law, Bertha "Berdie" Berger, to cook Thanksgiving dinner and sat with her in the hospital during her last illness.

As spring came to Southampton in 1953, the Porters made plans to stay home for the summer. The decision was an economy measure; going to Maine was simply too expensive. But Porter had issued many invitations to Southampton the previous winter, and the Porters soon found themselves being visited by increasing numbers of friends from New York, all eager for fresh air and country hospitality. Jane Freilicher recalled that Porter "was very generous and friendly. He loved to make friends. He was very social in a certain sense. The house out in Southampton sort of became a stopover, like a crash pad, in those days. Everybody would come out to Fairfield's for the weekend. His poor wife, I think, really suffered a great deal [laughs]. It was very enjoyable."[44]

All the company caused a strain on the household, which now consisted of four Porter children, Joe Rivers, two dogs, and at least one cat, as well as Porter and his wife. Anne wrote her mother in April: "I hear that in the city we're called 'Porter's Rest Home for Broken-down New Yorkers' – how can anyone rest here I wonder?"[45]

The difficulties of housekeeping were compounded by the age and impracticality of the house and by the lack of household help. As Laurence Porter recalled,

If you ask her, [my mother] always says that she willingly spent all her time doing housework and raising children, but the slowness and inefficiency with which she's always done housework strongly suggests unconscious resistance. ... *Every* day, at an invisible sink in the kitchen, my mother was washing all the breakfast dishes, the lunch dishes, and the pots and pans – and, oh yes, she did most of the cooking and cleaning most of the time. ... Fairfield didn't help with the dishes during the first twenty-five years of his marriage. One of the few times I dared argue with him, as a young man, was when I urged him to agree to Anne's request to get a dishwashing machine. He refused; he didn't care for the taste left on the dishes by the detergent.[46]

The daily struggle of maintaining the house, however grave in reality, was given superb comic treatment in a film made by Rudy Burckhardt in the summer of 1953 entitled "A Day in the Life of a Cleaning Woman."[47] Burckhardt and his wife, Edith Schloss, by now old and dear friends, arrived in Southampton with their four-year-old son, Jacob, and during the course of a several-week stay they created a fifteen-minute silent film starring Anne Porter.

The script evolved during the course of the filming, but according to Burckhardt, the basic scenario – in which a down-and-out cleaning woman named Mrs. Rocker purchases a magic dishmop – was conceived by Anne, who had a lifelong sympathy for the plight of women engaged as household help (many of her poems describe their lives). Like the surrealistic plays being produced by the Poet's Theater, the film, which is full of inside jokes, puts a Dadaist spin on conventional modes of storytelling, in this case fairy tales and silent film melodrama. Edith Schloss, Larry Rivers, and Fairfield Porter have supporting roles in the film, but Anne Porter is the star (which is itself something of an inside joke, since she was renowned among Porter's friends for her shyness).

The film offers a rare photographic document of the household that Porter painted over the next two decades. According to Burckhardt, "We didn't change anything in the house – what you see in the movie is pretty much how they lived."[48] Both the house and its disarray are given a prominent role, perhaps because the disorderliness of the Porter home was legendary among Porter's circle of friends (and perhaps because setting the untidy house in order with the help of the magic dishmop is one of the most satisfying and delightful aspects of the story).

Occasional moments of simple, relaxed domesticity make some of the most powerful moments in the film. At one point, the camera wanders into the backyard, where the Porter and Burckhardt children (who have no part in the plot) are listening to fairy tales read by Anne Porter. In the background, Porter mows the lawn. Eventually, he too reads aloud to the children.

What is perhaps most fascinating about the film is the physical beauty of both Anne and Fairfield Porter and their ease and rapport on film. (Porter, a quiet clown, takes the supporting role of Elmer Turnip, handyman and eventual suitor to Mrs. Rocker.) At age forty-six, Porter, wearing his usual workman's overalls (adopted in the early 1930s in solidarity with the labor movement and by 1953 a preferred manner of dress at home and in the studio), is handsome and boyish, with a lanky and imposing physical presence. Anne Porter, in her early forties but already gray-haired, has a clownish soulfulness; on viewing her performance in 1993, one former New York City commissioner of cultural affairs compared her to the Italian film star Giulietta Massina.[49] Throughout the film, the couple seem comfortable and relaxed; Schloss (who plays Nathalie, Comtesse de Caviar) observed, "It was wonderful to watch how funny and ironic [Fairfield] could become [in Anne's company], how his wit would match hers."[50]

The movie concludes, after a series of brilliantly funny plot twists concocted by Larry Rivers, with the loss of the magic dishmop, a return to housework, and, happily, the marriage of Mrs. Rocker and Elmer Turnip. This ending was gratifying to Anne Porter, for "it showed me as married to Fairfield, which is something I never really felt in real life."[51]

The chaos of the Porter house during the summer of 1953 is suggested by two letters that Anne wrote her mother during the month that Burckhardt was shooting the movie. In the first she wrote, "Everyone eats at different times and there are lots of beaux arts going on here, literature (Edith), cinema (Rudi), art and art-criticism (Fairfield), music (Laurence), and culinary (me)."[52] The second concerned "strange footsteps and strange mens' voices upstairs" at four in the morning. "I came out into the hall to see what it was and there was a young man who thought we were a rooming house and had put another young man to bed in his boots in Johnny's room and was searching for a room for himself! They were very apologetic and asked what they could do for us. 'Find the right house,' said Fairfield calmly."[53]

The Porters' other company that busy summer included two poets, Frank O'Hara and James Schuyler, and the piano duo of Arthur Gold and Robert Fizdale. Schuyler met Gold there at lunch, and the two became romantically involved. Schuyler spent the next four months traveling through Europe with Gold and Fizdale on a concert tour with venues in London, Paris, Brussels, Amsterdam, Rome, Palermo, and Milan.[54] He corresponded warmly with Porter, and their friendship resumed upon his return.

By the end of July the Porters felt the need to escape their many friends and abandoned their home and children to the Burckhardts. They drove together to the Catskills, where they visited the émigré Russian painter Nicholas Vasilieff (whom Porter had recently written up in *Art News*) and Jane Freilicher, who had taken a summer rental in Nyack. They returned home to find "the kleig lights blazing so we knew Rudi was filming some more of the 'Day in the Life of a Cleaning Woman.'"[55]

With their return came even more company, Anne writing her mother after Labor Day that "we had a very lively week-end lasting through Wednesday, and entertained at various times 5 painters, 4 poets, 2 concert pianists, an interior decorator, a dancer from Trinidad, a former archduke from Russia (or so he says), a very nice man who runs a skirt factory, and a doctor and family!"[56]

With the departure of their summer guests, the Porters realized that they were probably not cut out for summers on Long Island. Pleasant though the weather and the proximity to the beach made life, Porter had been too distracted to get much good work done. He had been able to paint a couple of interiors, but he would not have enough paintings for a show that season. He resolved that next summer he and his family would return to Great Spruce Head.

13
Poetry, Painting, and a
Very Busy Summer

Porter had always enjoyed poetry and literary criticism, which aided and complemented his thinking about contemporary visual art. As he observed, "As much as any articulation of ideas in words, it is literary criticism that led to the development of schools in modern art."[1] As he grew more assured of his painting technique, the friends he sought out most avidly for discussion were poets and critics rather than other painters, especially from the 1950s on. The delight he took in conversing with poet-critics like Frank O'Hara, John Ashbery, and James Schuyler probably had less to do with his interest in art criticism or poetry, however, than it did with the pleasure of their company. "The younger people I know, especially in literature, keep me alert," Porter remarked by 1956. "In painting, I do not find the same stimulus, because painters for some reason are inarticulate, perhaps even stupid."[2]

During the mid-1950s, Porter's conversations with Frank O'Hara and James Schuyler played an important part in establishing once and for all the aesthetic which defined Porter's mature work as both painter and critic. Their early conversations often concerned the work of the poet Stéphane Mallarmé, sometimes in relation to the painter Edouard Vuillard, for the two had been friends. Porter's discussions with O'Hara were frequent in the fall and winter of 1953–54, when O'Hara, then living at Larry Rivers's home in Southampton, dropped by in the afternoons to talk.[3] Their conversations included discussions about translating Mallarmé, a poet whose work is so complex and abstract that it, "like the Bible," as his translator Roger Fry once remarked, "should be translated only by committee."

Porter's friendship with O'Hara and Schuyler evolved partly out of an interest in their poetry, Mallarmé's poetry, and poetry in general but partly as well out of an interest in the relation between painting and poetry, which both Schuyler and O'Hara, poets who lived among painters, were interested in exploring. Porter wrote: "What interests me is the relationship between painting, or if there is no relationship, then the analogy between painting and the expert use of words. It is quite possible that I see writing as a painter, and that for me to admire Elizabeth Bishop's poems, or even [Wallace] Stevens' perhaps, is to admire a visual writer."[4] In time, Porter came to value Schuyler in particular as the creator of intensely visual poetry.

Porter's French, while far from fluent, was good enough that he spoke it to his wife when discussing delicate matters in front of the children, and he enjoyed the challenge of reading Mallarmé in French. Porter also enjoyed the intellectual challenge posed by translation; during the 1950s he translated five of Mallarmé's poems into English (as well as two by Apollinaire). Porter was aware of the influence that Mallarmé had in the shaping of modernist poetry, from T. S. Eliot to Wallace Stevens. And he was aware of the cross-pollination which had taken place in French painting and poetry during the late nineteenth and early twentieth centuries, which he saw as a model for his own small group of poet and artist friends.

In his art criticism, Porter mentions Mallarmé frequently enough that the poet comes to represent intellectual and artistic integrity, his ideas lending weight and importance to the artistic innovations of Degas,[5] Whistler,[6] Berthe Morisot,[7] and (particularly and most importantly) Vuillard.[8] Mallarmé had influenced artistic theory through his weekly salons on the Rue de Rome in Paris; Porter, now finding himself host of a (much more relaxed and irreverent) literary and artistic salon on South Main Street in Southampton, probably looked to Mallarmé as a role model.

But Porter was much more interested in Mallarmé's poetry than he was in the cult of Mallarmé's celebrity and influence or in the example he set for intellectual excellence. Porter's five translations of Mallarmé demonstrate that his own interest comes from a sheer love of the poetry – a difficult poetry which, allusive and indirect, often borders syntactically on abstraction.

To some extent, Porter's attraction to the poetry was based on temperament, for Mallarmé's poetry, despite its emphasis on intellectual experience and its assumption that poetry is a sacred art and spiritual quest, is often moody and sensual, full of unresolved longings, full of, as Porter would have it, "night, despair and precious stone."[9] Porter's Mallarmé translations, notably "Sea Breeze," revel in strong feeling.

Set in a maritime environment (one thinks of Great Spruce Head), "Sea Breeze" expresses sadness, ennui, and a desire for escape from mundane existence with the opening lines, "I have read all the books and my flesh is sad, alas! / Oh, to fly!" The narrator resolves that "Nothing ... / Can hold back this heart ... "

> Not even my young wife suckling her child.
> I will leave! Steamer balancing your rigged mast
> Weigh anchor for a wild exotic land at last.[10]

It is tempting to find a biographical resonance in these lines, but Porter's response to Mallarmé was spiritual and intellectual as well as emotional and situational.

In fact, Porter was grappling, through translation, with questions about the meaning of language and its relation to art, about just what it meant to describe or "translate" a work of art. Translation was, in this way (Porter felt), like art criticism. Through his thinking about Mallarmé's poetry, Porter came to realize the ultimate authority of the work of art over any sort of criticism, translation, description, or evocation of that work. So far as the work of art was concerned, he agreed with Tolstoy (an artist with whom he increasingly identified), and differed from the translator Roger Fry (and, through Fry, Goethe). As Porter put it: "In his translation of Mallarmé, Roger Fry tentatively agrees with Goethe that 'the fundamental quality of poetry is translatable into another language.' This means that the actual poem is less real than some essence to which it refers, and that you can get equally close to this essential reality in any language. But a poem does not exist until it is written in a specific language, and its significance is larger than anything, including meaning, that can be abstracted from it. A translation remains a substitute, lacking the wholeness of the original."[11]

Porter's critical writings on art are suffused with an awareness that in any work of art, the medium (paint or language) is so integral to the work that the object, not the idea or meaning which it is given by others, is and must always be of primary importance. As Tolstoy wrote, "A good work of art can in its entirety be represented only by itself." Porter's expression of this idea in his criticism, and his practice of this idea in his criticism of art, gave him enduring popularity among artists. Combined with ideas taken from Wallace Stevens (specifically, that the best criticism is the best description and proceeds, like poetry, chiefly by analogies),[12] Porter's ideas about art, developed through his study of Mallarmé and translations of Mallarmé, form the cornerstone of his personal philosophy of art and art criticism.

Porter was also interested in Mallarmé because of the poet's friendship with Vuillard, for he felt that Mallarmé expressed something of Vuillard in his poetry. Porter was taken with an idea which he encountered in Mallarmé about the evocative nature of objects, Mallarmé having observed that "the contemplation of objects, the image that rises out of the reveries those objects provoke – those are the song." It was an idea about which O'Hara, too, felt strongly, for, as he said in reference to his own work, "We choose an object and derive a state of mind from it by a sequence of decipherings."[13] Mallarmé's ideas about the evocative nature of objects reinforced another saying which Porter often quoted to his wife, William Carlos Williams's "no ideas except in things."[14] To an artist such as Porter, working at a time when representation was considered passé, Mallarmé's idea about "the contemplation of objects" was a much-needed affirmation of his own representational impulse.

Writing on the 1954 retrospective of Vuillard at the Museum of Modern Art, Porter found Mallarmé's poetry and Vuillard's painting similar in that they featured a kind of "atheism" in which "the Idea is an absence of idea"[15] (the latter statement is a paraphrase of Georges Duthuit). Both the artist and the poet, Porter felt, paid close attention to the immediate present, to the objects surrounding them, as a celebration of an ultimate reality. Porter's use of the term *atheism* and his later feeling that in Vuillard he had found a "revelation of the obvious"[16] suggest that, to his mind, Vuillard and Mallarmé shared his perception of immediate visual experience as a connection to a nonreligious spiritual awareness. Porter's preoccupation with metaphysics (through his father, who had been an atheist, and through Whitehead, whom he continued to read and reread throughout the 1950s and 1960s) informed this rather extraordinary reading of both Vuillard and Mallarmé as investigators of the metaphysical through the sensual medium of art. Porter's late critical writings on painting would describe a similar search for ultimate reality through painting.

O'Hara, whatever his virtues as a poet, was not much interested in metaphysics. "I am very materialistic," O'Hara wrote Porter. "[My poetry] is full of objects for their own sake, spleen, and ironically intimate observation ... egotistical cynicism masquerading as honesty ... sometimes I think that writing a poem is such a moral crisis I get completely sick of the whole situation."[17] O'Hara responded most enthusiastically to Mallarmé's juxtaposition of the abstract and allusive with the intensely personal. He also delighted in Mallarmé's inclusion of his own experiences and friends in his poetry.

Through Mallarmé, O'Hara and Porter began to see an aesthetic justification for creating works which were, in essence, radically autobiographical. O'Hara's "modern ethos of the anarchically personal"[18] created a delightful, uneven oeuvre describing events, real or imagined, in his own tumultuous life; throughout his career he looked back on the Symbolist, Modernist, and Surrealist circles of poets and painters as an inspiration of and justification for his own spontaneously autobiographical impulse.

Porter's commitment through Mallarmé to the inclusion of the personal is less readily apparent and perhaps less compelling because it was less ecstatic and less sexually transgressive. Still, like O'Hara, Porter was creating a body of work whose ostensible subject is (or can be read as) autobiography: the artist's family and home, a world of apparent settled bourgeois domesticity – in Anne Porter's words, his paintings were "a sort of family album." Such work was daring and rebellious, for while Porter may not have been challenging bourgeois sensibilities or accepted modes of sexual behavior (as O'Hara was), he was issuing a radical challenge to the New York avant-garde, for whom realism was unfashionable, celebrations of suburban domesticity were unthinkable, and narrative of any sort, lyric or otherwise, was distinctly unpopular. In a community dominated by Abstract Expressionism and its adherents (including the Pollock-besotted O'Hara), Porter had the courage of his own convictions. He was committed to an art that was immediate and representational and personal.

Encouraged by O'Hara and others, and learning from his discoveries as a critic, Porter was experimenting with more painterly techniques in his second show in April 1954, loosening his brushstroke and achieving a more liquid effect in his oils that made them seem at times like gouache. The general reception for this exhibition at Tibor de Nagy was good. O'Hara knowingly observed in a review for *Art News* that Porter "has moved beyond the earlier felicity of sentiment (which linked him to certain pictures of Vuillard) to a more abstract concern for the verity of painting itself." O'Hara's feeling for the work was such that, by the time these words were published, he was already at work on another article on Porter, "Porter Paints a Picture," a feature which ran in the January 1955 *Art News*.

The critic Dore Ashton, less preoccupied than O'Hara with abstract painterliness, noted the quiet, intimate subject matter (the show featured a number of still lifes and paintings of empty rooms). Porter, she said, "takes us into the chamber of his well-resolved esthetic soul, permitting us to enjoy the peace and order of it."[19]

While Porter and O'Hara shared a passion for Mallarmé, Porter's friendship with James Schuyler seems to have developed, at least in their correspondence, out of a shared enthusiasm for the work of the painter Leon Hartl, whom Porter had befriended on his rounds as an art critic. Hartl, born in Paris, had lost his father at the age of eight and been raised by his mother. He emigrated to New York in 1912, where he lived in poverty while doggedly working at his delicate representational paintings. By the time Porter met him, Hartl was consumed with the care of his wife, who was mentally ill.[20] Porter's profile for *Art News*, entitled "Hartl Paints a Picture," was published in April 1953.

While much of the profile is technical, describing the use of certain colors and brushes, the rest is among the most intimate and moving writing to be found in Porter's published criticism. This writing concerns Hartl's lingering memories of his Parisian youth, the example set for him by his practical, hardworking mother, and the difficult circumstances Hartl faced in New York in the present day, taking care of his wife while struggling to paint. Hartl's philosophy of life in the face of adversity was (according to Porter) that "too much contemplation, too much planning is 'shutting yourself out of whatever treasures life offers you every day. ... Intelligence has to be watched out for: many times it breaks up your own being.'"[21]

Porter responded with enthusiasm to Hartl's unfashionably gentle and pretty representational work, noting in a later gallery review that it "goes against the grain of the existentialist cult of sincerity that values violence, ill-adjustment and awkwardness."[22] Reflecting upon the artist's difficult circumstances, Porter composed two poems in his honor, one of which is a sonnet describing the artist's life through images derived from his paintings:

A white bird beside the lilacs in the vase,
The young trees with naked graceful girls,
Along the branches flow the running squirrels,
Marcelle is present with a younger face.

Behind the color in an unremembered place
Tenacious, patient, the French flag unfurls;
His mother's country courage firmly curls,
An ancient vine composed with ancient grace.

The light around the forms resolves the dread
His mother felt, his father newly dead;
The wilting petals gracefully applied
Contain his mother's delicate fierce pride;
And now the son takes on his mother's life,
And turned about, is mother to his wife.[23]

One of the poem's merits is probably invisible to those unfamiliar with Hartl's paintings and drawings: its evocation, through language, of Hartl's delicate, curling, broken lines: girls, squirrels, a flag unfurling. Other visual images throughout the poem have a curling aspect: vines, flower petals, lilacs.

Porter's empathy for Hartl surely came from a deep awareness of the difficulty and heartbreak of living with mental illness; it may also have come out of Porter's memories of his own charmed and long-vanished childhood and the nourishing memory of his own strong and capable mother. In one of his earliest letters to Schuyler, Porter sent along the verses. Schuyler responded,

I was so moved by your poem about Leon Hartel that I took it for granted I *undated* would have something to say about it when I saw you next day, beyond "It was beautiful" (not that one would necessarily ask to hear more than that about something one had made). Perhaps, though, it's the nature of that poem to imply that one doesn't speak, or write a poem, without having reflected on what one has felt, or without feeling certain that one *has* felt. I was struck last night by how "like" your poems the Hartels are; I think anyone who had read the poem, and never seen the pictures in your house, could go through and instantly pick out his (and for other, if not better, reasons than that they are of flowers).

Discussing Porter's recent exhibition, he continued,

It was dizzying to see your recent paintings so quickly all at once. I have always loved the intensity of your preoccupation with your subject matter, and the positive way in which you grasp it. There seems to me to be an excitement in your pictures created by your desire, as a painter, to have your own way with your subject matter, that is at odds with a desire not to lose what it was that drew you to it in the first place, by tampering with it. That, I think, is an excellent tension under which to work, in the interest of creating interest, and quite different from only seeing, in the subject, one's own painting (as I think some painters do) or having the painting take over, once it's launched.[24]

Schuyler's letter is elegantly perceptive, about both Porter's painting and his poetry. It is, in short, the kind of letter an artist could spend a lifetime hoping to receive.

In another undated letter, Schuyler wrote:

undated I was so glad you could come for drinks and stay to supper last night. It made a very pleasant event out of an evening from which I had expected, well, nothing. ...

I was thrilled when you said you thought you liked the Hartl more than the Vuillard (opinions can be thrilling!), because I do too, though I hadn't thought it out in words until you said it. I haven't anything to say in dispraise of V[uillard], whose paintings I love, but his pictures are about history, about how the sunlight came in at a certain time of day, and someone moving in the next room, which suggests to me a state of mind tinged with nostalgia, and a satisfaction that homely moments have been saved from the passage of time. Whereas Hartl seems to me all about joy and permanence, beyond a point of view, a comment or a moral, an exaltation in repose.[25]

Schuyler, perhaps in response to Porter, composed a poem in Hartl's honor.

Schuyler and Porter, both shy, troubled men dedicated to their art, seem destined to have been friends if only because they shared so many tastes and opinions. And, though more impressed by the poetry of John Ashbery, Porter was always fond and respectful of Schuyler's work. Porter's experience with Johnny had acquainted him with mental illness, and he may have felt an immediate affinity with Schuyler who, in 1953, had only recently emerged from hospitalization in White Plains.

Schuyler's early brilliance (he did not publish a substantial volume of poems until years later) is perhaps best displayed in "Salute," which he wrote while hospitalized:

> Past is past, and if one
> remembers what one meant
> to do and never did, is
> not to have thought to do
> enough? Like that gather-
> ing of one of each I
> planned, to gather one
> of each kind of clover,

daisy, paintbrush that
grew in that field
the cabin stood in and
study them one afternoon
before they wilted. Past
is past. I salute
that various field.[26]

This gemlike pastoral, the first poem Schuyler ever published, suggests the aesthetic connection between Schuyler and Porter. (Years later, "Salute" was the Schuyler poem that Porter chose to quote in his essay "Poets and Painters in Collaboration"). The works of Schuyler and Porter are similar in their elegaic qualities and similar, too, in their acceptance of inability and loss. Both find virtue or transcendence in acts of passive observation.

On both sides, the friendship grew out of need, but on the basis of letters, it seems to have been more avidly cultivated at the outset by Schuyler, who, as a young man of no very firmly established reputation and no means at all of financial support, traded heavily on personal charm. In 1954, Schuyler was working part-time in a bookstore and being partially supported by the pianist Arthur Gold. Schuyler did not hesitate to ask other friends for money, and certainly in many of his sexual relationships he expected and received financial support. In Italy he had relied on Auden (who was not a lover, but a friend) to pay for an operation for hemorrhoids; the poet James Merrill would pay for another of Schuyler's hospitalizations by the end of the decade, and many others would contribute to his medical expenses and to his general finances in the decades which followed, particularly toward the end of his life. While relying upon the generosity and hospitality of friends is a practice hardly unknown among poets (Rilke comes to mind), it was nonetheless extraordinary in Schuyler's circle and was viewed by many in that group as one of the most unfortunate aspects of his character.[27]

A real friendship certainly existed between Schuyler and Porter. But Schuyler was aware of Porter not just as a friend but also as a possible source of support, just as Porter was aware of Schuyler not just as a friend but also as a sympathetic critic and (perhaps) lover. Moreover, by this point Porter was used to being courted for his money. Schuyler took an immediate liking to the Porter home in Southampton and was intrigued by Porter's mention of an island home in Maine; his interest in these places expressed itself as an interest in Porter. A great deal of his interest in the two homes came from his simple admiration of the Porter way of life, for Schuyler had a lifelong love of family and children and the security of a settled domestic existence. He seems to have wished to become a part of the Porter family and eventually did establish himself among them, as an adopted uncle in some ways, in others as a fully grown child.

One of Schuyler's first extended visits to the Porters came in the summer of 1954, when at the beginning of July he invited himself to Great Spruce Head for a visit.[28] Of Porter's new, younger friends, Schuyler was thus the first to avail himself of the hospitality of Great Spruce Head.[29] He stayed several weeks and was delighted by the island. Two charming thank-you letters from Schuyler remain from that summer, the second venturing beyond politeness into a declaration of something more powerful: "I've been reading Delacroix's journals, and found this in it last night: 'Intercourse with decent or bad people is the good or bad education which goes on throughout one's life. The mind lifts up on contact with honest minds; it is the same with the spirit.' My friendship with you lifts up my spirit."[30]

Porter had recently sent his son Laurence off to college and would bid goodbye that autumn to Jerry (he had been enrolled in boarding school at Putney). Johnny was away in Vermont at his foster home. Increasingly aware of his age and isolation, Porter found Schuyler an articulate, talented, and emotionally available new companion whose inability to contribute financially to the household was easy enough to overlook. There was plenty of room for him in the Big House (which, after all, slept eighteen). For these and other reasons, Porter must have been pleased with Schuyler's grateful letter.

Schuyler's high esteem and goodwill were particularly welcome that summer, as Porter, returning to Great Spruce Head for the first time in two years, struggled to reconcile himself to the dismissive and domineering attitudes of his older sister, Nancy, and younger brother, John. Porter's younger brother, now a schoolteacher in Bronxville, New York, had taken on the hard work of maintaining Great Spruce Head Island in the years since Ruth Porter's death. Along with the burden of stewardship (he had been "mayor" of Great Spruce Head since 1946), John had inherited a righteous sense of proprietorship. He felt quite deeply that his older brothers Fairfield and Eliot did not contribute enough to island life. John was particularly irritated that Fairfield was slow to pay his share of the island's maintenance,[31] and that, when visiting the island, he relied on John for boat transportation.

Moreover, John and Nancy could not help resenting Fairfield's continued occupation of the Big House, a space sacred to the memory of Ruth and James Porter, and the grandest house on the island by far. Feelings about the unfairness of the arrangement (and other long-simmering sibling rivalries) came to a boil over the issue of the dragons.

In 1931, the year Ruth and Fairfield Porter traveled to Italy, James Porter had painted two enormous decorative panels depicting a male and a female dragon. He had mounted the panels along the ceiling of the main room of the Big House, and there they had remained ever since, to Porter's constant irritation. As Eliot Porter recalled in his memoir of island life, Fairfield told me that he did not like the dragons, that they dominated the room and were too much like something out of *The Wizard of Oz*. ... I immediately backed him up – the house was solely his to furnish as he chose – and offered to remove the dragons for him, since he did not want to take the responsibility himself ... .But this was not the end of the matter; the family became sharply divided on the removal of the dragons. ... [When] a friend rented the Big House from Fairfield the next summer, [she] insisted that she would not go through with the rental unless the dragons were put back. So back they went; they have remained up ever since.[32]

The underlying issue was control and proprietorship of the Big House, which had become increasingly decrepit during Porter's on-again, off-again habitation with his many Chelsea friends. In forcing Porter to keep the dragons on the ceiling, Porter's brother and sister were forcing Porter to admit that the house was not really his to do with as he pleased. John and Nancy's triumph was a bitter and humbling experience for Porter and typical of his interactions with his siblings on the island from the mid-1950s on. He was probably glad to return from that summer to his friends in New York.

During the fall of 1954, Porter resumed his strenuous rounds as an art critic, working two weeks full-time per month in New York City. While not remunerative, the work was gratifying; on the basis of his 1954 writing, he received Honorable Mention from the College Art Association for his work in magazine art criticism. This small scrap of recognition, so long in coming, delighted him no end.

Recognition of another sort awaited him in January 1955, when Frank O'Hara published a profile of Porter at work. "Porter Paints a Picture," with photographs by Rudy Burckhardt, was flattering, charming, and inaccurate (fig. 28).

28
Porter painting his daughter Katharine while Anne Porter reads to her. From "Porter Paints a Picture" by Frank O'Hara (*Art News*, January 1955). Photo by Rudy Burckhardt. Courtesy Rudy Burckhardt.

Porter was grateful for O'Hara's generosity, but nonetheless alarmed by his imaginative constructions, writing to one friend, "Frank O'Hara is very imaginative and really writes his own ideas, and he is not accurate, nor interested in being so."[33]

The article begins, "Fairfield Porter lives in Southampton, Long Island, a town which looks permanent for all its handsomeness and rather reminds you of Henry James ... Porter's rambling white house ... is Jamesian, too; its many rooms invite and impose privacy to a degree." Porter himself was likened to Henry James (an author whom he did not much enjoy). First, O'Hara quotes Porter as saying, "The avant-garde implies a protocol which is more a challenge than a guide ... not that the Academicians aren't even more ignorant!" Then O'Hara comments: "With such definite ideas about the historical as well as esthetic position of the artist, one finds Porter (like Henry James, again) both objective and prejudiced."[34]

Porter – who, unlike James or O'Hara, was temperamentally disinclined to make exclamations in print – probably disliked O'Hara's irreverent caricature of him as a Jamesian crank. He observed mildly in a letter to Anne's parents, "I find it embarassing, because I sound so much like the writer of the article. Now I can imagine how my subjects have felt."[35]

In all, the profile seems to suffer from what the poetry critic Helen Vendler has called O'Hara's "fantastic tinsel of reference."[36] In likening the Jamesian Porter to his Jamesian home and the Jamesian town in which he resided, O'Hara may have been responding (with some accuracy) to Porter's class and background; but he was also responding to his own recent immersion in Henry James – for it was O'Hara, not Porter, who was the Henry James enthusiast (Porter spelled out his dislike of James's fussy, speculative, and intrusive narrative presence in a later letter from Great Spruce Head). Besides, Porter surely did not think himself related to the town in which he lived; he disliked Southampton and felt unwelcome there.

Perhaps, in the end, distinctions of this sort are important only to critics. Porter, being very serious about his responsibilities as a critic, was distressed by the perceived irresponsibility of O'Hara's writing. Nonetheless, Porter knew O'Hara as a friend and accepted his limitations as a critic, merely thanking him by letter for the profile.

The O'Hara article was good publicity. Porter sold four paintings at his next show at Tibor de Nagy the following month. This good news was met by good news of a different sort: *Poetry* magazine had accepted three of Porter's poems for publication in its March 1955 issue. Anne Porter, who had been published in *Poetry* several times during the 1930s, was among the first to congratulate Porter on his rise to "professional level." She remarked as well on the increased rate of payment: "*Poetry: A Magazine of Verses* seems to have struck oil since the Depression when I remember my first paycheck for $9 for five poems. Fairfield got $68 for three poems, and I tell him I feel that a mink coat is only a few sonnets away (only I don't like mink, too bad)."[37]

Aside from his growing commercial success and his growing recognition as a critic and poet, Porter found by the spring of 1955 the new group of painters with whom he had begun to exhibit were on the brink of being named a "movement." Throughout the New York art world, an alternative to Abstract Expressionism – a form of painting influenced by European artists such as Bonnard, Soutine, van Gogh, Rouault, Matisse, Vuillard, and Monet – was beginning to gain notice.

Perhaps the most convincing case for the validity of this new form of European-inspired representational painting was made by Elaine de Kooning in "Subject: What, How, or Who?" an essay which appeared in *Art News* in April 1954. The essay was a rebuttal to a pronouncement made by Clement Greenberg in a talk at the Hansa Gallery. He stated that "abstraction is the major mode of expression in our time; any other mode is necessarily minor."[38] Picking up where Greenberg had left off in his crucial early essay "Towards a Newer Lao-coon," Elaine de Kooning asserted that abstraction was no longer a revolution-ary idea and that, given the widespread acceptance of abstraction, realism was just as valid a way of seeing – it was in fact revolutionary. "Docile art students can take up the Non-Objective art in as conventional a spirit as their predeces-sors turned to Realism," she observed. "The 'taste bureaucracy' ... all freely accept abstraction."[39]

Along with this insightful questioning of Abstract Expressionism came a popular and critical excitement about European painting in New York. The purchase and installation of Monet's *Nymphéas* by the Museum of Modern Art in 1955 created a sensation in the art world, and artists were exploring the pos-sibility of a new sort of painting based on this European precedent, some even going so far as to label this second phase of the Abstract Expressionist move-ment "Abstract Impressionism." "Optical unity [is] the dominant expression in their work," the critic and artist Louis Finkelstein observed. "By and large these artists are more colorists than draftsmen, and their works evidence a more sen-suous response than conceptual control. Subject as such is not the issue; seeing is." Porter, though a good ten years older than any of the other painters caught up in this new movement, found himself at the center of a group later dubbed Second-Generation Abstract Expressionists as the result of an influential show, curated by Meyer Schapiro, at the Jewish Museum.

With so many positive developments in his career, Porter decided once again, despite financial constraints, to spend the summer of 1955 on Great Spruce Head. The previous summer had been a productive one; rising at five-thirty in the morning, Porter had managed to do an enormous amount of painting in the course of a day. A number of his painter and poet friends, hav-ing by now heard all about the island, were planning trips there.

Though Schuyler had spent the winter in Europe with Arthur Gold, he had not lost contact with Porter. While traveling in Venice, Schuyler had visited the American Pavilion of the Venice Biennale to see Porter's large de Kooning, *Pink Lady* (circa 1944), on exhibition. "The one that belongs to you was one of the two I liked best,"[40] he wrote Porter in a postcard. Other letters written by Schuyler in January and May of 1955 continue to praise and reassure Porter, this time on his accomplishments as a poet. In late spring Porter invited Schuyler to visit him again on Great Spruce Head; Schuyler readily accepted.

By the end of the spring of 1955, Porter was part of a busy, downtown social circle (fig. 29). Many of these new friends were male and homosexual, as this letter to Frank O'Hara records:

June, 2, 1955   I called the museum yesterday, but the line was busy. If I seemed somewhat strange about calling you it was because I had a date with J [John Button] & A [Alvin Novak, Button's lover] for supper Tuesday and because I had a number of things to fit in otherwise. As it turned out I had less to do because Jerry [Porter] came down with German measles so we cannot go to Putney until he gets better. Also I had [Richard] Stankiewicz to see. At Jimmy [Schuyler] & Arthur [Gold]'s I stayed until 3 & when I left Alexei [Haiess, a composer] and Chester Kallman [W. H. Auden's lover] seemed prepared to stay on until dawn. That made me dopey yesterday, as on Wednesday I have to get up at 7:00. I will call up when I am in town next & hope to see you. I got a very pleasant and gracious note of rejection from Howard Moss [at *The New Yorker*] asking me to send something else.[41]

Porter's first houseguest in Maine that summer was the twenty-six-year-old Californian painter John Button. Handsome, capable, and hilariously funny, Button had caused a sensation among Porter's homosexual friends upon his arrival in New York in 1954. (James Schuyler, then living with Arthur Gold, had fallen deeply in love with him.)[42] An enthusiast for the outdoors, Button had eagerly accepted an offer from Porter to come up to Maine to paint. The two planned to open the Big House together, stopping off first in Putney, Vermont, to pick up Porter's youngest son, Jerry.

Button, new to the Porter world, described his trip to Maine to Schuyler in a letter which gives a candid glimpse of Porter's abrupt and taciturn manner:

June, 16, 1955   F. & I drove here via Putney in 2 days without speaking. When we got to Putney, Fairfield greeted Jerry by making a couple of violent side steps, rising on his toes, thrusting out his hand, and missing Jerry's, and finally kissing him and giggling. Then he said, "Let's take a walk," and we walked or rather stormed down 2 MILES and then turned around and stormed back refusing three offers of a lift. All this was, of course, done in absolute silence. I was so tired and sick that I didn't eat dinner.

Now, all that is passed. Since we've been here, F. has been terribly kind, thoughtful, active, happy, and, best of all, talkative. Jerry still doesn't say much, and when he does speak, the words are so carefully pronounced that I just sit and stare at his head.[43]

Button was moved by the beauty of Great Spruce Head and faced down the blustery winds and low temperatures of early June to do a great deal of alfresco painting. Even Porter was impressed with his perseverance. In his free time, Button helped with the cooking and collected the tiny wild blueberries that grew in the meadow beyond the vegetable garden. When Anne Porter and little Katie reached the island, Button became a great favorite among the Porter family, and all were sorry to see him leave.

After Button's departure in late June, Schuyler arrived. Hard at work on a first novel, published as *Alfred and Guinevere*, he stayed until the end of the season, much longer than any other guest did. During that summer, Porter painted *Portrait of James Schuyler* (1955, fig. 30), the portrait by Porter which Schuyler would cherish above all others in the coming years, perhaps because it shows Schuyler looking handsome, open, and forthright. In this radiant composition of muted greens and yellows, Schuyler sits in a wicker armchair on Porter's painting porch, the light a combination of reflected interior light and the direct sunlight of outdoors, some of which is reflected by the polished cement floor. There is a crisp, architectonic quality to the composition and a fresh, sketchy handling of paint, which gives the work a relaxed and spontaneous summery feeling.

The sculptor Richard Stankiewicz arrived next, at the end of July. Porter admired Stankiewicz's work, in which he conjured human and animal presences out of scrap metal and discarded bits of machinery. The two had recently become friends, but Stankiewicz was not at all prepared for the forced congeniality of island life and spent most of his time alone. He kept a journal describing his intense feelings of self-consciousness and alienation, noting at one point, "I am not very comfortable with anyone here and am again & again feel-

29
Porter and James Schuyler at the Second Street home of John Button and Alvin Novak, circa 1955. Photographer unknown. Courtesy Alvin Novak.

30
Portrait of James Schuyler, 1955.
Private Collection.

ing I have hit off a false note."[44] He also realized to his horror that there was no place on the island to buy cigarettes and that no one would be going to the mainland any time soon to buy them for him. By the end of his week, Stankiewicz wrote in his diary that he had been reduced to begging smokes one by one off a grudging Schuyler.

Stankiewicz also observed the close friendship between Porter and Schuyler, which sometimes excluded others. "F. read aloud Keats' *Hyperion* ... I didn't even get the thread of the story and had to take the book up to bed with me, together with Bulfinch to puzzle it out. Keats, I must admit, is very good, but it doesn't follow that I like him ... it is hard work. ... Jim [Schuyler] & FP seem not to consult me or take my opinions after these readings but are not offensive about it – I supposed there just isn't much point in trying to milk a bull."[45]

The next guests to arrive after Stankiewicz's departure were Porter's old friends Rudy Burckhardt and Edith Schloss. Another guest to the island at midsummer was John Ashbery, who wrote a series of acrostic verses using the names of other guests in the household, from which we know that Ellen "Pit" Auerbach was also visiting (the verses, which Ashbery told his friend Kenneth Koch were "strictly for domestic consumption on Great Rose Pebble Island,"[46] have been preserved in the Porter papers at the Archives of American Art). Porter wrote to Frank O'Hara, Schuyler's roommate, of Schuyler's happiness on the island and also of the awkwardness of Porter's current dealings with his brother John.

Richard Stankiewicz came yesterday, and seems to like what he has seen, Jimmy is writing a new novel, and sometimes I hear him typing and often I hear a woodpecker and think that it is he. He loves to canoe, and has been in the water, swimming slowly around for a time with a smile on his face, and remarking very gently after a bit, "Why Fairfield, it's the coldest thing I ever felt."

... Right now the difficulty is that there are two busted boats, one the *Penguin*, belonging partly to me, which has a cracked block so that salt water mixes with the oil, immersing the engine internally in a sort of unique salad dressing, and the other, John's, which we naturally depend on, and therefore do not want ever to make John feel how much we depend on.[47]

August 1, 1955

Eight days later, when Jane Freilicher and Joe Hazan arrived (without O'Hara, who had been detained in New York), Porter took them sailing, with unfortunate results. As Edith Schloss recalled, "Fairfield took out Rudy and Joe and Jane for a short trip in a sailboat. ... meanwhile on Great Spruxehead lunch came and went, teatime came and there was no sign of our dear ones. At seven Anne and I, though rather worried still, went to a cocktail party on a wide lawn. As we were standing, glasses in hand, Laurence, Jerry, Katie and Jacob [Burckhardt] happened to meander by in single file at the edge of the clearing. 'There,' pointed someone, 'There go the children orphaned by the sea.' Anne and I did not think it at all funny."[48] Anne Porter finally prevailed upon John Porter and Michel Straus to make a search party, for the two had been disinclined to give up their cocktail hour on behalf of Porter and his friends. As darkness fell, John located the chilled and bedraggled group on "a desert island (with an empty house containing half a box of corn flakes)."[49] Rudy Burckhardt, a passenger on the ill-fated excursion, recalled, "We just got caught in a strong West wind and couldn't make any headway. ... We were on the island all day, until it got dark." When they were rescued, "everyone got into John's boat except Fairfield, who stayed in his own as it was towed back to the island, very glum and humiliated."[50]

Hosting so many people in his rustic home must have been a challenge, considering the limited finances of the Porter household. Porter never discussed his finances with his friends (most assumed him to be wealthy), and he merely instructed his wife, "Just don't *buy* anything."[51] Even as their financial situation grew desperate during the late 1950s, few had any idea of Porter's growing financial trouble.

As summer drew to a close, Porter was surprised by one final guest, whose visit was the highlight of the season. After a week's delay, Frank O'Hara had managed to escape to Maine for two weeks, arriving in great style by seaplane. The arrival impressed everyone, including Porter's brother John.

During this vacation from his new administrative job at the Museum of Modern Art, O'Hara relaxed by reading the work of Laura Riding. He composed two poems during his visit, "Goodbye to Spruce Head Island," and another, "To an Actor Who Died." O'Hara's gift for conversation enlivened the Porter dinner table. Laurence Porter said later that "the New York School of painters and poets were friendly and respectful to children. To hear their conversations, which typically went on for a three-hour dinner over red wine and several pots of espresso coffee (our family drank five pots a day) was a privilege and a fascinating intellectual experience. ... Frank O'Hara was particularly charming."[52] One night after dinner, O'Hara entertained the Porters and their guests with a reading of his new play, *The Thirties*, which was unfortunately lost (along with his typewriter and suitcase) on the return to New York. O'Hara's charisma was such that the young Katie Porter, then six, doted on him. The two wrote a poem together, entitled "Katy," which Schuyler saved among his papers:

> They say I mope too much
> but really I'm loudly dancing.
> I eat paper. It's good for my bone.
> I play the piano pedal. I dance,
> I am never quiet, I mean silent.
> Some day I'll love Frank O'Hara.
> I think I'll be alone for a little while.[53]

14

A Summer Illness

Upon returning to Southampton in the fall of 1955, the Porters learned that their renter that summer, the poet and art critic Barbara Guest, had suffered a mishap. As Guest recalled,

When we rented it, the price for the summer was 500 dollars. It was a wonderful house, full of the most marvelous antiques. And somehow I burnt a beautiful old bookcase and desk. It was awful. But we put the fire out. ... I thanked the firemen for coming and said I didn't know what I would have done if the place was on fire, it was full of such priceless objects. And the fireman said, "What – this old junk?" ... Anyway when Fairfield came back – money matters were always handled by Fairfield, never by Anne – I took him to the desk and showed him the burn. And I said we would want to pay for the repairs. Mind you, this was a very old and beautiful piece of furniture. He looked at it and simply said, "Don't worry about it – my insurance takes care of it." ... Fairfield was like that.[1]

Despite this gentlemanly show of indifference, Porter (who was not at all indifferent to his possessions) was facing an increasing number of financial problems. Money from the Porter realty trust had been dwindling since the Depression, and though the family business was still in capable hands, Porter's brother Edward could do nothing to halt the decline of the American inner city. With Johnny in year-round special care, Laurence at Harvard, and Jerry at Putney, Porter had many expenses to cover. (Laurence, wanting to do his part to help the family finances, had won an NROTC scholarship to Rochester and a New York State Regents Scholarship, and together the two would have paid his tuition, but Porter, being antimilitarist, had insisted on Laurence's attending Harvard instead.)[2]

Additional anxiety entered the Porter household that fall when Anne, then forty-four, told her husband, then forty-eight, that she was going to have another child. Porter may have felt that another child meant that all hope of achieving a tranquil home in old age was now gone. He could no more blame his wife for the pregnancy than he could himself, and according to a letter from Anne to her mother, he was "very good about it,"[3] but he was nonetheless disquieted by the news. He was probably also anxious about Anne's health, for her doctor in Maine had told her that she would most likely miscarry within two months.

Anne Porter was therefore gratified by the felicitations she received from Porter's artist friends at a party held by John Button.

undated   Furl [Fairfield] and I went to New York ... to a cold-water flat in an old house, between two gutted fallen-down houses – this combination of talent and willing, rather carefree poverty has grown familiar to me as an artist's wife and I feel very at home in it. ... There were a lot of our young friends. Kitty's beloved Frank O'Hara played the piano ... the guests were mostly poets (including W. H. Auden, the only guest as old as ourselves) and some young composers and I had a wonderful time simply because I was made much of because of the [expected] baby – the last thing I expected! I think it's because our young friends are fond of our children and think it would be fun if there were more of them. (Poor Furl is known in art circles as the man with 8 children).[4]

Shortly thereafter, Porter was given that rare opportunity for a working art critic, expense-paid travel to an out-of-state art exhibition. Tom Hess at *Art News* had assigned Porter to cover the John Singer Sargent retrospective at the Museum of Fine Arts, Boston. The assignment may have grown out of a painting by Porter completed in the previous season, a miraculous large canvas entitled *Katie and Anne* (1955, fig. 31), which drew on Sargent's *The Daughters of Edward D. Boit* (and through it, Velázquez's *Las Meninas*) for inspiration but turns those compositions inside out by replacing their gloomy interiors with one of radiant spring light.

In the painting, Anne Porter reclines on a comfortable slipcovered chair, between a straight-backed chair in the foreground and a round table in the background, on which stands a partners desk lamp and a vase full of forsythia branches in full bloom. Katie Porter, approximately age six, sits on a rag rug at Anne Porter's feet in a party dress and red stockings. The beige walls, ocher floor, and blue sky at the windows are brightened by the whiteness of Anne's book, the sheer white curtains at the open windows, and the white frosted-glass lampshades. Anne, who wears a yellow blouse and a gauzy white apron over her black skirt, seems to be taking a break from her housework, and gazes across the room, caught somewhere between reading and daydreaming. Katie stares directly out toward the viewer, the lilac of her dress adding to the painting's bright, pastel Easter-egg hues. An orange blanket or shawl is thrown over the arm of the chair in the foreground, which is otherwise left incomplete, as if the painter has just left off work.

The painting is most remarkable for its light, which is the joyous, almost overpowering light of a clear spring day in the country. This cold, brilliant out-

31
Katie and Anne, 1955.
Hirshhorn Museum and Sculpture Garden,
Smithsonian Institution, Washington, D.C.,
Gift of Joseph H. Hirshhorn, 1966.
Photo by Lee Stalsworth.

door light is met by the warm still tones of the house's interior and furnishings and the equal stillness of Katie and Anne as they sit patiently for the artist. This is an Intimist composition (a figured interior not so far from the work of Vuillard, but replacing Vuillard's stuffiness with an airy chill), but it is given liveliness and presence by Porter's handling of paint, which brings an Abstract Expressionist awareness of medium and paint surface (with drips, spatters, and scrubbed-out areas) even to something as humble and familiar as the old-fashioned rag rug. The painting is also made contemporary by the scale of the work, which (at 80⅛ by 62⅛ inches) is the large-scale painting size preferred by Abstract Expressionists and rarely used by the Intimists.

Hess may have known that Porter had been thinking about Sargent's painting in his creation of *Katie and Anne*; but he may also simply have thought that Porter would write something provocative about Sargent, since, as Porter later observed, "I was typed as the person to write about American art, which I think was because I didn't like American art. ... My reviews were more critical, maybe more interesting, for that reason."[5] Porter timed his visit to the Sargent Exhibition so that he could drive up to Putney to have Thanksgiving dinner with his son Jerry.

Porter's awareness of paint handling – an awareness that distinguishes *Katie and Anne* as stylistically related to Abstract Expressionism and specifically to de Kooning – was much in his mind as he reconsidered Sargent: "In the 1920's Sargent was despised by vanguard critics who ... thought of 'form' as the most important and essential quality in art. ... Sargent's paintings were full of empty bravura, passages of 'just paint'. ... today, when the American style of abstract painting is based on a formality (or informality) which is less three-dimensional than expressive of the nature of paint ... a passage of drapery in a Sargent painting ... relates to certain American abstract painting more closely than do Cézanne, Picasso, or even Monet."[6]

Porter was not merely thinking about painting techniques in his essay on Sargent; he saw the essay as an occasion to reconsider Boston, where he had not spent much time since his friendship with Wheelwright in the late 1930s and which (since Laurence was at Harvard and Porter was doing research at Boston College) probably reminded Porter of his student days. The conclusion of this perceptive critical essay – which, like most of Porter's profiles of American artists, was essentially negative: in this case, Porter felt Sargent lacked vision and conviction – suggests that in examining the life of Sargent, Porter was in some measure reflecting on his own relation to the Boston he had known as a young man: "It is as though contemporary American abstract painters had at last justified those potentialities of Sargent's which he was himself unable to believe in, because there was no place for them in the Boston-English world which tolerated painting, not for the sake of art but for the sake of the graces and refinement of an upper-class life."[7]

Porter had faced a similar challenge, both at Harvard and after: the challenge of living in a world which condoned painting but saw no importance in it

32
Jerry, 1955, repainted 1975.
Private Collection.

(being an artist, he had been told as a young man, "meant deciding in favor of triviality").[8] Here, as in his other extended writings on American artists, Porter seems to have been examining the choices that artists made about their work in relation to society and finding in their choices an ultimate failure and disappointment.

The Thanksgiving dinner in Putney which followed Porter's trip to Boston was not simply a side trip. Porter was increasingly concerned about Jerry, whose unhappiness in Southampton had been considerable and had remained constant during his first year at Putney (fig. 32).

As a child, Jerry Porter had shown a brilliant ability for language, writing poems from an early age; he had also taught himself to play the piano and could compose music spontaneously. But, perhaps more sensitive than his older brother Laurence, he had responded adversely to the tension in the Porter home. As he recalled, his father "got very upset very easily ... he hated when anybody spilled things or broke things, or when the house wasn't clean. He was very particular about keeping things clean and neat." (Laurence Porter agreed with his brother here, noting that "Fairfield's anger was frightening ... because of its unpredictability and intensity. ... He had no idea how to be a father to a child over five.")[9] Jerry also felt that his father, by staying home to paint, was embarrassingly unlike other working fathers. As Anne wrote her mother in 1955, making light of the situation, "The *Southampton Press* ... sent a lady to interview Furl. This will be nice for Jerry, whose father isn't on view at a Main Street office desk or at the wheel of a potato-truck, and so must seem rather sinister. Now they'll know that the lights burning late in the barn aren't the lights of a distillery."[10]

Jerry had long kept aloof from his family. According to his brother Laurence, "From as early as I can remember, [Jerry] seemed to express a feeling of alienation by being drawn to poor kids who weren't very bright." A year in Southampton High School had proved a disaster, so Porter had enrolled him at Putney, a progressive boarding school well known for its work with troubled students. But even during the summer of 1955 on Great Spruce Head, Jerry had kept apart from his family and seemed irritated at the presence of his father's arty friends. In traveling to Putney for Thanksgiving, Porter was attempting to reach out to his son, who had made few efforts to keep in touch with his parents by phone or mail. But his son's silence left him at a loss.

Except for several weeks spent on jury duty, Porter worked hard through the winter to prepare for his next show at Tibor de Nagy. As the exhibition approached, so did Anne Porter's delivery date, and Porter was once again distressed and anxious about his wife's impending childbirth. A note from Anne Porter to Fairfield Porter at the time of Elizabeth Porter's birth shows that Porter was in New York on the date of her delivery, April 1, 1956; he was there making his rounds as a reviewer, writing a profile of Jane Freilicher, and hanging his show at Tibor de Nagy, which opened two days later, on April 3.

Anne Porter, by now reconciled to her husband's waywardness where childbirth was concerned, tended the new baby on her own and noted to her mother that "the *Herald Tribune* compared Fairfield's enormous portrait of Kitty and me [*Katie and Anne*] to Renoir's *Mme. Charpentier et sa Fille* ... I feel very cheerful."[11]

During the remainder of the spring, Porter made plans once again to go to Great Spruce Head, but finances were so limited that he would not be able to afford any household help, not even a local teenage girl to help with the cooking and washing up – posing a formidable challenge to his wife, for the house still had no hot water, rudimentary plumbing, and a wood-fired stove for cooking meals and heating water for dishwashing. Anne, now in her mid-forties with a newborn infant, had a hard time caring for the baby, a seven-year-old daughter, and a fifteen-year-old son all summer long in this primitive environment.

Perhaps because he had hosted so many guests the previous summer and perhaps also because of the lack of household help, Porter invited few guests for the summer of 1956. The poet Kenneth Koch and his wife Janice were invited, along with their daughter, Katherine. The photographer Ellen Auerbach, then collaborating with Eliot Porter on a photography book about churches in Mexico and the American Southwest, was expected to visit as well. James Schuyler would not be coming, for he was renting the Southampton house from Porter and intended to live there with his lover, Arthur Gold.

During the spring, around the time of Elizabeth's birth, Porter occasionally called on Ilse Mattick to talk about his feelings for Schuyler, for he was troubled

33
James Schuyler, circa 1957. Photographer unknown. Courtesy James Schuyler Papers, Archive for New Poetry, Mandeville Department of Special Collections, University of California, San Diego / La Jolla.

by the realization that he was in love with him. He had told Anne about his feelings for Schuyler but thought that her counsel on such a subject was limited (fig. 33). So he turned from his wife to Ilse Mattick. Whatever Porter's history with her, she had always been a sympathetic listener.

Ilse Mattick knew Schuyler. The artist Nell Blaine had come to live with the Matticks the previous summer at their small home in Jamaica, Vermont; Schuyler, in coming to visit Blaine, had imposed himself on the Matticks as well, and Ilse Mattick, who had a good eye for character, harbored few illusions about him. "Jimmy took advantage of the situation. He was not above that sort of thing. He'd done it before, with Auden. I liked Jimmy – he was very agreeable. But he was also very weak, and, like many weak people, he would manipulate others into doing things for him, giving him things, taking care of him. I'll say it: there was something sleazy about him. I told him so when he came here to stay. And I said, 'Now do me a favor and don't write a poem about it.'"[12]

Ilse Mattick did not believe that Porter was really in love with Schuyler. But while Schuyler was visiting O'Hara up in Cambridge (where the latter had won a fellowship to the Poet's Theater), Porter felt lonely and excluded; when Ashbery's play *The Compromise* was produced that spring, Porter wrote his son Laurence saying that he wished he could go, too. Porter's sense of being both used and excluded by his younger friends, particularly Schuyler, grew over the summer and in the coming year.

Schuyler's letters from the summer months have not survived, but an undated letter from Schuyler in New York, carrying a reference to John Button's party that fall, establishes the tone he took in his friendship with Porter during this period:

undated   Dear Fairfield,

How inaccurate of you to have told Frank and Kenneth that the reason you don't call me is that it is you who always call! Wasn't it I who called you in Southampton when I heard you were back and coming into town? And I who called you the day we were moving, when you and I went downtown and you bought us the beautiful white lamp that has given us so much pleasure and illumination? And often, when it has been you who called, wasn't it because we had arranged it so beforehand – as often at my suggestion as at yours – on the grounds that you would be out during the day, and I would be in? I did try to call you the week of John's party, and then gave it up because I was aware of a deliberateness in your silence. One's often tempted to test one's friends in these little ways – at least I am – but it's my experience that to do so is a challenge to the friend to show that he has the nerve and heartlessness to fail one; and most of us have. Besides, I think you exaggerate the degree of initiative you take in your friendships; I know, because I'm shy, that it often takes more initiative for me to bring myself to say yes to an invitation than it took for the inviter to issue it.

While I'm at it, I'm also rather put out by this youth and age stuff. Insofar as I think of you as "older," I feel honored and benefitted by your friendship; but if it turns out that you feel odd in bestowing it, I feel snubbed. I don't, though, think of you as "older" so much as I do [as] a friend who has had a life very different from mine (but if I must think about it, then I say that I think I'm a man over thirty, past which age one might hope to have gained the right to mingle with one's elders &/or betters). I wish I had thought you dwelt a little on the virtues in your behavior: and saw that if (as I hope you do) you take pleasure in the company of Frank and Jane and Kenneth and Barbara and the rest of us, it's because your mind hasn't sealed over, and that you've kept a fresh enthusiasm and curiosity. ... All I mean is that it seems to me merely another instance of American self-consciousness when confronted by one's oddness, when the oddness is what makes value. ... I wish instead of odd, you thought of yourself as unique; you seem so to me, in relation to your brothers and sisters, to other artists, to other men your age, to other members of the Class of '28 ... but then, they haven't had a long draught from the only spring that matters. You have.

I hope this doesn't seem impudent and fresh; which was no part of my plan. ... I hope soon I can come out and visit you ... I'll write more chattily another time, when you tell me you've forgiven me for anything in this letter that needs forgiving. None of it means anything serious, in the light of the joy it gave me to see your face light up when you finally saw me signalling wildly from that moving cab.

> As always,
> Jimmy.
> P.S. Would you call me next Tuesday?
> I expect to be in all day.

Schuyler had, by this point, made clear to Porter that he was involved with Arthur Gold and in love with John Button; but Schuyler seems to have wanted to give Porter mixed signals about his feelings, in part because he respected Porter as an artist and critic and friend, and in part because he wanted to retain Porter's good opinion, an opinion which was founded to some extent on Porter's love for him.

Schuyler's treatment of Porter, while manipulative, is best understood by the difficult circumstances in which he lived. For most of the 1950s he had very little money and eked out a living by working in a bookshop. He had little contact with his family and no support from them; he also had a history of mental illness and was prone to paranoia and incapacitating depression. Even as early as June 1956, Schuyler seems to have been aware that his relationship with Arthur Gold was coming to an end, that his love for John Button was destined to remain unrequited, and that he was once again facing a life in which he had no one to rely upon for financial and emotional support. Moreover, as the summer progressed, he again experienced episodes of schizophrenia.[13]

At the end of May, Schuyler arrived in Southampton to take possession of the house as the Porters left for Maine. In the previous weeks, Anne Porter had done her best to make the place presentable, writing her husband, then in New York on his rounds as a reviewer, "I've been working on the house and see dimly the outlines of a house that Jimmy and Arthur could live in, appearing from under the usual things."[14] After a final weekend together, during which Schuyler observed the agitated Porter "charging around the garden with a dangerous-looking spade,"[15] Schuyler and Porter said goodbye, and the Porters departed in their station wagon, Porter already feeling tired from the hard work of packing for the summer. Shortly thereafter, Porter fell into a depression.

Some time after arriving on the island, Porter developed a temperature. Feeling that his illness was psychosomatic, he blamed himself for being unable to leave bed to paint. Compounding his frustration was the Porter family philosophy that – the death of his maternal grandfather notwithstanding – one simply did not get sick while summering on Great Spruce Head Island. His exhaustion is evident in a letter to Schuyler: "I have been using your and John Button's room to write in, as my study of last year is now Elizabeth's room; but once the rain came right through the closed windows and rusted the typewriter and wet the checks and papers, so I decided to move across the hall to [another] room, that still is full of father's preserved sea life in glass jars, the throwing away of which seems such a tiresome chore that I still just leave them. Anne is doing all the work."[16]

Confined to bed, Porter began reading Proust. His mother had bought the original American editions of *Remembrance of Things Past* as they had appeared one by one in American bookshops. Porter's awareness of Proust in 1956 must have been filtered, therefore, through memories of his mother, for he was reading her books in her former bedroom – indeed, in her bed. Confined there in a feverish and dreadful state of mind, Porter abandoned himself to the novel, in which Marcel's obsession with Albertine may well have informed and magnified his awareness of his love for Schuyler.

Schuyler's letters to Porter during this summer no longer exist. Porter and Schuyler were meticulous about saving correspondence, so the absence of Schuyler's letters suggests that Porter lost, returned, or destroyed them[17] (though it was not at all like him to destroy anyone's letters). The letters from Porter to Schuyler do survive, however, and while slightly incoherent, they are perfectly expressive of Porter's distracted state during this period of illness. They are excerpted here. On the first was written "I do not know what day"; the others are also undated.

undated   You say you can understand the state of mind that made me send my letter, even if you cannot sympathize with it. What rubbish! If you understand without sympathy, then your understanding is not understanding, but manipulation.

I do not want to be everything to you, I wanted to be that which you said John [Button] was to you, which is not everything. I think I recognized the letter,

I think it was like one you once wrote me. I suppose one is especially possessive of what he is afraid of losing, and a miser's dominant emotion is fear of poverty. ...

The letter I wrote you one day all day, when Jerry and I were alone here, was about Proust and about writing, about what musicalness can be, about John A.'s, Kenneth's, Frank's and your poems, about the pollen blowing from the spruce trees, about Balbec, Maine, Northern California, Oregon and Norway, about my relief when after that awfully bitchy musical party at Mme. de St. Euverte's Swann fell out of love, and my elation and hope. I burned it up because it seemed pedantic at the rereading. I cannot rewrite it now. If this letter of mine does not prevent your sending that sensible letter you promised, then I will better be able to write to you in a different tone.

The different tone sometimes comes over me now: it is like a wave of faith and hope, which though secular, is not concrete.

Please do not take it amiss that I tell you that your letter touched me and moved me and made me feel stronger. You have the power (though I can see that you are feeling weak) of making me extremely happy. When I do not hear from you in answer to a letter of mine it makes me feel that I don't exist. When I hope for and do not find a letter from you, I get restless and depressed and want to break things and damage myself. ... My rudeness comes from an attempt to get rid of those positive feelings that are unwelcome to you. ... You find me wicked for both my positive feelings and the negative ones I substitute for them: when I feel wicked in relation to you, I lose hope and purpose; I can hardly concentrate. And when you find me wicked, it seems that like a child, I get worse, out of defiance. Of course I don't know this when I do it.

undated

And just as I ought to be gentle and kind to you, because only kindness is good for people, so I beg you, Jimmy, please, please, be gentle and indulgent and generous and make allowances out of whatever strength you have instead of scolding me out of your feelings of weakness.

... I have been ill with a high fever ... yesterday I was up for the first time, and at noon, when the mail was due, I had, in anticipation, my daily fit of despair: your letter came, and revived me.

Sunday, after the Kochs came, I felt, as usual, physically, mentally, emotionally and spiritually tired ... at supper time, feeling not in the least rested, I found out I had a temperature of 102½, and so I have been in bed since.

... I have the highest hopes for your psycho-analysis: you have the two qualities that are necessary for a good prognosis; you are very bright, and you have already "taken yourself in hand."

... I like the fact that you say (by implication) that I am a snob; because lots of people think I am not, and the fact that you know that I am, is another sign of that intelligence and understanding of me which gives me pleasure.

... I told Anne that you wanted to be analyzed, to which she said, "Jimmy is a person who deserves much better bringing up than he got, he has so much innate sweetness."

As for me, I love you very, very much. Anne and I send our love to you and Frank [O'Hara], and I include John [Button] and Alvin [Novak].

[An addendum to the letter:] Dearest Jimmy: I just got your second note in the mail. It makes me awfully happy. Last night, I was up, and feeling good, because I had heard from you. I was outdoors, talking to Kenneth, about the sunset and the birds; and Kenneth said to me, "You have such an air of new life, of beginning again, of taking an interest in things. I am so glad you are well at last." It was my emotional health he was talking about; I was feeling happy about you again.

undated I am in the hospital at Camden. I have been here two days and go home tomorrow (Saturday). We found out that I had mononucleosis & that I am recovering. I wrote the enclosed canzone during convalescence on the island. With my convalescence my mood has changed & when I am not completely bushed I like everything.

A viral illness often triggered by stress and fatigue, mononucleosis is rare in people over the age of forty, and Porter was lucky to have gone to the hospital; he might otherwise have ruptured his spleen. The hospital treatment and the relief of knowing that his unhappiness had an organic cause seem to have concluded the worst of Porter's emotional crisis. Still, on returning from the hospital to the island aboard the *Penguin*, the motor broke down, and Porter lay ill in the bottom of the boat "getting sicker by the minute from the wallowing and the smell of gas."[18] After an hour and a half, he was rescued by his brother John, another incidence of humiliation. When the Porters left the island that September, Porter was still seriously ill with mononucleosis; he remained so well into the fall.[19]

At the end of the summer of 1956, Schuyler wrote an angry letter to the painter John Button concerning Button's acknowledgment to Larry Rivers that Porter was bisexual. Schuyler, whose love for Button had prompted an intimate correspondence, was going through a difficult time. He had just suffered a schizophrenic episode during a weekend on Fire Island with O'Hara and had recently ended his relationship with Arthur Gold. Button, who already had a lover, had recently told Schuyler that he did not share Schuyler's feelings of love. Schuyler, angry and vulnerable, accused Button of a number of personal betrayals in the letter, concluding,

Labor Day, 1956 What is most serious (if true) is that you told Larry [Rivers] about Fairfield's private affairs. No matter what Larry may have surmised, he did not before really know anything (I got this from Jane [Freilicher]). I don't imply at all that you were motivated by malice, but you do provide people who are malicious with weapons: would you really care to take the responsibility for what Larry is capable of saying to Anne Porter, and do you think she deserves having it said to her? (Not that her nature isn't large enough to encompass it). And what about the obligations your friendship with Fairfield, John Ashbery and with me place on you?[20]

The letter is somewhat hypocritical, for Schuyler had, after all, told Button about "Fairfield's private affairs," which made him just as guilty of indiscretion. But Schuyler need not have worried about Larry Rivers's surprising Anne Porter with news of her husband's bisexuality. Although Porter had always stopped short of describing the extent and nature of his involvements to her,[21] Anne Porter was by now well enough aware of her husband's needs to understand Schuyler's importance to him. Both Anne Porter and her husband had already made many compromises with one another; since the late 1940s they had been working at rebuilding their marriage. A certain tension would, of course, always exist between Anne Porter and James Schuyler, since both were seeking the affection and approval of the same man, since both were living in such close and constant contact, and, finally (and this should not be underestimated), since both were poets with radically different politics, ambitions, and worldviews. But Anne Porter had been married to her husband for twenty-four years, loved him with singular devotion, and was mother to his five children. She had just spent a summer with him, taking care of him in his sickness and misery, and was quietly aware of the reasons for his unhappiness. She did not want him to be unhappy.

Shortly after Thanksgiving 1956, while Porter was still recuperating, she wrote Schuyler, "Thank you for your letter. This is an old, made-over typewriter which can be a guest-room typewriter whenever you come to visit 'the (ugh) Porters.' We hope sometime you can visit, and also Frank; we haven't seen either of you for so long and we miss you, though there's not much here for visitors to do except sleep, rake leaves and write poetry (and no one is really going to rake leaves, not even Furl)."[22]

A few days later she even made light of her marital situation, writing to her mother about a mutual friend, "I'm (confidentially) a bit horrified at Rosa and I told her so, for asking if Fairfield *lives* in the barn! We're naturally temperamental, and have had difficult conditions outwardly too, more often than not, but few people mean more to their wives and children than does our unique and beloved Fairfield! who is even very patient with us, 'in his own weird way,' as Laurence Porter puts it."[23]

The Porter household would be open to James Schuyler, just as it had been open to many other friends over the decades. The extent to which Schuyler availed himself of that hospitality, however, would be altogether different and eventually posed a great challenge to both Porter and his wife.

15

Portraits, *The Nation*, and
a Monograph

During the fall of 1956, while Porter recovered from mononucleosis in Southampton, an important magazine article appeared in the special annual edition of *Art News*, written by its influential editor Thomas B. Hess, to celebrate the magazine's twenty-fifth anniversary. "U.S. Painting: Some Recent Directions" featured twenty-one artists who were just then coming into their own. To be included on that list was a great honor, and Porter made the cut. Others in the group were Felix Pasilis, Milton Resnick, Miles Forst, Leland Bell, Joan Mitchell, Robert Rauschenberg, Nell Blaine, Stephan Pace, Robert Goodnough, Seymour Remenick, Michael Goldberg, Larry Rivers, Helen Frankenthaler, Wolf Kahn, Robert DeNiro, Gandy Brodie, Elaine de Kooning, Hyde Solomon, Friedebald Dzubas, and Ernest Briggs. In seeking to define the new "generation" (Porter was ten years older than anyone else in the group), Hess noted that they "insist on a greater role for the subject. The object being depicted does have, in itself, outside of art, a value, an electric charge or valence, which must be studied, isolated, and brought back into the painting. Its equivalence must be ascertained. There is something else than art, different but as valuable; the difference is vital."[1]

Though all had been influenced by European painting, Hess saw no single movement afoot, writing, "There is no 'Revolutionary Discipline'; each artist is a confirmed deviationist from his own time." Porter's inclusion despite his age marked a watershed in his career, for never before had he been considered part of the artistic mainstream, much less one of its most promising new talents. This recognition and acceptance must have gratified him enormously.

Apart from this moment of critical recognition in a magazine, however, Porter had a difficult fall and winter. He was recovering from mononucleosis until late in the fall; in January, Anne Porter entered St. Vincent's hospital in New York for an operation; in February, Porter's hayloft studio caught fire. The potbellied stove had been heavily stoked, and the chimney, which was improperly insulated, had grown so hot that the roof timbers burst into flame. Porter did not lose any paintings in the blaze – several were creased – but the reconstruction of the studio took three months. His nonproductivity due to illness and the fire meant that he was not able to have a show at Tibor de Nagy that year.

But the Porters' main concern during the spring of 1957 was their son Jerry. Porter had hoped that by going away to Putney, his son would settle down, and at first Jerry seemed content. Porter had written to the art critic Lawrence Campbell at the end of Jerry's fall term, "Jerry likes being home and is proud of his achievements at school, that is, of just being able to have in his background a life of his own, situations of his own that he solves somehow, and that he brings back to us like a cat bringing home a dead mole."[2]

But by the time of the studio fire a year later, Jerry seemed miserable again. Porter wrote his son Laurence, on whom he had come to depend for advice and emotional support, "Jerry hasn't written to us since Christmas, so I called him up just now, and got a few yesses and nos out of him, but hardly anything else. I remember that when I was sixteen I went to Milton Academy for a year, where I was so shy and homesick, that when I came home I was unable to talk to anyone older than twenty. But then I started out before I went there very shy anyway, and in that perhaps I was superficially a little like Jerry: what he is like underneath, I believe to be quite different (I don't mean different from shy, I mean different from me)."[3] In attempting to reconnect with his third son, whom he considered "brilliant,"[4] Porter sent Jerry a volume of Elizabeth Bishop's poems. Porter, who admired Bishop, felt that Jerry's poetry was something like Bishop's. But the gift was not received with much enthusiasm.

Laurence Porter was graduated from Harvard in May 1957; the Porters drove up for the ceremony, then returned to Southampton, for their financial circumstances were such that they were not able to go to Maine for the summer. Porter was hoping that by painting more (even if it meant giving up criticism) he would be able to improve his income. He wrote Ashbery, "I think this summer I will stay here, being quite broke again, meaning that I am living off capital which will reduce my income. This summer I expect to paint a lot for the show next year and I should stop reviewing: it is beginning to bore me, except that Jimmy [Schuyler]'s exaltation stimulates me."[5]

Porter instead set to work in his new Southampton studio, which was now painted pale pink. In addition to his usual landscapes, interiors, and still lifes, he began painting portraits; he hoped to attract portrait commissions (and income) by completing works of his friends. During 1957, Porter made portraits of Frank O'Hara, John Ashbery (then visiting from France), Elaine de Kooning, the piano duo of Arthur Gold and Bobby Fizdale, Bobby Fizdale's mother, two portraits of the painter Jane Wilson, a double portrait of James Schuyler and John Ashbery, and another double portrait of Katharine Porter and her friend Dorothy.

34 *(left)*
Portrait of Elaine de Kooning, 1957.
Metropolitan Museum of Art, New York,
Gift of Mrs. Fairfield Porter, 1978 (1978.296).
Photo by Lynton Gardiner © 1991
The Metropolitan Museum of Art.

35
Jimmy and John, 1957–58.
Barbara and Michael Kratchman.

The *Portrait of Elaine de Kooning* (1957, fig. 34) is one of Porter's most beautiful from the period and, typically enough, is one that never sold. In it, Porter's brilliant subject, a frequent visitor to the Porter house (and, childless, a special friend to the Porter girls), is portrayed seated on the old flowered sofa which Porter kept in his studio. (The sofa can also be seen in *Portrait of Frank O'Hara* [1957] and *Jimmy and John* [1957–58] as well as *The Mirror* [1960]). Porter views Elaine de Kooning from above and from the side, a flattering and dynamic compositional device probably borrowed from John Singer Sargent's portraits of grandes dames. The painting features none of Sargent's signature impasto, however, for rather than paint with a loaded brush, Porter created a washy image which seems about to break apart or dissolve in the radiant pink light (a new light, thanks to the newly pink-painted studio). The darkness of the floor anchors the image in space, and the painting of the printed slipcover gives the image a rich textural subtlety (again reminiscent of Vuillard) that it otherwise lacks. The vivid, clashing oranges of Elaine's dress – rich tones enhanced by the pink and black of the rest of the picture – match her fiery personality, a personality manifest in her game, watchful expression.

Even though Schuyler sat for Porter for his double portrait with John Ashbery that year (a successful venture showing Schuyler in elegant profile), that summer of 1957 his relationship with Porter seems to have cooled (fig. 35). Schuyler was now involved with the art dealer Donald Droll, living at Droll's garden apartment on the Upper East Side. Schuyler could be cruel about Porter in his letters to others and seems glad to have escaped Porter in this letter to John Ashbery (which was probably written at the beginning of the summer):

undated   Jane [Freilicher] read me a letter of yours with some amusing Fairfieldisms in it. Yes, in a sense the group has rather fallen apart … I certainly hope Frank [O'Hara] and Joey [LeSueur, O'Hara's lover] enjoy [Fairfield's] dropping in [to the Forty-ninth Street apartment]. Ha. The other evening he appeared at the Museum at exactly six o'clock (I had avoided an … opening the evening before just 'cause I knew he was laying in wait at it) so we had dinner at the Old Colony. … He showed me a rather dopey sestina about Greece, and then said, "It bears the same relation to my work that The Instruction Manual bears to John's." It's a sequence of those that leaves me feeling like an excerpt from the Smugglers' chorus in *Carmen*.[6]

Porter's tendency to lie in wait for people could be wearing, as Ilse Mattick knew. Porter's grave discussions of his own less accomplished poetry may also have exhausted his poet friend, whose temperament was more mercurial.

While Porter did not particularly like spending the summer in Southampton, he once again enjoyed the pleasure of an active summer social life, thanks in part to the painter Jane Wilson and her husband, the writer and composer John Gruen. Wilson, who supplemented her income by working as a fashion model, had met Porter through Jane Freilicher, with whom she shared a summer place (fig. 36). She had recently become a contestant on the popular television quiz show *The $64,000 Challenge*. (Unlike Larry Rivers, who appeared on the show and, supplied with the answers by Leonard Bernstein's sister Shirley, won the jackpot, Wilson lost her final round and was sent home with a thousand dollars and ten boxes of Kent cigarettes.)[7] As Porter wrote his son Laurence,

When mother was away [visiting her mother in Wareham] I had a night party to which 55 people came. The hosts were me and the Gruens, she (Jane Wilson Gruen) is a painter who missed out on the television contest that ran with Larry's – hers about renaissance art – and he [John Gruen] is a composer. They had wanted to have a party while renting the Hazan's house in Water Mill, to celebrate her expected $64,000 victory, and so asked to share a party with me. ... It was very expensive, costing for two cases of liquor, five bags of ice cubes and two cases of soda and quinine water more than $150 (shared with the Gruens). I don't know very much about the party, because in order not to look too worried about everyone, I decided to act like a guest. Larry [Rivers] said it was the best party of the year. There was much very wild dancing in the living room, and many people said over and over to me that it was a wonderful party. The dining room was a swamp of melting ice cubes and 72 glasses (bought for the occasion) quickly disappeared from the sideboard. But there was only one broken glass afterwards. I remember Frank [O'Hara] and Mrs. Harold Rosenberg dancing, and telling me that it was a wonderful party, at which I embraced them both: "I'm so glad!" which made them both giggle.[8]

July 25, 1957

36
Jane Freilicher and Fairfield Porter at the home shared by Freilicher, Jane Wilson, John Gruen, and Joe Hazan in Water Mill, N.Y., in the summer of 1959. Photo by John Jonas Gruen. Courtesy John Jonas Gruen.

Despite his active social life, Porter remained preoccupied with his son Jerry. As he wrote Kenneth Koch, "Jerry is [in Frank O'Hara's words] 'taking a stand' (he is getting silent, stubborn, as Joe Hazan says, 'interested in nothing but sex'). I asked him if he wanted to meet Elizabeth Bishop, who was at the Gold-Fizdale house a few weeks ago, and he replied, 'Why should I meet her? Is she pretty or ugly?' He has an adolescent snobbishness that nothing except a pretty girl is worth his time."[9]

By the end of summer, Jerry was spending lots of time with Larry Rivers's eldest son, Joe. Porter wrote his son Laurence,

Late August 1957   Jerry we are somewhat worried about. Last night he stayed away all night with Joe Rivers, and in the morning I called the police and Larry, and finally he came home. We learned first that he stayed out with Joe, in Joe's car, with two girls who had been missing from home since Sunday, and later from Lilian that these girls had been fought over by rival gangs from Southampton and Hampton Bays, and we were worried, because these gangs are very cruel and hurt each other. I talked seriously to him about the dangers he was getting himself into. He was serious in turn, and really very nice and reasonable, and tonight he wanted to go in town with Joe and Larry [Rivers], which I was against, but finally after lecturing him about Larry, who I do not consider a good mentor for a boy, and my disapproval of Joe, I let him go, because as Anne said, he might have been done more harm than good by being made to stay at home. I think he has essentially good instincts, and is kind and fairly strongminded. He let me know what he planned to do, which was harmless, and I warned him against drug addicts (Larry used to be one). He had done nothing with the girls that "he shouldn't," as Henry James would say. But we had been afraid that he might have got hurt, and were relieved that they were home. I told him he must not drink. It will have the effect of making him at least a little watchful.[10]

The Porters' concern for their son, combined with an awareness of the drug use and wild behavior of the Rivers household, caused a break between Porter and Rivers. In Rivers's words, Porter "just decided that I was some kind of villain."[11]

During the fall and winter of 1957–58, Porter continued to paint and maintained his usual reviewing schedule. He wrote his son Laurence, "In New York I am painting Jane Wilson in her studio, which is her bedroom too, and very crowded, so that I can't back far enough away from it. The face might be any-one most of the time, even Abraham Lincoln. This made her laugh, and she asked when I looked more contented, 'Is it now more like Wilson than Lincoln?'"[12]

At Christmas, Porter was delighted to receive a card from an old acquaintance. Arthur Giardelli, Porter's friend from Florence, was now an artist and teacher living in Wales. Porter's renewed correspondence with Giardelli, which lasted for over a decade, gave Porter, now fifty, the opportunity to review the course his life had taken since 1931 and to reflect upon events to an impartial stranger. It also gave Porter an opportunity to see another wayward artistic path.

Giardelli had been exposed to the teachings of Gandhi by his family's Indian lodgers in the late 1920s and became further involved with the pacifist movement at Oxford. At the outbreak of World War II, he had announced himself a conscientious objector. His pacifism and his Italian last name combined to make him a social outcast. He had found a sense of solidarity among the ethnic Welsh, many of whom were also conscientious objectors, and worked on a fire brigade in Wales during the war (dangerous work, since he lived in an area of fueling stations and refineries). After the Allied victory, Giardelli had decided to remain in Wales to practice his art, buying a home in Llethr, Pendyne. Dylan Thomas and his wife, Kaitlin John, who lived a village away in Laugharne, were his friends. Of Dylan Thomas, Giardelli wrote Porter, "Did you meet Dylan when he was in New York? ... We were appalled by what happened to him in America – so unlike his life here. He used to drink a lot of beer but no spirits, & there was no scandal about him as regards the women of these parts. And as you know in a village everyone knows everything ... here he was at home and understood how to get along. He was an even better talker when he was not showing off. He couldn't help using words as though they had been made specially for him & that occasion."[13]

Giardelli's casual but informed comments about Thomas are representative of his unassuming manner and great intelligence. Now a schoolteacher married to a musician and the father of two children, Giardelli supplemented his income in the summer by opening his home to language students from abroad, hosting as many as thirty at a time. But he was first and foremost an artist, exhibiting at London's well-known Grosvenor Gallery. Giardelli would meet Porter again in 1967.

Porter's May 1958 show was, in retrospect, an extraordinary one, featuring some of his best paintings. At the time, the exhibition of twenty-three works was a cause for some concern, because so many of the works were portraits – a distinctly unfashionable commodity among the avant-garde. Schuyler wrote of the exhibition that Porter is "one of the few modern American painters who transforms genre into high art. ... His special gift is catching the nuance of vacancy in a room, or landscape, the unseen presences that human use and cultivation create."[14] Of Schuyler's review, Porter wrote Giardelli, "The review in *Art News* (May) was by a friend on the staff [Schuyler] – he really likes my paintings, but also he knows what I have been influenced by, and so it is, in a way, more accurate than other reviews."[15]

The review may have been something of a peace offering. Schuyler's friendship with Porter had suffered in the past year because of Schuyler's preoccupation with Donald Droll, because of his general indifference to Porter's affection for him, and because of his mental condition, which had deteriorated substantially, leaving him little energy or ability for friendship. Even Schuyler's good friend Frank O'Hara (and O'Hara's lover Joe LeSueur) had grown exhausted with Schuyler, to the point of abandoning the exceptionally convenient and inexpensive apartment that the three shared in midtown Manhattan. As O'Hara wrote Kenneth Koch, Jimmy's analysis "seems to be going along okay, but confidentially I have found it rather depressing myself, and have reacted to certain things in recent months myself, probably neurotically but nevertheless really, and the necessity to consider his neural-emotional state as more vulnerable than my own has gotten to be quite a pressure ... his complete concentration on his own states of mind and a certain liberated aggressiveness from analysis (I suppose) amounts to an implicit overall demand which could only be countered if I were less fond of him than I am. So *lève l'ancre!*"[16]

Schuyler's sloppiness and disinclination to clean up after himself, combined with a need, symptomatic of his illness, to order others around in a gruff and abrupt manner and to exert control over the domestic environment, convinced O'Hara of the need to depart, despite the inconvenience of finding a new place. Schuyler's behavior toward O'Hara and LeSueur would, in time, repeat itself with the Porters.

Porter spent the summer of 1958 in Southampton, again prevented by money worries from traveling to Great Spruce Head. The exhibition at Tibor de Nagy had sold only three out of twenty-three paintings, and the Southampton house was in desperate need of repairs; one visitor recalled seeing a large patch of sky through a hole in the roof.[17] Porter began to consider teaching as a way of supplementing his income and to consider as well the sale of several of his paintings, one of which, a small orange and green abstraction by de Kooning, had been given on loan (at least so far as Porter understood) to Frank O'Hara.

The summer was marked by a quiet family crisis. Jerry, who was supposed to have been graduated from Putney that June, packed his bags and departed before the graduation ceremony without leaving behind any explanation or forwarding address. Later he explained that tensions at home had led him to run away; but throughout the early part of the summer, the Porters did not know where their son had gone or even whether he was alive.

Porter continued to work on portrait commissions and painted two of his best-known and most delightful family-related works that summer: *Anne, Lizzie, and Katie* (1958, fig. 37) and *Lizzie at the Table* (1958, fig. 38). Given Jerry Porter's absence, the first one is perhaps the more revealing; in it, Porter's wife stands in the living room holding Elizabeth in her arms while Katie sits on a nearby chair; behind them, on the living room wall, is an earlier painting by Porter of an unhappy Jerry (*Jerry*, see fig. 32). The color combinations (and the setting, the living room) recall *Laurence at the Piano* and *Katie and Anne* (see figs. 27 and 31). *Anne, Lizzie, and Katie* is a remarkably still and quiet painting in which one is aware of nothing so much as the emptiness of the house at a certain moment in late afternoon, and seems, like the valedictory painting of Laurence, another meditation on family and loss.

Lizzie at the Table, meanwhile, is an example of Porter's continuing examination of the randomness of everyday life, a cheerful, Intimist-inspired evocation of breakfast-table disarray featuring Elizabeth in her high chair. (Elizabeth's serene countenance, reminiscent of a portrait by Holbein, as well as her ready availability as an artist's model, would make her a favored subject in the years to come.) A random bouquet of flowers and beech leaves sits in a vase at the center of the table, which is littered with mismatched breakfast china (including some gold-rimmed Limoges porcelain which Porter had inherited from a relative, the first territorial governor of Minnesota, by way of his maternal cousins Nita and Laura Furness). Also on the table is a jar of marmalade, a white enamel coffeepot (an accessory to the Aga stove), an orange, a teaspoon, a napkin ring, and a volume of Wallace Stevens's *Opus Posthumous*. The coffeepot and orange suggest an homage to the opening lines of Stevens's "Sunday Morning" (an evocation of, "late / Coffee and oranges in a sunny chair"); but the image also suggests a visual pun on another Stevens poem, "Table Talk," which was first published (in the volume on the table) in 1957: the poem, which concerns itself with randomness and coincidence, is certainly related thematically to the painting. But Porter was neither a manifesto writer nor a manifesto painter, and it is significant that he titled the painting *Lizzie at the Table*, for it is surely Elizabeth at the table, not Stevens on the table, that is the subject of the painting. Still, Porter's interest in and preoccupation with Stevens are a part of this painting, just as they were part of his consciousness at the time that he brought the volume of Stevens to the table and, later, painted it.[18]

Porter received a pleasant compliment that summer. He wrote to Laurence, "Did Mother tell you of the Five Spot Cafe (a branch of one of the same name on the Bowery at Seventh Street) opened here? ... I have been only on 'official' occasions, except last night, when Bob Dash invited me as a compensation, I suppose, for his visit ... I saw Bill de Kooning, who gave me the most flattering compliment – he wanted me to know that he had been, in his painting, influenced by my painting."[19]

De Kooning, perhaps the most successful painter of his generation, had fallen out of touch with Porter; with this renewal of acquaintance, Porter may have resolved once again to write about the work of his favorite artist, for within a year he would write an essay on de Kooning that received a prize from the Longview Foundation for excellence in reviewing. He would also, perhaps coincidentally, paint and draw several nudes of de Kooning's girlfriend, Ruth Kligman.

By the end of the summer of 1958, the Porters were relieved to hear at last from their vanished son, Jerry. Porter, to improve his relationship with his son, decided that the two might share Porter's studio in New York, but to do so required moving. As Anne Porter wrote her mother that September, "Fairfield

37 (right)
Anne, Lizzie, and Katie, 1958.
Sheldon Memorial Art Gallery,
University of Nebraska, Lincoln,
Nebraska Art Association,
Thomas C. Woods Memorial
(1962.N-142).

38
Lizzie at the Table, 1958.
Metropolitan Museum of Art,
New York, Bequest of
Arthur Bullowa, 1993 (1993.406.2).
© Photograph 1994
The Metropolitan Museum of Art.

and Jerry are in town. Fairfield is looking for an apartment where he and Jerry can be more comfortable as their present one has no privacy (no doors) and scarcely room for 2 beds. Jerry wants a practice piano and Fairfield has had to rent *another* place for a studio."[20] The situation resulted in a move from Porter's old studio to a new one on Eleventh Street and Avenue A, not far from the bustling Tenth Street gallery scene; Porter planned to live with his son in the apartment for two weeks out of every month.

Porter's show in March 1959 reviewed well, and one of the works included in the show, *Plane Tree*, was accepted for exhibition in the 1959 annual exhibition at the Whitney Museum of American Art. Porter had already been exhibited in the prestigious Stable Annual; to be included in the Whitney Annual was very much a rite of passage (his paintings were included regularly in Whitney Annuals after 1959). Porter may have hoped that this honor would bring sales; he was growing reliant on the small income generated by sales to support his family, for he no longer had much of a trust income. "The fact is that decentralization of cities is catching up with the Porter Realty Trust," his brother Edward wrote him from Chicago, including with the letter one of the last dividend checks issued by the office and remarking plainly, "Father had the mistaken idea that we should not have to work and I think that idea has been bad for us. If one has to work one learns to be self-reliant and not worry."[21]

Porter's March 1959 exhibit at Tibor de Nagy was marked by a small crisis in his friendship with Schuyler, O'Hara, and John Button. Though all had said they would attend Porter's opening, none did, even though Schuyler and O'Hara worked just a few blocks away at the Museum of Modern Art. Porter's anger at this apparent snub was considerable and perhaps irrational, as a letter from Jane Freilicher to John Ashbery makes clear: "Uncle Furl, who was quite drunk, cornered me for a really Fairfieldian half hour of injustices against all the people who didn't show up at his opening, among whom were Jimmy, Frank and John Button. He did paint a rather black picture of their recent behavior to him as opposed to their previous gracious acceptance of his hospitality. He did not of course go into detail about his own lovely gestures of friendship, one of which consisted of his going over to Frank and stage-whispering, 'You're a shit.' However he seemed awfully upset and hurt by everybody."[22]

Schuyler himself wrote John Ashbery,

April 23, 1959 Honestly, if Furl hadn't failed the Taste (Good) Test aeons ago, I'd be faintly cross about his dishing us to Mme. Freilicher-Hazan. ... He did completely flip over that opening. Well. Frankly, I have fibbed so often about how Frank and I were in a meeting and didn't get out till after 6.30, I've quite come to believe it myself. Fact is, we *were* stupefied from work, and, along with Waldo [Rasmussen], met Donald [Droll] a bit after six on the opening night, when what you aptly characterized as "frozen piss" was falling from the skies. After ruining every garment we owned flailing about on the corner in the obscure hope that a celestial cab would appear, we decided to let the Madison Avenue bus go its over-crowded way and repaired to the Berkshire for a refreshing dry martini. We might have known what sort of stores we were laying up. ... Anyway, Furl was much meaner to Frank and to John Button (who didn't go of his own free will, and not because of any plot between us all) than to me, which I found a refreshing change. He has managed to recollect every occasion on which Frank ever broke a date or stood him up, over the last (let's not count them) years, and accused him of them in a lump. This caused Frank to fly off to the Cedar and tell Jerry [Porter], who shares – I think – Jane's old studio, the Auerbach one, with Joe Rivers, how mean Jerry's dad had just been to him. Then, at a party the boys [Gold and Fizdale] gave, more or less under duress, following Alice Esty's recent concert-debacle, Furl stalked up to Frank (which was quite a trick, since the guests were crowding each other out the windows) and said, "I'm very anxious that Jerry go back into analysis and I just hope *you* wouldn't say or do anything to prevent it." Not, you will admit, the most charming thing to say to a guy.

As for me, he just "hoped I would see the show before it closed," to which I ... but let's skip it. I did see it. It was very nice, though not so nice as last year's, perhaps.[23]

Porter's tantrum was probably fueled by his desire that the show be a critical and financial success. In the spring of 1959, aware of the imminent need to get a paying job, Porter decided to quit reviewing for *Art News*. Shortly thereafter, however, he learned from Robert Hatch at *The Nation* that he had been recommended by his old Harvard friend Lincoln Kirstein to write a monthly column on whatever topic he cared to choose. Porter had been an avid reader of *The Nation* since childhood; the opportunity to write for it was too intellectually exciting to pass up despite his financial obligations. His first column for the magazine appeared in June 1959, a definitive appraisal of Willem de Kooning. (Porter had not been able to publish on de Kooning in *Art News* because its editor, Tom Hess, had always been eager to write about the artist.) Over the next two years, a series of brilliant columns by Porter would appear in *The Nation*, on topics as far-flung as "art and rubbish," "Italy and France in the Renaissance," and "communication and moral commitment," until the desire to return to painting full-time led Porter to quit.

To make money, Porter decided upon a twofold course of action. First, he decided to teach, and, second, he resolved to sell his de Koonings, which were now much more valuable than when he had bought them in the mid-1940s ("I hope to realize a 1000% profit," he wrote his son in November 1958).[24] The decision to sell one of the smaller de Koonings came as a surprise to Frank O'Hara, who was under the impression that Porter had given him the painting. O'Hara (who had taken another small de Kooning on loan from Porter in 1954 and returned it) eventually gave back the orange-and-green abstraction, but not happily;

according to his friend the painter Mike Goldberg, who was present when Porter "gave"[25] O'Hara the painting, O'Hara, too, was in need of cash and had been thinking for some time of selling the work to support his poetry writing.[26]

Porter was relieved to find a buyer for the big de Kooning by midsummer, a buyer who said he wanted the painting for himself. "We sold the big de Kooning for $7,000, which means that I can have the roof fixed where it leaks, among other things,"[27] Porter wrote his son. His joy did not last long, for the buyer immediately resold the work to a gallery, which then offered it at more than twice the price. Though the man, a collector, had only done the sort of thing art dealers routinely do, Porter angrily instructed his dealers never to sell any more paintings to him.

O'Hara was still a good-enough sport about the return of the little de Kooning to come to a party hosted by the Porters that summer, which Porter described to his son Laurence:

August 12, 1959 We gave a huge party of which the Gruens and Hazans were co-hosts, that is they brought the liquor, we supplied the house, and bought ice and soda and tonic. Everyone said it was a marvelous party. Beforehand when I said to mother I would like the mantlepieces cleared up, she remarked, "That mantlepiece is

39
Fairfield Porter in the house at 49 South Main Street. Photo by John Jonas Gruen. Courtesy John Jonas Gruen.

clean enough, or my name is not Bob Rauschenberg" (he was at Larry's, and therefore came). Jimmy Schuyler afterwards told me that he and Jasper Johns – who is as avant-garde as Rauschenberg, liked my paintings very much. I guess that taste of theirs is part of their off-beatness, and they find my paintings so far out that they are in (or vice-versa.) ... We are all still tired from [the party] (it happened last Saturday).[28]

Porter felt an absence in his life toward the end of summer: Schuyler (who, as a weekend guest of the Kochs that summer, had attended the Porters' party) was deliberately avoiding him (fig. 39). Letters from Schuyler to John Button from the period indicate that Schuyler wished to remain on good terms with Porter and in fact hoped to live part-time with the Porters, but did not want a romantic involvement.[29] On receiving a short note from Schuyler in late August telling Porter that he was entering psychoanalysis, Porter wrote back, "Thanks for your considerate note ... I hope you have more insight into yourself always from psychoanalysis. I think of calling you when I am in the city but I don't, for fear you might not want me to. I was in town yesterday. What can I say?"[30]

Apparently, a reconciliation of sorts was effected, with Porter seeing Schuyler in New York. Porter wrote Schuyler afterward,

I was very glad to see you in New York. ... What I meant by manipulation was that you seemed to be trying not to tell me anything, and to keep yourself out ... and to instead cause an effect in me – to manoeuvre my feelings around to what you thought they should be. You were being closed in the guise of being open. But after I saw you, and saw that you were suffering, my emotions had an argument with my reason (stubborn inarticulate fellow!) and finally convinced reason that it should sympathize with you. And as a matter of fact, I do feel very proud of you, because it is as though you had achieved inside yourself something comparable to your new outward thinness.[31]

undated

With their friendship back on track, Schuyler – who had lost a great deal of weight during his bout with mental illness – once again became a frequent weekend guest at the Porter home; the Porters set aside a suite of rooms for him at the back of the house above the kitchen.

During the summer, to improve his finances Porter tried giving private painting lessons. As he wrote Laurence, "I had a pupil for one session, which I felt was quite successful, and she said again and again in amazement, 'This is fantastic,' but she won't continue, because her husband who is a golf pro named Van Johnstone says $25 a lesson is too expensive, and she must join a class. And so I feel miffed at being rejected, and this is cancelled by my relief at not having to be around for her every Monday afternoon for three hours for a lousy $25. And so my feelings are exactly where they were before I started."

Porter's financial trouble is evident in a letter he wrote to his sister-in-law the artist Aline Kilham Porter that fall:

October 8, 1959 De Kooning ... sold $125,000 worth at his last show – it was sold out – which means he got about $80,000. He is rich now for the first time in his life. ... I myself sold $2,900 worth of paintings last year, the best I have ever done. All but $750 was for portrait commissions – five of them. ... I am now worth $666.66 to John Myers [director of the Tibor de Nagy gallery], and [this] means that he will begin to think of me as a source for him of income.

I sold my large de Kooning for $7,000, and a small one [which had been lent to Frank O'Hara] for $2,000. The large one that I sold to a collector he immediately sold to a gallery, which is now offering it for $18,000.

This sudden interest in money is necessary, I suppose, what with the reduced Porter Realty income.

... I quit *Art News*, did I tell you? One or two portrait commissions make as much, and I hope I can get one or two. And they take only one week at most to do, not 15 weeks, as a year's work for *Art News* takes. *The Nation* pays about twice as much.

This letter seems to be almost entirely about money – I suppose that is chiefly what is on my mind.[32]

The need for money also led Porter to publish a monograph that year on Thomas Eakins, an artist toward whom he had no very positive feelings. The assignment came about almost by chance: George Braziller, a publisher known for quality art books, decided to commission a series of monographs on painters called the Great American Artists Series. Thomas Hess wrote on de Kooning, Frank O'Hara on Pollock, Lloyd Goodrich on Winslow Homer and Albert Pinkham Ryder, and E. C. Goosen on Stuart Davis. Porter was offered the last of the bunch. "Eakins was what there was," he later told an interviewer. "I thought, I need the money, so I'll do it. I remember I didn't like Eakins very much ... but anyway it was just a potboiler."[33] Interestingly enough, Porter had a family connection to Eakins: his great-aunt Rebecca, one of the two Little Aunts, had studied with Eakins in Philadelphia shortly before Eakins was dismissed from his post for having a male model pose in the nude before female students.

The monograph, for which Porter was paid $750, was commissioned in January, written in February and March, and published in October 1959. It was among the best received of the series. A violently opinionated work, it offers perhaps the closest thing in print to the argumentative tone for which Porter was both renowned and disparaged by his friends. As a monograph, it does its subject a disservice – monographs usually help a viewer appreciate the work of an artist rather than see the artist's flaws – but, taken on its own terms, *Thomas Eakins* is a perceptive document in which Porter examines once again the place of the artist in American society.

Porter described Eakins as a man who saw and painted American society for what it was – and thus neither found his own escape from that society through a highly personal art nor met the expectations of that society, which desired flattery and idealism above all else. Porter saw something heroic in Eakins's oppositional stance, even though he judged Eakins a failure both as a visionary and as a popular artist. Porter saw a final irony in the adoration that Eakins ultimately garnered for his moral qualities, noting that while it is always good to be adored, this sort of adoration was hardly the kind which Eakins – a painter, not a moralist – wanted or expected or enjoyed.

The monograph shows an almost complete lack of concern for Eakins's techniques and abilities as a painter and at times is quite funny and whimsical in its choice of biographical details – as when, mid-argument, Porter stops to observe of Eakins and his father that "Benjamin Eakins was an excellent skater, tracing calligraphic flourishes on the ice. Thomas could skate backwards as fast as most people could skate forwards."[34]

In truth, Porter disliked Eakins's painting style and had very little to say about it. Moreover, because all the paintings were in Philadelphia, Porter was not able to see them. As Porter recalled, he wrote the book "from photographs. Which you should never do. ... If I had a little more time, you see, I could have gone to Philadelphia and looked at all the paintings. ... A year ago I was in Philadelphia and saw these paintings and I saw that Eakins – one thing about him is that he could not paint a landscape, an outdoor picture. You know, they all look indoors. But that's a minor fault because his landscapes are a very minor part of his painting ... the light ... is like the light on the planet Pluto. He had no sense of light."[35]

Because Porter was much more moved by the artist's plight than by his work, his monograph abounds in observations about Eakins's life which seem to have relevance to Porter's own (indeed, all Porter's writings on American artists feature observations which have resonance with his own life and career). Porter notes, for instance, that Eakins lived all his life in his father's home. Porter, too, spent his life painting in the house in Maine, which was always, in his mind, the home of his father. Porter observed of Eakins, "Because his father's money enabled him not to have to work for a living, he had to convince his conscience that painting was work."[36] Porter, too, had struggled throughout the 1930s and early 1940s to convince himself that painting was work, realizing only later in life that he had been mistaken, that the best sort of painting was a sort of enlightened play which required "a more selfish character and a weaker conscience."[37] In short, Porter seems to have found in Eakins a symbol of his previous, miserable self. The startling vehemence of the monograph is comprehensible, then, not so much as disregard for Eakins as disregard for the failure, symbolized by Eakins, that Porter himself might have experienced had he not developed further as an artist and as a human being.

In the end, this monograph defines Eakins in his time by examining what he did not achieve because of Eakins's nature and because of the world in which he lived. As such, it is resoundingly negative. But, perhaps for exactly this reason, it is also an invigorating piece of criticism. As Porter observed later that year, "One likes to read [art criticism] if it's worth reading. ... But this has nothing to do with the correctness of its evaluations; nor with the painting to which it refers; just as it is not what painting and sculpture refer to, but what they present, that makes them worth looking at."[38]

The monograph was published in October 1959 with little fanfare. Lincoln Kirstein, writing in *The Nation*, observed, "Porter is himself an able painter, an admirable critic with an eye and mind as candid, penetrating and exact as his subject."[39] Other critics ignored the monograph almost entirely. Hilton Kramer, reviewing the series, observed merely that "Mr. Porter's *Thomas Eakins* ... [is] straightforward and reasonable, but leave[s] its subject confused and undefined."[40]

In the fall of 1959, Porter began teaching. In the coming decade he would teach and lecture frequently, both as a means of supplementing his income and as a way of broadening his exposure to art and art criticism. To his sister-in-law he wrote,

October 8, 1959 I teach at Great Neck, adult education, on Mondays. I have a morning class of beginners, an afternoon class of "continuers" and once a month, in the evening, I am part of a four-man panel on modern art in a high school auditorium. ... Milton Resnick, an abstract painter, is on the panel, and Helen Frankenthaler, abstract, young, wanting to enlighten the parents; and a former editor of *Arts*, who is intellectual (very) and very stupid. Milton's face is twisted into the most complicated expression of conviction that every remark is the preparation for a trap for him: so he says things that gradually completely contradict themselves, all indirectly and in parables.[41]

In another letter he observed, "I like [teaching] very much. It has nothing to do with the performance of the ladies I teach – they haven't much talent, it is only that I like to try to explain. I guess I am a natural pedant."[42]

By Christmas 1959, Porter had established a teaching schedule, and though he might have wished, at age fifty-two, to spend his days entirely in the studio, he was not unhappy in the classroom, for, as many of his friends knew all too well, he had a natural tendency to lecture rather than converse. Over the next decade, teaching became more than a paying job for Porter; it became a psychological release, just as political debate had been during the thirties and forties and reviewing and criticism were during the fifties and early sixties: an activity, away from the daily challenge of the studio, which had its own excitements and satisfactions.

At home, the Porter family had achieved a state of relative calm. During the spring of 1959, Laurence Porter had announced his engagement to a young woman named Betsy Hart, and the family looked forward to their wedding in

June 1960. Jerry Porter, living in Porter's studio on Avenue A, had enrolled in City College. Johnny Porter, now twenty-five, came down from Vermont for Christmas (fig. 40). Of him, Porter – who frequently retreated to his studio at holidaytime to compose long letters to distant friends and relatives – wrote Giardelli, "Christmas for me is much more a season of anxiety than of pleasure. Johnny comes home, and when he is home I can't help feeling somewhat tense all the time. He is so odd, I have to ignore it and my uneasiness with the opinion of people on the street and in the town. However people are usually very kind to him, and protective. He himself has no anxiety: it is only my opinion that he somewhat fears, which he shows by giggling too much, as if to appease me. But his little sisters like him."[43]

That winter, as this letter perhaps reflects, Porter began to devote time to developing his inner awareness. Through his old friend Ellen Auerbach, he had become aware of a movement called Subud. Auerbach had learned of the teachings of Bapak Subuh, an Indonesian mystic, during a visit to England, where Subud was then being popularized by J. G. Bennet.[44] Auerbach, impressed by Bennet, had urged Porter to attend one of his lectures in New York, which he did. Porter wrote Giardelli, "Have you heard anything about Subud, which has extensive membership in Great Britain? I have joined it here: I was deeply impressed by J. G. Bennet, when he came to New York two years ago to talk about it. I tell you this a little embarrassedly, not knowing what you might think about it if you have heard about it."[45]

Subud was not an Eastern cult. It merely advocated meditation and latihan, a series of physical relaxation techniques closely related to yoga, to help clear the mind. During the spring of 1960, Porter practiced latihan regularly, often before painting, and found that it helped his work, as well as his dealings

40
Johnny Porter as an adult, in the backyard at 49 South Main Street. Photographer and date unknown (but the camera used to take the photograph was Fairfield Porter's). Courtesy Mrs. Fairfield Porter.

with family. Describing Laurence's June 9 wedding to a friend, he wrote: "The trip [to Baltimore] was exhausting of course, but I did it without any mistakes – of driving, I mean, not of direction, which I expect not to make, all concentrated without impatience or disagreeableness to[ward] tired children, which I credit to latihan, and so it was not after all exhausting, or as much so as I expected. And Laurence's wedding was something I took with the proper choking back of tears."[46]

During the summer of 1960 the Porters were still being careful about money and so did not go to Great Spruce Head, though Porter confided to Giardelli that he missed the island very much; indeed, along with his many landscapes that summer he painted an interior of the Big House on the island from memory. Porter kept a great deal to himself in Southampton, had little company, and hosted no parties, rising early to swim naked on a deserted stretch of beach, and going early to bed. As he wrote a friend, the painter Robert Dash, "This condition [working in solitude] is something that I am just now beginning to know and to prefer, and curiously enough, it makes social life, when I have it, much more rewarding, in the sense, simply, of something that I do not look beyond, or for anything in. I like what I am doing, when I do it, and where I am, when I am there, more and more. I live more in a continuous present that I enjoy."[47]

Porter went on to explain that his one social indulgence that summer was hosting Subud meetings, which contributed to that ability to live in the present. He wrote: "Subud has caught up with me here, and two Easthampton members come here Tuesday mornings for latihan. They tell me that this studio, which I had, of course, once, to clean up, and mop, so one could lie down on the floor if one wished to without getting dusty, is ideal for the purpose."

Although Porter painted mostly landscapes during the summer of 1960, he also painted several portraits and nudes. The nudes were of Ruth Kligman, who, having been the girlfriend of Jackson Pollock and Franz Kline, was just then involved with Porter's old friend Bill de Kooning, who had separated from his wife, Elaine. Porter also did a double portrait of Andy Warhol and his friend Ted Carey. Warhol, just then on the brink of success and already an avid art collector, commisioned the work through Porter's gallery. Porter, as was usual with gallery portrait commissions, seems not to have had any opinion of or interest in Warhol; there is no mention of him in any of Porter's correspondence. Finally, he painted *Johnny* (1960, fig. 41), his only painting of his first son as an adult, now aged twenty-six. This somber image, uncharacteristic in its use of brown, portrays Johnny as younger than he actually was; many of Porter's images of his children do the same, for Porter often seemed to portray his children as much from memory as from life.

But Porter was less concerned, during this summer, with Johnny Porter than with James Schuyler. Despite Schuyler's absence and occasional cruelties, Porter still considered him a dear friend as well as an enthusiastic supporter of his painting and wrote him about the Maine picture he had just painted from memory: "My compulsive interior of Maine is bad. It is bad in the same way as my poems are bad: I guess it is bad like me. My badness consists of lack of courage, that is, an indecisive fussing-about that shows in the paint or word texture, all is muddiness, and muddier and muddier the more I adjust."[48]

Porter's need for a concerned and sympathetic critical presence in his life (apart from his wife) and his awareness of Schuyler's mental fragility may have led him to issue Schuyler an open invitation to the Porter home that summer. At any rate, Schuyler, judging from his letters to John Button, seems to have wanted to reconcile with Porter (and so accept his offer of hospitality) since late 1959: "Perhaps I won't become a public charge after all. (I haven't had any chat with Porter yet; but I think that will go all right.)"[49]

41
Johnny, 1960.
Courtesy the Estate of
Fairfield Porter.

16

A Yellow Van and
"The Four Ugly People"

In the fall of 1960, James Schuyler began spending weekends and sometimes weeks at the Porter home in Southampton. Porter's *Jimmy in a Black Rocker* (1960), painted at this time, came to be known among the Porters as "Jimmy Thin"; Schuyler's gaunt appearance was a result of a recent bout of mental illness.

Schuyler's deteriorating mental condition in 1960 is perhaps best chronicled by Frank O'Hara, who, though no longer Schuyler's roommate, was in contact with him through their work together at the Museum of Modern Art. Writing Ashbery, O'Hara observed,

October, 14, 1959   I have left off deliberately in previous letters mentioning Jimmy's mood (sic) of the summer, but now that you've seen Harry [Mathews] you probably have a wonderful idea. ... Now he seems to be much better since Fairfield has more or less officially adopted him – he spends part of each week there, usually quite more than the weekend – and I hear that the bossing that goes on in that poor benighted household is fearsome to behold. But I suppose it may provide an opportunity for sainthood to someone.

... [Jimmy's] period of megalomania-paranoia seems to have passed now, being replaced with a rather sinister air of purposefulness about trivia. I am still very fond of him, but I can't tell you how trying it's been, with little notes about me to Waldo [Rasmussen, a coworker at the Museum of Modern Art], etc. Sometimes, though, it seems hilariously funny – but those moments coincide with my not giving a shit for him, which is again depressing in itself.

... I will write at greater length very soon, and I'm sorry about my ill-temper over Jimmy, who actually is much better now.[1]

Schuyler used the Porter address to receive mail, for he was guest-editing the first issue of the short-lived poetry magazine *Locus Solus*, financed by the writer Harry Mathews.[2] From the Porter home, Schuyler wrote Chester Kallman, an old friend, requesting submissions from both Kallman and Auden: "I am going back to work Tuesday, but please write me here (and please do write, dear boy!) I intend to keep coming out here long weekends – quite possibly until well into next summer. ... Did you know that Fairfield Porter is a sort of cousin, quite close, of T. S. Eliot's? I guess that's why his older brother is named Eliot – though scarcely for T.S., who may be younger than Eliot, who is an attractive grandfather; for family reasons I mean."[3]

Porter, meanwhile, was glad for the company, writing his son Laurence, "The standing painting of you in the studio I completely repainted, partly with Jimmy Schuyler's help, he was stand in for you for the way the light falls. ... He is very sweet with the girls, both Lizzie and Katie adore him. He takes the place of those missing big brothers."[4]

When not immobilized by depression, Schuyler was a good houseguest: he made wildflower arrangements, played with the girls, and occasionally even helped with the cooking; certainly the large, rambling house benefited from his presence. To John Button, who was hospitalized for a cancer operation, Porter wrote,

42

A group photo, taken at Julia Gruen's third birthday party, at the home of her parents, the composer and writer John Gruen and the painter Jane Wilson, in Water Mill, 1961. *Back row, from left*: Lisa de Kooning, Frank Perry, Eleanor Perry, John Bernard Myers, Anne and Fairfield Porter, Angelo Torricini, Arthur Gold, Jane Wilson, Kenward Elmslie, Paul Brach, Jerry Porter, Nancy Ward, Katharine Porter, unidentified woman. *Second row*: Joe Hazan, Clarice Rivers, Kenneth Koch, Larry Rivers, Miriam Shapiro, Robert Fizdale, Jane Freilicher, Joan Ward, John Kacere, Sylvia Maizell. *Sitting and kneeling in front*: Stephen Rivers, Bill Berkson, Frank O'Hara, Herbert Machiz, Jim Tommaney, Willem de Kooning, Alvin Novak. Photo by John Jonas Gruen. Courtesy John Jonas Gruen.

October, 1, 1960 Jimmy has been spending a lot of time here as you know, often with Adele [Hoenig, a friend]. They came last night, Anne met them. Lizzy refers to him as "our dear Jimmy," which she made up all by herself: when he came first in August, Anne asked me privately, almost with tears in her voice, "Why is Jimmy so *thin*?" and to Katie she said, "Jimmy used to be one of our fattest friends." She has been inspired to cook all kinds of creamy eggy foods; and if something is gone from the icebox in the morning, she is very pleased, and says complacently that Jimmy ate it in the night. But Katie shouted, when something was gone, "You ate it in the night!" and would not be mollified. Lizzie said to Jimmy, which pleased him very much, "Jimmy, you have little laughs all over your face."

He will appear in three paintings in my show; one typewriting in the doorway of the studio, rather Diebenkornish ... ; another head-on in the black rocking chair – the new Jimmy, with romantically hollow cheeks and longish curly hair. ... He was a stand-in for a paralyzed portrait of Laurence, which immediately came to life, when I could see how the shadows go. We went often to the beach, where he practically never swam, but picked up things which he invested with a Rauschenbergian potential value.[5]

Porter's delight at having Schuyler in the house is clear in this and other letters (fig. 42).

In November 1960 Porter had his first show at the new, expanded Tibor de Nagy gallery space at 149 East Seventy-second Street. He sold eighteen of thirty paintings; Porter's son Laurence remembers being impressed by the "sudden, miraculous, and permanent improvement in his painting" at this time.[6] Important collectors attended the show. Encouraged by Alfred Barr and Dorothy Miller of the Museum of Modern Art, David Rockefeller put a painting on reserve. When Porter's old friend John Walker, now the director of the National Gallery in Washington, brought the wife of the president, Jacqueline Kennedy, to the exhibition, she asked to buy the picture reserved by Rockefeller. Porter refused on principle to give her precedence, and the painting went to Rockefeller.

Far from courting capitalists and socialites at the gallery, however, Porter was much more interested in meeting Russian communists, for a delegation of Soviet writers and critics had arrived in New York in conjunction with an exhibition of contemporary Soviet art at the Museum of Modern Art. Porter, along with the painters Ben Shahn, Mark Rothko, and Philip Guston and the sculptor Philip Lippold, was invited to meet them and converse about art issues over lunch. Porter, who was always spoiling for a good political argument, described the meeting to Aline Porter:

December, 12, 1960 The Russians were exactly the way they are always said to be: with the usual cliches. ... I had at my table the one woman who spoke English, and I set about immediately to attack her; and as I later was told by Alfred Barr that she is a Communist, and the one who keeps her eye on the others, I was not sorry I did.

She was interested in my attack much more than the others' politeness, and invited me to come to Russia (even taking my name to remember me) where we could continue the discussion, and I might see that in Russia the working class is not so horribly exploited as I thought. I tried to attack in ways that would take [her] off guard, and I somewhat succeeded; for instance I asked, "Is there a working class in Russia? And are they paid wages?" And since she assured me that the answer was yes, then [I said] in Russia the social situation was capitalism, since the wage system, according to Marx, is the essential system of Capitalism. Then when she asked if I had read Marx, I said, that since Marx described reality, it is not necessary to have read all of him, all one needs to do is to observe the reality he described.[7]

Apart from this meeting with the Russians, which was the high point of his autumn, Porter did little more than paint and supervise repair work on the Southampton house and prepare for a return to Great Spruce Head. Thanks to his sales with de Nagy that season, he was able to afford certain crucial acts of maintenance which had been impossible over the past four years.

Return to Great Spruce Head meant facing his brother John and sister Nancy once again over island issues. As Porter wrote his son Laurence,

When I hear how Nancy (it is she) redecorates our house by putting the dragons back, etc. it makes my blood boil, because Nancy will never get used to thinking of me as a person in my own right, but rather as an object of her directive instincts. If and when I do go back there, I will remove the dragons and burn them. ... For me the trouble is that John and Nancy's greater wealth makes them able to do things for me, like putting floors in the wood shed ... and this makes them feel that they have the right also to decide how everything shall look. Being an object of their charity, I am in a weak position about saying that I would like their charity to stop short of a certain interference.[8]

undated

During the winter, Porter began work on his first series of prints, offset lithographs with a fine, sketchlike quality made from drawings done of his home in Southampton during the many snowstorms that winter (during cold spells, Porter preferred to work in the house rather than the studio, which was particularly drafty). In New York he spent time in a little studio at Twentieth Street and Union Square East (later Porter would make several paintings of the area near Union Square and Park Avenue South); he shared the space with the painter Robert Dash. The apartment that he had shared with Jerry Porter on Avenue A was too socially busy a place for Porter to work; Schuyler, between apartments, was living there along with Jerry Porter when he came to town (though by March of that year, Porter was able to arrange a sublet on Schuyler's behalf at an Avenue A apartment recently vacated by the artist Phillip Pearlstein).

The winter of 1960–61 was cold and stormy, and Porter, at age fifty-three, was forced to shovel a great deal of snow. He had suffered from sciatica since the mid-1930s; but over the winter his aches and pains increased considerably. His exhaustion was made worse by a cold which lasted over a month. By spring, despite his love of exercise and healthy habits, he observed to Schuyler, "I have been sick with intense arthritis or rheumatism, but it has gone now. I can't drink anything any more without disastrous results. One cocktail at lunch cripples me."[9]

During early 1961, Porter immersed himself in recent art-historical scholarship on ancient, mostly Greek, sculpture, a topic which had interested him since his childhood visit to Athens on a Mediterranean cruise and about which he knew relatively little. Because of the enormous amount of reading involved, the article was troublesome for Porter and may well have contributed to his decision in May 1961 to quit writing his column for *The Nation*, though there were other reasons: "On the *Nation* I feel that since I am not assigned, I must assign myself, and present to the *Nation* readers my view of the essence of the season, so I have to see everything. And ... a lot of a certain kind of fashionable abstraction bores me, even when I think it is good, like Milton Resnick, often."[10]

Porter published a final article that spring, not in *The Nation* but in *Evergreen Review*, a literary magazine which had been developed several years earlier by Don Allen and Barney Rossett. Porter's article, "Poets and Painters in Collaboration," was a review of the recent joint publication of four oversized volumes of poetry and art by the Tiber Press, a literary outgrowth of the Tibor de Nagy gallery. Porter had been thinking a great deal about the relation of poetry to painting in the past decade; the topic was an important one, and he wanted to do it justice. At the same time, he had not wanted to involve himself in the project as either artist or poet (John Bernard Myers had proposed that Porter involve himself in a collaborative effort; Porter had declined absolutely). His essay is a brief but beautifully perceptive look at the work of O'Hara, Koch, Schuyler, and Ashbery; it was, in Porter's estimation, "the most difficult writing I ever did."[11]

Porter noted early in the review that the pairing of artist with poet in the series had been an external, rather than organic, decision, which was aesthetically troubling to him (and probably the reason he declined to become involved with the project). All the artists were in the "school of de Kooning ... tak[ing] as the subject matter ... workmanship as such, good and bad: ... the work, including the craft, of painting." The artists were related to the poets in that the poets, too, "partly do something similar [to what de Kooning does] in regard to all language from literary to inarticulate speech." Both poets and painters "try to begin poetry and painting again."

Porter's remarks on the four poets, all of whom were his friends, are brief but astute and remarkably distilled. He describes O'Hara's first-person odes as "prophecy set adrift," observes of Koch that "his ironical language is the animating principle of his emotions," sees in Ashbery that his simple sentences have "sibylline clarity," that his "words have more objective reality than reality of meaning," and notes that Schuyler "tends toward a deceptively simple Chinese visibility, like transparent windows on a complex view."[12]

Porter was not entirely convinced that the art which had been put together by the publisher was well suited to the work that it illustrated. The artists Mike Goldberg, Alfred Leslie, Joan Mitchell, and Grace Hartigan had worked in collaboration with the poets, but not out of any great understanding of their work. Of the four collaborations, Porter found that the Mitchell-Ashbery one worked best. Overall, he preferred an earlier collaborative venture created by two old friends, Edwin Denby and Rudy Burckhardt: *Mediterranean Cities*, published by the Tibor de Nagy gallery.

In the spring of 1961, after a period of instability, Schuyler suffered a complete mental collapse. His paranoid and delusional behavior had already distanced him from many of his friends, as a letter from O'Hara to Ashbery makes clear:

Jimmy got considerably sicker ... and it was arranged by John Myers with the help of Jimmy Merrill to get him into what is supposed to be an excellent clinic in New Haven (bio-chemical and psychiatric – I really didn't know much about it) about three weeks ago. A few people have gone up to visit him and [he] has already improved they say. Anyhow, since ... he has got quite a hate on for me ... I am not going to write or visit him until I hear that he has some desire for me to (if ever), so I thought he might like to hear from you ... John Myers spoke with his doctor who said he was showing marked improvement and would like visitors. ... John Myers has really been an angel to him and is now getting money from a few people so he'll have something to get by on when he gets out. It is strange to think that he and I will not be friends again, but that is my conclusion after hearing several unmalicious reports of his opinion of me. At first I thought that this was part of his illness, but now that he has improved it has only seemed to grow more articulate. ... I do not intend ... to be ridiculed and maligned behind my back by Jimmy to whatever new friends (like us once) he makes when he gets out. I don't mean that I blame or dislike Jimmy for what's happened – anyone's actions can be interpreted as amiable or hostile depending on your point of view and perhaps mine more than most – but I don't see any use in either of us going through the strain of pretending we like each other as much as we once did. I don't know why, for instance, he has singled me out for the accusation that I've put him in the shade as a writer. ... It's none of our fault ... that Jimmy has not written more and that he couldn't bring himself to let John Myers publish his poems, etc., but he apparently wants to blame it on me for damaging his self-confidence, and that's the way it is. I don't think it's a particularly bad thing for him, even, since that sort of spleenish feeling may lead him to write more, and he always writes so beautifully. Perhaps I shall have the glamorous position of being the villain in some future roman à clef from his typewriter – I suppose Tony Curtis will play me in the movie, I'm so pushy.[13]

May 1, 1961

O'Hara, the most generous and supportive of friends, was deeply hurt by Schuyler's behavior; his inability to decide where Schuyler's personality ended and his sickness began is characteristic of the confusion that many of Schuyler's friends, the Porters included, eventually faced.

In the early spring, Porter began corresponding with Howard Griffin, an English poet who worked as a secretary to Auden and was friends with Schuyler. Porter wrote him, "Jimmy is in a hospital in New Haven, taking a rather rush psychological cure that was recommended by Jimmy Merrill and David Jackson. I have seen him twice there, and he seems better: at least physically. The cure involves drugs."[14] A week later Porter, who was passing through New Haven on a return from Vermont, where he had been working on a portrait commission, stopped to see Schuyler. He wrote Button that Jimmy "was off one of his original, more relaxing drugs and so somewhat restless, but he looks well."[15] Soon afterward, Porter learned that Schuyler's illness may have been schizophrenia, the disease that Porter's son Johnny had ultimately (and probably incorrectly) been diagnosed as having. Schuyler wrote to Porter, and Porter responded by inviting him to either Southampton or Maine, for the Porters planned to return to the island for the first time in four years in July 1961.

During June 1961, another crisis was taking place. Anne Porter's mother, Katharine Channing, was dying painfully from leukemia. Hoping that her husband would join her, Anne Porter departed with both girls for Wareham in mid-June, expecting that her mother would die within the month. Porter went to pick up Schuyler, and together they drove to Maine in the expectation that, once established, Schuyler could be left there alone while Porter joined his wife in Wareham.

Porter picked up Schuyler in New Haven, finding him no longer gaunt but "well, cheerful, fat."[16] Schuyler recalled, "When Fairfield picked me up at the hospital in New Haven on the first day of summer in 1961 he said, 'I'll never let you down, Jimmy.' He never did."[17] But once they had arrived on Great Spruce Head, Porter realized that Schuyler's condition was still so precarious that he could not be left to fend for himself. So instead of going to Wareham to be with his wife as her mother died, he stayed with Schuyler on the island.

Being essentially alone in the Big House, Porter was necessarily much more in contact with his sister, Nancy, with whom he had never had an easy relationship and toward whom he already felt a certain animosity over the dragons. About her, Porter wrote Robert Dash, "My sister, who has a certain medical background (two years medical school) suggested to me that [Jimmy's] trouble is not psychological but metabolic. ... She contradicts every one of my opinions, and so I get sore, and don't talk to her, much to Mike [Straus, her husband]'s amusement. 'A Porter argument,' he observes to his guest of the moment. My role is to be the fool of the island, but though this is expected of me, and wanted, also it is wanted that I am grateful for all corrections and so on."[18]

Given the choice, Porter spent as much time as possible alone or with Schuyler and so managed to do a great deal of painting. Schuyler, who read and slept most of the time, was not a disruptive presence. Of the solitude, Porter wrote Robert Dash, "I rather like being alone," adding,

Maine ... is like this: each day is a different weather, and it is so intense, that by breakfast, you think that the weather has always been whatever it is that morning. One only remembers the other days of similar weather. And it is most changeable.

  July 27, 1961

  I painted another painting of this room (like the many in the Southampton studio) and each painting when I do it, and/if it is successful, fills me with loathing, that never, never again will I do this one again. But there are just too damn many subjects that I want to do, and as a result, I feel constantly impatient – impatient with people for wanting to talk to me – it wastes too much time – the weather might change.

  At night I am exhausted, after morning and afternoon painting, plus cooking, plus getting ice from the ice house, some exercise.[19]

Porter realized during this period that, as he wrote Leon Hartl, "this is the one place in the world where I have a sense of connection with my own past."[20] He began to think of relocating full-time to Maine, to either the island or the mainland, an idea which remained with him for the rest of his life.

  Anne Porter's mother did not die as soon as expected, so Porter, who wrote his wife a series of tender letters, was not joined by her. For a while he was alone, for Schuyler departed in late July for a checkup in New Haven. Then, in early August, the Big House came alive again as Katie Porter and her two cousins Annie and Ruth arrived in the care of a friend, Virginia Kniesel. They were joined shortly afterward by Schuyler and his friend Adele Hoenig. Jerry Porter and his girlfriend Suzanne arrived, then, following Katharine Channing's death, Anne Porter and Elizabeth at last rejoined the family. Porter described it as "a most inorganic and entertaining household, rather like a house party in a novel."[21] There were only a few outside visitors at the end of summer, including the artists Wolf Kahn and Emily Mason, a couple then residing on Deer Isle, who came for lunch.

  On returning to Southampton, the Porters hoped that Schuyler would be able to get on his feet again in New York. When Porter quit *The Nation*, he proposed Schuyler as his substitute, but Lincoln Kirstein chose Robert Rosenblum instead[22] (the position was ultimately filled by Max Kozloff). Schuyler was able, however, to return to his reviewing for *Art News*, a position which had originally been given to him when Frank O'Hara had stopped reviewing for the magazine. He again took up part-time residence in the Avenue A studio that Porter had found for him that March. Drugs had altered Schuyler's appearance and behavior, as a letter from O'Hara to Ashbery makes clear:

Jimmy is reputed to be in New York reviewing again for *Art News* and sharing that Avenue A apartment with Jerry Porter! What a combination! He is also said to weigh well over 200 lbs. ...

  September 20, 1961

... I saw Jimmy at Jane [Freilicher]'s house just after I got back and, though enormous, he seemed very friendly and charming. Then I saw him about two weeks later at an opening and he was very upsetting and had difficulty articulating, so I don't really know how he is. He told me he wanted to have lunch and discuss the next issue of *Locus Solus*, but that's the last I heard from him. I gather he is doing his reviews for *Art News* though, so I guess he is gradually improving. That time at the opening he had had a couple of martinis, which may have had some effect on him to cause what I described.[23]

Schuyler did not stay long at the Avenue A apartment; soon he was back in Southampton, relying on the Porters for financial and emotional support as well as housing. Jane Freilicher, a good friend to both Schuyler and Porter, recalled,

The situation was a difficult one for Anne. She would be funny about Jimmy, saying it was certainly very unusual to wake up in the middle of the night to the smell of frying bacon. But I always felt it was a sort of martyrdom. Then again, Jimmy was useful around the house, particularly at first. He wasn't incapable, not at all, at least not before his condition worsened and he really fell apart. For example, he was an excellent cook. I remember seeing him toss a salad with his bare hands. And it was part of his mania, I think, that he did things in the garden so well – he planted several things here that I still have, digging enormous holes for them and putting in all the things that would make them grow well. In the back of our minds, though, I remember we all had a sense that while Jimmy was ordering all these things from fancy gardening catalogues, Fairfield was getting the bill.[24]

Kenneth Koch, a good friend to Schuyler, agreed that before being paralyzed by mental illness, Schuyler contributed a great deal to the Porter home: "Jimmy had the best manners of anyone I ever knew. And really, he transformed that house. He would make areas of it liveable. He had a very strong sense of how things ought to be. I remember he once saw a magazine on the mantlepiece, and he shook his head and said, 'Magazine on the mantlepiece – can you believe it?' And took it off and put it someplace else. It was a house that needed that kind of help."[25]

But Schuyler's emotional vicissitudes were such that he could not be depended upon consistently to help around the house or even in the garden. Much of Schuyler's poetry concerns gardens and gardening, but as he himself said, "Because I've written about plants and flowers so much, people get the impression I was a gardener, but I wasn't. I was a gardening slave when I was a kid, being forced to weed or hoe or mow. So I'm very ambivalent about the actual physical work of gardening. I'd rather read about it."[26] Schuyler's friend Barbara Guest, the poet, may have summed up Schuyler's participation in household affairs best when she observed, "He may have planted a few rose-bushes, but he sure as hell never watered them."[27]

Porter's show in January 1962 came to be known among the Porter family as his Island Show because so many of the images were of Great Spruce

Head. The show was successful enough, with seven paintings sold, several to major collectors. Schuyler reviewed the show in *Art News*:

Part of Porter's originality lies in a complete reliance in the freedom of his hand. ... Also, there is his almost invisible mastery of structure, of composition. ... This gift he may have acquired from his father ... a Chicago architect whose houses combined an originality of plan with an exactitude of detail. ... [Fairfield Porter] can return to a subject year after year, finding new aspects, trying to penetrate more deeply to the core of his feelings about it. ... Porter, in the lyric solidity of his work, embodies the virtues of man: love of family, of carved fields, of the beauty of everyday. They have, after all, kindled our finest art for some centuries.[28]

The review marked the first of several which would explore the psychological content in Porter's paintings, a topic that Porter found tricky, perhaps disagreeable. While he went so far as to observe that in painting the Big House he was painting, in some sense, a portrait of his father, he seemed not altogether at ease with the idea of painting as a vehicle for emotional self-expression – even though he noted the psychological content of others' paintings, writing of Eakins, for instance, that "in the eyes of most of his sitters there is a defeated look that goes beyond objective realism."[29]

Porter had already argued about the point with Schuyler, stating in a letter that in painting "either neurotic or psychological as values are irrelevant. ... There is always psychological content ... the psychological content may be what it seems, or it may be the opposite. There is psychological content to a slap in the face, or a smile at a baby, but it does not follow from this that there is art."[30]

Following Schuyler's review, Porter wrote him:

My dialectical skill makes me say that emotion does not tell reason, though it may distort it; and though reason can tell emotion, it cannot tell you to sympathize, for unless sympathy is instinctive, deriving directly from emotion, it is something phony. Doesn't that sound eighteenth century? My dialectical skill (a talent for quibbling) is what makes me a good critic and a stinkeroo of a painter.   *undated*

When I disagree with you, which I often do, and say so too, what remains with me is your opinion; I express my opinion, and then I think about yours afterwards, not about my own any more, which being expressed to you, I am through with. Your opinion interests me more than my own, and I consider it without thinking about its place, so to speak, not my agreement or disagreement, I just turn it over in my mind because it has nourishment for me, where my own does not.

One day I told Anne, "I got a lovely letter from Jimmy," and she said, knowing how I miss you, "I was about to write Jimmy to write Fairfield a lovely letter."[31]

Schuyler, more to the point, replied:

undated It angers, bores and tires me (to exaggerate a little) when you write that you "are a good critic and a stinkeroo of a painter." Of course you are a good critic ... but, since you place no value at all on aesthetics, I don't see that being a good critic can be a very real satisfaction to you. Writing will never pain and distress you the way painting can, because you are a painter. And your criticism is good because you are a good painter, and therefore can see much in paintings, and trouble to write it. ...

I also object when you persist in misunderstanding what was meant when your painting was described as psychological; what *wasn't* meant is "neurotic" – I don't know anyone whose pictures are less neurotic than yours (besides, insofar as a work is a work of art, the neurosis is transformed, not just sublimated, but brought into the scope of the possible and actual world). I think what was meant is that, by means purely painterly, you invested your picture of the porch not only with the atmosphere of a particular place but a sense of the living that takes place on it, the atmosphere of the people whose it is; the people, in a sense, it (the porch) most takes for granted. It isn't anything literary or sentimental: it's the opposite of what Greuze, who went so clodhoppingly after Warmth, Simplicity, and Family Love, ever got, and very like what Chardin could get from a still life.[32]

Reading such a letter, one begins to understand why Porter so valued Schuyler's company: Schuyler was not just an observant poet and friend but a formidable critical presence, an articulate intellectual sparring partner with great emotional accuracy. Porter had the unconditional emotional and intellectual support of his wife, but in his work as an artist he seems to have felt the need for someone

43
Anne and Fairfield Porter breakfasting with James Schuyler in the dining room at 49 South Main Street, circa 1962. Photo by John Button. Courtesy Henry W. and Albert A. Berg Collection of English and American Literature, New York Public Library.

less unconditionally supportive – someone, moreover, with whom he had less of an emotional history. Schuyler, despite his many problems, provided Porter with a new source of encouragement, new perceptions, and a fresh critical eye.

Schuyler's review of Porter's 1962 show begs the question of just how objective a review he could write (and, by extension, how truthful a critic – and friend and lover – he could be in his dealings with Porter). Schuyler was, at the time he wrote this review, not just Porter's best friend; he was also living in Porter's house on an income provided by Porter (fig. 43). Both Schuyler and O'Hara had, in previous years, reviewed Porter's work appreciatively while maintaining close friendships with him and availing themselves of his hospitality both in Southampton and on Great Spruce Head. Robert Dash, who covered Porter's exhibitions for *Arts* magazine during the early 1960s, and the critic Lawrence Campbell, who reviewed Porter during the early 1950s, had also been guests at the Porter house; and so had John Ashbery, who also wrote glowingly of Porter's painting. Had Porter been more successful during his lifetime, the question of influence might have been raised. But he was not.

Porter himself observed in 1968 about *Art News*, "I think [Hess] did a lot of promoting, yes, but if he hadn't promoted [his artists] nobody else at the time would have. And they were painters who should have been promoted. They were the best painters around. And the conspiracy was, as far as I can see, that he recognized that they were the best painters around and deserved to be publicized."[33] The same could be said about the promotion that Porter received from his friends at *Art News* and elsewhere. Moreover, while all critics are open to some amount of persuasion, few are truly capable of misrepresenting their perceptions about the quality of art, their critical integrity being, after all, their stock-in-trade, and the material rewards of dishonest criticism being minor.

Porter seems to have become more self-observant about his painting in 1962, writing new friends, Lucien and Poppy Day,

It seems that at the beginning of a year, which means after the turbulence of an exhibition, when all effort seems to be false, I can paint in the manner of skill that I have acquired during the previous effort, that the exhibition has brought to an end, but no one is deceived, not even the dumbest philistine. And so I have to learn painting all over again, not to acquire skill again, but to acquire integrity, which is, after all, perhaps the only true skill. Have I acquired integrity again? Perhaps, but every year I feel more skeptical. At the same time, I get back every year that sense of virtue that comes from making a continuous effort.[34]

July 23, 1962

This depth of introspection is new to Porter's letters; one might assume that the death of his mother-in-law, the return to Great Spruce Head (with its flood of memories and sensations) and finally the mysterious, lingering fatigue that he had started to suffer from in the past year all prompted him to consider his own mortality. Free of the burden of reviewing, he found himself caught up in religious reading during the spring of 1962, noting to his son that he had just "finished *Essentials of Mysticism* by Evelyn [Underhill]. I like Plotinus and a lay 19th century married Frenchwoman named Lucie-Christine. I can't stand the blessed Angela da Foi (?) [Angela da Foligno] or Thérèse of Lisieux, or Charles Péguy."[35]

This new awareness of religious writing and thought is further reflected in a July 4 letter to the painter John Button, a devout Anglican, in which Porter observed, "I am still somewhat overcome by the intimate presence of this vast and unaccountable weather that both stimulates and exhausts one on the island, as if one were a constant communicant with the power of God."[36] Porter was, however, nowhere near a religious conversion.

Along with spiritual matters, there were material ones to preoccupy Porter that year – namely, a brand-new Chevrolet van, which Porter had ordered with excitement that spring. Porter's lifelong indifference to "American Dream kind"[37] of possessions seems to have found its one exception in this ungainly suburban vehicle, which Porter was able to purchase with profits from his gallery sales in the previous season. As he wrote his son Laurence, "With all my gains this year I am buying a new car, a Chevy bus, like a Volkswagen only larger and more comfortable, in which seven of us will drive to Maine. It is the first NEW car I have ever had. It is almost demoralizing waiting for it."[38]

Porter could not afford to indulge himself entirely; his original hope had been to purchase a two-tone van, Yuma yellow and white, but, for reasons of economy, he was forced to choose solid yellow. The car transported the family, including Schuyler, to Maine that June. Porter wrote, "I am thrilled with it. It is most capacious. Nine passenger – like the VW – but nine fat people instead of nine thin ones. Also I transported an easel and a huge roll of canvas with much baggage."[39]

Due to cold and overcast weather during the summer of 1962, Porter had trouble with his painting and did not work very successfully. Partly this was due to fatigue, which would be understood only after his death as a symptom of undiagnosed arteriosclerosis. Porter had always enjoyed going to bed early, but this summer he went to bed earlier than ever before. Schuyler maintained an opposite schedule, sleeping until noon on most days and staying up late to read and write, a habit Porter took in stride. "I hear applause from the kitchen below," Porter wrote at one point, "which means I think that Jimmy Schuyler got up for breakfast."[40]

Porter's difficulties with his painting may also have arisen from a change in media, for he was working for the first time with Liquitex, a quick-drying, water-soluble medium that lacks the transparency of oils but dries quickly. The speed with which Liquitex dries was a convenience for Porter, who had previously left his works on the island to dry for a month before returning to transport them to New York. Porter's letters from the summer note an increased ambition regarding color and disappointment with the results. His most successful work of that season, entitled *Summer Studio* (1962), featured his daughter Elizabeth "with an expression on her face that Anne says [means] 'When I grow up, I'm going to change all this.'"[41] Porter also worked on several night paintings and day paintings featuring artificial (that is, electric) light and depicting Katie Porter, her cousin Annie Channing, and James Schuyler. The best of these is entitled *A Day Indoors* (1962). Of it, Porter observed to a son, "I painted an immense canvas (six feet high) of the living room on a cold day, with Jimmy, Katie and Annie sitting around the fire, the Greek horse (or part of it), an electric light on, a bit of landscape through the window, and with all these conflicting lights and colors, the result is one of lovely darkness – the firelight and electric light against the daylight. It is in any case a tour de force, but I do not know if it is much more."[42] Porter used the term *tour de force* to describe a work to be praised more for its ambition than for its success (John Wheelwright had used the word in the same way to describe Anne Porter's May Day socialist anthem back in the 1930s). His uncertainty about this painting is justified; the colors are not Porter's most thrilling, perhaps because of the use of Liquitex; at the same time, the light, while complex, is also confused.

August brought disappointing weather. With only four days of sunshine, the island seemed less beautiful than it had in previous years, and so less inspiring. The overcast and rainy days made Porter irritable and fatigued, and company wore him out. A visit from his son Laurence, Laurence's wife, Betsy, and Betsy's parents proved difficult, Porter discovering that he disliked, and was in turn disliked by, his son's wife. Laurence Porter commented later that Betsy "is extremely intelligent, but so awkward from her own upbringing that she would blurt out her own opinions in an awkward, offensive way. As the person who was older, more established, wealthier, and the host, Fairfield should have been more gracious. But he never tried. Their mutual hostility was intensely painful to me ... these conflicts drove Fairfield and me further apart than ever during the last fifteen years of his life."[43]

After the departure of the Laurence Porters, Porter hosted his friend Carl Morse and after that the painter Alex Katz and his family. The listless, indoor quality of the summer is captured by Porter in a note to John Bernard Myers: "I play chess with Jimmy ... he passes on what I teach him to Katie's cousin Annie, who is Katie's age. We haven't really done much here except eat and read, and go to occasional cocktail parties at my sister's, which she holds to introduce her guests to the other island people."[44]

Nineteen sixty-two, while a moderately successful painting year for Porter, marked a turning point for his brother Eliot, who published a book with the Sierra Club that year. *In Wildness Is the Preservation of the World*, featuring text by Thoreau, was a successful and impressive volume of Eliot Porter's innovative color photographs. Fairfield Porter, who had used his position at *The Nation* to write a column praising his brother's work, took pride in Eliot's success and in the coming years sent copies of the book to artists he particularly admired, including Joseph Cornell. Porter looked forward to seeing Eliot during the next summer on Great Spruce Head, Eliot having decided to return there after an absence of eight years for a family reunion celebrating the fiftieth anniversary of James Porter's purchase of the island.

Porter's next show took place in January and February 1963. Despite the mediocre results of the 1962 painting season, Porter seems to have achieved enough of a presence by this point to be profiled by Jack Kroll of *Newsweek* about his work. The article, which was hastily and inaccurately appreciative, embarrassed Porter, who wrote, "If I am interviewed again, I will think more carefully before speaking and not be led by the interviewer's ideas or interests."[45] The show resulted in several impressive sales, but Porter took home less than six thousand dollars, and his irritation at the incidental charges surrounding the exhibit are reflected in his exchanges with the gallery. One letter of complaint concludes, "The above should give you an idea of my income for 1963, which is the total income for me, Anne, Johnny, Katie, Elizabeth, Jerry, and Jimmy Schuyler."[46] Porter's inclusion of Schuyler (for it was not in his nature to exaggerate) suggests that Porter was Schuyler's main support. Schuyler's financial dependence upon the Porters would continue for the rest of the decade.

But Porter's concern for money did not lead him to attempt to increase public awareness of his name or reputation. When contacted by the gallery to participate in the Art in Embassies program, which placed contemporary work in American embassies around the world, Porter refused on principle. He had a long-standing dislike of big government and hated bureaucratic arrogance (he had experienced it firsthand through his brother-in-law, Michel Straus) and he was particularly angry at that moment with federal indifference to environmental issues. As his son Laurence recalled, "You have to remember the lack of environmental protection in the 50s and 60s, the syphilitic black men who were deliberately untreated by the government, the Army's experiments with soldiers whom they ordered to run into nuclear clouds (during the 50s), and so forth, to recall the brutal arrogance of technocrats during the third quarter of this century – to say nothing of the U.S.'s carpet bombing of civilian populations in Germany and Japan, the firestorms we started in Hamburg and Nagasaki, MacArthur's and Goldwater's calls for the renewed use of atomic weapons."[47]

Porter's response to his gallery about the Art in Embassies program was therefore decisive: "I would rather not have any paintings of mine sent out on the Art in Embassies Program. Tell the [Museum of Modern Art] to count me out. ... I don't want to advertise the American Government abroad: I get nothing from such a program except a reputation for passivity and indifference."[48]

Porter did need money, however, so he sought out portrait commissions and asked de Nagy and Myers at the gallery to do the same. They were not successful, apart from one double portrait commission. In general, Porter's attempts to portray people whom he did not know were of limited success. His ability to catch a likeness was hardly a specialty, and those who were less interested in good painting than in flattering representations were usually nonplussed by his results. A number of commissions were completed only to be rejected by the clients.

At the beginning of the summer of 1963, Anne Porter came down with hepatitis, delaying the Porters' summer move to Great Spruce Head until August. They missed the fiftieth-anniversary celebration of James Porter's purchase of the island, which took place on July 20 in order to coincide with a solar eclipse in memory of James Porter's youthful interest in astronomy.[49] Porter instead worked on a painting of Anne sick in bed, which he entitled *July Interior* (1963, fig. 44).

The painting is less a representation of illness (Anne Porter shows no sign of the jaundice which usually characterizes her disease) than an intimate portrait. The setting recalls the bedroom portrait of Countess Anna de Noailles by Vuillard, an image which had long fascinated Porter and which he had discussed with Wolf Kahn the previous August on Great Spruce Head Island.

Porter's image of his wife contains the same letter from Emily Dickinson to Thomas Wentworth Higginson that he had included in his *Anne in the Living Room at 312 East 52nd Street* fifteen years before; it sits on the bureau at the far side of the room. An image of the Virgin Mary is mounted over the bed, and on the bed sit a sewing box, a pair of reading glasses, and several books. A clock stands on the bureau; over it hangs a photograph by Eliot Porter. In the foreground, beside the bed, sits a beautifully prosaic white plastic telephone, behind which a checked pink curtain sways in the afternoon breeze.

While it is tempting to read this picture as an artfully composed assemblage of objects and possessions which define its central subject (Porter was well acquainted with such practices in early Renaissance portraiture), Porter's discussion with Kahn of the previous summer and his devotion to the late Vuillard suggest that he was simply and respectfully transcribing things as he found them, trusting that such a composition had its own inherent symbolism. As Kahn recalled, "We were arguing about Vuillard, discussing which stage of Vuillard was better or more important. I mentioned that in Vuillard's portrait of the Countess de Noailles there were too many bottles of medicine in the background and it took away from the picture. Fairfield said, 'He had to put them in because they were there. Otherwise he would have had to be his own aesthetician.'"[50]

Porter had a violent dislike of sentimentality; by naming his portrait of his sick wife *July Interior* he was maintaining a characteristic distance between himself and his feelings. Indeed, Porter's feelings about his wife do not volunteer themselves in the image. Rather, the light, airy, highly keyed colors (variations on pink and mauve, with a surprising clash, at the right foreground, with a deep orange-red) seem inappropriate to illness, just as illness itself was inappropriate both to summer and to Anne Porter.

Writing John Ashbery, Schuyler noted that the image of Anne Porter was "a remarkably unflattering likeness. Anne called it, 'The Last Illness of Marvin Ginsburg' – but don't ever let on I told you. The title is awfully apt."[51] Nonethe-

44
July Interior, 1963.
Hirshhorn Museum and
Sculpture Garden,
Smithsonian Institution,
Washington, D.C.
Photo by Lee Stalsworth.

45
October Interior, 1963.
Private Collection.

less, the work sold quickly to the collector Joseph Hirshhorn for four thousand dollars, the highest price Porter had ever received for a painting.

Porter's other major painting for the year was *October Interior*, also an image from 49 South Main Street, describing the sharp afternoon sun as it slanted through the windows of the glassed-in sun porch (fig. 45). The room, occupied by a single woman and an abandoned rocking horse, is decidedly casual, suburban, and domestic; still, the deeply exciting play of yellow light – on autumn foliage outside; on houseplants, armchairs, tabletops, and floors within – makes this an image of exceptional, almost dazzling brilliance. In its subject (light) and composition (room with woman), the work recalls a similar one by Alex Katz, *Ten o'Clock* (1960), about which Porter had written, "The light is not for light's sake, but for color's sake, and even more for the painting's sake."[52] Yellow had always been a favorite color for Porter, as evidenced not only in his choice of a color for his new van but in the prevalence of yellows in his paintings throughout the 1950s and 1960s, from the bright yellow forsythia and yellow ocher floors of *Katie and Anne* (1955, see fig. 31) to the subdued Big House interior *Yellow Room* (1961). In the coming years, Porter would experiment with lighter and brighter yellows, from the intense yellow shadows of *Island Farmhouse* (1969, see fig. 54) to the daring, head-on painting of the sun, *Yellow Sunrise* (1974, see fig. 62).

Porter's precarious financial situation may have prompted his irritation with his gallery at this time, but he was having other problems. As he wrote John Bernard Myers and Tibor de Nagy two months before the 1964 exhibition,

January 10, 1964   I have Tibor's letter about the frame.

When I put strips around pictures, and the customer doesn't like them, if that will stop him from buying the painting, then please don't sell to him. I do not want to have to pay for frames ... if I buy a frame, I want to add the cost of the frame to the price of the painting.

There are a few other things I would like to put down here, for the record. Please do not send away to any exhibition any paintings that could otherwise be in my current show. If anyone wants a painting, let them take it away after the show. Please do not let the Museum of Modern Art or any other museum borrow a new painting for one of their purposes, no matter how worthy. I do not want my show that is coming up to be raided by the International Council, or Dorothy Miller, or Alfred Barr, or Mrs. Kennedy, or his Holiness the Pope, not even by the most important and arrogant collector on Manhattan Island. If anyone wants a painting for a show that runs at the same time as mine, give them a previously shown painting, not a new one.

May I have something to say about the catalogue? I did not like the one last year, so I don't want this year's to look like it.[53]

One way Porter found to offset his financial problems was by accepting lecture engagements at universities around the country, which suited his self-described

270

talent as a natural pedant. Schuyler observed to Ashbery in February, "Fairfield has been busy trotting about by jet to places like Alabama and Wisconsin, lecturing art students. He likes it."[54] Porter gave lectures and visited art students both at the University of Alabama at Tuscaloosa and at the University of Wisconsin at Madison and was able to observe how views and opinions that he had encountered in the art world seemed to have become standardized in little more than a decade. As he later observed with wonder, "The School of [Hans] Hofmann seems to have percolated into the remotest corners of the United States."[55] One stop on his travels was at Southern Illinois University at Carbondale, which offered him a yearlong appointment. In the end, he declined out of a dislike of the area's landscape and architecture.

When Porter's show opened in March, critics gave it their most enthusiastic response to date. Porter was given the cover of *Art News* for March 1964 and a feature entitled "Fairfield Porter: Minimum of Melodrama," by Michael Benedikt. Porter was also profiled in *Time Magazine* along with Wayne Thiebaud and George Segal as part of a contemporary trend away from abstraction and toward representation. Porter's recognition was short-lived; within a year, new movements, including Pop Art and Minimalism, began grabbing the headlines. But for a moment Porter found himself in the limelight. He was particularly pleased by the accuracy of the *Art News* profile, whose author noted that his style consisted of "great efficacy combined with considerable invisibility" and that his "identification of painting with seeking emotional as well as plastic simplicity is perhaps the most distinctive philosophical contribution to American painting today."

In the first week of June 1964, Porter and Schuyler opened the Big House on Great Spruce Head, spending two weeks there alone before being joined by Anne Porter and the girls. During the 1960s, Porter established the practice of arriving in Maine with Schuyler before the rest of his family in order to enjoy the solitude of the house and set up his studio for the summer and also in order to have some time alone with Schuyler, for, as Anne Porter knew, Porter and Schuyler had begun a sexual relationship.[56] Porter wrote his wife in June of that year, "There are Quaker Ladies on the island, which are apparently also called bluets. ... Jimmy ... does most of the cooking, making good brown bread, somewhat like the kind you sent to Jerry, only no molasses. He makes a little too much cake and pie."[57]

Porter's complex feelings about Schuyler, his daughters, and his wife are suggested by his major work of that summer, *The Screen Porch* (1964, fig. 46), which depicts Schuyler and the two girls in the studio and Anne Porter standing outside looking in. The image is rather thickly painted and has a flat, color-cartoonish quality suggesting the influence of Alex Katz (Porter had already written about Katz's work, owned one of his paintings, and enjoyed him as a friend).

46
The Screen Porch, 1964.
Collection of the
Whitney Museum of American Art,
New York,
Lawrence H. Bloedel Bequest.

The scene once again is Porter's painting porch in the Big House on Great Spruce Head. Katie Porter, an awkward fifteen years old, seems to be the focus of the painting. Her expression as she gazes into the distance, shown in one-quarter profile, is the most carefully rendered (just as it was in *Katie and Anne*); the uncomfortable way she holds her hands before her sets the tone for the rest of the painting. Beside her, with her back to the canvas, stands young Elizabeth, her hands on the back of Schuyler's chair; she stares down curiously at him or else at the book in his lap. Schuyler, seated, reads (perhaps aloud); his glance is downward, also toward the book. At the extreme right, beyond the screen, Anne Porter stands one step down from the porch itself, glancing in toward the viewer, but her expression is vague and hard to read, perhaps because of the intermediate presence of the screen.

One of Porter's best-known works, the image is remarkable for the odd tension which seems to exist among the four subjects and, by extension, the painter, whose perspective is taken by the viewer. The relationships and states of mind of the four are impossible to know, but it clearly describes a many-layered, inexplicable tension within what appears to be a family.

Porter's framing of his wife in the doorway is perhaps a quotation from Velázquez's *Las Meninas* – but not simply quotation for quotation's sake. Porter may have eschewed "neurotic or psychological values [as] irrelevant," but he enjoyed Velázquez's puzzling and psychologically resonant compositions (he quoted from *Las Meninas* again in *The Mirror* [1966]). What is perhaps most astonishing about the painting is that Porter should have allowed himself to create it, for despite its apparent simplicity it is an evocation of an intensely personal situation in which he invites the viewer to participate as a voyeur and thereby to respond to a parallel voyeurism on the part of Anne Porter, looking in through the screen. Yet, given Porter's personal history of complete and often disturbing honesty in criticism, poetry, and art, the work seems only one of many lifelong declarations of self-knowledge.

In the Porter family, *The Screen Porch* was not popular. In truth, it is not a beautiful painting, merely a powerful and unsettling one. Porter's visual statement of the complicated ambiguities – sexual, emotional, and personal – that ran through his family and his home was disturbing enough that within the group it was soon known jokingly as "The Four Ugly People."

During July, Porter and his wife traveled to Skowhegan, Maine, where Porter had been asked to lecture as a visiting artist. The Porters were delighted to go, for their old friend John Button was teaching there for the summer, and they were able to visit with him during the course of the weekend (Button and Anne Porter enjoyed a warm friendship). Porter read his lecture on art and science. Invited to attend a Beaux Arts ball on Saturday night, he and his wife appeared without costume, claiming to be characters from one of Porter's own paintings.

During the rest of the summer, Porter completed some of his most fluent and beautiful landscapes to date, which (along with the images of family members) were widely praised in Porter's February 1965 exhibition. Brian O'Doherty in *The New York Times* praised Porter for the "stoical sadness" of his work and observed that Porter had managed in works like *The Screen Porch* to achieve a "spontaneous response to subject matter rather than the employment of an artistic convention, relat[ing] not so much to things seen as to the meaning and significance they hold for him."[58]

Three years later Porter told an interviewer that "I used to sort of hate to go to [my] opening[s] ... because here I am with this shameful stuff all around being exposed."[59] But even with *The Screen Porch*, Porter's discomfort was not with the work's psychological content but with the quality of the painting.

Porter's earnings from the 1964 show totaled eleven thousand dollars. For the rest of his career, though he would never have very much money, Porter would at least be able to cover his basic expenses with a combined income from sales and teaching. Apart from teaching and painting, he found himself being drawn into ecological causes, as a letter to his dealer, John Bernard Myers, makes clear: "Right now I am rather upset because the village insists on spraying their trees along our sidewalk with DDT, though I say this is a health hazard, and shouldn't be done. They seem to think it is more important to save the elm trees from Dutch elm disease than to bother with risks to the population of the town. So now I have to gather together all the evidence I can for a letter to the mayor and the head of the tree committee – who Anne says is a classmate of Laurence. They think I am a foolish and annoying crank."[60]

Porter's spring ended in catastrophe. On June 8, he was driving in his Yuma-yellow Chevrolet van to visit a sculpture studio in Bridgehampton. When he turned off Montauk Highway onto Scuttlehole Road, he saw lights flashing at the railroad crossing just ahead. Rather than wait for the train to pass, Porter accelerated, expecting he would cross the tracks long before the train arrived; he had done so before on many occasions, frequently against the protests of his wife. "It wasn't that he was a risk-taker or daredevil," Anne Porter observed. "He was simply impatient. He didn't want to wait for the train to pass and he honestly thought he could get across."[61]

Porter described what came next in a letter to Howard Griffin:

November 27, 1965   The car was, as they say, completely demolished, though at the time it did not look at all so to me, though I was upside down when I got out, which, as it seemed to me, I did simply by opening the door and stepping out. As I looked back at it, I thought that all it needed was to be righted and towed away and started again. But the engine had sheared off the rear end. I saw that the train had stopped, so I thought I should show them I was all right, which so alarmed the conductor or engineer or whoever, that he ran towards me and put me in a waiting car; whose driver, a woman, felt too sick, at the sight of me all bloody, to drive, and took me to the hospital.[62]

According to the police, Porter, who was in shock, took the keys out of the ignition of the upside-down remaining half of the van so that no one would steal it and walked around in circles, saying over and over again, "My wife told me not to do this." When the train came to a halt, the engineer, seeing that Porter was all right, told him, "Don't ever do that again."[63] The Long Island Railroad sent Porter a bill for damages to the railroad engine, but he had a lawyer send them a threatening letter, and the railroad eventually sent him two hundred dollars in compensation for the destroyed new van and his hospital bills.

Porter, though chagrined, was essentially unharmed. "No bones were broken," he wrote Griffin, "only sustained cuts and bruises, which required a few days in the hospital for the principal cut to heal enough so that I could bend my knee and go home. [The artist] Paul Georges, who visited me in the hospital the same day, told me that this was the most interesting thing I had ever done in my life – which I suppose is true."[64]

The accident is marked in Schuyler's work by two references, one in "The Morning of the Poem" and the other in the short poem "Stun," which begins,

> If you've ever been hit by a car
> that was hit by a train
> whang
> (a tearing like metal shears)
> flip   spin
>   "Why I'm perfectly OK!"
> this streaming blood
> a euphoric sweat of thanksgiving [65]

Toward the end of his stay at the hospital, Porter found himself once again in need of a car. Knowing that he would be unable to afford another new one, he arranged with the man in the next bed to buy his white Ford station wagon. The white station wagon appeared in many of Porter's sketches and several paintings over the next decade. To his son Laurence, it had a symbolic significance: "When I drove his coffin to the graveyard [in 1975] in the station wagon he had bought after the crash, I thought of it as symbolizing a gift of an extra decade of life."[66]

17

Critical Success and a
European Vacation

Though Porter went to Maine as planned after recovering from his auto accident, the shock to his system had been considerable, and he spent the entire summer recuperating. Still, Porter completed several major paintings on Great Spruce Head, including *Morning Landscape* (1965, fig. 47), an enormous, brilliantly colored image of the harbor with nine-year-old Elizabeth Porter sitting in the foreground. Porter wrote Laurence, "I have one very large painting, the same size as the one last year that mother called 'the four ugly people,' which has Lizzie sitting on the front porch in Maine with all the morning harbor view behind her, all in pink, cerulean, pale orange and grey. Lizzie is in scarlet. And on the left of her are pink and purple canterbury bells and foxglove planted the preceding year by Jimmy. The island was very, very dry and the grass turned the color of the rock."[1]

The work is one of Porter's most joyous, in part because the open, almost mischievous expression of Elizabeth harmonizes so perfectly with the fresh, bright morning sun on the landscape behind her and the flowers to her right. In her funny scarlet hat and sweater, Elizabeth has the cheerful presence of a cardinal; here, Porter's color combination of scarlet and ocher is a departure, for he had frequently paired ocher with a deep, vivid orange during the 1950s. The porch architecture – its roofline and bug screens – frames the view beyond Elizabeth, which moves easily between representation and abstraction and is concerned primarily with color harmonies. The interior light of the porch gives way to the vivid daylight of the middle ground, with its "grass turned the color of the rock"; the soft, opalescent outlines of the misty harbor and cove finish off the view. There is a wonderful, airy casualness to the work; the complicated forms of the spruce tree to the left and the wall of trees on the far side of the cove seem merely to have been drawn in outline and then blocked in. The dry surface texture of the painting, along with its use of bright colors, recalls the glories of fine weather, particularly that specific moment in midmorning when

47
Morning Landscape, 1965.
Santa Barbara Museum of Art,
Santa Barbara, Calif.,
Gift of Rowe Gieson.

the soft haze begins to burn off and the dry summer landscape is revealed in all its splendor. Again, Porter's use of a large canvas, a convention among Abstract Expressionist painters, counts as an innovation and experiment in this work, which is essentially Intimist.

Other works of the summer were relatively small. A lovely portrait of Porter's wife, *Anne* (1965, fig. 48), celebrates her favorite and distinguishing colors of white, blue, and gray. Porter completed a rare self-portrait during this time, but primarily his work consisted of landscapes, seascapes, and floral still lifes.

During the summer Porter corresponded with Arthur Giardelli in Wales. Porter had invited the Giardellis to visit Great Spruce Head as early as 1961, but when they hesitated, he came up with a new plan: to take his family on a European tour and incorporate a visit to the Giardellis into the trip. Porter saw the journey as a part of his girls' education and a way to refresh his memory about the art and sights of Europe, which he had last seen thirty years earlier.

On his return to Southampton in the fall of 1965, Porter revised the lecture he had been giving, "Art and Knowledge," for publication in the February 1966 *Art News*. In the resulting short essay, in which he seeks an appropriate way to describe art, he concludes that art, as opposed to science and criticism, helps one to accept one's essential wholeness and connection to the world, a wholeness and connection that are suppressed in the individual by traditional forms of education. In this essay Porter finds in art a means of gaining access to what others might call the sacredness of everyday life. The essay is a key statement of Porter's artistic beliefs.

That fall, Porter also completed one of his best essays on a contemporary artist, Joseph Cornell. Cornell was legendary for disliking everything that was written about him, but he was delighted with Porter's essay, perhaps because Porter seemed to think that, like a great poem, a Cornell box – a "subjective container of the soul" – transcended criticism. In blending objects and language into art, Cornell certainly spoke to Porter's own Mallarmé-inspired aesthetic. Shortly after the piece was published, Cornell called the Porter house and told Anne Porter, "I'm so angry about your husband's review that I'm going to come to give him one of my boxes." He did come, with his sister, and left a box for Porter (who was away). In return, Porter sent Cornell a note of thanks and a copy of Eliot Porter's book, to which Cornell responded, "Please feel free to come by [the studio] any time and investigate." The Cornell box was soon hung in the Porter living room.[2]

Along with his writing and painting that fall, Porter took a job at the newly founded Southampton branch of Long Island University. The position was convenient to his home and, as such, irresistible, but Porter, upon meeting the students, soon realized his folly, noting in a letter that they "have no background and are such babies that my job is rather like being a nurse. That is a waste of time." In the future, Porter chose his teaching assignments carefully and, when given a choice, would lecture or appear as a visiting artist rather than

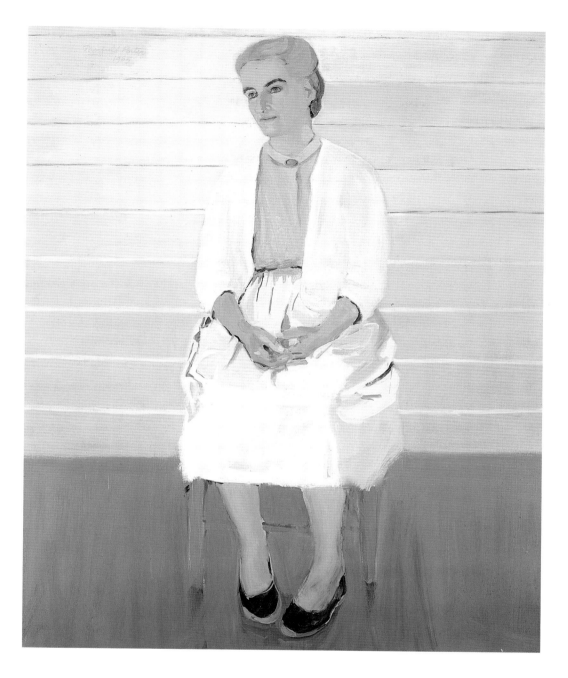

48
Anne, 1965.
Parrish Art Museum, Southampton, N.Y.,
Gift of the Estate
of Fairfield Porter (1980.10.6).
Photo by Noel Rowe.

teach full-time, for he disliked the forced conviviality of teaching and was particularly irritated at having to instruct people who were not really interested in art.

Luckily, teaching was no longer absolutely necessary to the Porter family finances, for during the fall of 1965, Porter received two final checks from the Porter realty trust when his brother Edward liquidated the family property holdings. Porter's share was just under forty thousand dollars, roughly equal to the amount he would make from his paintings in the coming year. Porter still had both daughters' educations to pay for and a grown son in special care, but from the mid-1960s on he was no longer facing debt or the forced sale of works of art. He continued to lecture to supplement his income (in the coming year visiting Yale, Skowhegan, and the Maryland Institute College of Art), but true financial hardship was now behind him.

Porter's February 1966 show was a critical success, prompting a major review from Hilton Kramer of *The New York Times*, a critic who became a persistent and influential champion of Porter's work. The exhibition took place in a new gallery space on 29 West Fifty-seventh Street, about which Porter observed, "It [the new Tibor de Nagy] doesn't have as good exhibition space, but it does have very much more storage space, so they won't constantly be sending paintings back here, and then demanding them again as they used to do."³ The new storage space meant that more works were available to buyers at all times. One happy result of this arrangement was that avid collectors immediately began buying up Porter's (cheaply priced) back stock of paintings simply because they were on hand at the gallery, ready for the taking.

Porter had a busy spring. Along with the usual work of preparing for his next show, he was putting together his strongest paintings for his first one-man museum exhibition, at the Cleveland Museum of Art. The exhibition, entitled "The Genre Art of Fairfield Porter," had originally been scheduled for the spring of 1966, but the date was changed to August, an inauspicious time for a museum exhibition. Even so, Porter wanted a strong show. He was not having much luck in persuading collectors to lend his best works to the exhibition, so he tried hard to come up with good new work. One result was *The Mirror* (1966, fig. 49), a painting of Elizabeth Porter sitting before a mirror in Porter's studio, with Porter standing alone in the mirror's reflection. The painting is somewhat mysterious in that the easel and canvas in the mirror image are noticeably absent from the composition. But Porter frequently observed from vantage points several steps away from his canvas,⁴ so there is no attempt at paradox in the painting, merely business as usual. Velázquez's *Las Meninas* is the inspiration for the work. But the image can also be viewed as a winter version of Porter's *Morning Landscape*. Elizabeth, again in red (this time red leggings and an orange red cardigan), again sits before a framed view. In this case, the view is interior: a framed mirror. The painting again takes color relations in near, middle, and far light as its subject. The near distance, where Elizabeth sits, is warm; then comes a silvery middle area, the mirror reflection of the studio, where Porter stands to

49
The Mirror, 1966.
Nelson-Atkins Museum of Art,
Kansas City, Mo.,
Gift of the Enid and Crosby
Kemper Foundation.

the right, before his potbellied stove, and a jug of water stands to the left. The distant view, through the studio window, is of bright, distant winter sunlight reflecting off the cottage next door. The chill of this work is matched by Elizabeth's expression: she wears, instead of the open, sunny smile of *Morning Landscape,* a cool and watchful look.

During early 1966, James Schuyler, who was still residing with the Porters, wrote John Ashbery about a disagreement he had had with Porter over the artist and poet Joe Brainard. Porter liked Brainard and his painting but took a violent dislike to his criticism and declined Schuyler's request of a recommendation for Brainard at *Art News.* Schuyler had befriended Brainard and his lover, the librettist Kenward Elmslie, several years earlier and on at least one occasion in 1964 the two had visited the Porters on Great Spruce Head Island.[5] Within a couple of years, Schuyler was dividing his time between the Porters' Southampton home and Elmslie's country home in Calais, Vermont. Schuyler enjoyed the change of scene, for both he and the Porters were less content with each other's constant company than they had been previously.

Anne Porter viewed her husband's open invitation to Schuyler to come and go as he pleased from the house on South Main Street as a typical act of generosity and kindness. But Porter's preference for Schuyler's company in her own home was difficult, and putting up with it daily left her feeling, in her own words, "terrible," for as she later explained in reference to an invitation once

50
Schuyler (*right*) and Ashbery on the porch of the Big House,
Great Spruce Head, circa 1966. Photographer unknown.
Courtesy James Schuyler Papers, Archive for New Poetry,
Mandeville Department of Special Collections, University
of California, San Diego / La Jolla.

extended to Porter and Schuyler but not to her, "I felt as if my relationship to F. was being severed. He and Jimmy were now the couple & I could be left out of F.'s social life even where we lived, like someone in another generation or of another social class, and not married to him at all. It was different from F.'s separate social life in New York, which I knew he needed."[6] From the mid-1960s, Schuyler's presence caused increasing tension within the Porter marriage, a tension which Schuyler tended to blame on Anne Porter rather than on his own continued presence.[7]

When Porter and his wife made their annual trip to Great Spruce Head in 1966, Schuyler once again came along. Porter's daughter Katharine, having completed high school in three years, was traveling to Europe with Laurence and Betsy Porter before attending Manhattanville College, a Catholic institution, in the fall. Porter, worn out from painting so intently all spring to prepare for his Cleveland show and suffering from arthritis of the knee, took a break from painting when John Ashbery, newly returned from France, came for a second visit to the island (fig. 50). Both Schuyler and the Porters were delighted to see him.

Shortly after Ashbery's departure in late July, Porter received tragic news. Frank O'Hara had been hit by a dune buggy on Fire Island in the early hours of July 23 and had died two days later of internal injuries. O'Hara was to be buried at the Green River Cemetery near East Hampton in three days. The Porters, like many in the art world, were devastated, for even though they had not seen much of him in recent years, O'Hara had been a good friend to the Porters since the early 1950s. But the Porters did not travel back to Long Island for the funeral, nor did Schuyler, whose mental condition was too fragile. Instead, some time later, Porter expressed his sense of loss to Ashbery, writing, "About a week ago I had a dream of Frank O'Hara, in which there were two Franks, one Frank dead, and the other Frank his own interpreter to me. In the dream I had the sad feeling that he had really been a sympathetic friend of mine in a different way to anyone else, in his unique way, that would be irreplaceable."[8]

Porter gave a lecture at Skowhegan but passed the rest of the summer quietly on the island. There was a visit from Kenneth Koch, his wife, Janice, and their daughter, Katherine, who was by now a good friend of Elizabeth Porter's. In August, Elizabeth and James Schuyler appeared in a major painting of that summer, *Iced Coffee* (1966, fig. 51), which features the two sitting quietly on Porter's studio porch (that is, the back porch) of the Big House.[9]

The painting marks a renewed interest in lighting effects, which had tended to become flattened out and "cartoonish" (the word is Porter's) in Alex Katz – inspired paintings like *The Screen Porch* (see fig. 46). But it was not a return to older renderings of light, like the lustrous, flickering light of the *Portrait of James Schuyler*, painted more than a decade earlier in the same room (see fig. 30). *Iced Coffee* gives a thorough and considered rendering of solid forms, with a wildflower arrangement – goldenrod, Queen Anne's lace, and black-eyed Susans – creating a moment of late-summer intricacy in an otherwise simple,

51
Iced Coffee, 1966.
G.U.C. Collection, Chicago.

solid, and straightforward composition. The tranquillity of the work derives in part from the specific light of late afternoon; the light of Porter's painting porch is even and gentle because the porch catches no light off the water but sits instead in a small area of luminous dry grass surrounded by spruce. In *Iced Coffee*, the area of brightest light, apart from the light falling on Elizabeth's pink blouse, emanates from the polished concrete floor at the edge of the porch. Just above that gleaming area is the small glass of iced coffee which gives the painting its name.

The Porters left the island in early September (fig. 52), and during the fall Porter began planning an extensive and ambitious itinerary for his trip to Europe with Anne and the girls in the summer of 1967. By December, Porter had booked passage on the *Michelangelo* departing on June 5 from New York and going to Naples; the return tickets would bring them from Southampton, England, on August 12 on the *France*. Both ports were familiar to him from his voyages to Europe with his parents – Southampton from the cathedral tour of England, and Naples from his voyage to Italy with his mother in 1931. Flying to Europe might have been quicker and more convenient, but Porter preferred to know, through the physical sensation of boat travel, just how far a distance Europe lay from America. He may also have wanted to reexperience the sensations that he had known as a young man traveling to Europe thirty-six years earlier.

But the trip was months away. In February 1967, Porter went to Kent State University in Ohio to participate in its Creative Arts Festival. His lecture was "Art and Knowledge," but he had been invited as well to participate in a round-table discussion entitled "The Arts Today: A Symptom of a Sick Society?" Porter, "stimulate[d] in opposition" by the topic, had a very good time. "There were other people – an architect, Stockhausen, the composer, Agnes de Mille, and other people. And they all talked before I did," he recalled. "And so that gave me more and more things to say."[10] Porter's main contribution to the discussion was an idea that increasingly preoccupied him during the last years of his life, an idea which he had seen earlier in Mallarmé and more recently in William

52
Anne, Fairfield, and Elizabeth Porter leaving Great Spruce Head on the mailboat, end of summer 1966. James Schuyler's head can be seen through the window. Photo by Per Voss. Courtesy Mrs. John Porter.

Carlos Williams's statement "no ideas except in things." Porter was "against the Platonic notion that what is real is an idea. That is *not* what is real. Plato is wrong. He's completely wrong ... I said that at Kent State University ... we ... talked to philosophy students. So that was what I said to them, that Plato was completely wrong, that art is not ideal, it's material and specific and actual. It's not an idea."[11]

Porter's idea that the material, specific, and actual was a sort of ultimate reality can be traced back to his father's atheism and to his father's belief in careful scientific examination of the natural world; indeed, many of Porter's late beliefs and interests were close to those of his father and became more so as he aged. Schuyler rearticulated Porter's theories about his painting in a 1967 article on Porter's show: "What we are given [in Porter's work] is an aspect of everyday life, seen neither as a snapshot nor as an exaltation. Its art is one that values the everyday as the ultimate, the most varied and desirable knowledge. What these paintings celebrate is never treated as an archetype: they are concentrated instances. They are not a substitute for religion, they are an attitude toward life."[12]

Porter's February 1967 show at Tibor de Nagy was marred by the theft of two paintings. James Schuyler wrote Joe Brainard about it in March:

March 1967   Fairfield has had another painting stolen from his show, this small one in the same room as yours called the *North West Wind*. ... It was his favorite, and he had reserved it for himself, the first time he has done that. I think he feels very depressed about it, too much so [to] say anything about it. It seems typically John Myers to have left small pictures in that room when one had already been taken. Nor did he bother to call F. up and tell him about it – I heard of it, told F., who called him. John said something like, "Oh, *yes*, isn't it *dreadful*?" That it was in any way his fault didn't of course occur to him.

Schuyler's 1967 article about Porter's show addressed itself less to the paintings than to an accusation that Porter's work was bourgeois, materialistic, and out of touch with the times. Porter's work during the late 1960s reveals a long-sought and hard-won inner serenity. Schuyler, knowing Porter as he did, felt the need to explain something of Porter's past to those who saw his work merely as a complacent representation of bourgeois suburban affluence:

A critic who found nothing to like (in fact, the contrary) in an exhibition of Fairfield Porter's paintings summed up his feelings about them in the epithet "bourgeois." Or perhaps he had the taste to say middle-class, though it's doubtful. ...

... While painting which can be called traditional, in whole or part, of course continues to be painted, its right to be considered on a level higher than that of genre – in the "mere" sense – is often questioned. [Porter's painting] is "illusionistic," a way of painting associated with a presumed wish to perpetuate its values and its possessions, which were much the same.

Schuyler's defense of his friend led him to explore Porter's past as a way of understanding his present style of painting. He noted that Porter's "factual and unromantic knowledge of ... Stalinism ... has left him with a distrust of idealism," adding that Porter's stance toward politics in art resembled that of the socialist Rosa Luxemburg, who felt that "any too obvious *purpose* in art – even social – meant automatic disqualification. Art was *sui generis*. ... What made art timeless was not vision but quality. As a means of social change [Luxemburg] preferred direct political activity [to political art]." Schuyler concluded, "What we are given [in Porter's paintings] is an aspect of everyday life. ... Their value is not one connected to class. ... These paintings have no concern with production. Their values are no more timeless than anything else, but they are values which exist in any society, whether they are embodied or not."[13]

Schuyler's spirited defense of Porter's work is significant. For the first time in print, the suggestion is made that it needed to be evaluated not just on the basis of how well it was painted but also in terms of the values represented by the subjects depicted – the immediate world of a "wealthy" "bourgeois" family. In essence, Schuyler suggests that Porter's work was being attacked not as painting but as a series of representations that defined the artist as a man of a certain background and class to viewers newly critical of "establishment" values. The issue of class content was not one that nonrepresentational painters like de Kooning had ever been forced to address; and even for representational painters, it had been less a matter of general concern among critics during the Eisenhower-dominated 1950s. But times were changing. Porter himself could hardly explain or defend the "bourgeois" content of his work, for he was addressing an entirely different set of problems and issues in his painting. Schuyler's defense of Porter – noting that the artist had a history of being politically aware but now felt that the practice of art must, to be successful, lie outside the realm of any specific political agenda – left a larger question unanswered: why such a politically aware artist should have deliberately chosen to paint, over and over again, provocatively private, privileged, and bourgeois subjects. The answer to this question was, simply, that Porter's paintings were like his home: deliberate in paradox. Given his often-stated belief in no ideas except in things, the question of whether these (valuable) possessions were the embodiment of a set of (conservative) values was an important one – and one that went unanswered in Schuyler's article, just as it does in Porter's paintings.

With the trip to Europe approaching, Porter found it increasingly difficult to concentrate on his work. He had written to Giardelli back in December to say, "I feel very excited about this trip, as much as the first time I went abroad when I was 14. ... I dream about it every night, the most happy dreams."[14] But the Naples of 1967 was nothing like the sleepy city that Porter had visited in 1931. To Schuyler, who was staying in the house in Southampton with Ruth Kligman, he wrote,

June 16, 1967 Naples is as noisy as a subway station through which an express train is passing, and where the Con Ed is drilling. Our first day was exhausting and we got lost ... Lizzie was frightened.

We took a trip in a hired car to Ravello and Amalfi and [Lizzie] was in ecstasy over the orange trees, mossy trunks, paths, flowers, outlooks over the Mediterranean with antique statues, as we all were. ... I feel altogether a strange mixture of feelings, extremely moved by the beauty of a foreign city with three ladies to protect [but] I miss being able to paint and I hate the noise. I hope Rome is more humane ... we plunge back and forth from ancient beauty to the present hellishness of traffic and smog.[15]

The Amalfi coast appealed to Porter as a place worth painting – "the landscape is very Bonnard"[16] – but the excavations at Pompeii and Herculaneum were not visually inspiring to him. The Porters stayed in Naples only long enough to visit "a duchessa cousin" of Anne Porter's; this distant relative on the Channing side was merely a "Christmas card acquaintance," but Anne's mother had always hoped she and her daughter would meet, and the Porters were charmed with their cousin, whom Anne Porter described as "a sort of Henry James heroine."[17]

From Naples the Porters traveled by rail to Rome, where Porter had unwittingly booked a room in a dormitory. But the Porters' old friend Edith Schloss, now divorced from Rudy Burckhardt and living in Rome, was able to find them an apartment on the Piazza Navona, which they used as a home base for the next two weeks. Porter wrote Schuyler, "We are almost acclimatized and it's ever so much nicer than Naples. ... I have to forgo Italian wine. It is as hot as a frying pan. Katie is sick and we haven't been around very much yet."[18]

Schloss, who introduced Porter to a number of Italian artists, later said that Rome had been difficult for him and his family: "The Porters were ill at ease and silent most of the time. ... I see them on a rainy Sunday, after having been blessed by the Pope at noon, standing sodden and miserable in crinkly raincoats under the awning of the cafe Tre Scalini, wondering what to do next."[19] Schloss was also disconcerted at the way in which, "walking through the crooked alleys of our neighborhood ... Anne and the girls would detach themselves to sign themselves in front of every Madonna picture we passed." Porter's response, if any, to these manifestations of faith has gone unrecorded; no doubt he was more interested in the art.

After seeing museums, churches, palazzos, piazzas, and an exhausting number of Roman ruins, the Porters traveled to Orvieto, where Porter was able to sketch the countryside as well as admire the cathedral's glittering facade and visit the famed Luca Signorelli frescoes in the chapel of San Brizio.

Porter's brief visit to Orvieto made him regret not visiting other towns which had been of such great importance to his art-historical education, including Arezzo (for the Piero della Francesca *Legend of the True Cross* frescoes), Sienna (Simone Martini's Guido Riccio fresco), and Padua (the Giotto frescoes of the Scrovegni chapel). Instead, from Orvieto, the Porters traveled to Florence, which had been ravaged the year before by the floods on the Arno. The family stayed at a pensione that Porter had visited with his mother – not the bohemian Casa Bertolini but the more expensive pensione Ruth found for her son on the Arno shortly before her departure, "a smoothly run old place full of sedate old Americans."[20] Unfortunately, they arrived during a heat wave and were troubled by the crush of tourists at the major artistic sights and by the heavy diesel emissions of the tourist buses, so much so that during a visit to the Medici tombs, Katharine Porter collapsed from the heat and lack of air.

One of the highlights of Florence was the Porters' visit to San Miniato al Monte, in the hills facing Florence. Porter had hiked to San Miniato with Giardelli during the cold winter of 1931; now he visited it at the height of summer with his wife and daughters, and they were equally delighted, preferring it "to all the churches in Rome."[21]

The Porters proceeded from Florence via rail to Venice. "Mother made a champion flat remark, when we arrived in Venice: 'Why, it's like some foreign city,'" Porter wrote, adding, "But this expressed the way we all felt and so it was the most appropriate remark also."[22] He said, "St. Mark's Square has a perpetually festive air that Johnny would love, with live music playing while one sips cool drinks, from 2 p.m. until, I guess, midnight. And San Marco is probably altogether the most interesting cathedral we saw." To Schuyler, Porter wrote, "I still like those Tintorettos as much as I did in 1931, but what I didn't see before are Tiepolo frescos; they have modern light. The light of Venice has not yet been adequately represented, not by anyone." In another letter, he expressed a sense of being overwhelmed by great art: "I will be glad to get home and back to painting. But Italian art and architecture reduce all of the Avant-Garde from Picasso on to a rather smallish bubble. Which does not in any way elevate the rear guard. There is no answer, if you know what I mean."[23]

From Venice the Porters traveled to Paris, where they visited museums and toured the city at a more relaxed pace. As Porter wrote Laurence, "We slowed down a little because of Lizzie and partly because of me, who found getting tickets and reservations and so on somewhat nerve-wracking."[24] From Paris the Porters, by now craving fresh air and a verdant landscape, traveled directly to Wales, where Porter was reunited after thirty-five years with his old friend Giardelli.

The Porters were surprised to learn that the Giardellis opened their home to language students and visitors during the summer to supplement their income. Arthur Giardelli, now a bald and grizzled man in his middle fifties, had slyly withheld the information from his old friend out of a fear that Porter would not want to intrude upon his busy season. Porter and his family were exhausted by their European travels and were not altogether comfortable in a house filled to bursting with unknown teenagers, but they managed to settle in. To Schuyler, Porter wrote, "In Wales the Giardellis have a heroic and entirely peculiar household of about twenty boys and girls from foreign countries there to learn English, old friends (four in a family) as well as four Porters. In the two months of summer Arthur does no painting at all, just the opposite of me."[25] He mentioned no personal response to Arthur Giardelli's change in appearance or manner, merely observing that he was delighted by some of his work, much of it reminiscent of the artist Joseph Cornell – an artist about whom, to Porter's surprise, Giardelli knew nothing, for he was attuned only to developments in contemporary European art and knew little about developments in New York.

Porter was also surprised to learn that Giardelli had made a number of life choices similar to those that Porter had made for himself. Opposed to governmental policies from World War II on, Giardelli had chosen a country life among the independent-spirited Welsh, who prided themselves on observing few distinctions between social classes. He was a passionate student of European literature. And his work was entirely free of "the urban and ironic attitudes of Pop art and other derivatives of surrealism," as one English critic observed, just as Giardelli himself disliked "the idea of an art made for art galleries rather than for personal rooms."[26] Even the Giardelli house had similarities to the Porters': many bedrooms, a tradition of come-as-you-are hospitality, plenty of art and books and musical instruments. There was even an Aga stove just like the one in Southampton. Experiencing the world of his old friend after so many years, Porter must have felt like Alice through the looking-glass.

During his stay with the Giardellis, Porter helped hang an exhibition of Giardelli's large assemblages in the Cathedral of St. David's, an eleventh-century structure, one of the oldest in Wales. This intimate connection with an old building turned out to be a highlight of Porter's trip. Porter was also fascinated by the low, active skies of Wales, where moments of brilliant sunshine appeared constantly out of the mist and drizzle, illuminating the moist, green countryside with moments of golden-bright light. In the evenings, after a simple meal, the Porters listened to Giardelli's wife, Judy, play the piano.

The last stop on the Porters' tour was London, but shortly after arriving they took a day-trip to Wells to see a cathedral that Porter remembered from childhood, and ended up staying the night, for they were tired of big cities and tired of traveling. As Porter wrote Schuyler, "Why is London depressing? Perhaps because we are all homesick and look forward to getting home again."[27]

Still, they enjoyed themselves. "The [London] parks are the best in the world, better than Paris," Porter wrote. "And Wren churches are really more beautiful than the small churches of Paris and Italy." They visited the National Gallery and the Wallace Collection, where Porter was impressed by *Boy Bringing Pomegranates* by De Hooch. Velázquez's *Don Carlos at the Riding School* was another painting that Porter found revelatory. At Arthur Giardelli's suggestion, Porter looked at contemporary art at the London galleries, including Giardelli's own Grosvenor Gallery; but Porter came away unimpressed, observing to Laurence, "On the whole, if I have any right to an opinion, I would say that British contemporary art does not interest me as much as what one sees in New York."

While in London, the Porters made a point of having a cup of tea at the ABC chain of tea shops, in homage to T. S. Eliot's line "Weeping, weeping multitudes / Droop in a hundred ABC's." Indeed, English melancholy would be Porter's chief recollection of his visit to England; he observed in several of his last letters home that "English niceness has a broken heart as its basis."[28] Porter's visit to Europe after a span of thirty-five years was heavy with memories of both deceased parents as well as his long-vanished youth. Seeing Giardelli, balding and wrinkled and worn down by a difficult life, must have made Porter sharply aware of the passage of time.

When the Porters returned to Southampton in mid-August, Porter returned to the studio eager to pick up the brush after so much time away. The most immediate effect of the trip was to make him realize how much he enjoyed the distinctive quality of the light in Southampton and New York. His exceptional awareness of Southampton's light – in this case, a summer twilight – is apparent in a double portrait that he painted shortly after his return of Jane Freilicher and her daughter Elizabeth, which features a sky of vivid lavender.

Porter also worked on a number of Southampton interiors and still lifes, including an image of Anne Porter standing at the north window of Porter's studio, entitled *Anne in a Striped Dress* (1967). His most singular work that fall of 1967 was *Nyack*, done from a painting made in 1953, itself done from a sketch that Porter had drawn during his visit to Jane Freilicher's rented summer home in that town. The painting, an image of Jane painting in her backyard and Anne seated on a treebench reading a volume of Ronald Firbank, has a languid, summertime quality, but its details are rough, its colors harsh and flat, and all in all it looks much more like a painting by Alex Katz. Porter observed that part of its distinctive quality "comes from the inevitable decision that if you don't remember something, you might as well make that area flat ... the rest is almost reasoned, conceptual, in a sense willed." Porter, aware that many people disliked the painting, said to Giardelli that it was "inconsistent, I am told, and I see that it is, but I like it."[29]

After the Porters returned from Europe, Schuyler, who had been watching the house, left for a month in Calais, Vermont, with Elmslie and Brainard. During his visit, he convinced the poet Ron Padgett, who was also visiting Calais, to drive him to Maine for a brief September visit to Great Spruce Head. They did so, bivouacking in the Big House, and there collaborated on a poem, "Under the Dome," about the prototypical geodesic dome constructed by Buckminster Fuller on the neighboring island, which belonged to the Fuller family. Schuyler's independent visit to the island and his lack of concern about being there without the Porters suggests the extent to which he considered the Porters' home his own.

In fact, by the beginning of 1968 the Porters were beginning to feel that Schuyler had stayed long enough with them. Early in 1968, Porter, who had never before been in the position of asking a houseguest to leave, broached the subject with him.[30] But one effect of Schuyler's depression and alcoholism was helplessness and inertia. With his basic needs provided for by the Porters, Schuyler had stopped seeking employment and had no savings; he filled his days with the difficult and demanding work of writing good poetry. When pressed to move out, Schuyler promised Porter that he would "think about it."[31] Porter, believing him, mentioned the situation to no one in his correspondence.

In January 1968, at roughly the time that Porter first asked him to leave, Schuyler began a journal in which he creates beautiful images of isolation and stillness in the Porter home, usually out of simple observations of weather and light. This strangely eventless journal creates nuanced prose images of scenes familiar in Porter paintings: the forsythia bush in the backyard, the clear blue of a winter sky in late afternoon. But even in these quiet reflections there is a shadow-awareness of buried anxiety: "I was going to go into the city today, but when I woke up to rain – the first rainy morning in weeks and weeks – I put it off until tomorrow, when Fairfield is going in too. This meant calling Kenward, which was uncomfortable, since I'd felt I was imposing or inconveniencing him in some way that wasn't clear to me – oh well, why be paranoid about it ... What a 'pore little feller' I make myself out to be sometimes."[32]

As Schuyler's depression and anxiety worsened, his desire to participate in household activities disappeared, and he reverted to the darker, more slovenly habits of his days at the Forty-ninth Street apartment with Frank O'Hara and Joe LeSueur, where LeSueur had complained of Schuyler's black looks and his empty coffee cups and crusted-over glasses of buttermilk left lying about for others to wash and put away. Robert Dash, who gave Schuyler dinner every Thursday at his Bridgehampton home, described him during this period as "completely senescent." If left to his own devices, the poet sat still for hours at a time, often listening to the same record over and over again. "I cooked him thousands of dinners, and not *once* did he ever clear the table."[33]

Dash worried that Schuyler was going to commit suicide; the Porters did, too. But his behavior was starting to dictate the mood of the Porter household in a most unpleasant way, and Porter worried about his effect on the rest of the family. Anne Porter, having seen the negative effect that household discord had had on her son Jerry during the 1940s and 1950s, was particularly concerned about her daughter Elizabeth, now fast approaching adolescence. While both Anne and Fairfield Porter cared for Schuyler, they were tired of the tension he had introduced into their life and home.

During the fall of 1967, at Liz Porter's request, the Porters drove to a kennel in Manorville, Long Island, and picked out a golden retriever pup. Bruno belonged to Elizabeth, but he quickly became a regular visitor to Porter's studio and was featured in many Porter paintings. Schuyler described the dog in his journals as a "most amiable dog, though perhaps not a genius." Unlike previous household pets, Bruno was well trained; Porter had made the dog's training a condition of his purchase.

But the dog was soon the cause of an accident. In early spring, Porter began taking the dog out on the leash for morning jogs – jogging had been recommended to Porter by his friend Dr. Kenneth Wright to combat his physical fatigue. While running, Porter tripped over Bruno's leash and fell, breaking his left arm. He spent several days in April in the hospital, several weeks in a cast, and the balance of the spring and early summer undergoing painful physical therapy. The broken arm limited Porter's ability to paint.

Owing to the trip to Europe the previous summer, Porter's exhibition in February and March 1968 had few paintings. The strange, large-scale *Nyack* was bought by the Cleveland Museum of Art. Schuyler once again reviewed Porter's exhibition, perhaps out of a desire to contribute to the household. Since joining the Porters in 1961, Schuyler had written two long articles on Porter as well as several reviews, in this way continuing, despite his illness, to give Porter his professional support. Porter had another show that season, at the Richard Gray Gallery in Chicago.

In late spring, just before departing for Great Spruce Head, Porter was visited by Paul Cummings from the Archives of American Art, who recorded an interview with Porter on the lawn outside the studio. The interview is a remarkably detailed autobiographical account of Porter's life from childhood on. Shortly after completing the interview, which took two days, the Porters welcomed Kenward Elmslie and Joe Brainard to Southampton – the two had rented the house from the Porters for the summer – and then departed for Maine.

Summer on Great Spruce Head in 1968 got off to a slow start. Porter was still experiencing pain in his broken elbow, and he also seems to have undergone a period of existential questioning. He wrote his friend Lucien Day, "Why make it? Who cares? In a short time we will be back in Southampton. It is more beautiful *here*, in fact this is one of the beauty spots of the world. But that too, puts me off. Why reproduce this, when what matters, if it does, is just to look. How does this beauty connect with everything else? I do not imagine that ugliness is more significant, as some puritanical artists seem to believe, but I seem to have lost a certain energy or will. ... I think I feel I have discovered my limits, which does not encourage me to do anything."[34]

The sense of purposelessness may have been caused, paradoxically, by Porter's success, for, now past sixty, Porter had achieved a certain plateau in his painting and in his life; he no longer needed to prove himself through his paintings, nor did he need to worry overmuch about selling enough paintings to support his family. His reputation was established, and moneymaking did not interest him enough to motivate him to paint. The question, then, of why one should continue to struggle with painting was a vexing one.

Porter seems, during this summer of listlessness and casting about, to have begun contemplating year-round living on Great Spruce Head, writing Joe Brainard, "When I am here, I gradually get to feel, why couldn't one live here all the time, with wood for heat and no electricity. It has so much natural character." Earlier, Porter had observed to Arthur Giardelli that "the choice [between Maine and New York] is almost between liveliness, violence and disorder on one side and quietness, beauty and stultification on the other. Southampton is in a way a compromise, and like all compromises, a second choice."[35]

Schuyler had accompanied the Porters to Great Spruce Head for the summer of 1968. His writing was going well, and within a year his first major book of poems, *Freely Espousing*, dedicated to Anne and Fairfield Porter, was published by Doubleday to good reviews.[36] Still, his moods were dark. He took a violent dislike to Laurence's wife, Betsy, and complained in letters that summer of other members of the extended Porter family. His humorous sketch of Porter's sister, Nancy, is vivid:

July 17, 1968   At the cove we found Nancy Straus, whose memory is one-ups-manship personified – Fairfield made the mistake of saying it was the hottest it's ever been on the island – "Oh, I don't know" (which is Nancy's version of, I know for a fact) "– it was really *much hotter* the summer the Browns came and brought summer flu. There were *four cots* out on the porch and it was so hot Father took everyone off in the Hippocampus during the day. Everyone who could go, that is." Then she chuckled a lot – perhaps at the last sentence, an instance of the Porter passion for accuracy, perhaps at the thought of four summer flu victims abandoned in their cots while the others went yachting.[37]

Schuyler's observation is no doubt accurate, but it is also slightly wicked. Porter's island relatives were never rude to Schuyler, but they were puzzled by his slothful ways and could see that he contributed little to life in the Big House. To at least one Porter relative, he was not just a perpetual houseguest but a "mooch."[38] Schuyler, sensing their reserve and probably not feeling particularly good about himself, suffered from self-consciousness and paranoia as a result.

The summer of 1968 was full of books. Reading Henry James, Porter found a further confirmation of his theory that the best sort of art consisted of closely observed reality rather than artfully phrased abstract ideas. Comparing James to his favorite Russian novelists, Porter observed to his son Laurence that "where a Russian novelist tells you only the particulars, as though each event were unique, James tells you what it means and keeps modifying this by new generalities." He likewise enjoyed the keen observations of George Eliot: "At night ... I read *Middlemarch* aloud to Jimmy and Anne. I like it as well as any English novel I have read."[39]

During the day, reading materials were of a different sort entirely: "Sometimes when I am painting on the porch Jimmy reads to me: he read two books by Frenchmen (in English) which you may know, or know of, *The Psychoanalysis of Fire*, by [Gaston] Bachelard who has strongly influenced (according to the jacket) contemporary French criticism; and *The Historian's Craft* by Marc Bloch, which is even more interesting to me ... I get ideas for my opinions on aesthetics."[40]

Porter was impressed with Marc Bloch's opinion that (in Porter's words) "we in the West think knowledge is not enough without understanding. And to me it seems that understanding, or one's desire for it, inhibits one's knowledge." Porter's theory, as expressed in "Art and Knowledge," was that there are two kinds of knowledge – scientific knowledge and artistic knowledge – and that the great threat to civilization was culture's choice of scientific over artistic knowledge. His thoughts on the subject were so much reinforced by Bloch's writing that six months later, when teaching a course on the philosophic underpinnings of late twentieth-century art, he included Bloch's work on the reading list.

The large amount of reading that Porter was doing during that summer was partly to offset his discouragement with his painting. He seems to have found no great joy in the inclusion of four of his works in the 1968 Venice Biennale exhibition entitled "The Figurative Tradition in Recent American Art," which showcased the work of Edwin Dickinson and included work by Leonard Baskin, Byron Burford, Robert Cremean, Richard Diebenkorn, Frank Gallo, Red Grooms, and Reuben Nakian, as well as Porter (Grooms's Pop work, the crowd-pleasing *City of Chicago*, was the entry which caught the public eye). No mention of the Venice Biennale exists in the Porter correspondence of the period.

Upon returning to Southampton that fall, Porter did a number of Southampton landscapes. They were included in his 1968 show to make up for the poor painting season on the island.

During the early winter, Porter traded his twilight portrait of Jane Freilicher and her daughter for two of Jane Freilicher's works. As she wrote Ashbery, "Fairfield ... couldn't make up his mind between a still-life and that unfinished portrait of you which he says is the best portrait of you extant so I gave him both the still life and the picture of you though there was something mumbled to the effect that if you should want the portrait you might have it. Still, why would you want it? It seems to be a picture only a Porter could love."[41]

Porter's idiosyncratic taste in pictures, his own and others, was by this point a running joke, Joe Brainard having observed that one of the things he most admired in Porter was his ability to come up, every so often, with a really bad painting. The remark is more significant than it seems, because it points to the fact that Porter remained experimental in his painting throughout his life and never settled into a steady production of paintings, as many others of his generation quickly did. A large number of Porter's surviving paintings, even from his best, late period are failures, and many, many more were burned by Porter during his lifetime rather than placed with any gallery. Porter destroyed so many of his works that he built a special incinerator for the purpose in his backyard.

Throughout his life Porter had seen beauty in failed efforts and imperfections and even treasured them in his own work, for he found that both pictures and poems that were deemed failures (his own among them) often had rare qualities – qualities which, despite the overall lack of success of the work, easily justified its preservation. As he matured, Porter found that his aesthetic did not insist upon overall beauty; sure of his taste and interested, as always, in particulars, he continued to indulge his eye.

Porter's show in January 1969 occasioned a deeply appreciative review of Porter's work by Hilton Kramer entitled "An Art of Conservation." The show also received a zippy and mildly derogatory profile by the critic Grace Glueck: "Neither abstract nor representational, but existing in a light struck zone between, these beautiful, well-mannered, WASP-y records of domestic felicity make up the umpteenth one-man show of – who else but the card-carrying realist beloved by the avant garde, Fairfield Porter!"[42] Glueck made pointed reference to Porter's affluence and class yet never addressed them directly as topics, preferring instead to insinuate that Porter's work was comfortably out of touch because of his wealth and Southampton address. (Porter disliked having the term WASP applied to him; as an atheist, not a Protestant, he felt the acronym was inaccurate.) Curiously enough, Hilton Kramer praised Porter's work for the same reason that Glueck dismissed it. About Porter's seeming lack of engagement, Kramer wrote, "We seek in [his paintings] a renewal of spirit that stands aloof from the very concept of dynamism."

Porter, who was happy with the show and grateful to Alex Katz for giving him a small party afterwards, had other concerns besides reviews: during the fall he had accepted a teaching position at Queens College in Flushing, and he was hurrying to put together a course syllabus in time for the first day of class. The course was entitled "Art Since 1945." Porter hoped not just to survey contemporary art but to conduct an intellectual examination of the philosophical discourse which surrounded and informed it. The reading list for the course was certainly a challenge to even the most advanced undergraduates, including works by Clive Bell, Bernard Berenson, John Ashbery, Harold Rosenberg, Meyer Schapiro, Isaiah Berlin, Marc Bloch, James B. Conant, Sigmund Freud, Roger Fry, Lloyd Goodrich, Robert Graves, G. H. Hanley, Suzanne K. Langer, Marshall McLuhan, Idries Shah, Thomas B. Hess, Alfred North Whitehead, and Ludwig Wittgenstein.[43] As Porter wrote Lucien Day, "I am desperately unprepared. I do not intend to list artists and discuss them individually, but instead be general: talk about what started the artistic explosion in New York, and afterwards elsewhere, and what it means, and what art is now, and has been, and why people are interested, etc. I feel like Scheherazade, that I must never end at the end of an hour, for fear that I might not be able to go on next week, and would therefore be executed. It seems to me that if I have any idea, I could say it all in four hours, and that's all."[44]

Porter's students quickly felt overwhelmed by the material and expressed that opinion in no uncertain terms. As Porter wrote a friend: "I read to them from David Pye [*The Nature of Art and Workmanship*] – started Bachelard, *The Psychoanalysis of Fire*, but then they objected. They told me to be more personal, that what they liked best was my anecdotes of the Abstract Expressionists I had known."[45]

In the end, Porter's class at Queens College served to introduce Porter to the intellectual limitations of most survey-course undergraduates, as well as to clarify in his own mind just what one did when one taught, for, as he told Giardelli, "What I read beforehand was some Whitehead and a little of Wittgenstein, as well as a lot about Wittgenstein, with whose teaching methods, I found, I identified, and with Whitehead's. I suppose I really felt I was teaching a branch of philosophy."[46]

Porter's other activities during the spring were minor. In early April he lectured at the University of Nebraska, where some of the U.S. entries for the 1968 Venice Biennale were on display in the university gallery. He got little painting done on account of the three-hour commute to Queens College. Still, teaching had its pleasures. By the end of the semester, Porter found himself a hit with his students. "I asked all 28 of them out to our house for a picnic," Porter wrote. "18 came ... when I introduced them all without a hitch to Anne and Lizzie, they applauded."[47]

Porter finished the semester looking forward to the teaching challenges which awaited him in the fall, for he had accepted a one-year visiting lectureship at Amherst College, in western Massachusetts, where he would teach studio art to liberal arts undergraduates. Porter and his wife had driven up to the college in February to meet with faculty but had been caught in a blizzard on the way and spent two days stranded outside Bridgeport, Connecticut, in a motel room, eating food from vending machines and reading the recently published collaborative novel by Schuyler and Ashbery, *A Nest of Ninnies*, which had taken the two poets over a decade to complete. Eventually, the Porters had reached Amherst and liked what they saw: a small liberal arts college, graced with late Federal architecture, set on a hill over the lush meadows, fields and apple orchards of the Connecticut River Valley.

Two mishaps colored the spring of 1969: the elm tree in Porter's backyard succumbed to Dutch elm disease and a painting of Porter's, a portrait of his daughter Katie, was stolen from an exhibition at Southampton College. But Colby College in Maine granted honorary degrees to both Fairfield and Eliot Porter; and Arthur and Judy Giardelli, who had traveled to Montreal to visit their daughter, were able to make a side trip to New York and Southampton to visit the Fairfield Porters at home.

Giardelli described the visit in an autobiographical essay that was published in a book about artists in Wales. Porter, he wrote,

took me to the private and public art galleries, and to see his friends Al Held, Alex Katz, and de Kooning. De Kooning, who had reached New York as a common sailor from Holland, had been having built for the last ten years a round studio like an airport in the middle of a wood. Paintings were on easels in various parts. He had an assistant who took excess paint off some canvases with paper towels which were laid on the ground and some of which were also regarded as works of art. De Kooning showed me a pile of drawings of women. These he leafed through quickly, saying that he did them with his eyes shut, or while he watched the television. Being nearly seventy, he was full of charm, zest and youth, but of all I saw, Titians, Rembrandts, El Grecos, Velázquezes, what most amazed me was the deep glass canyon of Park Avenue, where the clouds scurry across the sun in the reflecting walls.[48]

In the quiet of the Porter home (Schuyler was away; he and Giardelli never met), Porter and his old friend were able to renew their acquaintance in a way they had not been able to do in Wales. Giardelli thanked Porter afterward for the visit. "You gave us a wonderful welcome: it was like coming to our American home. And you took us to your friends who also treated us as friends ... then came the fabulous (don't criticise me for choosing the extreme word for after all what other word would be anything like appropriate) so fabulous stay in New York."[49]

18

"Brilliant, Crazy, Heart-Breaking, and Very Mysterious"

When the Porters departed for Great Spruce Head in the summer of 1969, they handed over the care of their house to the poet Ron Padgett and his wife, Patty, who, with their son, Wayne, were to house-sit for the Porters over the coming year. Schuyler planned to accompany the Porters not only to Maine but to Amherst as well, with visits planned to Brainard and Elmslie in Vermont and the Padgetts (at the Porters' home) in Southampton. Though Porter had repeatedly requested that Schuyler move out, Schuyler had not done so in 1969, apparently hoping that by spending only part of the year with the Porters and the other part visiting Elmslie and Brainard he was effecting an acceptable compromise. Schuyler's unhappiness is palpable in his 1969 letters, which give a valuable (if tangential and elliptical) appreciation of life with the Porters on Great Spruce Head while at the same time providing a prelude to the catastrophic breakdown which would monopolize the attention of Porter and his family over the next two years. On July 30, he notes in his journal,

Fog continues. Humidity in my hair, my knee, my ears, my sinuses, my clothes. More gracious rain for which we return ungracious thanks. Bruno taken to the garden while we pick peas, gets tied up and sits and barks reproachfully. Lizzie is in the kitchen wrangling with her mother about nothing at all. I'm as cross as two sticks – also about nothing at all. ... Only Fairfield goes irresistibly on absorbed in his painting: "I think I learned a lot from that de Hooch–Balthus picture." Of the living room, a real marvel of quiet beauties.

Not a day worth memorializing.

By the first week of August, Schuyler had asked Ashbery, who soon arrived on a visit, to bring hard liquor, for which he promised to pay in cash. The Porters, habitually temperate and worried by Schuyler's drinking, kept little alcohol in the house.

Porter painted steadily through the summer, pausing only during the first two weeks of August to teach at Skowhegan (fig. 53). His paintings were exceptionally strong. *Island Farmhouse* (1969, fig. 54) is an image of graphic simplicity in which a spotted white dog lies in the afternoon shade of the Greek-revival farmhouse designed by James Porter and transported to the island by barge in 1926. Beyond lies the boathouse, the harbor, and the southernmost of the Barred Islands. Porter's appreciation for architectural detail is obvious in his rendering of the pilastered corner of the farmhouse. But the image is most extraordinary for its use of yellow to express the shadows on the farmhouse wall. The marine brilliance of the light gives the entire painting a highly keyed, almost tropical sense of color and light.

Interior with a Dress Pattern (1969, see fig. 5), is among the most successful of Porter's Big House interiors, a daytime view of the main room of the house. Light filters in through the front porch and through various rooms at the kitchen end, giving the painting a sense of receding light and spaces reminiscent of Dutch interior paintings. The palette, however, is anything but Dutch, thanks to the color choices made by James Porter many decades earlier. The Ming yellow beaverboard walls give the light of the room a golden tint. The Chinese red of the floor and of the Chinese lanterns suspended in midair complete the design scheme of a room which Ruth Porter once likened to "a medium's parlor."[1] In the foreground, on the table that usually held books and magazines, a

54
Island Farmhouse, 1969.
Private Collection.

dress pattern has been spread out beside a dictionary. Chairs, including a high chair, stand about in a haphazard way. A fire burns in the fireplace, and a little girl stands before it; another girl peeks through the kitchen doorway. One of James Porter's Parthenon casts creates a picture-within-a-picture just above the mantle. This painting is the one that Schuyler described in his journal as "a real marvel of quiet beauties."

At the end of summer, Porter and his family drove directly from Maine to Amherst, taking up residence in a large clapboard house set in a pine wood well off campus, halfway between the college football field and the college observatory. Elizabeth Porter was soon enrolled at Amherst Regional High School. Though outsiders to the life of the college, the Porters quickly felt at home in its academic environment and were glad to be spending an autumn in Massachusetts. Anne Porter had grown up in the Massachusetts countryside, and Porter had a passion for New England architecture as well as for brilliant fall foliage. In his free time, he made local excursions with his wife and daughter to the surrounding villages, once driving to the little town of North Hadley, less than ten miles away from Amherst, where an ancestor, Moses Porter, had owned a general store.

The foliage and the hilly landscape were visually stimulating. Porter offhandedly remarked to a friend that "Amherst is very pretty, with mountain-shaped hills, somewhat like Cézanne's Mt. St. Victoire."[2] He set up his easel and went to work, observing to another friend that "it's nice to be in a place where it isn't eccentric to paint." He also enjoyed being part of the academic community. His studio was at the center of campus, a long walk from home, so he made a habit of lunching in the faculty cafeteria.

Porter had never resided in a college community as a faculty member, and he found the faculty more varied in their interests than his artist friends and more acute in their perception of issues that had yet to achieve recognition among the general public. Writing his son Laurence, now a professor of French in East Lansing, Michigan, and Laurence's wife, Betsy, he noted:

November 23, 1969   I meant to write to you earlier, about life here. I like it very much. It is ever so much friendlier than Southampton. ... What I like is the ghetto of academic life, something quite new to me, after the isolation of Southampton. I also like the beauty of the landscape, the pretty New England town surrounded by jagged hills.

... I have also found here, which I would have a hard time doing in Southampton, some people who share my concern about the proliferation of nuclear energy plants that threatens especially New England, with the accompaniment of a perpetual leak of radioactivity into the air and water. They include physicists from U Mass and Smith, biologists from Amherst and Hampshire, and only one other layman besides myself. It came up at lunch once, when there were at the table a psychologist and a couple of chemists and a political scientist. They were partly sympathetic and partly seemed to want to treat me as a figure of fun: "everyone has to die someday" and somewhat of an attitude of "who the hell are you?" But the dean of Hampshire College of Sciences told me, that's all right, every progressive step was initiated by laymen.3

Porter enjoyed teaching, too, writing to Giardelli, "The students I enjoy most are the most advanced ones … I can treat them like colleagues: I try to understand what they are doing and what they want to do, and then I can say things that they find interesting as it comes from my position of being about three times their age. … I do paint myself, but at the end of the day I am ready for supper and bed; I am exhausted."4

Though Porter may have complained of exhaustion, he painted quite well when not teaching, completing eighteen paintings in a single academic year. Perhaps because the winter was so bitterly cold, many of the paintings Porter created were views from the windows of Fayerweather Hall, which housed the Art Department and Porter's painting studio. Despite the beauty of the campus and its buildings (the campus had been designed by Frederick Law Olmsted, and Fayerweather was designed by McKim, Mead, and White), Porter never succumbed to the picturesque; his views are as likely to include parking lots and ugly modern buildings as they are to include towering maples and Federal gems (fig. 55).

Porter's paintings of fall foliage are brilliant and distinctive, but his most exciting images of the college campus feature snow and the light created by snow. Southampton, owing to its coastal climate, rarely has heavy or lasting snowfalls. Amherst's chilly winter thus gave Porter new color opportunities in his paintings. He noted in a letter to Giardelli that he had not experienced such prolonged snow, ice, and frigid cold since childhood.5

Along with his teaching duties and his painting, Porter contributed to the life of the college by giving a lecture to the faculty club about teaching art. In a letter describing the address, Porter wrote, "I was told to make it short and so I did, and it is perhaps too compressed, too elliptical. I want to expand it. I had the temerity to make a radical criticism of science and when I came home, feeling I had stuck my neck way out, Anne remarked that I had the expression of someone who had just proposed to Mae West, and been accepted. I needn't have worried however. The athletic coaches and one psychology professor especially were delighted. Also, the president even wrote me a note next day to say he liked it; and a professor of chemistry now wants my opinion on artistic matters."6

Confirmed in his work by the admiration of his academic peers, Porter seemed rejuvenated during his time in Amherst, Schuyler writing to Ashbery in October that Porter looked better and seemed more energetic than he had in years. Apart from revising his lecture on teaching art, Porter seems to have been preoccupied during the spring of 1970 with Wittgenstein's observation in *Philosophical Investigations* that "every sentence is in order as it is."7 Porter's delight in Wittgenstein's late insistence that the better part of communication lies out-

55
Amherst Campus No. 1, 1969.
Parrish Art Museum, Southampton, N.Y.,
Gift of the Estate of Fairfield Porter.
Photo by Jim Strong.

side logical propositions agrees in spirit with Porter's favorite (mis)quotation from Wallace Stevens, that "without imposing, without reasoning at all (one discovers) the eccentric to be the base of design."[8] These two statements accord with Porter's belief that the randomness of real life is always much more expressive than any willed or intentional arrangement.

Amherst's proximity to Vermont meant that Anne and Fairfield were closer to their son Johnny and could have him down to visit more frequently. His presence prompted Porter to reevaluate Johnny's living situation: "Saturday we drove to Rutland to see a new place where our Johnny might live, but it will cost us over $7,000 a year, twice what we have been paying. His former guardian is recently widowed and retiring. I suppose we will eventually have to get a place where it will be practical to have him at home."[9]

As the Porters contemplated the future of their household, Schuyler came and went from Amherst, borrowing money from Porter to finance his travels.[10] He spent a good deal of time with the Padgetts in the Porters' Southampton home, for he was close to the Padgetts and more comfortable in Southampton than Amherst, which reminded him, in its claustrophobic New England way, of *The Scarlet Letter*; he punned, "This place is not so much squaresville as Dimsdale."[11] Though he enjoyed taking Bruno for long walks through the college bird sanctuary, Schuyler also seems to have been experiencing trouble coping with the Porters. In March, faced with a visit by Katharine Porter and the Laurence Porters, Schuyler decided to flee Amherst by visiting his mother in East Aurora, New York.

During the spring of 1970, black student unrest at Amherst prompted a takeover of four buildings. Porter's sympathies were almost always with the students. He felt an enormous respect for alternative-lifestyle youth movements, in particular for communes, and had been delighted to discover a commune earlier that year at the Southampton home of his next-door neighbor, Dr. Ned Doscher (the commune was being run by Doscher's son, Peter).[12] But Porter was unimpressed by the Amherst protest and was taken aback by the rudeness and arrogance of the students. "I am for the strike's motives," he wrote Carl Morse, "but I don't go much for mass meetings, etc., which remind me of the worst aspects of radical actions in the '30's. A lot of rhetoric." Still, he tried to take the striking students seriously. "When I told my class that a strike usually meant producers stop making something or some service, and that students are not producing anything one wants, they laughed."[13]

Toward the end of the semester, Porter gave an exhibition of his work at Amherst College and held his usual exhibition at Tibor de Nagy. *Island Farmhouse* and *Interior with a Dress Pattern* were highlights of the de Nagy exhibition, which was, despite its brilliance, clouded by the announcement by de Nagy and Myers that the two would soon be parting company. Each hoped Porter would join him in a new gallery venture. Porter decided not to choose one over the other, but rather to accept an offer from Schuyler's ex-lover Donald Droll, who now headed the contemporary art department at Knoedler, a powerful and highly esteemed gallery. Porter signed with Droll in June 1970 in what seemed to be a very good arrangement, to the disappointment of both de Nagy and Myers (who nonetheless did remain friends with him).

Before packing up the house in Amherst and traveling to Maine for the summer, Porter journeyed to Maryland, where he gave the commencement address at the Maryland Institute of Art and received an honorary degree from that institution. His address was on the subject of portraiture; the speech was later adapted as an article. Leaving Amherst was difficult for the entire family, for Porter felt more at home in the academic environment of the college than he ever had in Southampton, and Elizabeth Porter had made a good friend at Amherst Regional High School.

Schuyler joined the Porters for the summer of 1970 on Great Spruce Head Island, where the Porter family was visited by the Katzes and the Kochs. Porter also saw his businessman brother Edward and Edward's wife, Audrey, that summer; Edward, now retired and living in North Carolina, came to the island to visit Michel and Nancy Straus. Porter was painting the foursome in a large composition, *July* (1970), featuring the two couples seated on Adirondack chairs in the bright summer sun, when Michel Straus made a visit to the mainland and died there of a heart attack. Porter's curious lack of a response to his death – his only mention of it in his correspondence is in a cool and parenthetical aside to his son Laurence – was typical of the Porter family, which habitually met death with silence.

During the summer Porter also began work on a painting of a game of tennis on the island's concrete tennis court, which, though built shortly before America's entry into the First World War and somewhat the worse for wear after fifty-five harsh Maine winters, was still serviceable enough for a game. Porter, who was never good at sketching the human figure in motion, struggled all summer with studies for the composition, which was finally realized two years later in *The Tennis Game* (1972).

James Schuyler described the island life of 1970 in his correspondence and journals. In the previous year his first book of poems, *Freely Espousing*, had been published, and his poetry was receiving favorable critical attention; but even a success which had been decades in coming (Schuyler was forty-six) did little to change his mood or alter his life. He was drinking heavily and smoking marijuana and also attempting to diet and quit smoking cigarettes. In a July 15 letter to Joe Brainard he wrote: "I haven't felt very energetic this summer, period. The Katzes came and went very quickly, and in the middle of their stay guess who came sailing in on the mailboat ... big jolly noisy boring Kenneth Koch. I've already lost my temper with him once ... I thought it would be easier to get along with him, but I find watching him trying to control his temper as irritating as having him lose it."

Increasingly, Schuyler's feelings toward even his closest friends were angry and unforgiving. Anne Porter was frequently the victim of his anger. Just as, years before, Schuyler had focused his hostility not on Frank O'Hara but on O'Hara's lover, Joe LeSueur, so now he clung to Porter while expressing anger toward his wife: at one point, Schuyler even informed her that he had saved her marriage.[14] Anne, ever sensitive to the possibility that her husband was not happy enough in his home or his marriage, forgave the comment but could hardly forget it.

The ultimate responsibility for making a decision about Schuyler's departure lay with Porter. For some time now, Porter's response to Schuyler had been one of appeasement. His hesitation to make a decision about Schuyler grew out of his enjoyment of his friend's company, for when well, Schuyler was not just a good companion but an "ambassador of culture"[15] to the Porter home whose awareness of music, literature, and art contributed enormously to the household environment. Porter valued his company, and by now most of the Porter children considered him a "de facto"[16] member of the family; and Schuyler, for his part, had been solicitous of Porter's happiness over the past decade, so his claim on Porter's assistance and attention came from many sources apart from the love relationship that had brought them together years earlier, a relationship which had faded during the intervening years as Schuyler (who had come to dread their liaisons) found other lovers, and Porter took on the more distant role of caretaker and provider.

Porter was becoming concerned, however, for his daughter Elizabeth, who was not looking forward to returning to Southampton and its high school after an exhilarating year in Amherst and who was susceptible to depression. Schuyler's emotional vicissitudes had come to dictate the mood of the house, and his darkness and anger, his inability to take care of himself or contribute to the life of the family, had become more than an occasional strain. Still, it was a strain that Porter was willing to endure and willing to inflict upon the rest of his family if it meant (as Porter felt it did) the difference between sanity and madness, between freedom and institutionalization, and ultimately between life and death.

Writing Giardelli from Southampton that fall, Porter observed, "I like being back in my own house, which is chilly, inefficient and charming."[17] The Padgetts had left the Porter home in excellent condition, with both house and garden looking better than they had in years; Ron Padgett, excited about country living, had even kept a vegetable garden. Whatever reservations the Porters may have had about the village of Southampton were dispelled by the house itself, with its familiar and welcoming art and clutter.

Ron Padgett's observations about the house contribute valuable information about Fairfield Porter's much-painted domestic environment.

The house was powerful and evocative. Already familiar to me through his paintings of it (and through several brief visits), it was imbued with his presence. Aside from being very beautiful in a big, rambling, old-fashioned, offhand way, it was also particular to Fairfield.

The coal stoves, for instance. The one in the kitchen was a large cast-iron model from Sweden or Norway. To protect it from rusting in the damp Southampton air, it had to be kept going day and night, which meant ordering coal, shovelling it from the bin into the scuttle, feeding the fire twice a day, and shaking down and taking out the ashes. I got to enjoy the routine. The main point, though, is that with that stove you knew exactly where your heat was coming from.

There was also Fairfield's bed, a four-poster with a horsehair mattress so hard that for the first several months I got up every morning sore and stiff. After a while, though, I grew to like its hardness, the soreness went away, and I slept soundly. That mattress had substance and character, and you always knew it was there.

The clocks around the house were mechanical – they had to be wound by hand with keys. You could hear them ticking and chiming, particularly the grandfather clock in the hallway, outside the bedroom door. If you didn't wind them you wouldn't know what time it was, because there were no radios or televisions in the house. (There *was* a good stereo with classical records.) There was no way to be distracted by the electronic media. You got the weather report by going outside and guessing. Although the *New York Times* could be bought only a block away, the real news was the news of daily life at 49 South Main Street. If you felt a craving for something less domestic and more spectacular, the ocean was just down the street. I went to the beach almost every day, the way Fairfield did to walk his dog.

I wrote poems and letters at his desk and I read the books in his library. These included some of his mother's books, such as *Remembrance of Things Past*, whose volumes she had bought one by one as they appeared in the first American editions. I ate at his table. I bathed in his tub. When I looked out the bedroom window, or the studio hayloft door, I saw the same view that he did.

His house, his bed, his coal stoves, his desk, the natural calm induced by the absence of radio and television – all tended to make him closer to the things around him. He was not removed from where he was. He was right there in the moment, attentive, open to whatever it was.[18]

A month after returning to Southampton, Porter received a letter from his brother John concerning Great Spruce Head. As the island family contemplated the incorporation of the island, John Porter came up with the idea of declaring the majority of the island forever wild, thus exempting most of it from taxation but also limiting all future building to the small area of land near the harbor that held the current Porter and Straus homes. The plan was accepted by those Porter family members still participating in island life, and the papers of incorporation were drafted a year later, in November 1971 (the incorporation itself took place in 1974).

Responding to John Porter's letter about the future of the island, Porter wrote:

November 13, 1970 Sometimes I think (now is such a time) that modern art is so silly that I would rather do something else; then I imagine that in this way I could be part of the example of what is the right way to do things in the world today when so much is the wrong way. I think environmental questions are tied up with the survival of the human race, nothing less, and therefore very much more important than any political issues. ... What has this got to do with a letter about the island? Just this: that if this ambition of mine were to supplant painting, then the island would be the obvious place for me to express it, and I would want to live there permanently and all the time. (If I bought a farm, I would then of course stay there.) When I think art is not silly – and this is not a question at all of "modern" art versus another kind of art, but of the whole activity – it is because I imagine that being an artist also sets an example in opposition to all of the evils and destructiveness of scientific technology, which ... I think is at the bottom of all the troubles of the world today.

There is no point in going into this at greater length. It is, though, the basis of what I teach, even though only implicit in my criticisms of students' work. I think we have to begin the world all over again, in opposition to technology and progress. We have to live in such a way that our lives do not separate us from the material world, as technology does. It seems to me that almost everything that is taken unconsciously for granted as important or valuable today is just idea and generality; there is nothing concrete there, no facts. When painting counts for me, there is at least the fact of the paint itself, and when I don't like it, it is because it is all idea, and this usually some sort of deferential bowing to technology.[19]

Throughout the 1970s, Porter was increasingly preoccupied with environmental issues. Along with the works of Lewis Mumford, he read Sir George Stapledon's *The Land, Now and Tomorrow* and similar books about land use and environmental awareness. His interest in organic farming had been piqued by the artist Neil Welliver, who ran a successful organic farm in Maine, heated his house with wood, and generated his own electricity with a windmill. As Porter, too, considered moving to a farm in Maine or possibly building a year-round house on Great Spruce Head, the possibility of adopting a new, more ecologically responsible way of life excited him. In fact, the idea of Great Spruce Head as a model world in microcosm was just as appealing to him now as it had been to his father in 1912.

During November 1970, Porter executed a collaborative artwork with a poet. The poet was Ted Berrigan, a young follower – like Ron Padgett and Joe Brainard – of the New York School poets (as O'Hara, Ashbery, Schuyler, and Koch had come to be known). Berrigan had moved briefly to Southampton and specifically asked Porter to work with him. Porter, who liked Berrigan's poetry, came up with a black-and-white line drawing of people and cars on Southampton's Main Street. The drawing was etched into a zinc plate along with the poem "Scorpion, Eagle and Dove (A Love Poem)," and 150 copies were created, 45 of them signed by the artist and the poet.

That fall Porter planned another venture into the world of letters: a December exhibition of literary portraits in the upstairs gallery of the Gotham Book Mart. The Gotham, a famed literary meeting place, welcomed the exhibition, which included portraits of Ashbery, Schuyler, Koch, O'Hara, and Ron Padgett. The exhibition received significant press attention despite the unevenness of the work, but even so, not a single sale was made.

Porter, by now impatient to have a date fixed for his first exhibition at Knoedler, focused his energy on a series of lithographs created at the Bank Street Atelier. He completed five lithographs during the course of the winter. Meanwhile, Porter's spring show was postponed; Knoedler had a new director, Xavier Fourcade, and the changeover in administration had caused some delays. As a result, Porter had no show in the spring of 1971; his next exhibition, according to Fourcade, would take place in March 1972, a situation that made him even more restless and impatient. A quickly organized exhibition of Porter's works would be presented while he was away on Great Spruce Head during the summer of 1971 by the Parrish Art Museum in Southampton, but the exhibition was no substitute for the yearly shows, which Porter depended upon for income.

During the spring of 1971, Ron and Patty Padgett and their son, Wayne, agreed once again to spend the summer in the Southampton house while the Porters were in Maine. The arrangement suited the Porters, since they had finally determined, after three years of asking Schuyler to leave, that they needed to part ways with him whether he left their home or not. They hoped that by granting him the use of the Southampton house for the summer he would be able to make a slow transition to a new life in the outside world. The Porters felt that they had done all they could on Schuyler's behalf and that their continuing indulgence of his needs and phobias was causing him to regress into a childlike state of angry dependence. Schuyler's rage when told of the Porters' plan to go to Maine without him was considerable.

The Porters were not unconcerned with Schuyler's condition or his anger; in fact, they were deeply worried that, with no one to take him in, Schuyler might attempt suicide (as he had threatened and later, he wrote, did attempt).[20] But they recognized that their situation with him had become unlivable for them. Moreover, they recognized that Schuyler's own needs were changing, for he had recently found a lover, a married man who worked in New York.

But these were private affairs, and Porter did not discuss them freely. Writing to an Amherst student, Garry Brown, in late May, Porter merely observed, "On the 25th of June, we go to Maine … Lizzie [will be] in Montana at a 'work camp' run by the Ethical Culture Society, or a derivative of it. Katie will live and work at The Catholic Worker on the lower East Side. So Anne and I will be alone mostly, which I look forward to. I won't have to have anything on my mind except painting."[21] (After running away from home in the late 1950s, Jerry came home only for brief visits. He led a wandering life, keeping no fixed address.) No mention is made in any correspondence, by either Porter or Schuyler, of the fact that Porter had suggested to Schuyler that he not come to Maine for the summer of 1971.

On June 21, two days before Porter and his wife left for Maine, Schuyler wrote John Ashbery, "Anne and Fairfield are in the midst of something they call 'packing to go to Maine.' I am sitting it out *right here*. Anne and Fairfield leave the day after tomorrow; in the afternoon, Kenneth is dumping his well-beloved ... Koko off for a visit ... Then on Thursday arrive the Padgetts ... [Ron] loves being head of a household, especially if it is this house. Good. I rather expect I will be on some sort of ghastly vehicle bound for NYC ... Fri. for sure (unless Bob —— 22 is busy: I am not going to think about that possibility)."23

The next day, Schuyler asked Donald Droll to return a project that Schuyler had been working on at Porter's request, a chronology of Porter's career. Droll did so, noting, "I am sorry you are not going to finish it, but I certainly understand the problems involved."24 About a week later, the Porters, who were just settling into their island routine, received the first letter notifying them that something had gone drastically wrong in Southampton.

According to Ron Padgett, Schuyler was agitated and preoccupied when he and his family arrived at the house; the Porters' leaving him behind had made him quite angry. As the Padgetts settled in, Schuyler departed for New York to visit his friend Bob, and when he returned shortly thereafter, his behavior became increasingly erratic. He began wandering around the house naked and talking to himself. According to Padgett, "The sixties had just ended, and lots of people were doing strange things, so we didn't think it too odd to see Jimmy walking around naked. I thought maybe Jimmy might have been undergoing a religious conversion. Patty thought not. She thought Jimmy was going crazy, and she was very upset about it."25

On the morning of July 2, Schuyler threatened to kill Wayne Padgett, and the Padgetts, not knowing what else to do, got into their car and left. After consulting with Kenneth Koch, they decided to go to Dr. Mary Johnson, the Porters' next-door neighbor and a friend of the Porter family's since 1949. Padgett felt he was betraying Schuyler by doing so but was worried that Schuyler might hurt himself or burn down the Porter house. Dr. Johnson told the Padgetts that they had done all they could and that it was time to go to the village police.

Ron Padgett, along with the village police, went over to the house. Upon seeing the police, Schuyler immediately began acting "normal." At this point, Padgett thought the police were going to think he had made a false report. But they didn't; they took Schuyler to the Southampton Hospital and sat him down with Padgett in an examining room. Padgett was terrified that Schuyler was going to attack him, and also felt deeply ashamed at having "betrayed" his friend; but a few minutes later, two physicians arrived and diagnosed Schuyler as schizophrenic. With their signatures, Schuyler was committed to the state mental hospital and taken away alone in an ambulance.

Porter, who received news of what had happened by letter, described the situation to his son Laurence:

July 8, 1971   Soon after Lizzie and Katie left for Montana and the Catholic Worker, Jimmy came back from the city where he had visited a new friend, and behaved very strangely, and menaced Ron: he thought he was Jesus, and that Frank O'Hara was still alive. Ron and Kenneth [Koch] finally got Dr. Mary Johnson to come over (and no other doctor would) – it was Friday, July 2 – and she told the police to take him in an ambulance to the hospital, from where he was transferred to Islip State Hospital, that is supposed to be a very good mental hospital, fortunately. Dr. Arnold Cooper ... [who] is a friend of Jimmy's, said over the telephone to me that he thought he would not have to stay very long, that is, not more than two weeks; but Kenneth seemed to think it would take longer to straighten him out. Then we hope that Kenward Elmslie, at whose house in New York Jimmy spent much of last winter, would take him to his house in Vermont.

When you wrote [in your article] of Apollinaire's shattering blow to his self-esteem in 1912, I could not help comparing it to Jimmy's breakdowns, of which this is his second. He has been writing very very good poetry this winter, the best he has ever done; and some were accepted by *The New Yorker* and another, his best poem ever, a long one, somewhat Whitmany, which John A. and Kenneth and I consider his best poem, and on its own account, excellent, he sent to the *Paris Review*. *The New Yorker* rejected it only because of its length. He has also been getting recognition beyond what he has ever had.[26]

To Lucien Day, Porter wrote, "Anne and I are here alone in this big house, which was restful until the news about Jimmy, which required trips to Deer Isle to telephone and make no decisions, for what decisions can one make?"[27] And to the shaken Ron Padgett, Porter voiced the opinion that Schuyler's trouble was "related in a funny way to his recent success, both worldly, and succès d'estime."[28]

After being transferred to the Suffolk Psychiatric Hospital in Brookhaven, Schuyler spent nine and a half days under sedation. Visiting him there, Padgett, still distressed, observed to Porter, "I would say [Schuyler] is making one of the all-time speedy miracle recoveries. ... It might seem strange to add that despite the rather unsettling events, we are having a good time here."[29]

Schuyler wrote the Porters on July 13, thanking them for sending him money and telling them, as best he could, that he was all right. He wrote again the next day, this time about the chronology of Porter's life, which he had promised to send up to Maine, and about the many visitors he had received at the hospital. In a letter written the following day he suggested to the Porters that his breakdown had been precipitated by the Porters' forcing him to share the house with the Padgetts. He then asked them for more money.

Several angry and offensive letters from Schuyler to Fairfield and Anne Porter from this time have not survived, Anne Porter having felt, after some consideration, that Schuyler was not in his right mind when he wrote them and that he would not have wanted them preserved.[30] A later apology for these letters, addressed to Anne and Fairfield, does survive: "I am not going to bed without apologizing for having written to you in anger. I am sorry. I am coming off Thorazine & can blow my top very easily. I think it is better if we do not correspond. F. & I *have* had a misunderstanding: anything that upsets me, *might* hurt Bob ——. That, I will not allow. You know I love you both – Jimmy."[31]

Schuyler left Southampton shortly afterward with Kenneth Koch to visit Brainard and Elmslie in Vermont. At first all seemed well, with Padgett reporting to Porter, "Jimmy sounds fine and I think he's in good hands at Kenward's. I think that, in the face of my first experience with a psychotic episode, I tended to exaggerate, and in retrospect I'm embarrassed by the dramatic light I saw everything in; though embarrassed only a little."[32] Schuyler, meanwhile, wrote Porter a postcard on August 3 taking back the suggestion that they not correspond; the card was sent five days afterward, on the eighth. Just a few days later, Schuyler's condition deteriorated again – in part, Schuyler later thought, because he had smoked marijuana with his friends.[33]

According to John Ashbery, who was visiting Brainard and Elmslie, Schuyler's breakdown began with Schuyler locking himself in the bathroom in the middle of the night and washing his money until early the next morning. "Jimmy's behavior could not have been intentional," Ashbery recalled. "He really was making no sense at all and there was no bringing him out of it."[34] Elmslie, worried for Schuyler, eventually called a doctor and the state troopers. But Schuyler, unwilling to be institutionalized, "pulled a Blanche DuBois," according to Ashbery, refusing to go peacefully to the psychiatric hospital in Waterbury. Ashbery finally accompanied Schuyler there in the back of a patrol car.

Schuyler wrote of the experience to Porter on August 7 from Vermont General Hospital in Waterbury, again asking for money and again making unkind remarks about both Anne and Fairfield.[35] Schuyler also sent notes to Ron Padgett and the Porters requesting small amounts of cash to buy cigarettes. Porter responded directly to a disparaging comment from Schuyler about Porter's habit of reading the small magazine *Fate* (an investigative publication on the paranormal which Porter had learned about through his son Jerry) with a postcard stating simply: "The reason I read *Fate*, is not in a search for magic, which can be boring, but because it pulls away a little from authoritarian science, the sort that tells you to limit your perception. Ghost stories and most 'miracles' bore me; there is something beyond this kind of entertainment."

In this sort of response, Porter seems to have been dealing with Schuyler in the way he had learned to communicate with Johnny, namely, by responding sincerely and carefully to specific observations rather than getting involved in larger statements or emotional responses.

Porter also wrote, in a separate letter, "We were very sorry to hear that you had had another breakdown. I hope very much that you will take extensive therapy. Perhaps it would be good if you could be in a good hospital in New York City where you could be visited by friends. All your friends are very much concerned and will do all that they can to help.

... Today Anne is taking Johnny to the bus in Portland, after a week's visit. He spent much time playing a tape recorder at Landing Beach, while shouting to imitate Beatles fans, as he explained, and camping out there often at night, and swimming, sometimes naked."[37]

Porter's mention of Johnny and the tape recorder was probably meant to bolster Schuyler's self-esteem, for Schuyler had not only bought Johnny Porter the tape recorder but taught him to use it and had encouraged him for years in his love of music. According to Anne Porter, Jimmy "taught him beautifully and with a lot of sympathy. He also solved Liz's block against learning to tell time by giving her a watch!"[38]

Schuyler responded to Porter's letter with a request that they "wait to discuss my head (& yours) with Bruno on the beach."[39] He also asked that Porter put the 1955 *Portrait of James Schuyler* on reserve until he and his new lover could buy it (see fig. 30).

The letter was soon followed by another from Schuyler, asking for a loan of five thousand dollars so that Schuyler could buy into his lover's company, which would otherwise go bankrupt. The letter concluded, "Thanks, Anne, for Arthur B[ullowa, the Porters' lawyer]'s address – I do indeed need a good lawyer (does one not have the right to freak out *at home* – 49 South [Main Street, the Porter address]? Yes, one does. Forget it.)." He added a postscript: "The check, the sooner the better!"[40] Schuyler presumably needed a lawyer for the court appearance in Southampton concerning the disturbance he had caused at the Porter house, but used Anne Porter's recommendation of Bullowa as an opportunity to remind the Porters that their home was his home as well.

Porter, perhaps sensing that Schuyler's mind was clouded, responded understandingly in another carefully worded letter:

August 19, 1971   First to answer your joint letter to Anne and me. I do not want to lend you $5,000. The atmosphere at the hospital sounds terrific: I should think it would be (as from your letter it seems to be) great, to be, as it were, private (writing letters, etc.) with everyone around also busy on their own things, plus the TV breaking loose with all hell.

In your letter to me you say you wish you could take time out to explain step-by-step that you have no nervous breakdowns, but crises, and that you would like to save this for our walks on the beach with Bruno, along with discussion of my head, too. I am very sure that you have all kinds of insights about me, which I want to hear from you. After all, you are right now inspired as you have not been, at least overtly, for some time. And your insights are something that I have always depended upon, always.

... Now, about my lack of comment on the chronology. Why no compliments? Well it is like this: a chronology of my life written by someone not me (or perhaps even by myself) affects me exactly as a photograph of myself does: I find it painfully embarrassing: it gives me a twinge of self-hatred. ... It particularly embarrasses me that you were for a while a kind of secretary to me in getting this chronology together. I don't fancy you as my personal servant, as it were. I do not like to dominate your life. What I do enjoy, however, is, as in "Light from Canada," when I recognize the island, or in "The Crystal Lithium," when I recognize myself putting out the garbage on a snowy morning. That is pure pleasure.

As to your and Bob ——'s buying the '55 portrait of you: I do not want to sell it to anyone else ... and as to my selling it to you, I would rather give it to you. So ... I will write to Donald's secretary to tell Knoedler's that this '55 portrait of Jimmy is not for sale.

I am also happy to read in your letter that you haven't time to take out from poetry and HEAVY correspondence. Whatever else I think about you now, I am very glad that you are writing a lot – and I, and Anne too, like your letters very much.

... I painted a portrait of Arthur [Bullowa, who was visiting the Porters on Great Spruce Head], which may be all right (as a picture). It had the quality that you prefer usually in my paintings, the quality of being directly from nature. There is something similar to that in what I like in yours: I like the poems that you could say are from your direct experience, of course if it is an experience that might be one I have had too, and like much less well your "conceptual" writings that are indirect, as the chronology of F.P.'s life necessarily is.

(I do not think of your novels as "conceptual.")[41]

Schuyler wrote Porter again on August 19, with a plan to bring a young man, Garry Greene, whom Schuyler had met at the hospital, to Great Spruce Head, for Porter to employ doing maintenance work. He said, "I want, in general, to stand in relation to [Garry] as Fairfield has to me, [to be] someone on whom he can unquestioningly rely."

Porter, meanwhile, wrote letters to Schuyler's friends asking their advice. In an undated letter to Schuyler's concerned friend Robert Dash, Porter wrote,

I agree with what Anne told you, that it would be best for Jimmy to be in a hos- *undated* pital in New York ... his family seems to me a rather feeble assurance for him. ... Kenward says that he doesn't think Jimmy is well enough for anyone (unless this person devotes his life to Jimmy) to look after him. In short, he needs a wife, and none of his friends would be willing to live in this capacity for him. ... It is also necessary for his friends not to be afraid of Jimmy's getting angry at them for their suggestions. One is too inclined to be afraid of Jimmy, and consequently to appease him in a bad way. I do not think I realized how sick he was, I tended too much to take him at his own word. ... I don't know what I can promise, except to say that I will do what I can. But what precisely is that?[42]

Dash apparently took offense at something in the letter and reported his anger to Ashbery, who in turn reported it to Porter. To Ashbery, Porter wrote:

August 20, 1971 What I said to Bob Dash was that I would be glad to do what I could to persuade Jimmy. I quoted a letter from Kenward to Anne, in which Kenward remarked that the only person Jimmy could live with would be one who would devote his *life* to Jimmy. I remarked to Bob that such a person is a wife. Jimmy needs a wife, in short; and which of his friends is willing to be Jimmy's wife? When he lives with us, it puts a strain on the family, of whom Lizzie remains. This strain in turn is bad for Jimmy: either he is put down, which places him in a bad position for his own ego, or the family succumbs to his imperialism, which is, to say the least, unhealthy for them. Lizzie, back from Montana, where she spent the summer up to now, says that when a person has been living with you for a long time, you can't turn them out simply because they are sick. But I realize now that Jimmy has been sick for a long time, and my bad habit has been to appease him in order not to endure his anger. This was not necessary, I am sure; and Anne wants to communicate with his doctor to find out what is the proper way to understand him, but she does not mean to guarantee that she will look after him for the rest of her and/or his life; our house should be a way station for him, and there should be clear understandings about the limits of his stays with us. We will contribute financially what we can to maintain him. His needs cannot supersede Johnny's perpetual ones, nor such things as Katie's medical school tuition, and Lizzie's future education, nor her present best development.

Jimmy asked me to lend him (he asked both of us) $5,000, to buy into Bob ——'s business and perhaps relieve his bankruptcy. I refused. Maybe this will make Jimmy angry. At the same time, I think that such grandiose ideas have a good side, for it is the opposite of his former complete dependency. I don't think he should revert to his former complete dependence on us.[43]

Anne Porter's letter to Ashbery followed several days later:

August 24, 1971 Thank you for your letter. ... With Johnny's expenses and Katie's and Liz's college later on, we can't take care of Jimmy indefinitely, but we *will* do what we can – we'd want to.

About Jimmy living with us – we're agreed that we can't go on *too* long. My own reasons are mostly selfish and personal ones, and I realize that I can't see too clearly. That's why I'd like advice from Jimmy's doctor and his friends. But if Jimmy needs and *wants* to stay with us after the hospital while something better is being set up for him, of course none of us here want to let him down in this emergency. (Also, if his doctor wants this for him.)

I'd rather talk this over with Jimmy himself, but I can tell by his letters that it just wouldn't work right now, he's so confused and it would be upsetting.

We expect to be back in Southampton about September 3rd. We hope we'll get to see you.[44]

The Porters had given Schuyler a thousand dollars free and clear, to ease his anxiety about money, before he departed for Vermont. What Schuyler never mentioned to Porter and what he later took pains to conceal was that upon his arrival in Vermont, Kenward Elmslie also gave him several thousand dollars. (Schuyler's own account of this gift appears in a letter to Kenneth Koch written more than a year later, for Schuyler had used some of Elmslie's money to purchase an edition of the *Oxford English Dictionary* for Koch.)[45]

Schuyler had enough money to cover his expenses when he left Waterbury, but he chose all the same to return to the Porters' house in Southampton, bringing along his lover, Bob.

Toward the end of August, Schuyler wrote the poet Barbara Guest, "I'm getting out this Saturday (the 28th), when my friend Bob —— is flying up to Burlington, then we will Hertz together to Southampton, getting there most likely late Sunday ... I think Anne and Fairfield are coming back the 3rd, a settling down date. Fairfield will march into the studio and paint paint ... and Anne will do her thing, which is, I believe, denominated 'housekeeping.' "[46] At the same time, Schuyler wrote Porter, "Thanks for not lending me the $5,000. After I mailed the letter I realized I had jumped the gun, which is dumb, because you [have] to go back to 'go.' ... Bob —— is flying up to Burlington, then we'll rent a car and drive to Southampton. So I'll probably be there when you get back, unless I'm in NYC for the day."[47]

The Porters' return to Southampton in September was not one that Fairfield or Anne was looking forward to. Schuyler's married lover was not popular among Schuyler's friends.[48] Schuyler planned on having him at the Porter house nonetheless. But when Schuyler requested that Anne Porter help deceive his lover's wife, Anne told Schuyler she would not have his lover in the house on those terms. Schuyler, quite angry with Anne Porter, canceled the visit. He maintained good relations with Fairfield Porter, however, and visited Southampton regularly that fall (without his lover), as Porter wrote Joe Brainard in an undated letter later in the season: "I enjoyed being at the island all alone. I had been afraid that I would be lonely, but I wasn't at all ... in fact, I was very sad to leave, and dreaded coming back here, partly because of my uncertainty about Jimmy, who, however, is nicer, more outgoing, etc. than I can ever remember, so that I am sad when he goes in town."[49]

To Lucien Day, Porter was more specific: "Jimmy Schuyler is released from the hospital in Vermont, and is here with us, when he isn't in New York. He's not entirely well yet, but the Vermont hospital couldn't legally keep him, as a resident of New York, nor could they send him to a hospital in New York, which he probably should have done. He, however, thinks he is now well: I hope he at least somewhat follows the doctor's recommendations. ... It is a delicate situation."[50]

Another letter to Brainard suggests that Porter found a method in Schuyler's madness but does not go so far as to indicate that Schuyler intentionally engaged in emotional manipulation of either him or his family: "Jimmy seems better now than when we went away to Maine. But then I, at least, did not think – at least seriously – that he might be sick. The letters he wrote from the hospital in Vermont were brilliant, crazy, heart-breaking, and very mysterious. What was he really saying, that is, what was the feeling behind the seeming ambiguities; was he satirical, was he partly so, or not at all? He is not bossy now, and it is as if he had talked over a lot about us at the hospital, and was thinking all the time and trying to be considerate."[51]

Schuyler did not immediately move out. Sometime that fall he arranged the loan of a small apartment on Thirty-fifth Street from the artist Neil Welliver so that he and his lover could meet (Schuyler eventually moved into the apartment and stayed six years). But throughout the fall and winter of 1971, Schuyler still clung to the notion of maintaining a primary residence at the Porter home in Southampton. His sense that 49 South Main Street would always be his home is evident in a September 13 letter to Harry Mathews proposing "a photo-offset magazine" which would take the name *49 South.*[52] (Schuyler went ahead with the project and listed the address as his own in the magazine's front matter.)

Schuyler also made sure to give his friends an account of why he was being asked to leave. In October, Schuyler told Ashbery that Fairfield was "quite irritable. He's also very jealous of Bob ——, & is afraid (I think) that I might move from here to N.Y.C. Well, & so I might."[53]

For Porter, Schuyler's breakdown marked the end of a period in which much of Porter's time and energy was taken up with concern for and care of his friend, just as, during the 1930s, his life had been chiefly devoted to his unwell son. The tone of Schuyler's letters during and after the breakdown suggests his ability to manipulate the emotions of the Porters and the unpleasant way his needs had come to dominate their lives.

Though the drama of Schuyler's breakdown would seem to preclude any other sort of activity during the summer of 1971, Porter had a quiet summer on Great Spruce Head with his wife as the only other immediate family member in residence. Apart from a number of day visitors, Porter hosted his lawyer, Arthur Bullowa, whose collection of Porter paintings would one day be given to the Metropolitan Museum of Art. Porter painted Bullowa's portrait, as well as a portrait of his brother Eliot's wife, the artist Aline Kilham Porter, sitting beside the screen door of her smartly decorated kitchen. He also painted landscapes and still lifes and began working more in watercolor, a medium which beguiled him in the coming years. The results with this new medium, particularly in landscape, were fresh and delightful.

But fall brought new responsibilities and concerns. Apart from the exhausting question of what was to be done for Schuyler and the sad awareness that by asking him to leave, Porter had changed their relationship forever, Porter had another crisis. Knoedler, Porter's new gallery, was rumored to be going broke. Xavier Fourcade, the new director, and Donald Droll, the head of its contemporary art department, had both tendered their resignations. Porter had not painted very many paintings over the summer, in part because of his concern for Schuyler, but suddenly the number of paintings was unimportant, because Porter was yet again without his promised yearly show.

19

An American Gallery and "Ultimate Reality"

When Knoedler was bought by the financier Armand Hammer, and Xavier Fourcade and Donald Droll were hired back, Porter – who had not had a gallery show in nearly two years (not counting the Gotham Book Mart show, where nothing had sold) – had completed twenty-six paintings and so was tempted to return to Knoedler for a show now rescheduled for May 1972. But in February, new complications arose at the gallery, causing Porter a great deal of stress. "Fairfield is jittering around like spit on a hot stove because of goings-on at Knoedler,"[1] Schuyler wrote Ashbery (Schuyler still visited on weekends; he would remain a guest with the Porters to the end of Porter's life). By mid-February, Knoedler's had canceled the May show.

Porter, who had been visiting New York frequently to work on his lithographs at the Bank Street Atelier, was then approached by Stuart Feld, director of Hirschl and Adler Galleries, about his problems at Knoedler. Hirschl and Adler, which specialized in nineteenth-century American art, had little experience in selling contemporary art, but when Feld and his partner, Norman Hirschl, offered to put together a show for Porter by April, Porter decided to take a chance on the less fashionable gallery.

The show, which opened on April 11, 1972, was the first to merit a catalogue essay. Up to now, Porter's catalogues had featured merely an artist's statement or else just a few illustrations. The young critic and poet Peter Schjeldahl, who had followed Porter's work for some time and had visited the Porter home with James Schuyler, wrote a thoughtful essay which suggests that Porter, if not wildly successful in the galleries or avidly collected by the museums, was at least becoming understood and appreciated by a new generation of artists and critics. Schjeldahl was also the first critic to note that Porter's philosophy of painting aimed at subduing "the merely intellectual" in favor of the sensual:

Porter ... is pitying of "revolutions" that seem to him to evade the question of how one is to live and work in some real relation to one's times. Most of all, Porter deplores the "professional," worldly, careerist brotherhood of modern art, which in its extreme form he sees as an imposition of the free exercise of sensibility, a kind of aesthetic Stalinism. ... It takes intelligence to make art simply. It takes more intelligence than that to subsume the traces of one's intelligence in the art one makes – to avoid, that is, the merely intellectual. And this, it seems to me, is the special achievement of Fairfield Porter ... his paintings celebrate the survival, in art, of personal feelings and, in society, of the happy, private life.[2]

Porter might have wondered about the choice of the word "happy," but he was pleased with the essay and also with the show, which sold well and received good press coverage. As he wrote Giardelli, who had undergone several similar crises of gallery representation in London, "I like my new dealers, Hirschl & Adler, who treat me very well and don't try to tell me how to behave or what to do, and are a sound business enterprise. I hesitated to go with them at first because they have a gallery full of the stuffiest, dreariest 19th Century American Paintings. But these paintings sell well now, and they, doing a good business with them, can afford to treat me with scrupulous indulgence."[3] Porter seems to have been resigned to the misunderstandings which representation by Hirschl and Adler would bring. Having written during his career of American artists who had struggled against a specifically "American identity" and having been pigeonholed through those assignments as a critic particularly interested in "American" painting, Porter was now being associated with a gallery specializing in the representation of the "American" art that he so frequently disliked.

Porter's awareness that he was not perceived in the gallery or museum worlds as a "major" artist, was apparent to the painter Wolf Kahn, who met Porter that summer while Porter was waiting for the mailboat to Great Spruce Head in Sunset, Maine. "I asked him, 'How does it feel in the new gallery?' He had just moved to Hirschl and Adler. He said, 'Very good. I take in my paintings; they send me checks.' I asked how he was doing with museums, and he looked at me and said, 'The museums have determined that I am not a significant painter.'"[4]

The summer of 1972 was the second summer that Porter and his wife had the Big House all to themselves, and they were looking forward to a quiet time after the many worries caused by Schuyler's breakdown the year before. Porter habitually relied on the fresh air, exercise, and sunshine of Great Spruce Head to revive his flagging energy; he cherished the long, cool, quiet nights so conducive to restful sleep. But the summer proved unexpectedly busy: "It seems that instead of getting, as it were, settled in my old age, I get more and more and more to do, which I bring on myself, and I suppose I wouldn't have it otherwise, but I must learn not to let this happen."[5] Porter had just set up his studio and begun painting when visitors started arriving. "This was supposed to be a summer alone – just Anne and me – it didn't turn out that way," he wrote Edith Schloss. "The [Paul] Georges just left. They came from Skowhegan."[6]

The Porters also hosted the young poet, musician, and scholar David Shapiro, and his wife, Lindsay. David Shapiro, who had been introduced to the Porters through Kenneth Koch, quickly fell in love with both Fairfield and his wife, finding them inspiring in every way. In his eagerness to learn from them, he apparently conversed nonstop for the duration of the visit, so much so that Porter, in a double portrait of the couple, celebrated David Shapiro's talkative nature by creating an image of him in mid-sentence, his mouth open.

Of all Porter's later acquaintances, David Shapiro seems to have understood and appreciated Porter best, and his memoir of the visit, later printed in part by the magazine *Art and Antiques*, gives an insightful account of Porter's philosophical and intellectual preoccupations during that summer:

[Porter] began to say that he would start every sermon with the following words: Pay attention, pay attention to the ultimate reality. He then laughed and said that John Ashbery had quipped: what does ultimate mean, Fairfield? I then said that I felt John came closest to a sense of the religious when he paid attention to "the surface of things." Exactly, Fairfield said, it is not behind everything, it is everything!

... because of his reputation as a kind of crank of causes, I was shocked by what was truly the reasonableness of Fairfield's politics. He told me that because his life was short, he could devote it to only a few things, and the issue he had decided on was the danger of nuclear reactors. He loved Barry Commoner's work. ... Fairfield was in touch with the small group of ecologists who were spreading alarm about the eco-system.

... We laughed as Fairfield told me stories about being excluded by the rest of the inhabitants of Southampton years past because of his association with bohemian types and homosexuals. Fairfield implied in the discussion of this isolation that he could care less. What remained was a life of vigilance and friends and a few "burning" issues.

... He was a natural teacher, but he once said to me that he had almost turned down any teaching jobs. "How can I teach, teaching is a great sin." He then went on in a wonderful and dry manner to describe the advice of a friend that he could at least show how a canvas was stretched. Here was Fairfield, master of an anti-systematic system, almost pretending that he had nothing to offer except a few craftsmanly details. But what this does show is his love of liberty.

... A lot of Fairfield's life and art ... are now misunderstood, it seems to me, as patrician and mild. There is a love of sensual pleasure that James Schuyler captures in a poem about Fairfield bathing nude in the sun. There is the element of excitement and vividness that he loved in color and that connects him more to de Kooning than to ... Vuillard.[7]

The Schuyler poem to which Shapiro makes reference is "The Morning of the Poem." In its account of Porter's nude sunbathing adventure, Porter encounters a couple of trespassers on the island, and both Porter and the trespassers are nude.[8]

After the Shapiros' departure, Porter wrote them several letters, one describing the visit of his son Johnny and the other describing his ongoing thoughts about moving to Great Spruce Head: "The island is being incorporated for various reasons, and also threatened with being taken over by the National Government as an extension of Acadia National Park. ... In the midst of this, Anne and I are contemplating (if we could afford it) building a small house that would be warm in the winter, for us, with naturally a guest room or two. I think it would be in the North Meadow near the Garden. This house would become the commune for the second generation [of Porter children] and their kids, who come here only a week or two at a time."[9] Increasingly, Porter felt that the Southampton house was no longer a place in which he wished to live; his new ideal was either a small and specially constructed farmhouse on Great Spruce Head or else an old and architecturally distinguished home somewhere else in Maine.

The house at 49 South Main Street was nonetheless still treasured by Schuyler, who was spending the summer there as a house sitter while the Porters were in Maine. He maintained his own little wing of the house, in the ell, over the kitchen, looking out over the back garden. Schuyler treasured the room, with its Schumacher "California Wildflower" wallpaper and Sheraton bed (Porter had tried to send the bed to Laurence Porter as a present – for it had been Laurence's bed – but Schuyler had insisted quite vehemently on keeping it, and Porter had eventually found a substitute for his son in a New York antiques shop). Schuyler memorialized his room in one of his less successful poems, "O Sleepless Night," just as Porter memorialized his continuing friendship with Schuyler in two more paintings, *Jimmy with Lamp* (1971) and an oil sketch, *Jimmy* (1972), both of which chronicle Schuyler's weight gain while on Thorazine.

By the summer of 1972, Schuyler had been on Thorazine for nearly a year, and perhaps out of consideration for his condition, Porter limited his correspondence to a few general observations mixed with necessary details of household finance. Schuyler's responses were equally brief and characterless, with the exception of this passage from a letter sent in late July:

Jerry [Porter] called up Saturday evening – he needed money to get from Denver to New York, and said something about his savings account, but that's out of my power. ... I wired him $150 ($158, with the telegraph charges). ...

July 17, 1972

John [Johnny Porter] calls up on Friday evenings and we have nice talks about thunderstorms, and the possibility of warm spells in December so one could swim at North Sea [an area north of Southampton on Peconic Bay]. He apologized (again) to me for blowing his top at Anne last November (he called her a tyrant – it had something to do with swimming), then said, "I get to blow my top more at Southampton than at Ottervale." From which I conclude that he finds it a release on the rare occasions when he does blow up. Who doesn't?[10]

The subtext concerns Schuyler's own feelings toward Anne Porter and about having blown his own top.

Schuyler's second volume of poems, *The Crystal Lithium*, dedicated to his lover, Bob, was to be published that year, and despite the distance between Schuyler and Porter, reading through the galleys for the book must have been a joy for Porter. The poems, with their homely and pastoral themes, bear a strong aesthetic relation to Porter's paintings. Moreover, the poems, like the art Porter described in "Art and Knowledge," can be described as attempts at rediscovering through art one's essential wholeness and connection to the physical world. Their celebration of the ordinary is matched in paintings by Porter which describe, for instance, the dishes left on the breakfast table. The critic Helen Vendler has observed that "Schuyler's unemphatic gestures – light, unpossessive, relinquishing – can make others' tones seem melodramatic." Porter, too, with no melodrama, sought out only that which surrounded him in everyday life. Vendler has also observed that "Schuyler's romantic impressionism has a morality behind it – a morality of receptiveness and absence of ego."[11] This carefully achieved state, which Porter aimed for in his own painting, and referred to on more than one occasion as "transparency" (a term he had credited to his wife and which he adopted after conversations with her), is one that Porter had discussed frequently with Schuyler and appreciated in all writing – poetry and prose, fiction and nonfiction – as well as in painting.

Finally, Schuyler's poetry and Porter's painting share a metaphysical awareness. Porter's painting, with its rapt attention to ultimate reality, is not far from Schuyler's poetry, in which, as David Shapiro has observed, Schuyler's "uneasy rapports with the personal, his delicate epistles, his reportage, his catalogue raisonné of the perishable, constitute paradoxically a transcendental poetry without the divine term." Both poet and painter are in the tradition of Thoreau, whose "fancy for referring everything to the meridian of [his home] was," according to his friend Emerson, "a playful expression of his conviction of the indifference of all places, and that the best place for each is where he stands."[12]

In later life, Schuyler discussed the "conscious relationship" between his highly visual poetry and painting: "I once showed some poems of mine to my dear friend Fairfield Porter, the painter, who read them and said, 'Jimmy, you're much more visual than I am.' To me, much of poetry is concerned with looking at things and trying to transcribe them as painting is. This is not generally true of poetry. As Virgil Thomson said the other day to me, 'Poetry and song are about feelings.' Personally, I think it's about anything you damn please."[13] The relation of some of his poems to Porter's paintings is occasionally more than one of a shared aesthetic; one section of Schuyler's poem "The Cenotaph," entitled "The Edge in the Morning" (named after a geographic feature, The Edge, on Great Spruce Head), was created, according to Schuyler, after a painting by Porter of the same name.

The poems in the first two sections of *The Crystal Lithium* are atmospheric evocations of life in and around the Porter homes. "Southampton and New York" refers in part to life at 49 South Main Street; "The Island," to Great Spruce

Head. The poems are intimately connected to the life Schuyler led with the Porters up to the point of his breakdown. The poem "Closed Gentian Distances" is a valediction to that time, which Schuyler later described as "much the happiest period of my life":[14]

A nothing day full of
wild beauty and the
timer pings. Roll up
the silver off the bay
take down the clouds
sort the spruce and
send to laundry marked,
more starch. Goodbye
golden- and silver-
rod, asters, bayberry
crisp in elegance.
Little fish stream
by, a river in water.[15]

Schuyler's literary leave-taking of the Porters was hardly final; it continued through several more volumes of poetry, ending, seventeen years later, in 1989, with "A Cardinal." In saying goodbye to his life with the Porters, Schuyler achieved some of his most haunting and beautiful poems. Schuyler was at his best when saying goodbye or saluting that which was past and gone. His slow departure from the Porter home, painful as it must have been, was as much an occasion for great poems as, in time, his loss of his new lover was the occasion for his most passionate.

Porter's jacket illustration for *The Crystal Lithium* was a watercolor of storm waves breaking on the winter beach, created to suit the recurring wave imagery in the title poem (fig. 56). It may also have been a tribute to their friendship, for they had walked the beach together on a nearly daily basis when Schuyler was living in Southampton. The image comes from the bleak "long poem, somewhat Whitmany," which Porter had so much admired the previous summer, taking "pure pleasure" in recognizing himself putting out the trash on a winter morning. "The Crystal Lithium" ends,

snow, wind

Lifted; black water, slashed with white; and that which is, which is
beyond
Happiness or love or mixed with them or more than they or less,
unchanging change,
"Look," the ocean said (it was tumbled, like our sheets), "look in my
eyes"[16]

Porter painted those waves breaking on the beach in Southampton again and again until the last year of his life. But he was not the beloved of the poem.

Porter's images of breaking waves may also have been inspired by a long, narrative poem of his own, written the previous year, entitled "The Wave and the Leaf." Schuyler had published the poem during the summer of 1972 in his magazine, *49 South*.

Though nowhere near as passionate, tumultuous, or vivid as Schuyler's great poem, "The Wave and the Leaf" was a substantial emotional statement for its author, one that perhaps holds the key to his essential character. Set on Great Spruce Head, the poem, written in the first person, begins with its narrator "alone in this house my father made," sunk into an end-of-season melancholy which he understands as his father's melancholy, "the melancholy of unrealized imaginings":

> It is a melancholy
> That is inherent to the beauty of the island.
> Sorrow lies down on the rocks
> Like a thin soil.

Everything about the island – the spruces, the rocks, the house – reminds the poet of his father:

> All these resemble my father
> Who did not like to be contradicted.
> His presence is in their arbitrary presence
> As it is in the monotonously passing waves
> Which infinitely different from each other
> Are waves after all, on the surface of the bay
> Unrepeatable as dry leaves
> Though the waves and the leaves for all their diversity
> Are recognizably themselves.

56
Porter's jacket illustration for James Schuyler's *The Crystal Lithium* (New York: Random House, 1972).

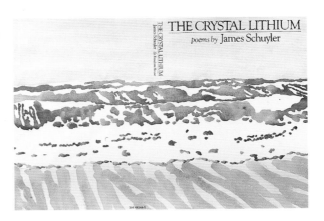

THE CRYSTAL LITHIUM
poems by James Schuyler

The poem ends with a revelatory vision, a "large bird flushed from a bay bush," whose "startled clatter filled me / With a pang of hope."[17] The narrator's quiet shift in mood when he is surprised by something unexpectedly beautiful and unknown is due to an event outside himself, in nature; the moment of epiphany comes not from an awareness of anything divine but from a chance encounter with the unexpected. The grace of this poem lies in its direct and unassuming simplicity, its respect for direct experience.

"The Crystal Lithium" and "The Wave and the Leaf" are similar in their contemplation of waves and, through them, the infinite. Porter's long walks along the beach in Southampton, both with Schuyler and alone, must have become particularly resonant as he contemplated his new, more solitary life away from both Schuyler and his grown children – and, with his wife, greeted the onset of old age (fig. 57). The wave paintings are among the most haunting of Porter's images despite their lack of drama. The art historian John Spike has

57
Porter on the Southampton beach in the early 1970s, about the time Schuyler wrote "The Crystal Lithium." Bruno lies in the distance. Photo by James Schuyler. Courtesy James Schuyler Papers, Archive for New Poetry, Mandeville Department of Special Collections, University of California, San Diego / La Jolla.

58
A Sudden Change of Wind, 1973.
Private Collection.

described them as "portraits of individual waves" (fig. 58).[18] Porter's artist friend Jane Freilicher appreciated them more insightfully: "His subject matter of sunlight on sea and ocean waves lent itself to an exalted, abstract look. I think that his last work was his best, which is very fortuitous for an artist, and alas, not always the case. He was able to undertake that kind of unpaintable subject, so difficult to do, because he had the confidence to attempt it. He was dealing with subject matter that is ineffable, and elusive, yet he managed to make it recognizable and interesting, and at the same time surprising. He seems to stir one's feelings about nature in a deeper way."[19]

The summer of 1972 was not much of a family affair on Great Spruce Head. Apart from the visit from Johnny, Fairfield and Anne Porter would not have the company of their children. From this summer onward, Elizabeth Porter's dog Bruno would be Porter's steadiest companion in the studio as well as outside (fig. 59). Jerry Porter had by now dropped out of City College and, after working as a laborer in the garment district, had begun a life of wandering, frequently staying out of contact with his parents for long periods of time; his random phone call to Schuyler from Denver was typical of his new life. Through his meditational practices in Subud, Jerry had also begun to realize that he did not like his name; in 1974, he changed it permanently to Richard (the decision recalls the very different experience of his father, who had been traumatized in childhood by his parents' changing his name). Katharine Porter, meanwhile, had progressed from Manhattanville College to medical school.

59
Porter naps with Bruno. Photo by James Schuyler. Courtesy James Schuyler Papers, Archive for New Poetry, Mandeville Department of Special Collections, University of California, San Diego / La Jolla.

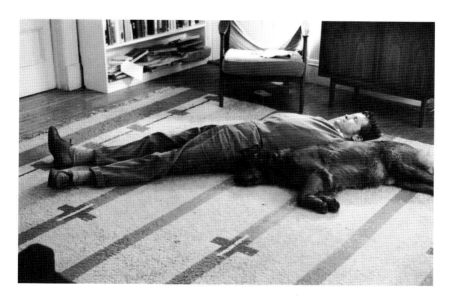

Elizabeth Porter, after three years at Southampton High School, had been accepted at Georgetown University in Washington, D.C.

When he returned to Southampton in the fall of 1972, Porter decided to paint a picture of the house at 49 South Main. The resulting canvas, *House with Three Chimneys* (1972, fig. 60), gives a private view of the house – that is, as seen from the back, not the front – with the section housing Schuyler's room and the kitchen facing the viewer. The intimacy of the view is balanced by the august proportions of the grand old house. The brilliant blue fall sky lends the image a distinctive clarity and vibrancy.

During that fall, Porter painted a local art student, John MacWhinnie, as well as his mother, Inez, the proprietor of a Southampton bric-a-brac shop. He also continued his project of intimate portraiture, painting Schuyler and, separately, a young English poet, Peter Ackroyd, who came to the Porters as a guest of Schuyler's. (Ackroyd wrote a biography of T. S. Eliot years later, apparently unaware of Eliot's relation to the Porters.) Porter also painted a small facial portrait of David Kermani, a young poet who was a friend of both Schuyler's and Ashbery's. Porter kept these small-scale portraits with their head-only or partial-head images mounted in the studio as if to create an environment filled with stimulating company as he painted there alone from day to day.

In January 1973, Porter's steady painting schedule was interrupted by two speaking engagements: one to introduce John Ashbery at a poetry reading held at the Guggenheim Museum for the Academy of American Poets ("Kenneth [Koch] said John probably asked for me," Porter wrote his son)[20] and another at the funeral service of Joseph Cornell. Porter was touched to learn after Cornell's death that Cornell had used Porter's article on him as a catalogue essay in a Los Angeles show.

During the spring of 1973, Porter also began the long search for a publisher for his essay "Technology and Artistic Perception." In it, Porter suggests that technology is totalitarian in nature and is destructive to society and the human spirit. Porter's son Laurence has suggested that Porter's opinions about the misuse of technology are similar to those of C. P. Snow in *The Question of Technology* and Martin Heidegger in his essay "The Question of Technology." They may also have been influenced by Porter's reading of Wittgenstein, who detested "the power of science in our age, which on the one hand encouraged the philosopher's 'craving for generality,' and on the other produced the atomic bomb."[21] But they are primarily an elaboration upon the critique of scientific materialism put forth by Whitehead in his *Science and the Modern World*, first published in 1925.

In his last years Porter was constantly alerting his friends and colleagues to the dangers inherent in technology. "I now think that the whole world is in a revolutionary situation where all previous radical (Marxist) tactics and strategies no longer count," he wrote the painter Rackstraw Downes. "That is because

60
House with Three Chimneys, 1972.
Alan and Laura Hruska.

of the immense power of technical progress, which threatens the world profoundly, and makes questions of governmental power different than they ever were. ... The enemy is our own skill, our own ability to run things."[22] Porter also traced the misuse of technology back to the flaws in America's fundamental philosophies, writing Joe Brainard, "It comes from living the idea of control, predestination and progress, all of which ideas dominate our activities."[23]

One of the difficulties that Porter faced in publishing "Technology and Artistic Perception" was that *Art News*, so long a supporter and publisher of his writing, had been sold. Porter wrote his son Laurence, "Tom Hess, John Ashbery and Henry LaFarge [were] all fired. Tom could have bought it (he is very, very rich) but he doesn't believe that the editor and owner should be the same person, and he likes being editor. *Newsweek* sold it to some vulgarian, who wants to make it more commercial, that is, he wants to emphasize gossip about the market. I didn't resubscribe myself, and I am glad to have one less magazine coming here."[24]

The last sentence is revealing of the fatigue which had recently begun to overwhelm Porter. During the seventies he started to repeat himself in his letters and often to seem tired and distracted, both in his writing and day-to-day life. His shorter essays, specifically one written about an idiosyncratic neighbor, the painter Albert York, have the directness and brilliance of his previous art criticism, but his long essays – particularly "Technology and Artistic Perception" – ramble. Many people who heard "Technology and Artistic Perception" read as a lecture found it nearly incomprehensible (in part, admittedly, because Porter was not good at public speaking).[25]

When not painting, reading, or writing, Porter campaigned against the proposed building of the Shoreham nuclear energy power plant on the North Shore of Long Island. To his daughter Katie, he observed, "I write to my congressmen and put ads in the Southampton, Hampton Bays and Westhampton, Riverhead and East Hampton papers, that were sent me by the national interveners – who now constitute groups in maybe half the states."[26] Just as, during the late 1930s, Porter had gone door-to-door in Winnetka to collect funds for Trotsky's legal defense, so now in 1973 he took to the streets of Southampton to campaign against nuclear energy. As he wrote Laurence in March: "A week ago, I went around Southampton trying to collect signatures on a petition in favor of a moratorium on the licensing and building of nuclear energy plants. I hadn't thought I could get any at all, and the people would only resent my busy-bodiness, but at my opening, Dorothy Wright asked me to say something about this to Odelle Corwith and her children, most of whom agreed with the idea, so back home I got signatures from Dorothy, the Corwiths, and from people who had either expressed agreement, or who seemed likely to be sympathetic."[27]

Laurence Porter, who was profoundly influenced by his father's opinions and himself became even more of an activist on behalf of energy conservation and related environmental causes, was glad to hear of his father's letter-writing campaign, but also somewhat skeptical, observing in a memoir that his father "seemed to feel that using a coal furnace and a Swedish coal stove instead of gas or electricity for heat and cooking was a contribution to conservation. He gave generously to environmental causes ... but his involvement was that of a spectator. Feeling concerned removed much of the need of doing much of anything else."[28]

In the spring of 1973, Porter decided to return to lithography, this time traveling to the Circle Gallery lithography studio, where the lithographers whom Porter had known at the Bank Street Atelier had recently relocated. Porter enjoyed the company of the craftsmen with whom he worked. Jane Freilicher remembered,

> During the last years of his life the work seemed to go humming along. I remember seeing Fairfield at the printers when he came in from Southampton in his commuting suit, carrying an attaché case. He would just put an apron on, roll up his sleeves and go to work. He knew the French artisans at the presses very well by then and they enjoyed a great rapport. He spoke to them in French and there was a certain camaraderie that must have been very nice for him. I don't think I ever saw him more at ease in a social situation than he was working around the lithograph machines ... I believe Fairfield thought that art was a kind of inspired play, and I think you get a sense of that felicitousness as he went about his business and just kept working.[29]

Along with the lithographs that Porter completed came a book jacket for Kenneth Koch's *Rose, Where Did You Get That Red?* The book, about teaching poetry to children, was one which both Anne and Fairfield Porter thought wonderful. Koch's playfulness and the glee with which the Porters entered into this spirit of play have both been memorialized in an exchange of letters in the form of poems (in Fairfield Porter's case, three sestinas and a sonnet).[30] For *Rose* and several other book jackets, Porter did his own hand-lettering. Porter had always been fascinated with lettering and signs, which appeared in his paintings as early as the 1930s and which he had enjoyed creating during his years as a draftsman for Walter Dorwin Teague.

Porter had no show during the spring of 1973; his next show at Hirschl and Adler was scheduled for March of the next season. Once again Porter invited Schuyler to stay at the house in Southampton while he and his wife traveled to Maine. During that summer, Porter painted pictures of his grandniece and grandnephew, Scott and Lisa, the grandchildren of his brother John. Scott and Lisa were the children of Porter's favorite niece Anina Porter Fuller, herself an artist.

Throughout the summer, Porter was flattered to find himself increasingly sought after by young people in search of mentorship and guidance. A former Amherst pupil named Garry Brown needed Porter's assistance when he was seeking to avoid the draft as a conscientious objector; Porter was pleased to sponsor him. In a letter to Brown that July, Porter observed, "It is perpetually amazing to me, now that I am old, to hear people say or get the evidence somehow that people respect me, for when I was even forty, I expected to be regarded with contempt; and it seems not to be so. I think this is a hangover from grammar school days. It took all this time to find out that I needn't expect so little."[31]

Adulation of another sort came from the painter and poet Joe Brainard, who, aside from writing to Porter, had taken to painting what he termed "faux Fairfields," paintings which came very close indeed to capturing Porter's style. On the phenomenon of mentorship, Porter wrote Schuyler, "I am having a rather extensive correspondence with Joe Brainard, who asks me lots of questions which I do not answer all of, not out of censorship so much as because I forget to, or I only answer the questions that interest me. It is all part of my new role as a mentor of the young, which I didn't seek, and do not seek, but has been growing anyway."[32]

During the summer of 1973, Porter's continuing interest in experiences outside those allowed by modern science led him to mysticism and spirituality. Along with *Fate* magazine, Subud, and transcendental meditation, Porter shared the general popular interest in the novels of Carlos Castaneda. The novels, which concerned traditional Mexican *curanderismo*, experiences of the paranormal, and the use of hallucinogens, prompted Porter's friend Richard Freeman to ask Porter if he had ever tried drugs. Porter responded,

July 16, 1973   I have to answer your letter, or rather I should say I feel impelled to answer it, because of your question as to whether I have engaged in "otherworldly trips." ... This is apropos of my telling you about Castaneda's books. ... The answer is no. My interest in these things is not so much that uncanny things interest me – I find most of them, in accounts I read, very dull and also trivial – as that I am much aware of how limited conventional science and logic are, how bigoted they tend to be, how often the conventional rational person seems to deny the existence of what he has no explanation for. I don't like the bullying attitude of "scientism." I think my interest comes from experience with "experts" who are the people who control the organization of our technical civilization. An example of my experience is the behaviorist idea of bringing up children, which was the fashion when Johnny Porter was a baby, and that though it did by no means cause his "backwardness," it did him a certain harm. I also remember the medical opinion about neurosis that "it's just your imagination," as though the imagination were something invalid, or even nonexistent. I have experienced being told that "if you have sciatica, you know that there is nothing you can do for it" and then being treated by an osteopath, who, as far as my feeling went, cured it.[33]

In a letter to another friend, again on the subject of Castaneda, Porter wrote, "All I know is that in my experience the usual description of the world is continually being abandoned by the experts, and also that it continually proves inadequate to my own experience. I have found that I have to be continually critical of what is told me by those who claim, with their very good reasons, to know what the actual case is."[34] In all questions relating to the spiritual or otherworldly, Porter kept a firmly open mind; his only certainty seems to have been that contemporary scientific theory was inadequate in its descriptions of the world and limiting to human perception.

Throughout the summer, Porter, whose major studio work was a portrait of his recently widowed seventy-three-year-old sister, Nancy, worked outdoors at a heroic new project of attempting to paint sun and sea head-on. To Schuyler, still on Thorazine in Southampton, Porter wrote, "I have painted several sunrises, with the sun in the picture, from the rocks below the house, except one from the porch. It works, more or less. I was trying to emulate the David Hockney painting I saw a few years ago, that amazed me."[35] Unfortunately, Porter never indicates specifically which Hockney painting he means (Porter never wrote about Hockney, probably because the artist, whom he admired, came to his attention only after he had stopped publishing art reviews in favor of longer essays).

Porter concluded the same letter with the news that "I am reading slowly Whitehead's *Concept of Nature* ... [and] acquiring a sense of what Whitehead is saying." He noted in another letter at the end of the summer, "I have read the Whitehead that I bought in June, and the book about Wittgenstein and Vienna, which is illuminating, and the last book of Castaneda, and have forgotten them, though they all relate to my perpetual ideas about esthetics." To his former Amherst pupil Armistead Leigh, then considering divinity school, Porter wrote, "I think ... that a strong religious feeling requires a strong sense of matter-of-fact. I have been reading philosophy this summer (at least this is the part of my summer's reading that has meant most to me), more Whitehead, and a book about Wittgenstein, which has the thesis that for Wittgenstein it was not logic but the ethical concern that meant most to him."[36] For Porter, too, most questions of religion and spirituality were tied to metaphysics and ethics.

So far as his career was concerned, Porter seems to have reconciled himself to the judgment of the museums. In an end-of-summer letter to Brainard, Porter observed with beautiful humility, "I think sometimes that as far as museums and patrons are concerned that I may be 'finished,' that is, that it has been decided that my work is not really any good. This partly stimulates me to be more critical, though not in the way 'they' might be. I try to work harder, to learn to be continuously interested."[37]

When the Porters returned to Southampton in the fall of 1973, they found Schuyler looking more relaxed than he had been in some time. Porter had helped finance Schuyler's therapy that summer and given him (and his friend Ruth Kligman) a place to live but otherwise had not supported him; other concerned friends (including Kligman) had rallied to help out and continued to do so until the end of Schuyler's life. Kenward Elmslie had established a trust fund for Schuyler that year which provided him approximately five thousand dollars per annum; in the decade ahead, others contributed money as well.[38]

Ron Padgett wrote Porter in November,

November 7, 1973   I haven't seen Jimmy since he moved into town, though we talked on the 'phone a couple of weeks ago. I keep telling myself I should go by and see him (as if he were in the hospital). ... Jimmy was a lot better when we saw him Labor Day weekend, in fact he looked about 90 per cent, as they say ... he dieted all summer, and, for all "practical purposes" stopped drinking. So he "looked" better, which made me *feel* better, which in turn helped Jimmy forget his anxiety about scaring us with his nuttiness. ... I've had few things deflate my spirit so much as Jimmy's episode that summer, so that his improvement now is equally inspiring.[39]

Porter's schedule during the fall of 1973 was a demanding one, because along with his work at the Circle Gallery lithography workshop, Porter had agreed to teach one night a week for three hours at the School of Visual Arts. It "makes a long day Thursdays – up at five, home at 11:30," he wrote a friend that November. One Thursday proved a particular challenge when, at Elizabeth Porter's request, Porter worked his long day while fasting for Oxfam.[40]

As a teacher, Porter was troubled by students he could not seem to reach: "My class at the School of Visual Arts is hard ... especially the Conceptualists, who are clever, and of whom I am a little afraid, and who produce chiefly ideas. I can't somehow get across to them ... that it is not ideas that I expect to see, but *things* they have made, and that is something I can say something about."[41] To these students, Porter quoted his favorite story about Mallarmé, related by Paul Valéry to Stravinsky, who had included it in his autobiography: "Degas, who, as is well known, liked to dabble in poetry, one day said to Mallarmé: 'I cannot manage the end of my sonnet, and it is not that I am wanting in ideas.' Mallarmé, softly: 'It is not with ideas that one makes sonnets, but with words.'"[42] Privately, however, Porter expressed his irritation with the teaching situation to the painter and teacher Neil Welliver, comparing it to "a French class [where a] student [insists] on being taught Spanish, or perhaps baseball."[43]

There was at least one small satisfaction in November 1973: Porter and his wife, having looked at homes in Maine on their previous two trips, had decided no place was quite so nice as the home they owned in Southampton. So rather than planning a move, they set about making renovations. Anne Porter recalled her reaction: "I've always been very conscious of how it's always the wife who has to say, 'No, you can't do that,' so I tried not to say" that we shouldn't move full-time to Great Spruce Head or to Maine. "But Fairfield was so sociable. He needed society. We could never have lived on the island year-round. He would have kept going off to New York."[44]

Fairfield Porter's first act in renovating the house was to replace the Aga stove, which had not burned properly since the summer of 1968, when Joe Brainard and Kenward Elmslie had rented the house and cracked its internal cylinder. Porter shared the news of the stove, which had been imported at great expense, with the Aga-loving Ron Padgett, writing, with great solemnity, "We are getting a new Aga Stove. It is here."[45]

Porter was delighted to learn in early January 1974 that his old friend Arthur Giardelli had been included in the Queen's list of New Year's Honors. Writing to congratulate Giardelli, Porter observed of his own life, "I like being alone with Anne; it is something I really never had, not even at the beginning of marriage."[46] But with this newfound comfort and calm, Porter also began to experience disquieting problems of concentration and memory loss. While a visiting critic at the School of the Art Institute of Chicago, Porter was unable to remember anything he had just said or any recent names. Weariness and low energy were also becoming a problem for him. His neighbor and friend the surgeon Dr. Kenneth Wright had recommended jogging to Porter years earlier as a way to revive his system, but Porter had broken his arm while jogging with Bruno and now contented himself with a long walk every morning.

In March, Porter held his second exhibition with Hirschl and Adler. The show was a financial success. As Porter wrote his son Laurence, "As of yesterday, they have sold 24 paintings in the last three weeks, and are extending the show for another week, of paintings that there weren't room for at first. Some of these are better than some they had hung ... in fact, Hirschl & Adler told Aline [Porter], who was in the city with Eliot, that it was their most successful exhibition of a living artist they had ever had." A month later he added, with a typical truthfulness, "This is not so grand as it sounds, as Hirschl & Adler gallery has a bad taste in living artists; they make their business out of a dreary but fashionable selection of nineteenth-century artists."[47] The show was the most remunerative of Porter's career, in part because Porter had nearly two years' worth of paintings to sell; he sold twenty-five.

The previous fall, Porter had created a book jacket for Schuyler's latest book of poems, *Hymn to Life*, which was published in March 1974. (Porter had also collaborated with Schuyler on a small project, a poem entitled "A Sun Cab," in 1972.) The *Hymn to Life* collection contained poems that Schuyler had begun writing while in the psychiatric hospital in Waterbury, Vermont, as well as a series of love poems to Bob ——, many of them describing Schuyler's life away from Bob —— in Southampton. The title poem features images taken from the garden view from Schuyler's bedroom window. To celebrate the title poem, Porter created an image for the book jacket of the old pear tree in blossom set against a hedge of blooming forsythia.

During the rest of the spring, Porter divided his time between painting and campaigning against nuclear power in Southampton. "I have been spending most of my emotional energy on collecting signatures on a petition for a nuclear energy moratorium ... today, for instance, I collected 13 signatures between 4 and 5:30 PM," he wrote a friend in April.

The summer of 1974 was again spent quietly on Great Spruce Head Island, with Porter completing an exceptional number of canvases, including one of his best-known paintings, *The Harbor – Great Spruce Head* (1974, fig. 61), which captures the dock and the boats in the harbor on a clear, brilliant day. Porter's other major paintings of the summer were a moody portrait of his wife, *Anne in the Doorway* (1974), and a series of landscapes and bayscapes. Porter continued his project of painting the sun head-on with one of his most successful efforts, *Yellow Sunrise* (1974, fig. 62). He memorialized a visit by his daughter Katharine and her boyfriend (and, later, husband) Dan Fishbein in *Katie and Dan* (1974), and began preparatory sketches for the portrait of his older brother Eliot that would be completed in the coming year. The summer was colored by one comical incident involving Bruno. As Porter wrote his friend Richard Freeman: "early in the summer our bed collapsed, during a thunderstorm, when Bruno tried to get on it and on top of our heads as the most secure imaginable (to him) sleeping place. Since then we have been sleeping in a dusty corner of the floor, and since Bruno, being such a person-centered dog, identifies with me, he has started sneezing endlessly every morning when we get up, or are about to."[48] The collapse of the bed gave Porter the opportunity, when not painting, to undertake his last woodworking project, the construction of a solid new bedstead for the master bedroom of the Big House.

In July, Porter wrote his son Laurence with news of the island: "Great Spruce Head Island is now a corporation, worth about $340,000. I naturally own ¼ of this, that is, $85,000 worth of stock [which] I [will distribute] among my five children. ... Johnny ... is considered legally incompetent. And since Jerry is somewhat incommunicado – (c/o General Delivery, Denver, Colorado, and his name is now Richard) perhaps you could also keep his certificates, as well as John's."[49]

Porter's matter-of-fact observation of his youngest son's new name is typical of him; so far as his children were concerned, their lives were their own, to do with as they pleased. Even where religion was concerned, his intervention had been minimal. Katharine Porter had decided to convert to Catholicism at the same time her mother did, but waited a year out of deference to her father before following through with it (she converted, but ceased practicing Catholicism while in medical school; she now raises her children as Jews, and they attend a Quaker school.)[50] Elizabeth Porter was baptized Catholic as an infant and has remained devout. Johnny Porter "*very* independently converted [to Catholicism], after reading the gospels and interviewing members in several denominations."[51] Laurence Porter, meanwhile, "vacillate[s] between being an atheist and an agnostic, but whatever kind of God there may be isn't one that [he] like[s]."[52]

Porter's interest in guiding his children's religious beliefs was minimal, but his interest in religion was evident to his wife in their many conversations on the subject. During 1974 he began reading Juliana of Norwich's *Revelations of Divine Love* and planned soon to begin William James's *Varieties of Religious Experience*.

During August, Porter was pleased to learn that Alan Wald, a professor of English literature and American culture at the University of Michigan at Ann Arbor, was planning to write a book about Porter's old friend John Wheelwright and his associate Sherry Mangan. Wald (who eventually also published a book about many of the New York intellectuals whom Porter had known while mingling with the editors of *Partisan Review*) sought Porter out for an interview; Porter responded with a long letter about Wheelwright detailing their interests and activities during the 1930s.[53]

Porter took a short break from his painting on Great Spruce Head to be a visiting artist at the Skowhegan School of Painting and Sculpture during the summer of 1974. "We were in Skowhegan school for a weekend (one weekend ago – my brother [Eliot] the photographer is there now) and it exhausted me only completely,"[54] he noted to Richard Freeman.

After returning to the island, Porter packed up his studio and belongings and returned to Southampton, but in a state of such fatigue that he decided, after some thought, not to bring his oils to the island next year, but to plan instead to work exclusively in watercolor, a more portable and less taxing medium.

During the fall of 1974, Porter continued to teach Thursday night classes, each three hours long, at the School of Visual Arts, and he finished the lithographs started the previous spring. "Since coming back from Maine, I still don't have enough time to do my primary work, that is, painting," he wrote Laurence at the end of November. "However, I suppose that the hiatus may even work out in my favor, because I think about painting all the time and, feeling dissatisfied with my recent work, will perhaps do all the better when I can paint again."[55] Porter made a total of thirty-one prints in varying edition sizes in his lifetime; only fourteen of them were color lithographs. Brooke Alexander, who showed the graphic work at his gallery, occasionally dropped by while Porter was working, and the two went to lunch at Beatrice, a restaurant on West Twelfth Street which had been a favorite of Porter's twenty years earlier, during his reviewing days. Over a bottle of wine, according to Alexander, Porter "would become expansive; he spoke of artists he admired, found interesting, and knew: de Kooning, Larry Rivers, Alex Katz, Red Grooms, Neil Welliver, Jane Freilicher."[56]

Occasionally, Porter met Schuyler at the end of the workday, and the two commuted together back to Southampton for the weekend; once, in late November, the two narrowly escaped injury when "at Center Moriches the train derailed. We were in the front car, which almost overturned."[57]

In December, a retrospective exhibition of Porter's work opened at the Heckscher Museum in Huntington, Long Island. The show contained sixty works, the earliest, *Roofs of Cambridge*, dating from 1927. David Shirey of *The New York Times* called Porter's paintings "achievements of major significance" and described him as "one of the most outstanding contemporary American

61
The Harbor – Great Spruce Head, 1974.
Andre Nasser.

62
Yellow Sunrise, 1974.
Collection of Daniel B. Fishbein.

artists." Though the show would travel only to small, regional museums – the Queens Museum in Flushing, New York, and the Montclair Museum of Art in Montclair, New Jersey – it was, apart from the small Cleveland show of 1968, the only one-man retrospective Porter received in his lifetime.

During the winter of 1974, Porter returned again to a project which had interested him in Amherst: snowscapes. One result was *Snow on South Main Street*, a view of the street in front of the Southampton house rendered into a nearly abstract composition in grays, whites, and blues by a snowfall. The wet, heavy coastal snow has a textural analogue in Porter's uncharacteristic use of a thick white impasto.

By March, Porter's retrospective exhibition had moved to Flushing. Porter, now nearly sixty-eight, described the surreal experience of attending the opening alone in a letter to friends:

March 28, 1975   The Queens Museum opening, to which I was begged to come by *their* directors who had come to the opening at Huntington, so I thought I had to go, is in an inaccessible place, especially after dark when the opening was; you take the Flushing line subway to the next to the last stop which is *nowhere*, not a soul in sight, not even a mugger, but instead miles and miles of concrete paths lined with benches and lamp posts. I struck off in what seemed to be a southerly direction and finally came to a dark shape near the Unisphere, which when I approached had written on it "Queens Museum." So I went up to a blank wall, which did have a door, went in, and there was Anne's portrait in the doorway. I had called up to say I didn't think I could come, so they said they would get me a ride home. The ride home was in the car of friends of the directors who live in Deer Park – which is next to Huntington. Those kind people drove 120 miles out of their way to take me to Southampton.[58]

Porter was disappointed by the exhibition, writing Rackstraw Downes, "My show looked terrific in Huntington, and disastrous in Queens. In Queens they added about seven paintings, some of which I plan to withdraw from exhibitions, and of these, repaint a few."[59] Among the paintings that Porter chose to revise was the 1955 portrait of his son Jerry (now Richard) sitting unhappily at a table with his head in one hand; Porter had included an image of that painting in *Anne, Lizzie, and Katie* (1958), the year Jerry had run away from home.

Schuyler's comings and goings from the Porter home, meanwhile, were increasingly complicated by his psychiatric condition. By January his behavior had become erratic; in February he suffered another breakdown and was hospitalized, first at Bellevue, then at Payne Whitney. By April, Schuyler had recovered enough to write Porter, "Sometime I would like to bring my girlfriend, Joyce Coe, out for a weekend or overnight. ... I met her at Payne Whitney, where she seemed to have suffered a breakdown similar to mine, though not quite as serious (I was really 'out of it' my first five days at Bellevue)."[60]

Schuyler's condition vacillated over the coming year; he was rehospitalized during the summer of 1975.

Porter continued to travel to New York, even after he had completed work on his last lithograph, in order to paint cityscapes. He liked going to the city. Since returning from Europe in 1967, Porter had become convinced that New York City had some of the most beautiful light in the world, and in returning to the challenge of portraying that light, he was in a sense taking up where he had left off in 1949, when he had done cityscapes of "New York disguised as Venice." The new works were much more accomplished than those earlier efforts and much more successful in capturing city light. *Broadway South of Union Square* and *Near Union Square – Looking Up Park Avenue* are extraordinary in their combination of solid renderings of architecture with highly specific atmospheric effects. In late spring, Porter also began a portrait commission that would take him until midsummer to complete. His subject was Albert Gordon, the president of the Harvard Club in New York City. Porter painted Gordon in his apartment home on Gracie Square.

As a result of these New York projects, and also because Schuyler suffered another breakdown and needed Porter's help in finding hospitalization, the Porters made a late arrival on Great Spruce Head that summer, arriving only on August 8, 1975. Porter worked, as planned, exclusively in watercolors until the first week of September, noting to Lucien Day that watercolor "is roughly to oil what the harpsichord is to the piano. Except I like the harpsichord better than watercolor, and oil better than the piano."[61]

The Porters had a letter from Schuyler, then at the New York Hospital psychiatric center in White Plains, discussing the possibility of going off Thorazine and starting lithium treatment, which Schuyler did not want to do, since it was "usually indicated for manic depressives, which I'm not." Schuyler concluded: "The main thing here, as in all hospitals, is the monstrous boredom. Very therapeutic. Please write soon."[62]

The Porters returned to Southampton after the first week in September. Southampton, now a busy vacation spot for New Yorkers, had emptied out after Labor Day. The weather continued fine, hot, and summery, but the village was quiet. Porter quietly resumed his painting schedule, taking Bruno for a walk every morning before breakfast. There was good news waiting for Porter in the mail upon his return; he had received a commission to paint Cardinal Krol of Philadelphia, a project which delighted Porter less because the sitter was important in the Catholic church than because a church commission would allow him to consider his art-historical precedents in the red-robed figures of Velázquez and El Greco. Ever happy to travel to New York, Porter resolved to make copies of several Old Master paintings in the Metropolitan Museum in preparation for the commission.

On September 18, Porter began his usual day by taking Bruno out on his brisk morning walk. The day was clear and warm. Anne Porter went to church, as was her custom.

Porter was walking Bruno on Herrick Road when he collapsed. He fell hard on the sidewalk. Sometime afterward, a motorist spotted his body and the dog beside it and summoned the police.

Porter was declared dead on the scene, but because he had died away from home, an autopsy was needed. He had hit the ground so hard that at first the doctors thought the blow to his head had killed him, according to his son Laurence; but the town medical examiner determined that Porter had died of a massive coronary brought on by severe and undiagnosed arteriosclerosis. His life had ended quickly, with no lingering distress, out in the fresh air and sunshine.

Porter's death caught his family and friends unawares, for his youthful looks, vitality, and habits of healthy living were so universally remarked upon within the art community that he had hardly seemed a candidate for early death.

Anne Porter's friend Claire White, who had written about Porter, and her husband, Robert Winthrop White, a sculptor who had made a portrait head of Porter in 1970, helped with the funeral arrangements. The Whites "had just been through all this with their daughter, and it was [Claire] who advised me on what to expect – how I didn't have to do everything the funeral home suggested, what my rights were, how to set everything up," Anne Porter recalled.[63]

Porter's children were summoned home, but Richard could not be found, and so was unable to attend the funeral. A wake for Porter was held in the house at 49 South Main Street, Anne Porter having deciding against cremation since it was discouraged by the Catholic church. She wrote to Schuyler, whose condition was such that he could not attend,

September 1975   I know that you & I & Furl's children are the ones that will miss him most, because he was part of us so I've been thinking especially of you & worrying a little about the pain for you.

... We sit & talk & laugh about things Furl said & did & then we suddenly put our heads down on the table and sob. Katie the most. ... We didn't want to leave Furl's body in the funeral parlor – we brought it home & in front of the box is a vase he decorated at RISD [Rhode Island School of Design] with roses in it that you grew. Fr. Christopher, who was a friend, will say a mass and Liz & her friends will play classical guitar & recorder music.

... I was just so lucky to be with him so long – it could so easily not have happened! And of course, you were one of the very dearest & most important parts of his life – which I know makes it hard for you to have him die –

... If I can do anything comforting please let me know.[64]

Artist Jane Freilicher gave an account of the funeral:

I had been to the funeral for Claire White's daughter, so I had a sense of why Anne chose to do what she did. But the way Claire did it was much more in the Stanford White style: the children had ivy in their hair, and the pickup truck was decked with wildflowers, and it was all very beautiful. Incidentally, that was the last time I saw Fairfield – when we went to that funeral [of Claire White's daughter].

It was a surprise that Fairfield had been laid out in the house. At first I walked right past him, into the dining room, where people were sitting. I didn't even notice that he was there. ... Anne remarked that a ... friend had asked her if she wanted a Valium. ... She said, "Why on earth would anyone want not to have feelings at a time like this?"

The funeral was well attended. Many, many people came, and we all brought food – I think I brought a ham. I don't think Jimmy [Schuyler] came. There was a plainness to the whole thing that was difficult to come to terms with. They put the casket in the station wagon, and the station wagon sagged as it drove off. The church was an ugly church, the cemetery an ugly cemetery. The plot was just a space in a row.[65]

Nobody spoke at Porter's wake. There was a service for him at the Church of the Sacred Heart of Jesus and Mary on Hill Street in Southampton, but since Porter had not been a Catholic, his body was not allowed inside the church. "Claire White stayed behind with the body and the rest of us went to the church," Anne Porter recalled. "The Parish priest spoke, and Fr. Gormely, the college chaplain at Southampton LIU [Long Island University]– he was a friend of Fairfield's – and Father Huntington, who went to seminary on the G.I. Bill. Then Gail and Jimmy Lennon [friends of the Porters] played classical guitar." Among the many artists and old friends who attended the service were Roni McCleod and Lydia Tate, the women who had lodged with the Porters during the mid-1940s while studying at Hunter College.

Porter's body was conveyed from his home to the church, and then to the town's Catholic cemetery, in the old white station wagon that Porter had purchased ten years earlier, after his collision with the Long Island Railroad train. His son Laurence drove, stopping matter-of-factly along the way to put gasoline in the car.[66]

There was no guest register at the wake, so no record survives of the funeral except for one, currently lost: Porter's Southampton neighbor, Larry Rivers, stood on the fringe of the assembled party, recording the burial with a video camera. "At that time Larry was videotaping everything," Jane Freilicher remembered. [67]

The grave is a simple one. A headstone gives Fairfield Porter's name and life dates and, underneath, the name of his wife, which Anne Porter had placed there in advance to save time and expense for her children.

Porter's last years had been good steady years of artistic production, and his engagement in painting in preference to criticism during these final years suggests that the vocation he had chosen in youth, that of a visual artist, had ultimately proven more satisfying to him than his secondary vocation as a critic. Porter's extraordinary intellect and lifelong awareness of politics, philosophy, and the visual arts gave him a talent for criticism, and his late writings reflect a deep sense of responsibility to culture and to society as a whole. But from the 1950s onward, partly through psychoanalysis and partly through his admiration for Velázquez, Tolstoy, and Chekhov, Porter had been striving to attain what he described as "impersonality," "transparency," or "openness"[68] in both his painting and his life. The cultivation of this "transparent" state in art and life was what Porter concentrated on most deeply during his final years.

Indeed, painting had invaluable meditational and metaphysical aspects for Porter, for it gave him a daily opportunity, like prayer, to reflect upon his relation to the world and to consider the nature of "ultimate reality." Porter's repeated late-life use of this term (which appears not only in Whitehead but also in any number of writings on religion, both Eastern and Western) suggests an abiding interest in spiritual and metaphysical issues. Though the son of an atheist and an atheist himself, Porter had nonetheless grown up in a family with a long history of religious awareness and (in his immediate family) a strong interest in the spiritual and metaphysical questions raised by science, philosophy, and religion. During his last decade, as Porter turned away from the certainties of science and sought inspiration and enlightenment elsewhere, the question of spirituality interested him more deeply than ever before. Painting, with its emphasis on the sensual and immediate, had given Porter a new way to approach and consider questions of the spirit; his celebration of the "ultimate reality" of the natural world in his art (a project which unites him, incidentally, with the photographic work of his brother Eliot) can in fact be seen as an extension of the interests of his nature-loving father.

Moreover, painting helped Porter to engage in life through his senses and emotions rather than his intellect, and so to explore certain aspects of everyday life – nature, family, and home – in a celebratory and instinctual rather than critical and analytical medium. His best paintings (including his last) record, in a clear, direct, and nonsentimental way, the world which Porter had created for his family and the world which they, in turn, had created for him.

Porter's great disappointment late in life was that his work had received so little sustained and careful attention. Porter's representational style remained unfashionable throughout his lifetime, and, perhaps as a result, his work never received the intellectual scrutiny brought to other, more fashionable forms of visual art during the 1970s. In fact, few critics were aware of the philosophical and intellectual questions which had inspired Porter to paint as he did, and, of those, even fewer cared. Porter accepted the lack of attention with humility and, ultimately, with a beautiful indifference; great fame and big money had never really been his ambition, and by the end of his life he knew that his work not only sold moderately well but also had won the admiration of a well-informed group. When he died, Porter was painting as well as he had ever painted, and he was as happy in his personal life as he had ever been. In that sense, his end was good.

The images that Porter created during his last years reflect the ongoing sensual pleasure he found in his relatively simple life from sixty on: specific images of his house, garden, friends, and dog; of the beach at Southampton and of Great Spruce Head Island in Maine. In his paintings and drawings of the ocean at Southampton, Porter seems to have been engaged in a contemplation of the infinite; but these are not awe-inspiring images. Rather, they are particular observations of weather and light which suggest that Porter accepted the infinite as yet another aspect of everyday life. And it is probably significant to note that the majority of his last works are drawn not from such oceanic imagery but from images closer to home – for home was, in those last years, a more comfortable place than it had ever been before.

Perhaps the greatest comfort to Porter in later life was the renewal of his marriage. While in Amherst, Porter had purchased a wedding ring for Anne Porter to replace an earlier one which she had lost, and the purchase suggests a revival of intimacy and a new sense of commitment between the two. Porter's references to Anne in his correspondence during his last five years confirm that he was rediscovering the pleasure of her company now that the children were grown and the daily conflicts of household life had lessened. For his wife, these late, long-awaited years of quiet intimacy were precious and all too brief.

The years that followed Porter's death were difficult ones for his wife. Schuyler stayed at the house once after Porter's death but was so distressed that Anne Porter thought it best not to have him back, though he sometimes dropped by while staying nearby with the poet Barbara Guest or the painter Darragh Park. Living on at 49 South Main Street with her daughter Elizabeth, Anne Porter found the big house difficult to maintain. Assorted friends came and went, much as they had in earlier years, but by 1979, she realized that she needed a smaller home and sold the house to neighbors, subdividing the property into three parcels, and keeping the one in the middle, including Porter's studio, for herself. She commissioned young architect friends to build her a modest house in which she would be able to look after Johnny and accommodate guests.

Selling the house forced Anne Porter to consider the many paintings by her husband which remained in the house and studio. A small number of Porter's paintings were, according to Porter's wishes, set aside to be distributed yearly to museums around the country. As for the rest, Anne Porter briefly considered buying a two-family home and keeping the remaining paintings in the unoccupied half. But then a friend suggested to her that she donate the paintings to the Parrish Art Museum in Southampton. Ron Pisano, director of the museum, was an active supporter of Fairfield Porter's work. Anne Porter, in consultation with her lawyer, Arthur Bullowa, approached the museum.

In an agreement dated June 4, 1980, Anne Porter donated 186 paintings to the museum, along with thirty thousand dollars to cover the expense of maintaining the collection and making the work available to interested scholars, and paid six thousand dollars toward writing a catalogue raisonné of Porter's work. In return, the museum agreed to "supervise and seek grant funding for the publication of a catalogue raisonné of paintings and possibly works on paper."[69] The museum never did find public funding for the catalogue raisonné, so fifteen years after the agreement, the Porter family, with the help of the art dealer Betty Cunningham, arranged to have a catalogue, written by Joan Ludman, published privately at the family's own expense.

A month after signing the agreement with the Parrish, Anne Porter suffered another loss. On July 11, 1980, Johnny Porter, who had recently developed epilepsy, died of what is believed to have been a combined epileptic seizure and heart attack. The death occurred three days before he was to have returned to Southampton for his summer vacation. Anne had last seen her son, to whom she had expected to devote the rest of her life, at Easter. According to her, he had telephoned the day he died to say, "Mom, if I ever don't call you, don't worry, it's because I'm busy."[70]

Schuyler's life, too, grew more difficult in the years following Porter's death. After leaving the Porters, Schuyler lived first in an apartment owned by Neil Welliver on East Thirty-fifth Street, where he stayed for about six years before moving into a series of cheap single-room-occupancy hotels. He was hospitalized twice in 1975 because of mental problems. He also suffered increasingly from other health problems, including pneumonia and diabetes. In 1979, while taking medication as a treatment for mental illness, Schuyler fell asleep while smoking in bed. The bed caught fire, and Schuyler, though rescued, sustained a number of injuries, including third-degree burns, and had to be resuscitated. After recovering at Bellevue, Schuyler moved into Room 625 at the Chelsea Hotel, a landmarked building which was (and remains) well known for its bohemian clientele.[71] It provided permanent accommodation for Schuyler as he recovered from the worst of his ordeal, then suffered again from tranquilizer poisoning and yet another nervous breakdown.

In 1981, Anne Porter set aside a fund for Schuyler, using interest on the proceeds of the sale of a group of Fairfield Porter paintings and donating the money to the Committee on Poetry to go directly to his support. Her gift remained anonymous during Schuyler's life.[72] Schuyler by this time had attracted a supportive circle of young poets and artists. After winning the Pulitzer Prize for *The Morning of the Poem* (1980) he was able to support himself for a while, in part on the sale of his papers to the University of California, San Diego / La Jolla. "When Jimmy had money from the sale of his archives," Anne Porter later said, "he several times sent us beautiful flowers as well as postcards."[73]

Though Schuyler did not communicate frequently with Anne Porter in the last years of his life, he visited Southampton occasionally. On one visit he passed by 49 South Main Street and saw that the new owners had chopped down the old horse-chestnut trees which once stood at the front of the Porter house. He wrote a poem describing his anger, "Horse-Chestnut Trees and Roses," which was published in *The New Yorker* in 1985. In a sense, it became a trademark poem: in 1986, Schuyler informed a radio host that his collected poems would be given the same title, and in a rare public appearance at the Poetry Center in 1989, the poem prompted a spontaneous ovation. But Schuyler did not conclude that evening's reading with "Horse-Chestnut Trees and Roses." Instead, he selected another recent poem:

> *A cardinal*
>
> in the branches of
> the great plane tree
> whistles its song:
>
> or is it that mimic
> Fairfield
> saluting the day
>
> under the branches of
> his great plane tree
> in his springtime yard?

Schuyler noted in his journal that "A Cardinal" was a poem "in which, finally, I said something of what I feel about Fairfield, and how he comes back and back to me."[74]

Schuyler had a religious conversion toward the end of his life; his assistant, Tom Carey, introduced him to the Episcopal church. After Carey became an Episcopal Franciscan friar, Schuyler often accompanied him to the Little Portion friary in Mount Sinai, Long Island, for contemplative weekend retreats.

After finding religion, Schuyler reestablished contact with Anne Porter. Sending her a note congratulating her on a poetry reading, he wrote,

Dear Anne,   *May 24, 1989*

Your reading was so beautiful – your poems *and* your reading – I cannot imagine anything lovelier. Coming home I knew something was brought to mind and this morning I remembered it: this little quotation from Baruch, which was in a reading for morning prayer recently: "the stars shone in their watches, and were glad; he called them, and they said, 'Here we are!'

Love,
Jimmy[75]

Schuyler died on April 12, 1991. A memorial service was held for him at the Church of the Incarnation, on Madison Avenue and Thirty-fifth Street, where Schuyler had first thought about joining the Episcopal church. Anne Porter attended the service with Hadley Guest, the daughter of Barbara Guest. Schuyler was later buried at the Little Portion friary at Mt. Sinai.

After Fairfield Porter's death, Anne Porter, who had never ceased writing poetry, began to write more of it and to send her poems to *Commonweal* magazine at the suggestion of David Shapiro. *Commonweal* published many of them; on several occasions, Anne Porter received the Catholic Journalism Award for Best Poetry from the Catholic Press Association. *An Altogether Different Language: Poems, 1934–1994*, a manuscript assembled by Anne Porter at Shapiro's insistence, was published by Zoland Books in 1994 and was a finalist for the 1994 National Book Award in poetry. She is currently at work on a second volume.

In recent years, Porter's reputation as a major American artist and art critic has grown. Rackstraw Downes began compiling Porter's critical essays shortly after his death. The collection was published by Taplinger in 1979 as *Art in Its Own Terms: Selected Criticism, 1935–1975*, and it went through several printings. Critical praise for the book was unanimous. Hilton Kramer, reviewing the collection for *The New York Times Book Review*, said, "This is an extraordinary book, one that places [Porter] among the most important critics of his time. ... [It is] the most consistently sensitive and thoughtful writing on new art, and on the art of the recent past, that any critic of the time gave us. ... Fairfield Porter was pre-eminently a critic of New York, the artistic capital of our time, and 'Art in Its Own Terms' gives us the best account of the art seen and produced here that I have yet read."[76] Peter Schjeldahl, now a well-established critic, called *Art in Its Own Terms* "a marvelous, revelatory book," noting that "the necessary connection between an artist's particular, material decisions and art's general significance is what Porter's criticism teaches again and again, by example as much as by precept. ... He offers evidence of what a richly civilized and civilizing occupation criticism can be when practiced by someone who both knows and cares."[77] The book has proved enduringly popular; after briefly going out of print, it was reissued by Zoland Books in 1993 and has remained in print ever since.

Porter's reputation as a painter has likewise grown through the years. His work was given a major retrospective originating at the Museum of Fine Arts, Boston in 1983. John Ashbery contributed a lively and perceptive essay for the catalogue, as did the curator, Kenworth Moffett; additional contributions were made by John Bernard Myers, Porter's former dealer, as well as by Paul Cummings, who had interviewed Porter for the Archives of American Art, Prescott Schutz of Hirschl and Adler Galleries, Rackstraw Downes, and Louise Hamlin. In 1981 a catalogue raisonné of his prints was compiled by the art historian Joan Ludman.

Porter's painting has proved enduringly popular not just with critics but with the general public. According to Hilton Kramer, the Porter retrospective exhibition at the Museum of Fine Arts broke all previous museum attendance records. A *Boston Globe* editorial, reacting to a somewhat negative review of the show (and the artist) by John Updike, compared the works to the writings of John Cheever and recommended the show heartily. A somewhat truncated version of the exhibition traveled to four other cities, ending in New York, where it was shown at the Whitney Museum of American Art in 1984.

In 1993 a second major exhibition, "Fairfield Porter: An American Painter," organized by a Hunter College professor, William C. Agee, opened at the Parrish Art Museum in Southampton, New York. The show, which received a strong critical reception, traveled to the Mead Art Museum at Amherst College; the Snite Museum of Art at the University of Notre Dame in South Bend, Indiana; the Albright-Knox Museum in Buffalo, New York; and the Colby College Museum of Art in Waterville, Maine. The same year, Harry N. Abrams published the monograph *Fairfield Porter: An American Classic* with text by John T. Spike, an expert on Italian art of the sixteenth through eighteenth centuries.

Porter's poetry received small-press publication in 1985. It was edited by the poet and art critic John Yau with David Kermani, who had organized the project. The long delay in bringing the book out was due in part to Schuyler. After Porter's death, Schuyler had said he would write an introduction to Porter's poetry. Anne Porter sent him the manuscript, but Schuyler did not respond, nor did he return the manuscript. Anne Porter understood Schuyler's nonparticipation in the project as a symptom of his illness. After several years and many requests from her for a response, Anne Porter turned to John Ashbery, who wrote an appreciative introduction to her husband's poems. The book was published, with thirteen selected Porter drawings as illustrations, by Tibor de Nagy Editions in association with the Promise of Learnings.

Fairfield Porter's artistic achievements have, to date, been appreciated as those of an American painter who combined the intimate, sensual, and representational style of the French artists Vuillard and Bonnard with the violent, colorful, gestural style of de Kooning – and in the process created a body of paintings which, perhaps more than any other of the second half of the twentieth century, defines the look, feel, and texture of American family life through the medium of paint. But this classification, while it does justice to Porter's work as a painter, necessarily ignores the much richer relationship that Porter had with painting and, in a larger sense, with art. Only in the context of his critical writings, personal correspondence, and poetry do the importance and complexity of that engagement (at once intellectual, emotional, and spiritual) become apparent. Up to now, few have appreciated the complexity and depth of his work, because few art critics or art historians have cared to involve themselves in the relation of Porter's homely and unassuming paintings to (among other things) nineteenth-century French poetry, metaphysical philosophy, Unitarian ethics, Italian Renaissance portraiture, or Freudian psychoanalysis, much less to the artist's own intimate relationships with his family and friends. But Porter's work as a writer, critic, poet, and painter is remarkably coherent and needs to be considered (as it has not been considered up to now) as a single, complex, lifelong project – an essentially diaristic project in which the artist perpetually sought to define for himself his relation to the world. Only when that project has been appreciated in its literary, critical, and artistic entirety will Porter be given the recognition that he is due as – in his friend John Ashbery's words – "perhaps the major American artist of this century."

Notes

Abbreviations

AEP: Anne Elizabeth Porter

AIIOT: *Art in Its Own Terms: Selected Criticism, 1935-1975, by Fairfield Porter*, ed. Rackstraw Downes (Cambridge, Mass.: Zoland Books, 1993)

Cummings interview: Fairfield Porter interview with Paul Cummings, June 6, 1968, for the Archives of American Art, Washington, D.C.

FP: Fairfield Porter

FPP-AAA: Fairfield Porter Papers

Freilicher, Schikler interview: Jane Freilicher interview with Barbara Schikler, August 4 and 5, 1987, for the Archives of American Art, Washington, D.C.

JA-HOU: John Ashbery Papers

JDS: Justin D. Spring

JS-UCSD: James Schuyler Papers

JW-JHL: John Wheelwright Papers

KMC: Katharine Minot Channing

NPS: Nancy Porter Straus

RWP: Ruth Wadsworth Porter

Archives

John Ashbery Papers, Houghton Library, Harvard University

John Button Papers, Henry W. and Albert A. Berg Collection of English and American Literature, New York Public Library

Kenneth Koch Papers, Henry W. and Albert A. Berg Collection of English and American Literature, New York Public Library

Anne Porter Papers, in the Fairfield Porter Papers, Archives of American Art, Washington, D.C.

Fairfield Porter Papers (1888-1981), Archives of American Art, Washington, D.C.

James Schuyler Papers, Archive for New Poetry, Mandeville Department of Special Collections, University of California, San Diego / La Jolla

John Wheelwright Papers, John Hay Library, Brown University, Providence, R.I.

Letters

The letters of Fairfield Porter have been assembled and are being edited for publication by Armistead Leigh. The manuscript, still in preparation, will be published in the year 2000 by the University of Michigan Press. Unless otherwise noted, all letters by Fairfield Porter in this book are quoted from Armistead Leigh's unpublished manuscript and/or from photocopies of original letters by Fairfield Porter given to Justin Spring by Armistead Leigh. Some letters or extracts of letters which appear in Leigh's current manuscript may not, in the end, be published in the book.

Many of the letters to Fairfield Porter used in this biography come from the Fairfield Porter Papers. Unless otherwise noted, letters to Fairfield Porter quoted here (except letters from James Schuyler) are in the Fairfield Porter Papers.

James Schuyler's letters are currently being assembled for publication by Bill Corbett. Unless otherwise noted, letters by James Schuyler quoted here are from Corbett's collection, which includes the letters of James Schuyler in the Fairfield Porter Papers at the Archives of American Art.

Extracts of the letters of Anne Porter to her mother, Katharine Minot Channing, relating to Fairfield Porter were compiled by Anne Porter in an unpublished manuscript several years after Fairfield Porter's death. Anne Porter then destroyed the original letters. She recently donated the unpublished manuscript of letter extracts, as part of the Anne Porter Papers, to the Fairfield Porter Papers at the Archives of American Art.

The letters of Ruth Wadsworth Porter to Nancy Porter Straus are currently in the possession of Nancy Porter Straus's daughter, Margaret Straus.

Additional letters relating to Porter and his circle can be found in the Kenneth Koch Papers and the John Button Papers.

1

Family and Home

1 Fairfield Porter, interview with Paul Cummings, June 6, 1968. Archives of American Art, Washington, D.C. (hereafter Cummings interview, 1968).

2 "Days That Were: The Autobiography of Gerald Warner Brace, 1901-1978" (typescript, 1979), vol. 2, p. 48. From a citation in John T. Spike, *Fairfield Porter: An American Classic* (New York: Abrams, 1992), p. 274.

3 Barbara Guest, interview with Justin D. Spring (hereafter JDS), summer 1993.

4 Longfellow died in 1882. Details of the meeting were recollected by Anne Porter, who had the story from Ruth Porter. Anne Porter, interview with JDS, 1996.

5 Anne Porter, interview with JDS, 1996. Evidence of Ruth Porter's interest in meeting and learning about other people can be found in a cruise itinerary belonging to Ruth in the Fairfield Porter Papers at the Archives of American Art, Washington, D.C. (hereafter FPP-AAA), which features check marks next to each name on the passenger list.

6 "Gleanings" is preserved, along with other Ruth Porter memorabilia, in the FPP-AAA.

7 Anne Porter, interview with JDS, 1996.

8 From "An appreciation of Ruth Porter written by George Packard and read at a gathering of friends at the home of Mr. and Mrs. Morris L. Greeley, Sunday, June 7, 1942." FPP-AAA.

9 Ellen Auerbach, interview with JDS, 1997.

10 Eliot Porter, *Eliot Porter*, exh. cat. (Boston: Little, Brown; Fort Worth: Amon Carter Museum, 1987), pp. 12-13.

11 For further information on Unitarianism, see Marta Flanagan, "We Are Unitarian Universalists" (Unitarian Universalist Association: Boston, 1992); and "Protestantism: The Major Protestant Denominations," Britannica CD 99 Standard Edition).

12 Ruth [Wadsworth] Porter, *Lucy Fairfield, My Mother and My Granddaughter* (privately printed, n.d.), pp. 13-14. FPP-AAA.

13 "An appreciation of Ruth Porter written by George Packard."

14 William Eliot Furness, in his unpublished autobiography. Manuscript in the collection of Katharine Porter (Fairfield Porter's daughter), quoted by Anne Porter. Anne Porter, interview with JDS, 1997.

15 From the essay "Hints for the Education of Very Young Children" by Ruth Porter's mother, Lucy Fairfield Furness. Ruth had the essay published as a pamphlet by Fergus Printing Co., Chicago (n.d.). Anne Porter Papers. The Anne Porter Papers were assembled in 1997 by Anne Porter and JDS and donated to the Fairfield Porter Papers.

16 "Children's Reading," an unpublished manuscript by Ruth [Wadsworth] Furness Porter, p. 6. FPP-AAA.

17 Eliot Porter, *Summer Island: Penobscot Country* (San Francisco: Sierra Club, 1996), p. 54. Other descriptions of Ruth Porter's reading can be found in his *Eliot Porter*, p. 14.

18 Printed in the *Chicago Tribune* on February 10, 1916, this poem and ten others appear in a memorial pamphlet put together at the time of Ruth's death in 1942. FPP-AAA.

19 Anne Porter, interview with JDS, 1996.

20 Anne Porter, interview with JDS, 1996.

21 Anne Porter, interview with JDS, 1996.

22 "Father is acting about [the trip to Ann Arbor] as grandmother used to act over company. I think maybe it's psychologically better for him to go anyway as not going anywhere is getting to be a possession. I do wish I knew how to make him happier!" Ruth Wadsworth Porter (hereafter RWP) to Nancy Porter Straus (hereafter NPS), April 16, 1936.

23 Anne Porter, interview with JDS, 1996.

24 Ruth Furness [Porter] to Elizabeth [?], October 9, 1897, sent from the Furness home at 417 Orchard Street in Chicago. FPP-AAA.

25 Anne Porter, interview with JDS, 1996.

26 Eliot Porter, *Eliot Porter*, pp. 11-13.

27 Cummings interview, 1968.

28 Cummings interview, 1968.

29 Cummings interview, 1968.

30 See "The Wave and the Leaf" by Fairfield Porter in *Fairfield Porter: The Collected Poems, with Selected Drawings*, ed. John Yau (New York: Tibor de Nagy / The Promise of Learnings, 1985), pp. 3-7.

31 Cummings interview, 1968.

32 Cummings interview, 1968.

33 See the James Schuyler Chronology of Fairfield Porter, with revisions by Fairfield Porter. James Schuyler Papers, Archive for New Poetry, Mandeville Department of Special Collections, University of California, San Diego / La Jolla (hereafter JS-UCSD).

34 Laurence Porter, letter to JDS, July 24-September 22, 1996.

35 Spike, *Fairfield Porter*, p. 21. Spike cites a personal interview with Eliot Porter as the source of this recollection.

36 Anne Porter, interview with JDS, 1996.

37 Lucy Fairfield Furness, "Hints for the Education of Very Young Children." FPP-AAA.

38 Laurence Porter, letter to JDS, July 24-September 22, 1996.

39 Laurence Porter, letter to JDS, July 24-September 22, 1996.

40 Cummings interview, 1968.

41 Cummings interview, 1968.

42 Letter to Laurence Porter, October 5, 1970. Unless otherwise specified, all letters are by Fairfield Porter.

43 Cummings interview, 1968.

44 Anne Porter, interview with JDS, 1996.

45 Anne Porter, interview with JDS, 1996.

46 Anne Porter, interview with JDS, 1996. One of the Porter children, Elizabeth, inherited this trait.

47 Cummings interview, 1968.

48 Letter to Rebecca and Laura Furness, December 31, 1918.

49 Cummings interview, 1968.

50 Laurence Porter, letter to JDS, July 24-September 22, 1996.

51 Cummings interview, 1968.

52 Cummings interview, 1968.

53 Cummings interview, 1968.

54 Letter to Claire White, April 24 [1973?].

55 Cummings interview, 1968.

56 Eliot Porter, *Summer Island*, p. 22.

57 "Father paid $10,000 for the island in 1912." John Porter to Fairfield Porter (hereafter FP), October 3, 1970.

58 Eliot Porter, *Summer Island*, p. 19.

59 See the James Schuyler Chronology of Fairfield Porter. A copy of this document and correspondence concerning it can be found in JS-UCSD.

60 See the James Schuyler Chronology of Fairfield Porter. JS-UCSD.

61 Eliot Porter, *Summer Island*, p. 51.

62 Eliot Porter, *Summer Island*, p. 29.

63 RWP to NPS, Wednesday, June 17 [1925].

64 RWP to NPS, September 17, 1925.

65 Eliot Porter, *Summer Island*, p. 55.

66 Ellen Auerbach, interview with JDS, 1996; Ilse Hamm Mattick, interview with JDS, 1997. See also Eliot Porter, *Summer Island*, p. 44.

67 Eliot Porter, *Summer Island*, p. 28.

68 Laurence Porter, letter to JDS, July 24-September 22, 1996.

69 RWP to NPS, June 11, 1925.

70 Laurence Porter, letter to JDS, July 24-September 22, 1996.

71 Anne Porter, interview with JDS, 1996.

72 Anne Porter, interview with JDS, 1996.

73 Quoted in John Neary, "Profile: Eliot Porter," *People*, December 10, 1979.

74 Laurence Porter, letter to JDS, July 22-September 24, 1996.

75 RWP to NPS, September 17, 1925.

76 Eliot Porter, *Summer Island*, p. 63.

77 RWP to NPS, June 26, 1925.

78 RWP to NPS, July 9, 1926.

79 RWP to NPS, July 17, 1926.

80 Anne Porter, interview with JDS, 1996.

81 RWP to NPS, July 4, 1925.

82 Cummings interview, 1968.

83 Cummings interview, 1968.

84 Letter to John Ashbery, [n.d.] 1957.

85 Fairfield Porter's Harvard transcript contains Porter's application to Harvard.

86 James Porter's letter is preserved with Fairfield's Harvard transcript.

87 Fairfield is related to T. S. Eliot through his mother, Ruth Porter, whose paternal grandmother's brother, W. G. Eliot Jr., was T. S. Eliot's father. Thus T. S. Eliot is technically Ruth Porter's second cousin. Stephen Porter confirmed this information by letter in response to a letter of surmise from JDS.

2

Milton and Harvard

1 Anne Porter, interview with JDS, 1996.

2 Letter to RWP, [n.d.].

3 Letter to RWP, April 14, 1925. The words about Milton Academy come in an aside to a description of a similar situation at Harvard.

4 Letter to RWP, November 20, 1923.

5 Letter to Margaret Furness, November 28, 1923.

6 Cummings interview, 1968.

7 Letter to Laurence Porter, "Sunday Mid Feb 1957."

8 Margaret Straus, letter to JDS, 1996.

9 Laurence Porter, letter to JDS, July 24-September 22, 1996.

10 Laurence Porter, letter to JDS, July 24-September 22, 1996.

11 Ruth Porter later remarked to Anne Channing, Porter's fiancée, that the only thing she regretted about Anne was "that she wasn't Jewish." Anne Porter, interview with JDS, 1996.

12 Letter to Arthur Giardelli, March 22, 1958.

13 Letter to Arthur Giardelli, May 25, 1958.

14 Letter to RWP, October 14, 1924.

15 Letter to RWP, November 12, 1924.

16 Letter to RWP, November 12, 1924.

17 Letter to RWP, quoted in John T. Spike, *Fairfield Porter: An American Classic* (New York: Abrams, 1992), p. 23.

18 Letter to RWP, December 9, 1924.

19 Letter to RWP, November 26, 1924.

20 Letter to RWP, December 9, 1924.

21 RWP to Michel Straus, July 23, 1926.

22 Letter to RWP, March 26, 1925.

23 Cummings interview, 1968.

24 Letter to RWP, March 19, 1925.

25 For an extensive examination of the relationship between Porter and Wallace Stevens, see Glen MacLeod, "Fairfield Porter and Wallace Stevens: Kindred Spirits of American Art," *Archives of American Art Journal*, 24, 1 (1984): 2-12.

26 David Shapiro, interview with JDS, 1998.

27 MacLeod, "Fairfield Porter and Wallace Stevens," p. 11.

28 Barbara Guest, interview with JDS, 1993.

29 Letter to RWP, March 1, 1925.

30 Fairfield Porter, "Technology and Artistic Perception," in Fairfield Porter, *Art in Its Own Terms
Selected Criticism, 1935-1975*, ed. Rackstraw Downes
(Cambridge, Mass.: Zoland Books, 1993)
(hereafter *AIIOT*), pp. 272-73.

31 RWP to Margaret Furness, July 9, 1925.

32 RWP to Margaret Furness, July 7, 1925; RWP to NPS,
August 30, 1925.

33 Letter to RWP, October 16, 1925.

34 Letter to RWP, October 28, 1925.

35 Letter to RWP, November 12, 1925.

36 John Walker, *Self Portrait*, p. 22, cited in Spike,
Fairfield Porter, p. 28.

37 Letter to Alan Wald, August 5, 1974. Porter mentions
first reading Wheelwright in *Hound and Horn*.

38 Raymond Foy, unpublished interview with James
Schuyler, March 2, 1990, at the Chelsea Hotel.
JS-UCSD. "Lincoln [Kirstein] had big eyes for Fairfield
[when they were at Harvard together] which scared
the shit out of Fairfield. [Laughs]. This great huge
towering brute positively leering over him." Schuyler
crossed out the observation in the typescript. Paul
Cadmus's reminiscence comes from a discussion
between Cadmus and JDS in May 1997.

39 Letter to RWP, January 8, 1926.

40 Letter to RWP, January 11, 1926.

41 "The dignity and modesty [of Chicagoans] is that of
a people who for a long time have accepted that
they are second rate, second rate to New York, second
best at best. This gives them a style similar to that
of the negro bourgeoisie, and probably explains why
when I am in a setting where there are well-to-do
negroes I feel so much at home." Letter to Arthur
Giardelli, May 5, 1965.

42 Letter to RWP, January 22, 1926.

43 Letter to RWP, March 17, 1926.

44 RWP to NPS, July 2, 1926.

45 Letter to RWP, March [n.d.] 1926.

46 Letter to RWP, March 11, 1926.

47 Letter to RWP, March 1926.

48 Porter had described his intended profession as
"painter" on his senior questionnaire.

49 RWP to NPS, July 5, 1926.

50 I am indebted to David Shapiro for directing my
attention to this information.

51 Cummings interview, 1968.

52 Letter to Anne Elizabeth Porter (hereafter AEP),
Rome, [n.d.] 1932.

53 Anne Porter, interview with JDS, 1996.

54 Eliot Porter, *Eliot Porter*, exh. cat. (Boston: Little,
Brown; Fort Worth: Amon Carter Museum, 1987),
p. 24. Porter may be mistaken; his mother's letter
concerning T. S. Eliot suggests that during the summer of 1926 Eliot Porter was planning to depart
for Cambridge, in which case his marriage to his
first wife would not have taken place until 1927.
Eliot Porter's memory is often at odds with facts
noted in family correspondence; but one should
assume that his marriage took place in the year
he notes in his memoirs and that Ruth's letter concerns another trip to England being planned by
Eliot Porter.

55 Barbara Birch (née Barbara Channing), interview
with JDS, 1996.

3

Russia and New York

1 In a letter to his mother that September, Porter
remarked that he was returning "on the *Leviathan*
from Cherbourg" (Letter to RWP, September 15,
1927). Porter would not have made a special trip
from Paris (or Le Havre) to Coutances in western
Normandy just to see the small cathedral; he
must have stopped there on his way south from
Cherbourg toward Mont-St.-Michel.

2 Cummings interview, 1968.

3 Anne Porter indicated that Fisher was a lawyer;
Fairfield Porter wrote to Alan Wald in 1974
that Fisher had been a conscientious objector.

4 Letter to RWP, August 1, 1927.

5 Anne Porter, interview with JDS, 1996.

6 Cummings interview, 1968.

7 Letter to RWP, September 15, 1927.

8 Letter to RWP, September 15, 1927.

9 Cummings interview, 1968.

10 For information on the 1927 installation of the Morosov and Shchukin collections, see Beverly Whitney Kean, *French Painters, Russian Collectors* (London: Hodder and Stoughton, 1988), p. 244.

11 Cummings interview, p. 37.

12 Letter to Alan Wald, August 5, 1974.

13 Letter to Alan Wald, August 5, 1974.

14 Letter to RWP, September 15, 1927.

15 Letter to RWP, September 29, 1927.

16 Cummings interview, 1968.

17 Letter to RWP, September 15, 1927.

18 Cummings interview, 1968.

19 Letter to RWP, September 15, 1927.

20 Letter to RWP, November 28, 1927.

21 See Nicky Mariano, *Forty Years with Berenson* (New York: Knopf, 1967).

22 This correspondence is preserved with Porter's Harvard transcript.

23 Cummings interview, 1968.

24 *New York Panorama: A Companion to the WPA Guide to New York City* (New York: Pantheon, 1984), p. 196.

25 Ilse Hamm Mattick, in an interview with JDS, 1997, recalled warm conversations between Porter and Stieglitz at An American Place in 1941.

26 Cummings interview, 1968.

27 *The WPA Guide to New York City* (New York: Random House, 1982), p. 135.

28 *The WPA Guide*, p. 128.

29 Cummings interview, 1968.

30 Letter to RWP, [n.d.] 1935.

31 Cummings interview, 1968.

32 Cummings interview, 1968.

33 Cummings interview, 1968.

34 See the James Schuyler Chronology of Fairfield Porter and its revisions by Porter, which features these names in conjunction with the Bryner-Schwab art collection. JS-UCSD.

35 Cummings interview, 1968.

36 Cummings interview, 1968.

37 AEP to Katharine Minot Channing (hereafter KMC), November 6, 1932.

38 Cummings interview, 1968.

39 Eliot Porter, *Eliot Porter*, exh. cat. (Boston: Little, Brown; Fort Worth: Amon Carter Museum, 1987), pp. 27-29.

40 Cummings interview, 1968.

41 AEP to KMC, May 11, 1931.

42 Anne Porter, interview with JDS, 1996.

43 Ilse Hamm Mattick, interview with JDS, 1997.

44 Anne Porter, interview with JDS, 1996.

45 Anne Porter, interview with JDS, 1996.

46 Barbara Birch, interview with JDS, 1996.

47 Anne Porter, interview with JDS, 1997.

48 John Bernard Myers, *Tracking the Marvelous: A Life in the New York Art World* (New York: Random House, 1981), p. 143.

49 Barbara Birch, interview with JDS, 1996.

50 A letter from the Radcliffe secretary of admissions in Anne Channing [Porter]'s undergraduate transcript reads: "Unless you fall heir to the disease which I understand from Barbara your relations at Harvard have suffered through, you will graduate from Radcliffe with the class of 1934."

51 Anne Porter, interview with JDS, 1997.

4

Travel and Study in Italy

1 "Mother is very sad these days; I think she regrets her lost youth. I feel depressed and then I think about a possible story about someone like Mother ... growing old by getting sad at her children leaving her. ... And Father (not Father but imagined from Father) would be in it: a man who is innocent of the world and who is therefore not a successful father to his sons and Mother trying to be her sons' father without success because she is not a man." Letter to AEP, September [n.d.] 1932. In another (undated) letter of September 1932, Porter mentions to Anne that Ruth, not James, wants to discuss money matters with him.

2 Eliot Porter, *Eliot Porter*, exh. cat. (Boston: Little, Brown; Fort Worth: Amon Carter Museum, 1987), p. 27.

3 Eliot Porter, *Eliot Porter*, p. 27.

4 Porter cites the description of Colleoni with admiration in his essay "The Short Review" (published in 1958, containing a citation to *The Necessary Angel*, which was published by Knopf in 1951; see *AIIOT*, p. 167) but goes into more depth about Stevens's abilities as a critic and observer in the essay "Art and Scientific Method" (published in 1969; see *AIIOT*, p. 265). The quotation from Stevens (which is actually a misquotation) can be found in *AIIOT*, p. 268. But in "Fairfield Porter and Wallace Stevens: Kindred Spirits of American Art" (*Archives of American Art Journal*, 24, 1 [1984]: 8) Glen MacLeod observes that Porter synthesized the quotation from two disparate sources: "the eccentric to be the base of design" is taken from the poem "Like Decorations in a Nigger Cemetery," and "Not to impose, not to have reasoned at all" is taken from "Notes Toward a Supreme Fiction."

5 Letter to AEP, [n.d.] 1931.

6 RWP travel notebook. FPP-AAA.

7 Letter to AEP, September [n.d.] 1932.

8 See Nicola Beauman, *E. M. Forster: A Biography* (New York: Knopf, 1994), p. 104.

9 Letter to RWP, [n.d.] 1931.

10 James Merrill, *A Different Person: A Memoir* (New York: Knopf, 1993), pp. 204-17.

11 For further information on Berenson, see Sylvia Sprigge, *Berenson: A Biography* (Boston: Houghton Mifflin / Riverside Press, 1960); R. W. B. Lewis, *Edith Wharton: A Biography* (New York: Fromm International, 1985); Umberto Morra, *Conversations with Berenson* (Boston: Houghton Mifflin, 1965); Nicky Mariano, ed., *The Berenson Archive: An Inventory of Correspondence* (Cambridge: Harvard University Press, 1965); and Nicky Mariano, *Forty Years with Berenson* (New York: Knopf, 1968).

12 Lewis, *Edith Wharton*, pp. 505-6.

13 Information on the layout, furnishings, and daily rituals of the Villa I Tatti in 1931 was kindly provided to me by Susan Wilson at Villa I Tatti.

14 Mariano, *Forty Years with Berenson*, pp. 105-6.

15 Mariano, *Forty Years with Berenson*, pp. 97-99.

16 Cummings interview, 1968.

17 Morra, *Conversations with Berenson*, p. vi.

18 Mariano, *Forty Years with Berenson*, p. 101.

19 Letter to RWP, November 28, 1931.

20 *Bryan's Dictionary of Painters and Engravers* (Macmillan, New York: 1903), p. 523. The Annunciation altarpiece in the Uffizi originally hung in the church of San Giorgio Sulla Costa.

21 Letter to RWP, November 28, 1931.

22 Letter to RWP, November 28, 1931.

23 Letter to RWP, December 12, 1931.

24 Anne Porter, interview with JDS, 1996. Anne Porter was certain that Porter had told her that Giardelli had one Jewish grandfather. Giardelli did not mention his mixed religious background in the interview with JDS of October 1996, merely that he had been baptized, according to conventions of the day, in the Church of England.

25 Arthur Giardelli, interview with JDS, 1996.

26 Giardelli to FP, November 2 [1933].

27 In Giardelli's letter to Porter of November 2 [1933] he wrote, "Before I send this letter I shall re-read the poem you gave me to see how time has changed – if it has – my thoughts in that." He added later in the letter, "I have re-read your poem again and feel that you paint better than you write."

28 Fyodor Dostoyevsky, *The Possessed*, trans. Constance Garnett (New York: Modern Library, 1936), pp. 632-33.

29 Dostoyevsky, *The Possessed*, pp. 632-33.

30 Letter to Giardelli, [n.d.] 1958.

31 See André Gide, *The Immoralist*, trans. Richard Howard (New York: Vintage, 1996); Jean Genet, *Querelle*, trans. Anselm Hollo (New York: Grove, 1989).

32 Arthur Giardelli, interview with JDS, 1996.

33 Arthur Giardelli to FP, "2nd November" [1933].

34 The Piot frescoes have recently been "rediscovered"; they are now visible by appointment in the Biblioteca Berenson.

35 John Walker to FP, October 1, 1952: "I hope some day you will come to Washington and that we can look at the pictures in the gallery together. You remember the fun we had in Vienna?"

36 Arthur Giardelli, interview with JDS, 1996.

37 Letter to Arthur Giardelli, [n.d. 1957].

38 Giardelli to FP, February 2, 1958.

5

Home to America and Marriage

1 Letter to John Ashbery, [n.d.] 1957.

2 Letter to RWP, February 11 [1932].

3 Letter to Alan Wald, [n.d.] 1974.

4 Letter to RWP, December 12 [1932].

5 Letter to AEP, [January 1932].

6 Letter to RWP, February 11 [1932].

7 Letter to RWP, February 15 [1932].

8 Letter to RWP, [n.d.] 1932.

9 Frank Rogers to his family, 1932. FFP-AAA.

10 Letter to RWP, [n.d.] 1932.

11 Letter to RWP, February 22 [1932].

12 James Merrill, *A Different Person: A Memoir* (New York: Knopf, 1993), pp. 108-9.

13 Letter to RWP, Sunday, February 28 [1932].

14 Merrill: *A Different Person*, pp. 108-9.

15 Porter misquotes Dickinson; the word "doors" should be "valves." The punctuation and indentation are also inaccurate.

16 Letter to RWP, March 25, 1932.

17 Letter to Alan Wald, [n.d.] 1974.

18 Letter to AEP, [n.d.] 1932.

19 "Morra accompanied us on most of the trip [through Spain in 1929], sometimes driving with us, sometimes going by train to places not included in our program. A delightful companion and a helpful one too through his fair knowledge of the language." Nicky Mariano, *Forty Years of Berenson* (New York: Knopf, 1968), p. 207.

20 Arthur Giardelli, interview with JDS, 1996. Information on Giardelli can be found in Meic Stephens, ed., *Artists in Wales* (Gwasg Gomer: Ilandysul, 1971), p. 80.

21 Arthur Giardelli, interview with JDS, 1996.

22 Porter's reference to "naming the cow" describes their introduction five years earlier, when Ruth Porter brought Fairfield Porter to lunch at Anne Channing's home (see Chapter 2).

23 Letter to AEP, May 21, 1932.

24 Barbara Birch, interview with JDS, 1996.

25 Anne Porter, *An Altogether Different Language: Poems, 1934-1994*, (Cambridge, Mass.: Zoland Books, 1994), p. 22.

26 Anne Porter, interview with JDS, 1996.

27 Anne Porter, note to JDS, 1998.

28 Anne Porter, note to JDS, 1998.

29 AEP to KMC, [Summer 1932].

30 AEP to KMC, July [n.d.] 1932.

31 Letter to AEP, September 9, 1932.

32 Letter to AEP September [n.d.] 1932.

33 Anne Porter, note to JDS, 1998; AEP to KMC, September [n.d.] 1938.

34 AEP to KMC, October [n.d.] 1932; Anne Porter interview with JDS, 1996.

35 AEP to KMC, November 1, 1932.

36 Anne Porter, interview with JDS; see also David Shapiro, "Fairfield Porter's Quiet Revolution," *Art and Antiques*, n.s., 7, 3 (1990): 110-15, 166-68.

37 Anne Porter, interview with JDS, 1996.

38 Anne Porter interview with JDS, 1996.

39 Anne Porter, interview with JDS, 1996.

40 Anne Porter, note to JDS, 1998.

41 KMC to RWP, April 13, 1933. Anne Porter Papers.

42 Letter to AEP, April 22, 1933.

43 Anne Porter, interview with JDS, 1996.

44 AEP to KMC, May 4, 1933. "Fairfield's show looks well at the jewelry store. I am proud of it." AEP to KMC, Spring 1933.

45 AEP to KMC, May 25, 1933.

46 Howard Devree, "In the Galleries," *The New York Times*, May 14, 1933, a review of dual exhibition with Simeon Braguin at the offices of Theodore A. Kohn and Son.

47 AEP to KMC, June 1933.

48 Letter to Dick Freeman, October 28, 1972.

49 Letter to Alfred Stieglitz, July 31, 1933.

50 The poem cycle published by Anne Channing in the October 1934 issue of *Poetry* magazine was entitled "Five Songs of Growth." The poems are "The Mother," "Wife of Time," "Conspiracy," "Early Respite," and "Evening Song."

51 AEP to KMC, October 30, 1933.

52 AEP to KMC, November 19, 1933.

53 AEP to KMC, [n.d.] 1934.

54 AEP to KMC, [n.d.] 1934.

55 AEP to KMC, January 25, 1934.

Murals and Babies

1 Statement of *Rebel Arts* dated January 24, 1936, and featuring Fairfield Porter, Artist and Critic, as a member of its national advisory committee. John Wheelwright Papers, John Hay Library, Brown University (hereafter JW-JHL).

2 David Shapiro and Cecile Shapiro, "Abstract Expressionism: The Politics of Apolitical Painting," in *Pollock and After: The Critical Debate*, ed. Francis Frascina (New York: Icon / Harper and Row, 1985), pp. 135-36.

3 Leon Trotsky, "Art and Politics," *Partisan Review* (August-September 1938): 10.

4 Letter to Alan Wald, [n.d.] 1974.

5 The mural is now lost.

6 AEP to KMC, [n.d.] 1934.

7 Letter to RWP, April [n.d.] 1934.

8 AEP to KMC, May 1, 1934.

9 Fairfield Porter, "Murals for Workers," *AIIOT*, p. 242.

10 AEP to KMC, June [n.d.] 1934.

11 Anne Porter, note to JDS, 1999.

12 AEP to KMC, August 6, 1934.

13 AEP to KMC, August 20, 1934.

14 AEP to KMC, [n.d.] 1935, reference to Alex Haberstroh.

15 "Hail Mary" and "Sun, Moon, Star," Alfred Kreymborg, Lewis Mumford, and Paul Rosenfeld, eds., *The American Caravan* (New York: Harpers, 1935), pp. 65, 66.

16 AEP to FP, [n.d.] 1934. Anne Porter Papers.

17 Letter to RWP, January 22, 1935.

18 Anne Porter, interview with JDS, 1996.

19 Anne Porter, letter to JDS, 1998.

20 AEP to KMC, February 13, 1935.

21 Letter to AEP, [n.d.].

22 Letter to RWP, [1935].

23 Letter to RWP, March 13, 1935.

24 Two mural designs were done by Porter for art competitions in 1933-34 for the Interior Department, the first for the Treasury Department Art Projects and the second for the Justice Department competition. This information comes from the National Archives (RG 121 - Public Buildings Service) and was brought to my attention by Joan Ludman, author of the Fairfield Porter catalogue raisonné (manuscript in preparation).

25 Cummings interview, 1968.

26 Letter to AEP, [n.d.] 1935. Anne Porter Papers.

27 Letter to RFP, March 13, 1935.

28 AEP to KMC, December 1935.

29 Anne Porter, note to JDS, 1999. See Anne Porter, *An Altogether Different Language: Poems, 1934-1994* (Cambridge, Mass.: Zoland Books, 1994), p. 67.

30 AEP to KMC, January 11, 1936.

31 Letter to AEP, [n.d.].

32 Cummings interview, 1968.

33 A very good biography that chronicles Wheelwright's radical politics is Alan Wald, *The Revolutionary Imagination: The Poetry and Politics of John Wheelwright and Sherry Mangan* (Chapel Hill: University of North Carolina Press, 1993).

34 John Ashbery, "In the American Grain" (review), *New York Review of Books*, February 22, 1973.

35 Wald, *The Revolutionary Imagination*, p. 314.

36 "[Wheelwright's] only explicit statement about his sexual views in later life is in a letter he sent to Kenneth Patchen after reading a draft version of

The Journal of Albion Moonlight. He bitterly attacks those 'who split the monism of love into the dismal triad of heterosexuality, bisexuality, and homosexuality.' … [but] homoerotic imagery is evident in the sonnet sequence *Mirrors of Venus* and sexual themes are explicitly manifest in the Doubting Thomas 'novel.' Elsewhere Wheelwright's complex illusions symbols and systems embody tensions that may be correlated to sexual energies." Wald, *The Revolutionary Imagination*, pp. 100-101.

37 On Wheelwright's tragic family history and his melancholia see Wald, *The Revolutionary Imagination*, p. 101.

38 Wald, *The Revolutionary Imagination*, pp. 316-17.

39 Letter to John Wheelwright, [n.d.]. In the last years of his life, when reviewing Wheelwright's letters for the historian Alan Wald, Porter mistakenly wrote Wald that the poem written for Porter by Wheelwright was the poem "Mirror," which describes a lovers' quarrel. But Wheelwright wrote many letters and poems on the verso of draft versions of poems (to save paper), and the poem he wrote about Porter is "Eye Opener." Porter's confusion can be explained by the fact that the original of this document (which can be found in JW-JHL) features "Eye Opener" handwritten in Wheelwright's hand, inscribed at the bottom "FP from JB," on the back of a typewritten draft of "Mirror."
    Both poems were privately published in 1938 in *Mirrors of Venus: A Novel in Sonnets.* The final version of this poem, published as "Eye-Opener," is much more coherent than the version sent to Porter. For both poems, see *The Collected Poems of John Wheelwright*, ed. Alvin H. Rosenfeld (New York: New Directions, 1972) pp. 82, 95.

40 Cummings interview, 1968.

41 Wald, *The Revolutionary Imagination*, pp. 316-17.

42 Joan Ludman, *Fairfield Porter: A Catalogue Raisonné of His Prints* (Westbury, N.Y.: Highland House, 1981), p. 57.

43 Ludman, *Fairfield Porter*, pp. 48-59.

44 Wald, *The Revolutionary Imagination*, p. 93.

45 John Wheelwright to FP, [n.d.]. JW-JHL.

46 Letter to Wheelwright, [n.d.] 1936.

47 Letter to Wheelwright, [n.d.] 1936.

48 Wheelwright to FP, [n.d.]. JW-JHL.

49 Letter to Wheelwright, [n.d.].

50 Letter to Wheelwright, January [n.d.] 1936.

51 Letter to Wheelwright, [n.d.].

52 Anne Porter, interview with JDS, 1996.

53 Anne Porter, note to JDS, 1998.

54 Reports of Porter's sciatica exist throughout Anne Porter's correspondence with her mother.

7

Winnetka

1 Letter to John Wheelwright, October 29, 1936.

2 RWP to NPS, April 16, 1936.

3 AEP to KMC, October 15, 1936.

4 Anne Porter, interview with JDS, 1996.

5 RWP to NPS, April 4, 1936.

6 "We are selling my building at 2510 Cottage Grove Ave & James is cheerful about it. For $45,000, $15 down, $5 for the next 6 years. The land was bought by Dr. John F. Foster from the government. It was one of the few pieces of property in the city to have stayed so long in the same family." RWP to Michel Straus, December 14, 1936.

7 "Last month when all my money had to go for taxes I thought I ought not to spend the money. But perhaps it would be all right. It is hard to find out from James what the situation is." RWP to NPS, April 4, 1936.

8 AEP to KMC, October 15, 1936.

9 Letter to John Wheelwright, [n.d.].

10 Letter to KMC, January 18, 1937.

11 Anne Porter, interview with JDS, 1996.

12 "You would have been interested as Fairfield and I were, in meeting the head of the Chicago Bauhaus, and his wife, and hearing about the Bauhaus school … where Gropius teaches, I think … the course includes such things as learning to enlarge one's signature to 9x its visual size … it sounds perfectly sensible *when* Moholy-Nagy (the teacher) tells about it." AEP to KMC, January 31, 1938. Anne Porter remembers Porter's dislike of the Bauhaus and all that it stood for. Anne Porter, interview with JDS, 1996.

13 Letter to Arthur Giardelli, May 5, 1965.

14 Letter to John Wheelwright, November 5, 1937.

15 Letter to John Wheelwright, March 13, 1937.

16 RWP to NPS, April 1, 1937.

17 AEP to KMC, [n.d.].

18 Letter to John Wheelwright, [n.d.].

19 *Fairfield Porter: The Collected Poems, With Selected Drawings*, ed. John Yau (New York: Tibor de Nagy / The Promise of Learnings, 1985), p. 19.

20 Letter to James Schuyler, September 14 [1956?].

21 AEP to KMC, January 19, 1938.

22 Anne Porter, interview with JDS, 1996.

23 AEP to KMC, May 2, 1938.

24 Anne Porter, note to JDS, 1998. Anne Porter also indicated in this note that her untidiness was lifelong and had nothing to do with her relationship with her husband, despite a differing view by Laurence Porter in a letter to JDS, July 24-September 22, 1996.

25 RWP to Michel Straus, December 14, 1936; RWP to NPS, December 7, 1936.

26 RWP to NPS, March 21, 1938.

27 AEP to KMC, "April 6 and 8," 1937.

28 AEP to KMC, November 5, 1937.

29 Ilse Hamm Mattick, interview with JDS, 1997; Ellen Auerbach, interview with JDS, 1996.

30 RWP to NPS, April 4, 1936.

31 RWP to KMC, January 18, 1937.

32 Letter to John Wheelwright, March 13, 1937.

33 RWP to Michel Straus, December 25, 1936.

34 When revising an article, "New York Painting Only Yesterday," from *Art News* in 1957, for his collected essays *Art and Culture* (1961), Greenberg added a parenthesis: "Abstract art was the main issue among the painters I knew then [the late 1930s]; radical politics was on many people's minds but for them Social Realism was as dead as the American Scene. (Though that is not all, by far, that there was to politics in art in those years; someday it will have to be told how 'anti-Stalinism,' which started out more or less as 'Trotskyism' turned into art for art's sake, and thereby cleared the way, heroically, for what was to come.)" Greenberg, "New York Painting Only Yesterday," in *Pollock and After: The Critical*

Debate, ed. Francis Frascina (New York: Icon / Harper and Row, 1985), p. 98.

35 Leon Trotsky, "Art and Politics in Our Epoch," cited in Alan Wald, *The New York Intellectuals: The Rise and Decline of the Anti-Stalinist Left from the 1930's to the 1980's* (Chapel Hill: University of North Carolina Press, 1987), p. 145.

36 Letter to John Wheelwright, [n.d.].

37 Cummings interview, 1968.

38 "F. & his mother & his wife were sued by the Hearst papers for contributing to a boycott over their support of Franco in the Civil War in Spain while F. was living in Winnetka." Anne Porter, note added to Eliot Porter's letter to FP, February 24 [1939?]. FPP-AAA.

39 Eliot Porter to FP, February 24 [1939?]. FPP-AAA.

40 Papers filed by JDS on behalf of Anne Porter under the Freedom of Information Act revealed that while the FBI never kept a file on Porter himself, a file containing his name, identifying him as an officer of the American Artists' Congress in 1936 and listing his home address as 1077 Sheridan Road, has been kept on file with the U.S. Government to the present day.

41 Cummings interview, 1968.

42 Cummings interview, 1968.

43 Ilse Hamm Mattick, interview with JDS, 1997.

44 For more on Mattick, by a colleague, see Michael Buckmiller, "Paul Mattick," *Root and Branch: A Libertarian Socialist Journal*, 10 (February 1982). Most of the issue is devoted to Mattick and his work.

45 Ilse Hamm Mattick, telephone conversation with JDS, 1998.

46 Cummings interview, 1968.

47 Ilse Hamm Mattick, interview with JDS, 1997.

48 Letter to Alfred Stieglitz, May 22, 1939.

49 Cummings interview, 1968.

50 Ilse Hamm Mattick, interview with JDS, 1997.

51 Letter to John Wheelwright, March 13, 1937.

52 Letter to John Wheelwright, [n.d.].

53 John Wheelwright to FP, November 26 [1938?].

54 John Wheelwright to FP, November 26, [1938?].

55 Cummings interview, 1968.

56 RWP to NPS, February 15, 1939.

57 "Fairfield has all his paintings - oil & watercolors -
    at the high school. Quite a good chance for him with
    the State Convention of the L[eague of] W[omen]
    V[oters] in Winnetka this week & all the delegates
    going to look in the art department of the school."
    RWP to NPS, May 9, 1938.

58 Cummings interview, 1968.

59 Eliot Porter, *Eliot Porter*, exh. cat (Boston: Little, Brown;
    Fort Worth: Amon Carter Museum, 1987), p. 27.

60 Eliot Porter, *Eliot Porter*, p. 27.

61 Cummings interview, 1968.

62 Cummings interview, 1968.

63 Fairfield Porter, "Vuillard, Bonnard," *AIIOT*,
    pp. 169-70.

64 Cummings interview, 1968.

65 Letter to KMC, January 9, 1938.

8

Three Homes in Westchester

1 RWP to AEP, [n.d.]. Anne Porter Papers.

2 AEP to KMC, November 21, 1938.

3 AEP to KMC, November 21, 1938.

4 "[James] speaks of the island & of taking things –
    like plates for the *Hippocampus* – so I think there's
    no doubt about [our going this summer]. But he
    does less & less & so I think the trips on the
    Hippocampus will be gentle ones, & we shall have to
    make his scullery work light – as light as he will
    let us!" RWP to NPS, February 15, 1939.

5 AEP to KMC, June 29, 1939.

6 Cummings interview, 1968.

7 AEP to KMC, July 19, 1939.

8 Anne Porter, interview with JDS, 1996.

9 AEP to KMC, August 1, 1939.

10 *New York Panorama: A Companion to the WPA
    Guide to New York City* (New York: Pantheon, 1984),
    pp. 479-80.

11 AEP to KMC, October 2, 1939.

12 Letter to Paul Mattick, October 3 [1939].

13 Letter to Paul Mattick, October 3 [1939].

14 Cummings interview, 1968.

15 Letter to Alfred Stieglitz, [n.d.].

16 Anne Porter, letter to JDS, 1998.

17 Anne Porter, interview with JDS, 1996. Ilse Hamm
    Mattick and Ellen Auerbach, also in interviews with
    JDS (1997), agreed that this was the consensus among
    the Council Communist group.

18 T. J. Clark, "Clement Greenberg's Theory of Art,"
    in *Pollock and After: The Critical Debate*, ed. Francis
    Frascina (New York: Icon / Harper and Row, 1985),
    p. 49.

19 Paul Mattick to FP, September 23, 1940.

20 Fred Orton and Griselda Pollock, "Avant-Gardes and
    Partisans Reviewed," in *Pollock and After*, pp. 167-81.

21 Letter to Paul Mattick, September 20, 1940.

22 Cummings interview, 1968.

23 Letter to Alan Wald, August 5, 1974.

24 Jane Freilicher, interview with JDS.

25 For the full text see *AIIOT*, p. 239.

26 John Crowe Ransom to FP, December 22, 1942.

27 Anne Porter, conversation with JDS, September 1998.

28 Porter to the editors of *Partisan Review*, in *Partisan
    Review* (January-February 1941): 77. Cited in John T.
    Spike, *Fairfield Porter: An American Classic* (New
    York: Abrams, 1992), p. 67.

29 Letter to Paul Mattick, July 4, 1941.

30 Clement Greenberg, "Avant-Garde and Kitsch," in
    Pollock and After, p. 51.

31 Letter to Paul Mattick, December 20, 1939.

32 Rudy Burckhardt and Edith Schloss both remark
    upon Ilse Hamm's beauty. Rudy Burckhardt,
    interview with JDS, 1996; Edith Schloss Memoir, 1984.
    The Schloss memoir was read by Schloss on June 2,
    1984, at the Parrish Art Museum, Southampton, N.Y.
    A copy exists in the Anne Porter Papers and is
    reprinted by permission of the author.

33 Ilse Hamm Mattick, interview with JDS, 1997.
    Given her background, she had experienced, she said,
    "neither childhood nor adolescence."

34 Ilse Hamm Mattick, interview with JDS, 1997.

35 Ilse Hamm Mattick, interview with JDS, 1997; repeated
    in phone conversation with JDS, September 1998.

36 Ilse Hamm Mattick to Fairfield Porter, September 16 [1940].

37 Anne Porter, letter to JDS, 1998.

38 Anne Porter, interview with JDS, 1996.

39 Letter to Paul Mattick, December 5, 1940.

40 Letter to RWP, March 26, 1941.

41 Letter to Paul Mattick, July 27, 1941.

42 Ilse Hamm Mattick, interview with JDS, 1997.

43 Ellen Auerbach, interview with JDS, 1996.

44 Ellen Auerbach, interview with JDS, 1996.

45 Ilse Hamm Mattick, interview with JDS, 1997.

46 Two of these poems have survived in the Anne Porter Papers.

47 Ilse Hamm Mattick, interview with JDS, 1997.

48 Ilse Hamm Mattick, interview with JDS, 1997.

49 Anne Porter, interview with JDS, 1996.

50 Letter to Paul Mattick, July 4, 1941.

51 Letter to Paul Mattick, July 27, 1941.

52 Paul Mattick to FP, August 1, 1941.

53 AEP to KMC, September 22, 1941.

54 Ilse Hamm Mattick, interview with JDS, 1997.

9
Househunting and a "Bivouac"

1 For a brief biography of Rexroth, see Eric Mottram, introduction to *The Rexroth Reader* (London: Jonathan Cape, 1972).

2 Letter to AEP, [n.d.].

3 Letter to AEP, October 23, 1941.

4 Ilse Hamm [Mattick] to FP, October 26, 1941.

5 Ilse Hamm [Mattick] to FP, October 26, 1941.

6 Letter to AEP, [n.d.].

7 Letter to AEP, [n.d.]

8 Letter to Paul Mattick, November 27, 1941.

9 Letter to Paul Mattick, [n.d.].

10 Anne Porter, note to JDS, 1998.

11 Anne Porter, interview with JDS, 1996.

12 Ilse Hamm Mattick, interview with JDS, 1997.

13 AEP to KMC, January 21, 1942.

14 Ilse Hamm Mattick, interview with JDS, 1997.

15 Anne Porter, interview with JDS, 1996.

16 Ilse Hamm Mattick, interview with JDS, 1997.

17 According to a letter to Arthur Giardelli (May 5, 1965), Porter did not return to Chicago for twenty-two years after his mother's death. This timeline suggests that Porter returned to Chicago, if only briefly, at the time of his mother's death or shortly thereafter. Porter mistakenly recalls in the same letter that his mother died in 1943.

18 "We wish to think that the analysis could help you a bit. Let us help healing the wounds. We love you very much. Pit and Walter." Ellen and Walter Auerbach to FP, June 2, 1942.

19 Letter to AEP, June 21, 1942.

20 Letter to AEP, June 15, 1942.

21 Letter to AEP, [n.d.] 1942.

22 Anne Porter, note to JDS, 1998.

23 Ilse Hamm Mattick, interview with JDS, 1997.

24 AEP to FP, [n.d.] 1942; letter to AEP, August 25, 1942.

25 AEP to FP, [n.d.] 1942.

26 AEP to FP, [n.d.] 1942.

27 Anne Porter, note to JDS, 1998.

28 Anne Porter, interview with JDS, 1996.

29 Edith Schloss Memoir, 1984.

30 Anne Porter, interview with JDS, 1996.

31 Anne Porter, conversation with JDS, 1996.

32 Letter to Arthur Giardelli, January 23, 1958.

33 Affidavit from the Studios of Walter Dorwin Teague, 444 Madison Avenue, March 13, 1944. FPP-AAA.

34 John T. Spike, *Fairfield Porter: An American Classic* (New York: Abrams, 1992), p. 75.

35 Cummings interview, 1968.

36 Barbara Birch, interview with JDS, 1996.

37 Edith Schloss Memoir, 1984. Schloss's memory is faulty concerning dates, so though she thinks the first meeting took place in 1942, it was probably later.

38 Ilse Hamm Mattick, interview with JDS, 1997.

39 Ilse Hamm Mattick, interview with JDS, 1997.

40 AEP to KMC, December 20, 1945.

41 Thomas B. Hess, "U.S. Painting: Some Recent Directions," *Art News Annual*, 25 (1956): 75-76.

42 Edith Schloss Memoir, 1984.

43 Ilse Hamm Mattick, interview with JDS, 1997. Ilse's son, Paul Mattick Jr., also remembers Porter giving him a chess set at age five, roughly the time that Anne Porter gave birth to her daughter Katharine (1949).

44 Anne Porter, letter to JDS, 1998.

45 The man's identity has been withheld as a courtesy to Anne Porter.

46 Anne Porter, letter to JDS, 1998.

47 Anne Porter, letter to JDS, 1998.

10

Living and Painting in New York

1 Rudy Burckhardt, interview with JDS, 1995.

2 Letter to RWP, [n.d.].

3 Anne Porter, interview with JDS, 1996.

4 Anne Porter, interview with JDS, 1996.

5 Anne Porter was mistaken for a governess when she went to retrieve her son Laurence from the Dalton School (Anne Porter, interview with JDS, 1996); Mary Johnson, the Porters' neighbor in Southampton, mistook Anne and Fairfield for caretakers at their first meeting, in 1949 (Dr. Mary Johnson, interview with JDS, 1995).

6 AEP to KMC, July 14, 1943.

7 AEP to KMC, June 24, 1943.

8 Anne Porter, letter to JDS, 1998.

9 Anne Porter, letter to JDS, 1998.

10 AEP to KMC, October 11, 1945.

11 AEP to KMC, March 28, 1945.

12 Anne Porter, interview with JDS, 1998.

13 Edith Schloss Memoir, 1984.

14 Edith Schloss Memoir, 1984.

15 Edith Schloss Memoir, 1984.

16 Anne Porter, interview with JDS, 1996.

17 Anne Porter, interview with JDS, 1996.

18 Maroger's recipe was more confusing; this one was developed by his assistant, Frank Redelin, who sent the recipe to Porter in a letter dated December 29, 1966. Anne Porter recalled black lead being used rather than white lead during the 1940s. Anne Porter Papers.

19 Anne Porter, interview with JDS, 1996.

20 Laurence Porter memoir, 1996.

21 Cummings interview, 1968.

22 Porter preferred the Venetian variety of Maroger's medium: "Also during the War he studied in night classes at the Parsons School with Jacques Maroger, whose 'recreation' of a 'Venetian Medium' he still uses." Schuyler Chronology of Fairfield Porter. JS-UCSD.

23 Cummings interview, 1968.

24 James Schuyler Chronology of Fairfield Porter. JS-UCSD.

25 I am indebted to the painter Stuart Shils for this observation, made as we examined the Tiepolo picture together in the Metropolitan Museum of Art in the spring of 1997.

26 Cummings interview, 1968.

27 James Schuyler Chronology of Fairfield Porter. JS-UCSD.

28 Cummings interview, 1968.

29 James Schuyler Chronology of Fairfield Porter. JS-UCSD.

30 John T. Spike, *Fairfield Porter: An American Classic* (New York: Abrams, 1992), p. 277 n. 129.

31 Cummings interview, 1968.

32 "I still like those Tintorettos as much as I did in 1931, but what I didn't see before are Tiepolo frescos; they have modern light. The light of Venice has not yet been adequately represented, not by anyone ... I will be glad to get back to painting again in the U.S." Postcard to James Schuyler, [n.d., postmark 1967]. JS-UCSD.

33 Letter to KMC, February 6, 1947.

34 Letter to KMC, February 13, 1947.

35 AEP to KMC, December 3, 1946.

36 Cummings interview, 1968.

37 Anatole Broyard, *Kafka Was the Rage: A Greenwich Village Memoir* (New York: Vintage, 1997), p. 45.

38 Anne Porter's bill for psychoanalysis in 1944 was $1,230, suggesting that she received over two hundred hours of treatment, breaking down to roughly four hours per week over the course of a year. Statement signed by Dr. Erich Kraft in the Anne Porter Papers. In Anne Porter's recollection, "He charged five dollars an hour, which was eventually raised to twelve when he became famous." Anne Porter, interview with JDS, 1996.

39 Letter to Rackstraw Downes, May 16, 1974.

40 Cummings interview, 1968.

41 Cummings interview, 1968.

42 Letter to KMC, February 6, 1947.

43 Dr. Erich Kraft to Anne Porter, [n.d.] 1953. Anne Porter Papers.

44 Dr. Margaret Mahler to Anne Porter, June 5, 1952. Anne Porter Papers.

45 AEP to KMC, January 2, 1947.

46 Broyard, *Kafka Was the Rage*, p. 45.

47 AEP to KMC, February 1, 1947.

48 AEP to KMC, November 11, 1946.

49 Anne Porter, interview with JDS, 1996.

50 The *Pink Lady* (circa 1944) appears as a color reproduction with a photo credit attributing the work to the collection of Fairfield Porter, in Thomas Hess, *De Kooning* (New York: Braziller, 1959), plate 37. Porter's 1955 reference to *Pink Woman* (1943) – *AIIOT*, p. 180, in his 1955 essay on de Kooning – is clearly in reference to the *Pink Lady* (circa 1944).

51 Edith Schloss Memoir, 1984.

52 Fairfield Porter, "De Kooning," *AIIOT*, pp. 180-81.

53 "There is the element of excitement and vividness that he loved in color and that connects him more to de Kooning than to … Vuillard." David Shapiro, "Fairfield Porter's Quiet Revolution," *Art and Antiques*, n.s., 7, 3 (1990): 110-15, 166-68.

54 Edith Schloss Memoir, 1984.

55 Edith Schloss Memoir, 1984.

56 Ilse Hamm Mattick, interview with JDS, 1997.

57 Broyard, *Kafka Was the Rage*, p. 29.

58 Edwin Denby, cited in Hess, *De Kooning*, p. 116.

59 Eliot Porter, *Summer Island: Penobscot Country* (San Francisco: Sierra Club, 1966), p. 19.

60 Eliot Porter dates the building of the farmhouse (1926) with the arrival of the Howards and says they stayed twenty-five years (*Summer Island*, p. 32). But records kept by Stephen Porter say the Howards departed in 1944.

61 Eliot Porter, *Summer Island*, p. 33.

62 AEP to KMC, August [n.d.] 1946 .

63 AEP to KMC, July 16, 1946.

64 Edith Schloss Memoir, 1984.

65 AEP to KMC, September [n.d.] 1949.

66 Laurence Porter, letter to JDS, July 24- September 22, 1996.

67 AEP to KMC, July 14, 1947.

68 Anne Porter, note to JDS, 1998.

69 Ilse Hamm Mattick, interview with JDS, 1997.

70 Ilse Hamm Mattick, interview with JDS, 1997; Anne Porter, interview with JDS, 1996.

11

Moving to Southampton

1 Anne Porter, interview with JDS.

2 Porter had purchased two other homes during the 1940s, one in Westchester and another in Sand Brook, New Jersey, but financial complications had prevented his moving into either. Anne Porter, interview with JDS, 1996.

3 Prescott Schutz, quoted in Whitney Balliet, "An Akimbo Quality," *The New Yorker*, March 14, 1983, pp. 140-45.

4 Jane Freilicher, interview with JDS, 1997.

5 Letter to Arthur Giardelli, October 28, 1970.

6 Balliet, "An Akimbo Quality," p. 140.

7 Balliet, "An Akimbo Quality," p. 140.

8 Copies of the deed of purchase and a survey of the property can be found in the Anne Porter Papers. Additional information about the house was given by Anne Porter (interview with JDS, 1996).

9 Letter to James Schuyler, [n.d.].

10 Anne Porter, note to JDS, 1998.

11 See, for example, *Le Lampe* (circa 1899), *Les Poires* (1899?), and *La Table* (1925) in Sara Whitfield, *Bonnard*, exh. cat. (London: Tate Gallery Publishing, 1998), plates 12, 14, and 50.

12 Anne Porter, in a note to JDS, wrote that Porter did remove at least one stove from the house, but John Button's photographs of the house, taken in the early 1960s, show Anne Porter standing in a kitchen with three stoves: one cast-iron, one electric, and the Aga. John Button Papers, Henry W. and Albert A. Berg Collection of English and American Literature (hereafter Berg Collection), New York Public Library.

13 Barbara Guest, interview with JDS, 1993.

14 Fairfield Porter, "Graham," *AIIOT*, pp. 214-19.

15 Fairfield Porter, "Graham," *AIIOT*, p. 214.

16 Anne Porter, interview with JDS, 1996.

17 See Schuyler letter to Donald Droll accompanying the incomplete James Schuyler Chronology of Fairfield Porter. JS-UCSD. Also see Cummings interview, 1968, for Porter's eventual lack of interest in John Marin.

18 Laurence Porter, letter to JDS, July 24-September 22, 1996.

19 Jane Freilicher, interview with JDS, 1997.

20 Cummings interview, 1968.

21 Edith Schloss Memoir, 1984.

22 Penny Wright, interview with JDS, 1993.

23 Anne Porter, interview with JDS, 1996. Princess Obolensky, née Alice Astor, was the daughter of John Jacob Astor and the second wife of Prince Serge Obolensky. Prince Serge Obolensky was also a frequent visitor to Southampton during the 1950s. See Serge Obolensky, *One Man in His Time* (New York: McDowell, Obolensky, 1958).

24 Letter to Claire White, [n.d.] 1973.

25 Laurence Porter, letter to JDS, July 24-September 22, 1996.

26 Laurence Porter Memoir, 1996.

27 Anne Porter, letter to JDS, 1998.

28 Laurence Porter, letter to JDS, July 24-September 22, 1996.

29 Laurence Porter, letter to JDS, July 24-September 22, 1996.

30 Letter to Kee and Hal Channing, January 8, 1950.

31 Laurence Porter Memoir, 1996.

32 Letter to Arthur Giardelli, [n.d.] 1958.

33 Anne Porter, interview with JDS, 1996.

34 Anne Porter, letter to JDS, 1998.

35 Anne Porter, letter to JDS, 1998.

36 Laurence Porter Memoir, 1996.

37 AEP to KMC, March [n.d.] 1951.

38 Anne Porter, interview with JDS, 1996.

39 Anne Porter, interview with JDS, 1996.

40 He was in Rome for a year on a G.I. scholarship. Letter to Aline Kilham Porter, [n.d., circa 1950-51].

41 Jane Freilicher, interview with Barbara Schikler, August 4 and 5, 1987, Archives of American Art (hereafter Freilicher, Schikler interview, 1987).

42 Ellen Auerbach, interview with JDS, 1996.

43 Freilicher, Schikler interview, 1987.

44 John Gruen, *The Party's Over Now* (Wainscott, N.Y.: Pushcart, 1967), pp. 130-31.

45 Freilicher, Schikler interview, 1987.

46 Carl Little, "An Interview with James Schuyler," *Agni*, 37 (1993): 152-82.

47 Laurence Porter Memoir, 1996; Anne Porter, interview with JDS, 1996.

48 Porter spoke on the panel "The Artist as Writer" in early 1953, according to a letter from the period. AEP to KMC, [n.d.].

49 Cummings interview, 1968.

50 Cummings interview, 1968.

51 James Schuyler Chronology of Fairfield Porter. JS-UCSD.

52 Cummings interview, 1968.

53 AEP to KMC, September 3, 1951.

54 AEP to KMC, [n.d.] 1951.

55 On Tibor de Nagy, see Laura DeCoppet and Alan Jones, *The Art Dealers: The Powers Behind the Scene Tell How the Art World Really Works* (New York: C. N. Potter / Crown, 1984); and James Merrill, *A Different Life: A Memoir* (New York: Knopf, 1993), p. 253.

56 Jane Freilicher, interview with JDS, 1996.

57 Freilicher, Schikler interview, 1987.

58 Thomas B. Hess, "U.S. Painting: Some Recent Directions," *Art News Annual*, 25 (1956): 76.

59 David Shapiro and Cecile Shapiro, "Abstract Expressionism: The Politics of Apolitical Painting," in *Pollock and After: The Critical Debate*, ed. Francis Frascina (New York: Icon / Harper and Row, 1985), pp. 143-44.

60 Shapiro and Shapiro, "Abstract Expressionism," p. 147.

61 Peter Schjeldahl, foreword to *Recent Work by Fairfield Porter*, exh. cat. (New York: Hirschl and Adler Galleries, 1972).

12

Young Friends

1 Larry Rivers with Arnold Weinstein, *What Did I Do? The Unauthorized Autobiography* (New York: Aaron Asher Books / HarperCollins, 1992), p. 270.

2 Letter to Lawrence "Larry" Campbell, June 15, 1952.

3 The Vuillard monograph, published in France in 1946 and written by André Chastel, remains (in tatters) in the Anne Porter Papers.

4 Fairfield Porter, introduction to John Ashbery Reading at the Guggenheim, January 1973. FPP-AAA.

5 David Shapiro, conversation with JDS, spring 1997. Porter made this comment to Shapiro.

6 Jane Freilicher, interview with JDS, 1997.

7 This version of "The Young Man" (there are several) comes from the Anne Porter Papers.

8 Letter to Larry Rivers, [n.d.].

9 Letter to James Schuyler, July 7, 1960. Porter revised the poem throughout the 1950s; the draft he sent in the 1960 letter had been written in 1958. The earliest draft of the poem dates from shortly after Porter's first meeting with Ashbery in 1952 and was mentioned to Larry Rivers in a letter dating from shortly after Rivers's suicide attempt in November 1952.

10 Cummings interview, 1968.

11 Letter to Arthur Giardelli, May 25, 1958.

12 Cummings interview, 1968.

13 Letter to Aline Kilham Porter, December 25, 1952.

14 Laurence Porter letter to JDS, July 24-September 22, 1996.

15 Anne Porter, interview with JDS.

16 Laurence Porter letter to JDS, July 24-September 22, 1996.

17 Laurence Porter, letter to JDS, July 22-September 24, 1996.

18 Laurence Porter, letter to JDS, July 22-September 24, 1996.

19 Fairfield Porter, "The Loved Son," in *Fairfield Porter: Collected Poems, with selected Drawings*, ed. John Yau (New York: Tibor de Nagy / The Promise of Learnings, 1985), p. 18.

20 Letter to Aline Kilham Porter, Christmas, 1952.

21 Letter to Aline Kilham Porter, Christmas, 1952.

22 Jane Freilicher, interview with JDS, 1997.

23 AEP to KMC, October 1, 1952.

24 Anne Porter, note to JDS, 1998.

25 Cummings interview, 1968.

26 Edith Schloss Memoir, 1984.

27 Lawrence Campbell, "Reviews and Previews," *Art News* (October 1952): 45.

28 James Fitzsimmons, "Fifty-seventh Street in Review," *The Arts Digest*, November 1, 1952, pp. 19-20.

29 Letter to Aline Kilham Porter, Christmas, 1952.

30 See Brad Gooch, *City Poet: The Life and Times of Frank O'Hara* (New York: Knopf, 1993), p. 228.

31 Cummings interview, 1968.

32 Rivers, *What Did I Do?* p. 266.

33 Anne Porter, note to JDS, 1998. It is also possible that Porter, in an act of discretion, spoke in veiled terms of his relationship to Ilse Hamm and Paul Mattick and that Rivers took this description to be a description of his relationship to Anne Porter.

34 Letter to Lawrence "Larry" Campbell, June 14, 1952.

35 Letter to Larry Rivers, [n.d.].

36 Letter to Larry Rivers, [n.d.].

37 Rivers, *What Did I Do?* p. 267.

38 Rivers, *What Did I Do?* p. 269.

39 Rivers, *What Did I Do?* p. 269.

40 Rivers, *What Did I Do?* p. 272.

41 Letter to Larry Rivers, [n.d.].

42 Letter to Lawrence Campbell, June 1952.

43 Letter to James Schuyler, Wednesday, [n.d.]. JS-UCSD.

44 Jane Freilicher, Schikler interview, 1987. The brackets are in the original transcript.

45 AEP to KMC, April 28, 1953.

46 Laurence Porter Memoir, 1996.

47 There is a copy of the film at the Parrish Art Museum, Southampton, N.Y. Burckhardt still has the original.

48 Rudy Burckhardt, interview with JDS.

49 Henry Geldzahler, conversation with JDS, July 1993.

50 Edith Schloss Memoir, 1984.

51 Anne Porter, interview with JDS, 1996.

52 AEP to KMC, July 1953.

53 AEP to KMC, July 1953.

54 Gooch, *City Poet*, pp. 241-42, 244.

55 AEP to KMC, August 31, 1953.

56 AEP to KMC, August 31, 1953.

13

Poetry, Painting, and a Very Busy Summer

1 Fairfield Porter, "Joseph Cornell," *AIIOT*, p. 49.

2 Letter to Laurence Porter, March 10, 1956.

3 AEP to KMC, February 27, 1954.

4 Letter to Thomas B. Hess (his editor at *Art News*), December 19, 1955.

5 Fairfield Porter, "Impressionism and Painting Today," *AIIOT*, p. 113.

6 Fairfield Porter, "Whistler, Morisot, Corinth," *AIIOT*, p. 153.

7 Fairfield Porter, "Whistler, Morisot, Corinth," *AIIOT*, p. 154.

8 Fairfield Porter, "Vuillard, Bonnard," *AIIOT*, p. 170.

9 Fairfield Porter, "To Travelling as the Sole Concern," in *Fairfield Porter: The Collected Poems, with Selected Drawings*, ed. John Yau (New York: Tibor de Nagy / The Promise of Learnings, 1985), p. 82.

10 Fairfield Porter, "Sea Breeze" (translated from Mallarmé), in *Fairfield Porter: The Collected Poems*, p. 79.

11 Fairfield Porter, "Art and Knowledge," *AIIOT*, p. 261.

12 Fairfield Porter, "The Short Review," *AIIOT*, pp. 167-69. Porter quotes Tolstoy's essay "What Is Art?" in *AIIOT*, p. 236.

13 Mallarmé, quoted in letter to James Schuyler, [n.d.]. Frank O'Hara, quoted in Thomas Meyer, "Glistening Torsos, Sandwiches, and Coca-Cola," *Parnassus: Poetry in Review* (Fall-Winter 1977): 248.

14 Anne Porter, interview with JDS, 1996. In a letter to Arthur Giardelli, July 24, 1965, Porter credits "no ideas except in things" to William Carlos Williams.

15 Porter, "Vuillard, Bonnard," *AIIOT*, p. 170.

16 Cummings interview, 1968.

17 O'Hara to Porter, quoted in Gooch, *City Poet: The Life and Times of Frank O'Hara* (New York: Knopf, 1993), p. 268.

18 Helen Vendler, "Frank O'Hara: The Virtue of the Alterable," *Parnassus: Poetry in Review* (Fall-Winter 1972): 237.

19 Dore Ashton, "Fortnight in Review," *Art Digest*, May 1, 1954, p. 16.

20 Anne Porter, interview with JDS.

21 Fairfield Porter, "Hartl Paints a Picture," *Art News* (April 1953): 46.

22 Fairfield Porter, "Hartl," *AIIOT*, p. 184.

23 Fairfield Porter, "Sonnet," in *Fairfield Porter: The Collected Poems*, p. 57.

24 James Schuyler to FP, Monday [n.d.].

25 James Schuyler to FP, Friday [n.d.].

26 *James Schuyler: Selected Poems* (New York: Noonday / Farrar, Straus & Giroux, 1988), p. 3.

27 Schuyler's financial neediness and dependence is remarked upon in interviews by JDS with Ilse Hamm Mattick, Anne Porter, Jane Freilicher, and John Ashbery, among others.

28 A series of letters documents Schuyler's self-invitation: Schuyler to FP, July 2 [1954] ("Would you, after all, like me to come and visit you?"), Schuyler to FP, July 7 [1954], and Schuyler to FP, July 8, [1954] ("I look to see you a week from today, on Friday, July 15th at 6:22 PM in Camden, Maine, at the yacht club"). FPP-AAA.

29 John T. Spike, *Fairfield Porter: An American Classic* (New York: Abrams, 1992), p. 112, mistakenly claims that Jane Freilicher and Joe Hazan visited the Porters in 1954. Freilicher (interview with JDS, 1997) remembered quite clearly that she visited Great Spruce Head only once during the 1950s. Anne Porter (interview with JDS, 1997) agreed.

30 James Schuyler to FP, July 29 [n.d.].

31 "Since receiving that large check from the Porter Realty Trust you may feel a little more like contributing towards your island share now than you will in the summer. I would like to suggest part payment of your 1951 dues: can you afford $250 now?" John Porter to Fairfield Porter, January 29, 1951. FPP-AAA.

32 Eliot Porter, *Summer Island: Penobscot Country* (San Francisco: Sierra Club, 1966), p. 51.

33 Letter to Arthur Giardelli, May 25, 1958.

34 Frank O'Hara, "Porter Paints a Picture," *Art News* (January 1955): 39.

35 Letter to Kee and Hal Channing, [n.d.].

36 Vendler, "Frank O'Hara," p. 238.

37 AEP to KMC, March 19, 1955.

38 Greenberg, quoted in Elaine de Kooning, "Subject: What, How, or Who?" *Art News* (April 1954): 26.

39 Elaine de Kooning, "Subject: What, How, or Who?" p. 26.

40 James Schuyler to FP, October 16 [1954]. FPP-AAA.

41 Letter to Frank O'Hara, June 2, 1955.

42 Schuyler's correspondence with Button in 1955-56 is housed in the John Button Papers, Berg Collection, New York Public Library.

43 John Button to James Schuyler, June 16, 1955. JS-UCSD.

44 Richard Stankiewicz, Journal Entry, Wednesday, August 3, 1955. Richard Stankiewicz Papers (1948-1984), Archives of American Art, Washington, D.C.

45 Richard Stankiewicz, Journal Entry, Wednesday, August 3, 1955.

46 John Ashbery to Kenneth Koch, August 4, 1955, quoted in David Lehman, *The Last Avant-Garde: The Making of the New York School of Poets* (New York: Doubleday, 1998), p. 328.

47 Letter to Frank O'Hara, August 1, 1955.

48 Edith Schloss Memoir, 1984.

49 AEP to KMC, [n.d.].

50 Rudy Burckhardt, interview with JDS, 1997.

51 Anne Porter, note to JDS, 1998.

52 Laurence Porter Memoir, 1996.

53 Frank O'Hara and Katharine Porter, "Katy." JS-UCSD. Reprinted by permission of Maureen Granville-Smith.

14

A Summer Illness

1 Barbara Guest, interview with JDS. Guest's residency was in 1954 or 1955, probably 1955 based on Porter's correspondence with Frank O'Hara that summer. O'Hara, who was friends with Guest, spent time at the Southampton house before departing for Maine.

2 Laurence Porter Memoir, 1996.

3 AEP to KMC, November 1955.

4 AEP to KMC, [n.d.].

5 Cummings interview, 1968.

6 Fairfield Porter, "Sargent," *AIIOT*, p. 204.

7 Fairfield Porter, "Sargent," *AIIOT*, p. 204.

8 Porter's recollection here is taken from Fairfield Porter, "Technology and Artistic Perception," *AIIOT*, p. 272.

9 Laurence Porter Memoir, 1996.

10 AEP to KMC, January 1955.

11 AEP to KMC, April 1956.

12 Ilse Hamm Mattick, interview with JDS, 1997.

13 Gooch, *City Poet: The Life and Times of Frank O'Hara* (New York: Knopf, 1993), p. 287.

14 AEP to FP, [n.d.].

15 James Schuyler to John Button, "Last weekend in May" [1956], John Button Papers, Berg Collection, New York Public Library.

16 Letter to James Schuyler, [n.d.].

17 Anne Porter destroyed a handful of abusive correspondence from Schuyler to the Porters dating from Schuyler's hospitalization in the mid-1970s, but nothing else. Anne Porter, interview with JDS, 1997.

18 Letter to James Schuyler, [n.d.].

19 Letter to Laurence Porter, October 1956.

20 James Schuyler to John Button, "Labor Day" [1956]. John Button Papers, Berg Collection, New York Public Library.

21 Anne Porter, interview with JDS, 1996.

22 Anne Porter to James Schuyler, November 28, 1956. JS-UCSD.

23 AEP to KMC, December 1957.

15

Portraits, *The Nation*, and a Monograph

1 Thomas Hess, "U.S. Painting: Some Recent Directions," *Art News Annual* 25 (1956): 75-76, 80.

2 Letter to Lawrence Campbell, January 2, 1956.

3 Letter to Laurence Porter, "Sunday night Mid Feb 1957."

4 Letter to Arthur Giardelli, January 23, 1958.

5 Letter to John Ashbery, February 20, 1957.

6 James Schuyler to John Ashbery, [n.d.]. John Ashbery Papers, Houghton Library, Harvard University, AM 6 (hereafter JA-HOU). This collection is not yet fully catalogued.

7 John Gruen and Jane Wilson, interview with JDS, 1997.

8 Letter to Laurence Porter, July 25, 1957.

9 Letter to Kenneth Koch, July 1957.

10 Letter to Laurence Porter, "late August 1957."

11 Larry Rivers, conversation with JDS, spring 1997. Rivers initially agreed to an interview but, when asked in writing about Jerry Porter, chose not to respond.

12 Letter to Laurence Porter, January 17, 1958.

13 Arthur Giardelli to FP, November 4, 1958.

14 James Schuyler, "Reviews and Previews," *Art News* (May 1958): 13.

15 Letter to Arthur Giardelli, May 25, 1958.

16 Frank O'Hara to Kenneth Koch, January 10, 1957. Kenneth Koch Papers, Berg Collection, New York Public Library.

17 Jane Wilson, interview with JDS, 1997.

18 The volume of Wallace Stevens poems was first identified in Glenn MacLeod, "Wallace Stevens and Fairfield Porter: Kindred Spirits of American Art," *Archives of American Art Journal*, 24, 1 (1984): 2-12.

19 Letter to Laurence Porter, August 17 (1958).

20 AEP to KMC, September 1958.

21 Edward Porter to FP, September 17, 1959. FPP-AAA.

22 Jane Freilicher to John Ashbery, March 27 [n.d.]. JA-HOU.

23 James Schuyler to John Ashbery, April 23, 1959. JA-HOU.

24 Letter to Laurence Porter, November 13, 1958.

25 The word is Mike Goldberg's. Mike Goldberg, conversation with JDS, 1997.

26 Mike Goldberg, conversation with JDS, 1997.

27 Letter to Laurence Porter, August 12, 1959.

28 Letter to Laurence Porter, August 12, 1959.

29 "I enclose a sample review of Furl's from the *Nation* (the next time you write him, whenever that will be, do mention that I sent it ... he's been very friendly lately but I don't like the quizzical, ruminative look he gets now and then." James Schuyler to John Button, November 2, 1959. John Button Papers, Berg Collection, New York Public Library.

30 Letter to James Schuyler, August 27 [1959].

31 Letter to James Schuyler, [n.d.].

32 Letter to Aline Kilham Porter, October 8 [1959].

33 Cummings interview, 1968.

34 Fairfield Porter, *Thomas Eakins* (New York: Braziller, 1959), p. 15.

35 Cummings interview, 1968.

36 Fairfield Porter, *Thomas Eakins*, p. 28.

37 Fairfield Porter, *Thomas Eakins*, p. 28.

38 Fairfield Porter, "The Short Review," *AIIOT*, p. 169.

39 Lincoln Kirstein (untitled book review), *The Nation*, December 12, 1959, p. 448.

40 Hilton Kramer, "Critics of American Painting," *Arts* (October 1959): 26.

41 Letter to Aline Kilham Porter, October 8 [1959].

42 Letter to Laurence Porter, "Early November," 1958.

43 Letter to Arthur Giardelli, Christmas Eve, 1959.

44 See J. G. Bennett, *Concerning Subud* (London: Hodder and Stoughton, 1958).

45 Letter to Arthur Giardelli, Christmas Eve, 1959.

46 Letter to Robert Dash, Sunday, June 26, 1960.

47 Letter to Robert Dash, July 23, 1960.

48 Letter to James Schuyler, July 7, 1960.

49 James Schuyler to John Button, September 8, 1959. John Button Papers, Berg Collection, New York Public Library.

16

A Yellow Van and "The Four Ugly People"

1 Frank O'Hara to John Ashbery, October 14 [1959]. JA-HOU.

2 The name for the magazine came from a Raymond Roussel novel of the same title, and it was chosen by Schuyler, who edited two of the five issues. Information on the magazine can be found in Jeffrey Julich and Geoffrey Young, "Locus Solus." Kenneth Koch Papers, Berg Collection, New York Public Library.

3 James Schuyler to Chester Kallman, September 3, 1960.

4 Letter to Laurence Porter, September 1960.

5 Letter to John Button, October 1, 1960.

6 Laurence Porter, written interview with JDS, September 1996.

7 Letter to Aline Kilham Porter, December 12, 1960.

8 Letter to Laurence Porter, [n.d.].

9 Letter to James Schuyler, June 6, 1961.

10 Letter to Lawrence Campbell, August 25, 1961.

11 Cummings interview, 1968.

12 Fairfield Porter, "Poets and Painters in Collaboration," *AIIOT*, pp. 220-24.

13 Frank O'Hara to John Ashbery, May 1, 1961. JA-HOU.

14 Letter to Howard [Griffin], May 12, 1961.

15 Letter to John Button, May 19, 1961.

16 Letter to Howard Griffin, June 20, 1961.

17 *The Journals of James Schuyler*, ed. Nathan Kernan (San Francisco: Black Sparrow, 1997), entry for October 3, 1965.

18 Letter to Robert Dash, July 27, 1961.

19 Letter to Robert Dash, July 27, 1961.

20 Letter to Leon Hartl, July 11, 1961.

21 Letter to Robert Dash, August 10, 1961.

22 James Schuyler to John Ashbery, May 15 [n.d.]. JA-HOU.

23 Frank O'Hara to John Ashbery, September 20, 1961. JA-HOU.

24 Jane Freilicher, interview with JDS, 1997.

25 Kenneth Koch, interview with JDS, 1997.

26 Raymond Foy, unpublished interview with James Schuyler, March 2, 1990, at the Chelsea Hotel. JS-UCSD.

27 Barbara Guest, interview with JDS, 1993.

28 James Schuyler, "Exhibitions for 1961-62," *Art News* (January 1962): 13.

29 Fairfield Porter, *Thomas Eakins* (New York: Braziller, 1959), p. 28.

30 Letter to James Schuyler, August 1959.

31 Letter to James Schuyler, [n.d.].

32 James Schuyler to FP, [n.d.].

33 Cummings interview, 1968.

34 Letter to Lucien and Poppy Day, July 23, 1962.

35 Letter to Laurence Porter, June 10, 1962.

36 Letter to John Button, July 4, 1962.

37 The word is Anne Porter's: "F. loved physical possessions (only not the American Dream kind of things)." Anne Porter, note to JDS, 1998.

38 Letter to Laurence Porter, June 10, 1962.

39 Letter to Carl Morse, August 1, 1962.

40 Letter to Lucien and Poppy Day, July 23, 1962.

41 Letter to Carl Morse, August 1, 1962.

42 Letter to Laurence Porter, August 17, 1962.

43 Laurence Porter Memoir, 1996.

44 Letter to John Bernard Myers, July 18 [1962].

45 Letter to Laurence Porter, [n.d.] 1963.

46 Letter to Tibor de Nagy, February 15, 1963.

47 Laurence Porter, letter to JDS, July 22-
September 24, 1996.

48 Letter to John Myers and Tibor de Nagy,
January 31, 1963.

49 Eliot Porter, *Summer Island: Penobscot Country*
(San Francisco: Sierra Club, 1966), p. 97.

50 Wolf Kahn, interview with JDS, 1996. A related
comment concerning Vuillard can be found in
AIIOT, p. 170.

51 James Schuyler to John Ashbery, February 24, 1964.
JA-HOU.

52 Fairfield Porter, "A Realist," *AIIOT*, pp. 90-91.

53 Letter to John Myers and Tibor de Nagy,
January 10, 1964.

54 James Schuyler to John Ashbery, February 22, 1964.

55 Cummings interview, 1968.

56 Both Anne Porter and Tom Carey, James Schuyler's
former secretary (and now an Episcopal Franciscan
friar) have confirmed that Porter's relationship with
Schuyler was at some point sexual (Schuyler told
Carey about it; Anne Porter knew it). According to
both, Porter and Schuyler did not pursue that relationship in the house in Southampton. Aside from a
poem by Schuyler ("O Sleepless Night," describing a
wake-up kiss from Porter, which does take place in
Schuyler's room in Southampton, and which is a kiss
of greeting), there is only elliptical documentary evidence of their sexual relationship. Surviving members of Porter's circle from the 1950s and 1960s have
privately acknowledged Porter's bisexuality during
that period.

57 Letter to AEP, June 5, 1964.

58 "Art - By Fairfield Porter: His School of Paris Works,
Which Bring the Outdoors In, Shown at De Nagy's,"
The New York Times, March 24, 1964, p. 32.

59 Cummings interview, 1968.

60 Letter to John Bernard Myers, [n.d.].

61 Anne Porter, interview with JDS, 1996.

62 Letter to Howard Griffin, November 27, 1965.

63 Anne Porter, interview with JDS, 1996. The police
gave Anne the report when she arrived at the hospital.

64 Letter to Howard Griffin, November 27, 1965.

65 James Schuyler, "Stun," in *James Schuyler: Selected
Poems* (New York: Noonday / Farrar, Straus and
Giroux, 1988), pp. 34-35.

66 Laurence Porter, letter to JDS, July 22-
September 24, 1996.

17

Critical Success and a European Vacation

1 Letter to Laurence Porter, October 29, 1965.

2 The Cornell box was given to Schuyler by Anne
Porter after Porter's death; Schuyler sold it soon after.

3 Letter to Laurence Porter, October 29, 1965.

4 See Jane Wilson's statement about Porter's painting
techniques in John T. Spike, *Fairfield Porter: An American Classic* (New York: Abrams, 1992), pp. 128-30.

5 A series of dated snapshots made by Kenward Elmslie,
now in the James Schuyler Papers, records the visit,
which goes unnoted in the correspondence. JS-UCSD.

6 Anne Porter, note to JDS, 1998.

7 Schuyler expressed his resentment of Anne in subtle
ways, such as "whistling cheerfully" and "decorating
the house with flowers" whenever Anne was to depart
on a trip. Anne Porter, conversation with JDS, 1998.

8 Letter to John Ashbery, [n.d.].

9 The girl in the picture seems to resemble Katie
Porter, but Porter himself states (Cummings interview, 1968) that the girl is Elizabeth Porter.

10 Cummings interview, 1968.

11 Cummings interview, 1968.

12 James Schuyler, "An Aspect of Fairfield Porter's
Paintings," *Art News* (May 1967): 18.

13 Schuyler, "An Aspect of Fairfield Porter's Paintings,"
p. 18.

14 Letter to Arthur Giardelli, December 13 [n.d.].

15 Letter to James Schuyler, June 16, 1967.

16 Letter to James Schuyler, [n.d.] 1967.

17 Anne Porter, interview with JDS, 1996. The phrase
"a duchessa cousin" comes from a postcard from
Porter to Schuyler, [n.d.] 1967.

18 Postcard to James Schuyler, [n.d.]. JS-UCSD.

19 Edith Schloss Memoir, 1984.

20 Edith Schloss Memoir, 1984.

21 Letter to James Schuyler, July 9, 1967.

22 Letter to Laurence and Betsy Porter, [n.d.].

23 Letter to James Schuyler, July 9, 1967.

24 Letter to Laurence and Betsy Porter, [n.d.] 1967.

25 Letter to James Schuyler, July [n.d.] 1967.

26 Stephen West, *Arthur Giardelli: Between the Tides* (Aberystwyth, Wales: Aberystwyth Arts Center / Arts Council of Wales, 1983), pp. 1-21.

27 Letter to James Schuyler, July [n.d.] 1967.

28 Postcard to James Schuyler, July 27 [n.d.].

29 Letter to Arthur Giardelli, November 2, 1967.

30 Anne Porter, interview with JDS, 1996.

31 Anne Porter, interview with JDS, 1996.

32 *The Journals of James Schuyler*, ed. Nathan Kernan (San Francisco: Black Sparrow, 1997), entry for October 7, 1968.

33 Robert Dash, interview with JDS, 1995.

34 Letter to Lucien Day, August 20, 1968.

35 Letter to Arthur Giardelli, March 16, 1965.

36 Schuyler's *Freely Espousing* was preceded by the collaborative work with Grace Hartigan, *Salute*, published in 1960 by Tiber Press, but that work was privately printed with a very small distribution. De Nagy printed a chapbook, *May 24th or So*, in 1966. *Freely Espousing* included the poems of *Salute* and *May 24th or So*.

37 James Schuyler to Jane Freilicher and Joe Hazan, July 17, 1968.

38 Trudy (Mrs. John) Porter, in conversation with JDS, 1993.

39 Letter to Laurence and Betsy Porter, August 23, 1968.

40 Letter to Laurence Porter, August 23, 1968.

41 Jane Freilicher to John Ashbery, December 16, 1968. JA-HOU.

42 Grace Glueck, "Nature with Manners," *The New York Times*, January 19, 1969.

43 Letter to Garry Brown, [n.d., 1970]. Porter included the reading list with the letter.

44 Letter to Lucien Day, February 14, 1969.

45 Letter to Arthur Giardelli, July 9, 1969.

46 Letter to Arthur Giardelli, July 9, 1969.

47 Letter to Arthur Giardelli, July 9, 1969.

48 Arthur Giardelli, "[Untitled Statement]," in *Artists in Wales*, ed. Meic Stephens and Gwasg Gomer (Llandysul, 1971).

49 Arthur Giardelli to Fairfield Porter, [n.d.].

18

"Brilliant, Crazy, Heart-Breaking, and Very Mysterious"

1 Eliot Porter, *Summer Island: Penobscot Country* (San Francisco: Sierra Club, 1966), p. 51.

2 Letter to Carl Morse, October 5 [n.d.].

3 Letter to Betsy and Laurence Porter, November 23, 1969.

4 Letter to Arthur Giardelli, Christmas Eve, 1969.

5 Letter to Arthur Giardelli, Christmas Eve, 1969.

6 Letter to John Bernard Myers, February 3, 1970.

7 Letter to Lucien Day, [n.d.].

8 Letter to Arthur Giardelli, February 3, 1970. See Chapter 4, note 4, for details regarding the misquotation.

9 Letter to Lucien Day, October 22, 1969.

10 James Schuyler to John Ashbery, December 12 [1969].

11 James Schuyler to Joe Brainard, January 4, 1970.

12 Peter Doscher, conversation with JDS, 1994.

13 Letter to Carl Morse, May 5, 1970.

14 Anne Porter, interview with JDS, 1996.

15 Anne Porter's phrase. Anne Porter, interview with JDS, 1996.

16 Laurence Porter's phrase. Laurence Porter Memoir, 1996.

17 Letter to Arthur Giardelli, October 28, 1970.

18 Excerpted from "Remembering Fairfield Porter," an unpublished memoir by Ron Padgett, courtesy of the author.

19 Letter to John Porter and "the island family," November 13, 1970.

20 See the unsent letter to John Ashbery in the Schuyler notebooks (1971-73). JS-UCSD.

21 Letter to Garry Brown, May 20, 1971.

22 While Schuyler includes his lover's last name in this and other unpublished documents, I have chosen to withhold it from this manuscript for fear that its publication could cause harm to him or his wife.

23 James Schuyler to John Ashbery, June 21, 1971. JA-HOU. This chronology is the incomplete James Schuyler Chronology of Fairfield Porter, with revisions by Fairfield Porter. JS-UCSD.

24 Donald Droll to James Schuyler, June 22, 1971. JS-UCSD.

25 Ron Padgett, interview with JDS, 1997.

26 Letter to Laurence Porter, July 8, 1971.

27 Letter to Lucien Day, August 14, 1971.

28 Letter to Ron Padgett, July 13, 1971.

29 Ron Padgett to FP, July 8, 1971. FPP-AAA.

30 Anne Porter, interview with JDS, 1996.

31 James Schuyler to FP, [n.d.]. FPP-AAA.

32 Ron Padgett to FP, July 28, 1971. FPP-AAA.

33 James Schuyler to Barbara Guest, August 25, 1971.

34 John Ashbery, interview with JDS, 1997.

35 James Schuyler to FP, July 7, 1971 [actually August from the postmark], Vermont General Hospital, Waterbury , Vt. FPP-AAA.

36 Letter to James Schuyler, August 12, 1971.

37 Letter to James Schuyler, August 11, 1971.

38 Anne Porter, note to JDS, 1998.

39 James Schuyler to FP, "Friday 13th, 1971," Vermont State Hospital, Waterbury, Vt.

40 James Schuyler to FP, [August 1971].

41 Letter to James Schuyler, August 19, 1971.

42 Letter to Robert Dash, [n.d.].

43 Letter to John Ashbery, August 20, 1971.

44 Anne Porter to John Ashbery, August 24, 1971.

45 James Schuyler to Kenneth Koch, February 7, 1972. Kenneth Koch Papers, Berg Collection, New York Public Library.

46 James Schuyler to Barbara Guest, August 25, 1971.

47 James Schuyler to FP, August 23, 1971.

48 He was "not at all what one would expect." Jane Freilicher, interview with JDS, 1997.

49 Letter to Joe Brainard, [n.d.].

50 Letter to Lucien Day, September 9, 1971.

51 Letter to Joe Brainard, September 13, 1971.

52 James Schuyler to Harry Mathews, September 13, 1971.

53 James Schuyler to John Ashbery, October 6, 1971. JA-HOU.

19

An American Gallery and "Ultimate Reality"

1 James Schuyler to John Ashbery, February 6, 1972. JA-HOU.

2 Peter Schjeldahl, foreword to *Recent Work by Fairfield Porter*, exh. cat. (New York: Hirschl and Adler Galleries, 1972).

3 Letter to Arthur Giardelli, May 17, 1972.

4 Wolf Kahn, interview with JDS, 1996.

5 Letter to Lucien Day, January 19, 1972.

6 Letter to Edith Schloss, August 3, 1972.

7 David Shapiro, "Fairfield Porter's Quiet Revolution," *Art and Antiques*, n.s., 7, 3 (1990): 111. The complete text of this memoir can be found in the Anne Porter Papers.

8 James Schuyler, "The Morning of the Poem," in *The Collected Poems of James Schuyler* (New York: Farrar, Straus and Giroux, 1993), pp. 287-88.

9 Letter to David and Lindsay Shapiro, August 27, 1972.

10 James Schuyler to FP, July 17, 1972.

11 Helen Vendler, "New York Pastoral: James Schuyler," in *Soul Says: On Recent Poetry* (Cambridge: Harvard University Press / Belknap, 1995), p. 62.

12 Ralph Waldo Emerson, preface to Henry David Thoreau, *Walden* (New York: Walter J. Black, 1942), p. 12.

13 James Schuyler, phone interview with Jean W. Ross, March 27, 1980, in *Contemporary Authors* (Detroit: Gale Research, 1981), vol. 101, p. 445.

14 James Schuyler, phone interview with Jean W. Ross, in *Contemporary Authors*, vol. 101, p. 445.

15 James Schuyler, "Closed Gentian Distances," in *The Collected Poems of James Schuyler*, p. 102.

16 *The Collected Poems of James Schuyler*, p. 119.

17 Fairfield Porter, "The Wave and the Leaf," in *Fairfield Porter: The Collected Poems, with Selected Drawings*, ed. John Yau (New York: Tibor de Nagy / The Promise of Learnings, 1985), pp. 4-7.

18 John T. Spike, *Fairfield Porter: An American Classic* (New York: Abrams, 1992), p. 245.

19 Jane Freilicher, interview with Fred Deitzel, in Joan Ludman, *Fairfield Porter: A Catalogue Raisonné of His Prints* (Westbury, N.Y.: Highland House, 1981), p. 33.

20 Letter to Laurence Porter, January 11, 1973.

21 Ray Monk, *Ludwig Wittgenstein: The Duty of Genius* (New York: Penguin, 1991) pp. 485-86. Porter's enthusiastic reading of late Wittgenstein works, which question scientific method, suggests as much.

22 Letter to Rackstraw Downes, November 8, 1973.

23 Letter to Joe Brainard, [n.d.].

24 Letter to Laurence Porter, January 11, 1973.

25 The artists Susan Shatter Brown and Mack Chambers, in conversation, recalled hearing Porter speak at the New York Studio School and being unable to comprehend "Technology and Artistic Perception."

26 Letter to Katharine Porter, [n.d.].

27 Letter to Laurence Porter, March 31, 1973.

28 Laurence Porter Memoir, 1996.

29 Jane Freilicher, interview with Fred Deitzel, in Ludman, *Fairfield Porter: A Catalogue Raisonné*, p. 34.

30 Koch wrote sestinas in response but did not keep copies. Three other related sestinas by Fairfield Porter, one cowritten with Koch, continue the game. Another sestina-letter by Anne Porter to her husband exists but has never been published. Porter also wrote sestinas not related to the Koch correspondence, liking the form, according to Anne Porter, because of the challenges it posed. Porter's sestinas to/with Koch can be found in *Fairfield Porter: The Collected Poems*, pp. 71-77.

31 Letter to Garry Brown, July 9, 1973.

32 Letter to James Schuyler, August 20, 1973.

33 Letter to Richard Freeman, July 16, 1973.

34 Letter to David [?], [n.d.] 1973.

35 Letter to James Schuyler, July 26, 1973. A James Schuyler letter to FP dated July 18, 1973, indicates that Schuyler was still on Thorazine.

36 Letter to Armistead "Ted" Leigh, September 12, 1973.

37 Letter to Joe Brainard, August 17, 1973.

38 A James Schuyler letter to FP, August 17, 1973, makes it sound as if Fairfield was paying for Schuyler's therapy (as Anne Porter confirmed that he was; Anne Porter, interview with JDS, 1996). Papers in the James Schuyler Papers detail the Elmslie trust for Schuyler. JS-UCSD.

39 Ron Padgett to FP, November 7, 1973.

40 Letter to David [?], [n.d.] 1973.

41 Letter to Laurence Porter, November 24, 1974.

42 *Igor Stravinsky: An Autobiography* (New York: Norton, 1996), p. 117, cited by Anne Porter, who recalled the anecdote as a favorite of her husband's.

43 Letter to Neil Welliver, February 16, 1975.

44 Anne Porter, interview with JDS, 1996.

45 Letter to Ron Padgett, November 4, 1973.

46 Letter to Arthur Giardelli, January 2, 1974.

47 Letter to Laurence Porter, March [n.d.] 1974; letter to Laurence Porter, April [n.d.] 1974.

48 Letter to Richard [Freeman?], September 13, 1974.

49 Letter to Laurence Porter, July 15, 1974.

50 Laurence Porter, letter to JDS, July 24-September 22, 1996. Katharine Porter chose not to participate in the writing of this biography.

51 Anne Porter, note to JDS, 1998.

52 Laurence Porter, letter to JDS, July 24-September 22, 1996.

53 Letter to Alan Wald, August 5, 1974.

54 Letter to Richard Freeman, [n.d.].

55 Letter to Laurence Porter, November [n.d.] 1974.

56 Brooke Alexander Memoir, September 1979, in Ludman, *Fairfield Porter: A Catalogue Raisonné*.

57 Letter to Laurence Porter, November 27, 1974.

58 Letter to Mildred and Ralph LaMarr, March 28, 1975.

59 Letter to Rackstraw Downes, March 20, 1975.

60 James Schuyler to FP, April 16, 1975.

61 Letter to Lucien Day, August 21, 1975.

62 James Schuyler to FP, August 5, 1975.

63 Anne Porter, interview with JDS, 1996.

64 Anne Porter to James Schuyler, September 1975.

65 Jane Freilicher, interview with JDS, 1997.

66 Anina Porter Fuller, conversation with JDS, 1995.

67 Jane Freilicher, interview with JDS, 1997. Rivers, in conversation with JDS, agreed that he had videotaped the funeral, adding, "But so what?" He did not know what had become of the videotape.

68 Cummings interview, 1968. The words in quotation marks are Porter's own.

69 A copy of the agreement can be found in the Anne Porter Papers.

70 Anne Porter, interview with JDS, 1996.

71 See Richard V. Schenkel, "The Chelsea: A Once and Forever Shrine," *Art Times* (June 1988): 1, 16.

72 Documents pertaining to these gifts are included in the Anne Porter Papers.

73 Anne Porter, note to JDS, 1998.

74 *The Journals of James Schuyler*, ed. Nathan Kernan (San Francisco: Black Sparrow, 1997), entry for November 14, 1989.

75 James Schuyler to Anne Porter, May 24, 1989.

76 Hilton Kramer, "Unexpected Linkages," *New York Times Book Review*, June 3, 1979, p 16.

77 Peter Schjeldahl, "Perceptions of Fairfield Porter," *Portfolio* (June-July 1979): 77-78.

Index